MANCHESTER UNLIMITED

MANCHESTER UNLIMITED

THE RISE AND RISE OF THE WORLD'S
PREMIER FOOTBALL CLUB

Mihir Bose

TEXERE

NEW YORK · LONDON

To my darling daughter, Indira, who was taken to White Hart Lane at the age of five, but now says, 'Daddy, when Tottenham don't play, can we support Manchester United?'

Copyright © 2000 Mihir Bose

First published in Great Britain in 1999 by Orion Business

This edition published by

TEXERE LLC
55 East 52nd Street
New York, NY 10055
Tel: +1 (212) 317 5106
Fax: +1 (212) 317 5178
www.texerepublishing.com

UK subsidiary office

TEXERE Publishing Limited
71–77 Leadenhall Street
London EC3A 3DE
Tel: +44 (0)20 7204 3644
Fax: +44 (0)20 7208 6701

Library of Congress Cataloging in Publication Data

ISBN 1-58799-008-3

Printed and bound in Great Britain

This book is printed on acid-free paper

10 9 8 7 6 5 4 3 2 1

CONTENTS

ACKNOWLEDGEMENTS

Like all good ideas this one came out of the blue and was, at first, quite shocking. When Martin Liu of Orion Publishing first approached me with the proposal it had never entered my head to write a business study of Manchester United.

However, the more I looked into the subject the more convinced I became that there was a story which, despite the many books on Manchester United, had not been told and needed to be told. I was fortunate that two months after Martin approached me Manchester United started a season which nobody could have predicted and has proved to be quite the most amazing in its history. If that at times made my task much harder and writing the book more complicated, it radically changed the way I had originally thought of approaching the book, and the end product has been more rewarding. So my first thanks go to Martin Liu.

This book could not have been written without the help I have received from many people connected with Manchester United. I would in particular like to thank Martin Edwards, Maurice Watkins, David Gill, Peter Kenyon, John Bick, Ken Ramsden, Sir Bobby Charlton, Mike Edelson, Glen Cooper, Edward and James Freedman, Keith Harris, Rupert Faure Walker, David Blake and Greg Dyke.

I would also like to thank Mark Booth, Martin Stewart, Richard Campbell-Breeden, Tim Allen, Lord Tim Bell and Chris Haines.

My thanks are also due to Peter Leaver, Peter Robinson, Ian Stott, Irving Scholar, Sam Chisholm, Peter Hill-Wood, Danny Fiszman, Neil Bennett, Colin Gibson, Bodo Mueller, Lennart Johansson, Gerhard Aigner, Frits Ahlstrom, Guido Tognoni, Patrick Cheney, David Davies, Graham Kelly, Keith Wiseman, Geoff Thompson, Yasmin Waljee and Peter Crowther. My old friend Harry Harris was as ever both impish and helpful and my thanks go to him as well.

Michael Knighton is also due my thanks as are the Manchester United supporters who so vigorously opposed the bid. I am particularly indebted to Andy Walsh who despite the fact that he was writing his own book, answered my queries with great patience. Jim White found time for me and Michael Crick was generous with his time and even spoke to me from Australia in the midst of his research into Murdoch. Roger Brierley and his son were both gracious and very helpful. These people may not agree with all my conclusions, but I hope they will accept I have presented their case.

Paul Greengran, who made the 1980 Granada programme on Manchester United, kindly lent me his research. I am grateful to him and to David Conn for his help in this matter.

I would also particularly like to thank David Welch, sports editor of the *Daily Telegraph*, his assistant Keith Perry and the sports desk for all their help.

One man felt he could not talk to me. That was Sir Roland Smith who told his friend, the legendary PR man Brian Basham, that he did not talk about football. I hope after reading this book he changes his mind.

I did not seek out Alex Ferguson because I was aware he was telling his side of the story in his own book.

My godson Daniel Mokades, who is showing the business skills that make him an ideal future director of Manchester United, provided wonderful research help.

Caroline Cecil deserves my gratitude first for lending me the services of Juliet Latham, who brought some order to my paper work when it was on the point of overwhelming me, and also for Caroline's own non-fussy pragmatism which, curiously, is very like the style Manchester United prefer.

Nigel Dudley did much to keep me sane and remind me that, contrary to what Bill Shankly said, there is not only life after football but it is important to realise that however important football may be, there are other things in life worth considering.

I am grateful to Rod Dadak for providing the necessary legal expertise and preventing me from committing too many errors. Needless to say the errors of commission or omission that remain are my responsibility.

Mihir Bose
London, Autumn 1999

PREFACE

Two weeks before the start of the new millennium my publisher held a press conference to launch the UK hardback edition of this book.

The publicist who handled it invited all the national newspapers, radio, television and any other media contacts he could think of.

But much to his chagrin, the press conference was poorly attended. There were understandable reasons: it was just a week before Christmas and yet another book on Manchester United did not, on the face of it, seem exciting. It also may not have helped that the hotel chosen was called My Hotel, a name which may have seemed to some media representatives as a bit of a tired pun.

In the event only three newspapers sent their representatives: my own paper the *Daily Telegraph*, the *Sun* and the *Mail*. No other paper, let alone television, bothered to turn up and the room only looked reasonably full because of the presence of several of my friends and their children. Nigel Dudley brought along his two young boys; the wonderful Caroline Cecil, herself a PR lady, came just to make sure I did not feel too lonely; and Hugh Pym, the former political correspondent of *ITN* and now a parliamentary candidate for the Liberal Democrats, was also there. None of them had any professional interest in the book; they were to support me. But how glad I was of this for their presence meant that when I took the podium to talk about the book I was not addressing a blank wall.

The press conference did not seem to be going anywhere when Hugh, his reporting instincts still very sharp, asked me the question that ignited the most furious media storm I have known. Since the Manchester United story had often been told, what made my book special, what was new in my book? I pointed to the revelations about BSkyB's attempted takeover of United and, in particular, the relationship between Martin Edwards and Sir Alex Ferguson. My book had details of this relationship which had never before been disclosed, and as I turned to these pages, I could see the *Mail* and the *Sun* reporters, who until then had looked bored, come alive with excitement.

The fuse was lit and the next day the *Mail, Sun* and *Daily Telegraph* led with stories based on the revelations I had made about the relationship between Edwards and Ferguson. As it happened I had long booked to take my daughter Indira for a holiday to Australia to see in the new millennium and that night, not long after the press conference, I left for Sydney.

Little did I realise how the curious timing of my holiday, which had been booked some seven months earlier, would now look. For while my daughter and I stopped over in Singapore on the way to Sydney, radio, television and all the other media, including the weekend papers, which had not even bothered to acknowledge the invitation to my press conference, now tried furiously to catch up with the tale. They knew they had a story to follow up and did so with a vengeance.

My secretary in London was inundated with calls, my mobile phone was jammed, and having promised my daughter that I would not do any work, I found myself holed up in my Singapore hotel room being interviewed on the phone by radio and television stations from all over the UK and some in Ireland. The whole experience made me realise yet again the tremendous power of Manchester United but also how media myths are made.

I did not, of course, need to be told of the power and influence of Manchester United. I was well aware of it. However, as the British press lavished attention on my revelations and the papers in the Far East and Australia followed their lead, I found myself re-reading material from my own book. It served to remind me that although British sporting influence is on the decline, when it comes to Manchester United, Britain does have a sports brand that is in a world of its own.

The media myth that developed was very different and made me realise with some dismay that, although I have been a journalist for more than a quarter of a century, there is much about my own profession that I do not know. For the most extraordinary story to emerge from the publication of my book was the myth which denied that the press conference in the basement of My Hotel had ever taken place.

Jim White in the *Guardian*, having first seen the story in the *Sun*, came to the extraordinary conclusion that the revelations had some-how been leaked to the *Sun* in advance of other papers and even sympathised with me, saying I must be feeling awful that as a *Daily Telegraph* writer the story had first appeared in a rival paper. In the curious way such myths can take hold, some four months after the press conference I meet Stephen Fay, an old friend and distinguished journalist, at the Wisden annual dinner who solicitously came up to me and offered me his sympathy, saying that in his experience he had never known a book to be so extensively leaked even before it was published. It must have ruined the publication. My book was written to dispel the many myths about Manchester United; little did I realise that the publicity surrounding it would spawn such a curious myth about the book itself.

In the nine months since the hardback was published the Manchester United story has rolled on. The year 2000 began badly for United with controversy over the club being allowed to opt out of the FA Cup for the sake of the World Club championship, and to help England's bid for the 2006 World Cup; but as so often with United these days, it ended well with yet another Premiership title.

I can only hope that this edition has just as great success and, in dispelling myths about Manchester United, this time I do not generate any more myths about myself or the making of the book.

Mihir Bose
London, Summer 2000

INTRODUCTION

They had come to the land of make-believe, where rich people retire to hide from the tax man and an American film star can become a fairy princess, to celebrate football. But as they gathered on a balmy night, so hot that ladies in shimmering dresses longingly eyed those lounging by the beach in a bikini, it turned into a celebration of Manchester United.

It was an appropriate place, for the occasion itself was the ultimate in football make-believe, the draw for the opening round of matches in a new season of European competition now converted into what television men called an 'event'. Even two years ago an 'event' like this staged on such a scale in Monte Carlo would have seemed like a fantasy, even more of one than Grace Kelly, a girl from Philadelphia, becoming the wife of His Serene Highness Prince Rainer III of the 700-year-old House of Grimaldi.

For years the draw had been made in the Atlantis hotel in Zürich, the same half a dozen journalists reporting, the same dozen or so club officials from across Europe attending, and the whole thing enveloped in cosy self-satisfaction as the participants hugged to themselves what they saw as their much-prized secret of football.

Then, in August 1998, the draw had been moved to Monte Carlo and suddenly it was no longer a case of drawing balls from different glass bowls to decide which European club played which other European club in the first round – generally an obscure East European one against a famous one from Italy or Spain – but was now invested with such glamour that even the Americans, who had taught the world how to convert athletic endeavour into showbiz extravaganza, would find it impossible to understand, let alone better. In this Monte Carlo reincarnation, the drawing of balls from glass bowls was the least important part of the whole event, and the football match that was supposed to pit the two best club teams of the previous European season was almost an afterthought, a postscript that concluded the whole thing.

Before all this came the most important event, the dinner, and it was at this dinner (what UEFA – European's football governing body – called the UEFA Gala) on that balmy night in August 1999 that what was meant to be European football gathering together ostensibly to congratulate itself became an honour parade of all the wondrous things Manchester United had achieved in its remarkable season of 1999.

In the previous August, in 1998, the first year such a Gala had been held, UEFA felt pleased Real Madrid had proved the best club in Europe. It had been the first team to win the European Cup, that most coveted of European trophies, it was the club with the most enviable of European records and in May 1998, after a long torturous gap of 32 years, it had won the European trophy again. But what should have been a joyous Madrid night had turned into one of sombre introspection for Europe's football hierarchy, overshadowed by the fear that not only might this be the first and last Gala, but it may well turn out to be the last year of UEFA's existence itself.

UEFA had come to Monte Carlo in August 1998 nursing one grievous wound and wondering whether the other might prove fatal. In June 1998 UEFA's President, Lennart Johansson, had failed to regain for Europe the presidency of FIFA, world football's governing body, which England's Stanley Rous had lost to the Brazilian Joao Havelange back in 1974. Johansson had been beaten by Sepp Blatter, Havelange's protégé, and the clever Swiss had not only secured the votes of the Asian, African and Latin American coalition that had sustained Havelange, but, the ultimate indignity for Johansson, many European ones including England. Unlike Real Madrid there was to be no comeback for Europe and, what was worse, the election had demonstrated to the world that European football was a house divided against itself.

Then in July news emerged which suggested that the house itself may collapse completely and UEFA lose everything it had built up over the previous 40 years. A hitherto unknown sports management company based in Milan had succeeded in luring the top European clubs into secretive talks about starting up their own European Super League and breaking away from UEFA. Real Madrid themselves were heavily involved in these shadowy talks and the Milan-based company had also gone to Brussels to complain to the European Commission about what it alleged were anti-competitive policies followed by UEFA.

In any other industry such freelance activity by a private company might have been easily dismissed. But such was the fragile nature of UEFA and the precarious, not to say non-existent, relationship it had with clubs, that as UEFA gathered in Monte Carlo in August 1998, it seemed that the Milan-based company might succeed and UEFA collapse almost as dramatically as the Berlin Wall.

The European Cup, the first and greatest of European competitions, which had started as a result of an idea floated by Gabriel Hanot, the then editor of *L'Equipe*, and his colleague Jacques Ferran, now seemed certain to be hijacked by the marketers. Where Hanot and Ferran, in the great tradition of journalists seeking to answer the question, 'Which was the greatest club side in Europe?', had spawned the most magical of European sporting contests, marketers, seeking more money for a select group of clubs, were now threatening to so transform their tournament that it would be more a vehicle to earn money from television rather than meet the romantic yearnings that had inspired the men from *L'Equipe* back in 1955.

But now, on the night of 26 August 1999 – a year later and after many meetings and many hours of fraught talks behind closed doors – UEFA had come to Monte Carlo to proclaim its victory over the intruders from Milan. As the retractable roof of the Sporting Club de Monte Carlo swung open, and the waiters served champagne, Gloria Gaynor, the American singer, urged everyone to forget the stiff-upper-lip reserve cultivated by the English and just hang loose. It seemed an unlikely invitation to extend to ageing Europeans but UEFA's top officials, most of them octogenarians with white hair, stood up instantly and, waving their white handkerchiefs in the air, danced to her music. The movements of these Europeans, swaying to rhythms that were so unfamiliar to them, was awkward and the gesture of the white handkerchief seemed borrowed (it is what fans in Spain do when they want to get rid of an unpopular coach). But for the UEFA bosses, however difficult it was to imitate Gaynor's seductive motions, the gestures were important and a powerful message to what they called the men from the world of filthy lucre. UEFA was proclaiming: We are here, we have survived. Within minutes the sky over the Sporting Club was a riot of colour and noise as the fireworks were let off and UEFA's message was writ large: after the most traumatic year in its history everything had, almost magically, come right in its world. UEFA's house had not collapsed.

True, many parts of it had to be rebuilt, but like a good institution it had reinvented itself and so successfully that new competitions had been created, clubs were getting more money than ever before and the Milan-based marketers were reduced to writing letters to the clubs asking for a share of the increased money they were getting as a result of the ideas that had forced UEFA's decision to revolutionise European soccer. To rub in UEFA's triumph one of the clubs, which had been at the centre of the shadowy talks with the Milan-based company, was now the champion club in Europe: Manchester United.

Manchester United, of course, knew all about rebirth and reinvention. Long before UEFA it had had to rebuild itself; coping with a crisis that completely put in the shade anything ever faced by UEFA. UEFA's crisis in 1998 had been a paper crisis of money; United in 1958 had faced a real human tragedy which had led to the club being rebuilt from the ashes of a horrific air crash that could well have totally destroyed a lesser club. In that year, when Hanot and Ferran were still at *L'Equipe*, and the European Cup a three-year-old idea, Manchester United, led by the great Matt Busby, had defied the insular ways and scorn of much of the English football world, and gone into Europe to play in this new competition. In the spring of 1958 Busby had taken his team to the semi-final, only to see the magnificent team he had built destroyed in a plane crash in Munich as it was on its way back to England.

Few other institutions could have survived such a disaster but Busby, conquering his own terrible injuries, rebuilt his club and a decade later it went on to win the European Cup, the first English club to do so (and the second British one following Celtic's success the previous season).

But that prodigious effort had exhausted Busby and his team. Busby had retired, his team had broken up, seven years later United were relegated, and it was another 30 years before Manchester United reached another European Cup final – now known as the Champions League.

And exactly three months to the day before the balmy night in the Sporting Club of Monte Carlo, United had gone to Barcelona and on the very day that Busby would have celebrated his 90th birthday, it had won the Cup. The timing was amazing and, like many such great triumphs, this was all the sweeter for being so unexpected.

In Barcelona's Nou Camp, United was without its captain and crucial midfielder Roy Keane and also another key player Paul Scholes. After six minutes United had gone behind to a free kick from Bayern's Mario Basler. Bayern Munich had then hit the United post, and followed that by rattling the United bar, and with two minutes to go and Bayern leading 1–0, Lennart Johannson was asked by his officials to go down to the touch-line so as to be ready to present the Cup to the Germans. As he left he consoled Bobby Charlton, who had scored the night United had first won the Cup at Wembley in 1968, and then as he took the lift at Nou Camp to make the long journey down through the tunnel to get to the touch-line, he rehearsed what he might say to the victorious Germans. As he emerged he saw on the electronic scoreboard, 'Bayern Munich 1 Manchester United 2', and thought there had been an electrical failure at the Nou Camp. It took him some time to be convinced it was no Catalan electrician's fault but United's ability to magically transform certain defeat into thrilling victory. It was then that he learnt that while he was in the Nou Camp lift, cocooned from the tumult of the drama taking place a few yards from him, first Sheringham had equalised and then Solksjaer had scored the winner.

Now, three months later, in Monte Carlo, Johansson could joke about his experience, 'I very nearly became the first UEFA president to present the cup to the losers', and United could join in the laughter that was produced. It was laughter that mingled relief with joy for men who knew how close they had been to the precipice and how they had, quite miraculously, wrought their reinvention that night. United's joy was all the more pleasurable because it knew that its Barcelona reinvention had been a culmination of many reinventions through the long years that followed the triumphs of Busby and his men in Wembley in 1968. And what is more, at the long table near the stage where United was seated, there were many United men who had their own stories of reinvention to tell.

Martin Edwards, the club chairman was on holiday in Alaska, where he had gone to celebrate the 30th birthday of his son, and so United's Board of directors was represented by Mike Edelson, one of its longest-serving directors after Edwards. Ten years ago, almost to the day, Edelson had been in the middle of a titanic struggle with his great friend Edwards to stop him selling the club to Michael Knighton for just £20 million. For all their friendship Edwards had not told Edelson before he made his deal with Knighton, which involved Knighton buying Edwards' 50% stake for £10 million, and in August 1989 Edelson was busy making his plans with his fellow directors, including Bobby Charlton, to reverse United into a company he was associated with called Conrad.

In the end these plans had come to nothing: Knighton had gone away, Edwards had had his lucky escape, as he puts it, and Edelson, having seen his fur business collapse, had reinvented himself as the 'shellmeister', the man who formed shell companies that were used to bring other unquoted companies to the stockmarket. He was to do this most notably with Sheffield United.

Along the table with him was a younger man who also knew how to reinvent himself. Just a year earlier David Beckham had returned from the World Cup in France as the most reviled man in England, his sending off in the Argentinian game being held to be responsible for England's defeat. As United opened its 1998–99 season at West Ham, fans were encouraged to boo and heckle his every touch. But he had survived that and prospered so well that by the time he met his nemesis Diego Simeone (Beckham's kick at the Argentinian had led to his sending off), Beckham had long been forgiven. Now in Monte Carlo he was with his wife Victoria (Posh Spice) Adams, the most sought-after couple in England, whose wedding had been the society event of the year with *OK* magazine paying a million pounds for the wedding photographs.

Perhaps the most remarkable reinvention had been by the man who had masterminded United's triumph in Barcelona and the unique treble – Alex Ferguson. Ten years ago, as Edelson, Bobby Charlton and the other United directors were trying to stop Edwards selling Manchester United to Knighton, Ferguson was trying to stop the Board listening to the baying fans who wanted him sacked. He had been at United for three years and the doubts the United Board had had when appointing him, that no-one who had managed in Scotland had succeeded in England, seemed to be coming true. At that stage he had nothing to show by way of trophies and in that 1989–90 season his team were flirting with relegation, had lost 5–1 to Manchester City at Maine Road, lost 3–0 in a humiliating defeat at home to Tottenham in the League Cup and faced a tricky away fixture in their first match in the FA Cup to Brian Clough's Nottingham Forest. But he won that match, went on to win the FA Cup, followed it with the Cup Winners Cup the following season – United's first European trophy since the Wembley triumph of 1968 – and then in 1993 came the first of his Premier League triumphs.

Now, as the waiters in their immaculate black ties switched from serving Bourgogne Chardonnay to a 1996 rouge from Château haut-Baillan – to match the sautéed local sea bass followed by médaillion de veal – the men who had reinvented themselves, and in the process reclaimed the crown United had sought for 31 years, got up to receive their individual honours from the revered names of European soccer.

First was Edelson, representing the Board, and escorted on to the stage by a lady in a body-hugging cerise dress to receive the replica of the Champions League Trophy United had won in Barcelona.

Then Japp Stam, the Dutch defender, receiving the award for being the best defender in Europe, ahead of Bayern's Lothar Mathaus, who had barely been able to accept his losers' medal in Barcelona, and Lillian Thuram from Parma, who had been at the heart of France's World Cup-winning team in 1998.

Then David Beckham, who had to go up not once but twice, once for the best midfielder, ahead of Stefan Effenberg, the man who had run the game for Bayern in Barcelona until the final minutes when United took over, and then for the most valuable player of the season, ahead of Zinedine Zidane, who had led France to their World Cup triumph but had been bested by United in an epic semi-final against Juventus on their way to Barcelona.

As with all such gala events there were those moments when football likes to present itself as something more than a mere game. So UEFA made much of the one million Swiss francs it had given to the anti-personnel land mines campaign which Princess Diana was so actively involved with – but even here United starred. Thus when the blind Cypriot fan Andreas Chapoupis was honoured as the best supporter, he was presented with his award by Beckham; when Arsene Wenger, the Arsenal manager, was given the Fair Play Award for offering to replay the FA Cup match against Sheffield United because of the 'unsporting' winner Arsenal scored, he was presented with his award by Bobby Charlton; and even the United tea lady, Nesta Burgess, who had come to Old Trafford just after the Munich crash and still made tea for the players, was honoured as one of the vital backroom staff of European football.

But the most telling moment came when Alex Ferguson went up to receive the best coach of the year award, ahead of Valery Lobanovsky, the coach of Dynamo Kyiv, which had come so close to winning the Champions League, and Alberto Malesani, the coach of Parma, who had guided his team to the UEFA Cup.

Even a couple of seasons ago, such an award for an English coach would have seemed fantasy. English football was reviled on the continent as primitive, a throwback to the dark days of long ball, endless running and kicking and players whose only asset seemed to be the athleticism involved in running from one penalty box to another, bereft of any capacity for even basic skills, let alone magic or invention.

But now Ferguson received his award from Rinus Michels, whose Dutch team in the 70s and 80s had invented 'total football' and had been Europe's answer to the beauty and fantasy that the Brazilians and South Americans had brought to the game. It demonstrated that while the English national team was still trying to recover its lost glories – two weeks later a dismal draw in Poland would dim its hopes of qualifying for Euro 2000 – United was leading the English clubs back to the pre-eminence it had once enjoyed.

There was one other presentation which showed how United was leading English football, at least at club level, away from the dark days of the 80s. This was when Beckham received his award for best European midfielder from Michel Platini, one of only three men to be thrice voted European footballer of the year. In making the award to Beckham, Platini and UEFA were not only honouring United's favourite son but redeeming English football and removing some of the shame that will always cling to it.

Before that night in Barcelona, the last time an English team had been in a European Cup Final was in Brussels in May 1985 when, just before the match was due to start, a charge by some drunken Liverpool fans against Juventus fans had led to the collapse of a wall and the death of 39 Juventus fans and injuries to 600 others. It had been a night of infamy, one of the most wretched in the long dark tunnel through which English football had travelled in the 70s and 80s, spreading havoc and terror in the football stadiums and cities of Europe. Platini had been the playmaker for Juventus that night in Brussels and scored the winning goal from a penalty that won the Italians the title. After that English clubs had been banned from Europe for five years but, as Platini presented the award to Beckham, that night in Heysel seemed to belong to a barbaric pre-history from which the English game, at least at European club level, had long emerged into light and footballing civilisation.

In the late 60s and the 70s Manchester United's fans had pioneered the wretched hooliganism that was to become known in Europe as the English disease. In the very season after United had won the European Cup in 1968, its semi-final against Milan was halted when a brick was thrown from the Stretford End and hit the Italian goalkeeper Cudicini. UEFA later ordered United to erect a screen at the Stretford End. Then in 1977–78, when Dave Sexton's side played in Europe, a riot by United fans in the match against the French club St Etienne led to UEFA initially banning United from Europe and, although reinstated after a fine, it was forced to play the second leg at a neutral stadium 200 kilometres from Manchester. But two decades on from that, in Barcelona, this was truly a new United which showed it could win the field and whose fans would not shame the club off it.

Long before the match, United's fans had taken over the city of

Barcelona, that symbol of Catalan nationalism. Europe, well aware of the English disease, had watched this invasion by United with fear and apprehension, with the Catalan police closely observing their every gesture as the fans moved from the elaborate fountains of the city to the over-crowded bars. Such was the state of nerves in Barcelona that day that the smartest hotels kept a wary eye for the English and even the official UEFA hotel refused to allow some of them to enter their premises, fearing they might go on the rampage. But on the night, despite the fact that they had outnumbered the German fans almost two to one in the Nou Camp, there had been no trouble, the only moment of anxiety coming when news emerged that a travel firm in England had collapsed and some fans might be stranded. Indeed, so restrained had been the United fans, so keen to display not the hooligan spirit of the English fans but the more celebrated English ability to suffer in silence, that they had stoically borne the many idiocies of the charter travel trade, even when they were herded outside airports like cattle, with armed police watching their every move, denied even basic amenities like food and water, and transported back to England long after they were due to return. What is more, United had displayed the new multi-racial face of England with their most eye-catching fans being Sikhs in multi-coloured turbans.

Just after Bayern had scored, a United fan sitting not far away from the VIP seats had got up and recreated Charlie Chaplin's imitation of Hitler giving the Nazi salute. But this merely underlined the old atavistic rivalry between the English and the Germans and in no way dimmed the way the fans had proved that the detested image of English fans was not a mould that could not be broken. That night in Barcelona United's fans had demonstrated that, despite the rampages of the fans of the national team, there was a very different, more appealing face of English soccer following for the world to appreciate.

And now in Monte Carlo the world could not get enough of this face and of United.

Nothing illustrated this more than the match that followed the night after the Gala dinner. The match belonged to Lazio, who having won the Cup Winners Cup had won the right to play United in the Super Cup. The following day's papers made much of Lazio's triumph, how the Italian team had outplayed United, could have won by more than a single goal and how Veron, who won the man-of-the-match award, showed Beckham how to run the midfield.

But this merely underscored that it was Lazio who had come to Monaco as the hungry outsiders. Before its Cup Winners Cup triumph,

Lazio had won nothing in Europe, while United, seemingly satiated by its triumphs in 1999, treated this match more like a practice event as symbolised by the fact that its leading goal scorer, Dwight Yorke, never took the field.

For United the match had so few resonances that many fans could dimly remember that the last time it had won a European trophy, in 1991, United had won this corresponding match beating Red Star Belgrade, then European champions. But that was on a cold November night at Old Trafford when barely 22,000 had turned up to cheer Brian McClair's winning goal. Nobody apart from the die-hard faithful had even noticed the event and the world had been so dismissive of it that *Rothmans*, English football's bible, had buried the result in the smallest print size it could find on page 924. Indeed, the last time an English club had contested the match as champions, (Liverpool in 1984) Peter Robinson the vice chairman of Liverpool, had spun a coin in a Zürich hotel room with Gianpierti Boniperti, head of Juventus, who was momentarily confused by seeing the Queen's head on the coin, but called correctly to give Juventus home advantage and the resulting 2–0 triumph.

But now, as opposed to earlier seasons, UEFA had got sponsorship from Nissan and it was billed as the greatest European contest between the team that had won the 1999 Champions League and the team that had won the 1999 Cup Winners Cup, to herald the first season of European football in the new millennium. BBC had tried hard to hype up the match, which was perfectly understandable, for it was one of its rare live football matches for the season. But United knew this was yet another new event created for television and which would soon be forgotten. Victory or defeat meant nothing.

Nothing emphasised this more than the behaviour of the fans. In Barcelona United fans had, like their team, displayed a hunger and a determination that one could almost touch. Here they were few in number, outnumbered by the Italians, and they were content to just display their banners which, proclaiming their origins from places as diverse as Colchester and Benidorm, only served to prove United's amazing appeal.

In contrast, it was the supposedly more cosmopolitan Italians who, like outsiders seeking to break into the big time, looked tacky, mean and, at times, frighteningly nasty. When Salas scored what proved the winner a couple of swastikas were waved and every time Cole, the only black amongst the 22 players, touched the ball the Italians hissed and booed, indicating that the mixture of fascism and Nazism that is always bubbling beneath Italian football was still alive.

But perhaps the banner that summed it up was the one that draped the Italian section. It read in Italian:

Noi siamo qui pr la Supercuppa Europea
Voi sul una priate dura con diorrea

We are here for the Super Cup
You are on the hard road to diarrhoea

In another age, English fans might have been provoked by such Italian words and gestures. But United, aware it was the best in Europe, ignored it, content that it was Lazio that, having been on the hard road for so long, was trying to get on to the super highway of football that United already occupied.

So how had Manchester United reinvented itself?

This is the burden of this book. The story of United's rise to glory since the Second World War under Busby had often been told. But the story of how the club, which in 1989 was nearly sold to a man described as an 'educationalist' for £20 million, has since become the richest club in the world with a stock market valuation of more than £600 million has not been told.

Or rather, it has been told as the story of one man. Just as in the standard United myth, before Busby came to Old Trafford in 1945, there was darkness and then he said let there be light and Old Trafford was bathed in glory, so all the success United has had since 1990 has been put down to just one man: Sir Alex Ferguson. This is certainly the view of the fans and also many neutrals.

The creation of the Ferguson myth has come more quickly than that of Busby and it has been helped by football occupying a position it has never before had in this country.

Football, a game whose laws and institutions were created by public school boys, following on from the educational and sporting revolution produced by Thomas Arnold, the founder of the modern public school system, at Rugby, had always been popular. But it is only now, in the closing years of the 20th century, that it has become the ultimate populist game, one ideally suited to be used by the present Labour government as a political weapon. So while the greatest sportsman this country had ever produced, the cricketer Dr WG Grace, a Victorian of such towering stature that his only rival for public popularity was said to be Gladstone, was never knighted, Ferguson was knighted within a month of United's triumph at Barcelona. If Grace did not get an honour because Queen Victoria did not rate sportsmen highly, the present government is only too aware of the power of football and is keen to harness it.

However, this rise of football at the centre of British life, replacing all other sports and often many other forms of entertainment, has in the process spawned its own myths, many of which have distorted the story of football and in particular Manchester United, and done much to prevent us from understanding what has happened at Old Trafford and in English football in general.

Even at the best of times the Manchester United story, made of many complex strands, would be difficult to unravel and explain. It is now, at times, almost impossible because the level of public discourse on football is conducted with such frenzy that almost all rational argument seems useless.

A vivid, but disheartening, illustration of this came on the day England played Poland in Warsaw in September 1999, in a match England had to win to be sure of making the play-offs for Euro 2000. The *Daily Mirror* had a huge, one-word headline across its back page: 'Traitor'. The accusation was being hurled by the paper against Graham Kelly, the former chief executive of the FA, who had just published his book, *Sweet FA*. Kelly in his book, serialised the week before England went to Poland, had alleged that just before the World Cup in France Alan Shearer had threatened to give up the England captaincy and boycott the World Cup if the FA went ahead with a misconduct charge against him for his foul on Neil Lennon of Leicester City.

Shearer, who always claimed the kick was accidental, was asked about Kelly's comments at the press conference the day before the match and said, 'This season has seen some serious, untrue accusations against myself', and then said Kelly was trying to sell his book 'off the back of me' and that he had to question Kelly's timing in publishing the book just as England was due to play a vital match. Its timing, said Shearer, would cause 'maximum damage to myself and disruption to an England side'.

Although Shearer had never used Kelly's name during the press conference, let alone called him a traitor, all this was enough for the *Mirror* to say this was what Shearer had done. The charge of traitor was ridiculous. Britain is one political nation but has four footballing nations, all of whom at any one stage could be opposed to each other on the field of play and, on this spurious logic, all of them and their supporters could at some stage or the other be labelled as traitors. For the *Mirror*, such realities did not matter. The story was good fun, its main rival the *Sun* (which had not even reported Shearer's comments) had serialised the Kelly book, and this was the *Mirror* getting its own back. It knew that in a few days there would be something else to work up synthetic steam about on the back pages. However, it indicated the fevered, and at times completely illogical, nature of the public discourse on football in this country – evidence, perhaps, of the dumming down of the country.

Manchester United has been the classic victim of such fevered, illogical debate. The result has been a picture that has been built of the club and the men who run it which, at times, bears no relation to the truth. Manchester United has not helped matters by having wretched public relations which would shame a company a quarter of its size and which, for a club supposed to be the richest in the world is quite staggering. But even with the best public relations, United would have found it difficult to escape from the myths that have built up round it. For they are connected with the wider myths about English football and how it has developed in the 1990s.

The most corrosive of these is that English football, once the people's game played for fun by lion-hearted men and watched by the most radiant souls on earth, has now been massively corrupted by money and greed. Men of commerce have taken the game away from its true owners, the real salts of the earth.

Every nation and every sport treasures a golden age, but in so romanticising football's golden age, we are in danger of completely losing all sense of reality of where English football has come from and where it is going.

The fact is that English football has always reflected English life. English football has more than its share of xenophobic, racist supporters, whose distrust of anything they see as not truly English, runs deep. And if the money in the game now seems excessive, and United the most commercial of clubs, then what has changed is not that money has come into football – it was always there – but the sheer volume of it and the way it affects individual clubs.

As Professor James Walvin points out in *The People's Game*, even in the halcyon days before and just after the Second World War – when modern myth would have it that money had not yet corrupted football – football was already a well-established business and industry. There was money to be made from football, plenty of it was made. However, it did not go into the football clubs as it does now, but to a few commercial people outside it, in particular the pools companies.

In 1935 football pools raked in £20 million, and by 1939 it had risen to £50 million. By the early 1950s pools and related gambling concerns had become the nation's seventh largest industry, employing some 100,000 people, and in 1948 pools paid £12.5 million in taxes alone. However, this money did not go into football, because football did not want anything to do with what many in the sport saw as tainted money, tainted from gambling. As Simon Inglis points out in his *League Football and the Men Who Made It*, the 1936 pools war showed the bankruptcy of the then football administrators. Their public position was that they did not want a penny of the pools money, since they felt betting was immoral. But privately they tried to get some of it and this contradiction, which they could not resolve, led to a humiliating defeat at the hands of the pools companies. It was another 20 years and the more worldly-wise leadership of Alan Hardaker that brought football money from the pools.

By then the man who had been seen as the great enemy of football, the man of commerce who would supposedly ruin the game, was inside the hallowed walls of football. In the 1936 pools war John Moores – founder of Littlewoods – had sworn on a bible that the League had asked for £100,000 and had been opposed by Will Cuff of Everton. But then Moores, having built his fortune through pools, took over Cuff's Everton and for good measure also owned Liverpool and nobody batted an eyelid about it. The man once so reviled in football as the evil man of commerce now owned not one but two clubs. In some ways Moores was the Rupert Murdoch of his times. The pools relationship with football was a little like the one football now has with television, but, reflecting a different age, unlike Murdoch he did not generate the sort of hype and hysteria that the Australian does.

As so often in English life change came slowly and was often forced on the football world. So it took the defeat by the Hungarians in 1953 for English football to realise that in other European countries, such as Hungary, the money made from pools went back into the game (between 1946 and 1953 alone the Hungarian Ministry of Sport had financed the building of some 600,000 sports stadiums). This remains the norm abroad, even in America where local taxes are used – as for instance in the stadium built in Denver for the Colorado Rockies baseball team – but the government here has never looked kindly on it and the Inland Revenue has never allowed tax breaks for building stadia as opposed to buying players.

But even after 1953 nothing much changed in the way football was run. In 1966, Len Shipman, then President of the Football League, could airily dismiss the idea that money should be spent on renovating stadiums which would encourage women – who had begun to be attracted to football following England's World Cup victory in 1966 – to attend games.

It required the horrific tragedy of the 1985 Bradford fire, which killed 56 people who were caught in a death trap of a Victorian stand that should have been demolished years ago, to begin the changes that finally came after Hillsborough and have since swept English football into the 90s. Although £200 million of public money has gone to rebuilding English and Scottish football since Hillsborough, Manchester United, in common with other Premiership clubs, has received £2 million, a drop in the £112 million spent on ground development and other capital spending by United since 1991. Clubs can argue with no little conviction that they have had to go down the commercial route to raise the money to rebuild grounds and fund the ever-increasing cost of players.

It is against this background that one must judge the commercialism that has undoubtedly come into the game.

That football fans should react against such commercialism is not surprising. As Jim White, the *Guardian* writer who loves Manchester United as passionately as he hates Martin Edwards, admits, football fans suffer from a kind of schizophrenia: 'When you are watching a match you want it to be an easy victory but afterwards you relish the tight finish. Take United's FA Cup semi-final against Arsenal – we would have liked an easier victory, but afterwards, we revelled in the way we won through the Giggs goal. You enjoy the tight finish, but when the match is going on you want it to be easy.'

Such a schizophrenia can become even more marked when it comes to both asking for good facilities at the ground and the best players on the park, and refusing to accept that it might cost more money.

As Martin Edwards puts it: 'You see, this is the crazy thing about supporters, they want the best players, they want the best stadium. We spent £28 million in 1998, we are spending £30 million on the stadium in 1999, we are just building a training ground for £14 million. If you want all these things you must be commercial. Unfortunately in this world, you need money to buy players, you need money to expand stadiums, you need money to set up operations whether retail or whatever. Without money you can't do these things, so we are commercial. We do not make an apology for that, as long as we don't charge ridiculous prices or rip people off. We make no apology for being commercial. We will continue to be commercial. We still hope to be the wealthiest club in the world in ten, 20 years' time, but think of the things that it does for you, think of the things that it gets you. Players' wages today are going through the roof, but supporters want the best player, so we have to be prepared to be commercial because we want to afford those players.

'All I can tell you is that in the 1998–99 season, of the 20 clubs in the Premier League, I think that we were the fifteenth in terms of price, so we were the sixth cheapest in the Premier League. We believe we have got the best stadium, the most expensive stadium and no other team spent £28 million on the team in 1998. For the 1999–2000 season we did put up prices by £2 per seat. Now you have to ask the supporters, for that £2 what are they getting? Have they got an improved team? Do they want the expansion of the stadium or do they want to stay at 55,000, 'cause it has got to be paid for. Do they want us to build that training ground where we hope to continue to get the best players, like the Ryan Giggs, the Butts and the Scholes and the Nevilles of this world, because by having what we feel will be the best training facilities or the best academy, that's the way you are going to do it.

'So we are spending our money in the right areas. Do they want that or not? Because if they don't want it and they vote with their feet, fine, we don't need to have it. We can be further down the League, we won't bother expanding the stadium, we won't bother doing the training ground and all these other things. At the end of the day things have to be paid for and apart from a dividend, which the club pays to its shareholders which amounts to about £5 million a year, every other penny that this club makes is ploughed back into the club. So the supporters are actually paying for their own future and I will say that for the 1999–2000 season we'll still be in the bottom half of the League for prices.' United's highest season ticket price of £418 is only £48 more expensive than of Wimbledon, half that of Tottenham's most expensive season tickets (£796) and a third that of Chelsea (£1,120).

However, such words and facts do little to appease fans and much of the fans' anger and frustration, which is often inchoate, reflects more a distrust of change and a sense of bewilderment that in a changing world their football club, which they thought was unchangeable, is being transformed so completely.

The focus of their anger has been the 'plc'. The three initials are now used almost as a swear word and it is seen as the fount of all evil, the ultimate triumph of money men over men of football.

Yet the arrival of plcs is the end result of a route English football took when professional clubs were first formed in this country and there is nothing more sinister than that. Indeed all the evidence suggests that in English football, plcs, far from being bad, have been beneficial. The best illustration of this comes from a comparison of the contrasting fates of Manchester United and Crystal Palace during the 1998–99 season.

Just as Sky was trying to buy United, which was considered an alien thing in the English game, Crystal Palace had what was a very traditional change of ownership. A life-long fan, Mark Goldberg, having made his money elsewhere, came to invest nearly £24 million in his beloved club and promised to float it on to the stock market in five years with a possible valuation of £150 million.

By March 1999, even before the Monopolies and Mergers Commission had reported on the Sky bid, Palace was forced into administration, and with the 1999–2000 season under way, there is no definite news as to who the new owners might be or how Palace will emerge from administration.

As Peter Kenyon, deputy chief executive of Manchester United, puts it: 'The whole question of plc destroying football is wrong. How many non-plc clubs have done a great deal? What has gone on with Goldberg cannot be healthy for the sport. Football is moving on. Somebody should look at the structure of football. Can we afford four divisions? The economics do not work. Football cannot override economics. Look at Blackburn. Jack Walker had spent a lot of money. They have got relegated and he has got to be disappointed after spending all that money.'

What Goldberg's experience at Palace demonstrates is that what is crucial is not so much the structure of the club, whether it is a plc, a private company, a trust or a mutual, but how it has been managed. And it is here that Manchester United has lessons for all in football.

But even here United's sheer success both on and off the field has led to myths that are quite remarkable. So the image presented of United is that it is a pioneer of commercialism. The reality is United has been true to its cautious, pragmatic northern roots and it has more often followed than led, but having seen the opportunities created by others it has often done it better.

It was not the first football club to come to the stock market. United followed Tottenham's lead, and having learnt from it, avoided the mistakes Tottenham made.

Again, when it comes to marketing, such as shirt sponsorship, it was Liverpool which showed the way. In 1978 Peter Robinson noticed in the FA minutes that it had relaxed the rules about carrying logos on shirts and in a fortnight did a deal with Hitachi for about £150,000. United's deal with Sharp came much later.

Where United has scored is in its commercial drive coming at the right time. Two years after Tottenham floated came Bradford and Heysel, and then Hillsborough in that long awful period through the 80s when English clubs were banned from Europe, and it seemed the game here might be so marginalised by hooliganism as to become worthless.

If United is now the supreme club in the land and in Europe then, through the late 70s and early 80s, so was Liverpool. Liverpool was one of the first clubs to build up a huge television following in Scandinavia on the back of its domestic league triumphs and the fact that it won four European Cups, still a British record. But then domestically BBC and ITV ran a cartel and there was hardly any money to be made from television. In 1985, the last year Liverpool was in the European Cup, the club made little over £250,000 from television, since none of its matches were shown live except the Final.

And when the BBC did show matches it laid down stringent conditions as to the ground advertisements Anfield could have. No company was allowed to have more than four advertising boards, no two of them together, and the BBC producer Alec Weeks would go round Anfield before the game checking to make sure the advertising boards conformed to BBC standards.

United's rise in the 90s has come in a very different era when such restrictions sound prehistoric. Sky and its money revolutionised televised football. UEFA's Champions League now brings in the sort of money Liverpool could not even dream of in the mid-80s and United, as champions, have gone into the 1999–2000 season's competitions aware that the riches they will bring are more than at any other time in the history of football. It provides United the ideal commercial platform to exploit.

But if United has been at the right place at the right time, it has also had men at the helm who have been able to exploit the opportunities created by the others.

The best example of this is Matt Busby himself. In United folklore, he is described as the great innovator for taking United into Europe to play in the European Cup, despite the disapproval of the Football League. But Busby was not the true innovator of the European Cup. The revolutionary idea, as we have seen, belonged not to Busby but to the two French journalists Gabriel Hanot, the then editor of *L'Equipe*, and his colleague Jacques Ferran, who dreamt up the idea of the European Cup.

Where Busby's skill lay was that, once he had been presented with this French idea, he could see what no-one else in England could: that this was a great opportunity, an idea whose time had come and which would catch on. The idea may not have been his but he knew how to exploit it.

In the same style, his successors at United have been able to exploit ideas dreamt of by others. This does not diminish what they have achieved, just as it does not make Busby a lesser man because he did not think of the European Cup idea. It is in the nature of great ideas that while there must be an inventor, for it to work there must be people who take it up and run with it as Busby did so brilliantly.

Only once has Manchester United strayed from this path of exploiting other people's ideas and charting a new route on its own. That was in July 1998 when an American approached Edwards and offered to buy the club. That led to the Sky bid for United.

Such vertical integration is quite common in Europe, where media companies own football clubs. But in Britain it is unknown. True, ICI owned 25% of Middlesbrough and local brewers have owned clubs such as Oldham, but they are essentially passive investors where the Board is run by a single man, for instance Steve Gibson in Middlesbrough.

United, seeking to emulate something common on the continent and in America, decided to strike out boldly and, as we know, failed. It not only proves that change comes slowly, but that United is at its best when it follows a lead or an idea of someone else's and then demonstrates how much better it is in exploiting it.

It is with this story of United's decision to do something revolutionary and the bid from Sky that we now begin.

PART ONE

MOORE AND BEST
Three Months that Shook United
and the World of Football

1

A LUNCH FROM THE CANTEEN

On the morning of 1 July 1998, two middle-aged men flew down from Manchester to the outskirts of London and a meeting with an American in a former biscuit factory. The American had not long arrived in this country but what he had to say to these two men not only shook them, but for a time, was to threaten to change the century-old face of English soccer.

The two men were Martin Edwards, chief executive of Manchester United, and Maurice Watkins, a senior partner in James Chapman & Co., a Manchester law firm, and also a non-executive director of United.

A couple of weeks earlier Mark Booth, chief executive of BSkyB, had rung Edwards to suggest a lunch to talk about pay-per-view television. Edwards wrote down in his gold-embossed Manchester United diary: 'Meeting with Mark Booth, Sky TV, Isleworth [headquarters of BSkyB], re pay-per-view.'

It seemed very natural that Booth would want to talk about pay-per-view. Sky had run into problems on this subject with the Premier League and Manchester United's sympathies were with Sky, not with the Premier League and certainly not with the way Peter Leaver, chief executive of the Premier League, had handled the issue.

A pay-per-view option had been part of the first television contract Sky had negotiated with the Premier League in 1992. Nothing had been done about it in the first contract, but as Peter Leaver took over from Rick Parry as the chief executive of the Premier League, Sky began to suggest that in the 1998–99 season it would like to start pay-per-view. Sky intended to launch its own digital channels in the autumn of 1998 and saw pay-per-view as the ideal vehicle to drive the sale of its digital channels. Pay-per-view would do for digital what live Premiership football had done for the main Sky channels since 1992.

In the summer of 1997 when Leaver had gone to Isleworth to meet

Sam Chisholm, then chief executive of BSkyB, and Vic Wakeling, head of Sky Sports, they had told Leaver that 'they would make a proposal for pay-per-view. I heard nothing more about it until I had my breakfast meeting with Mark Booth'.

That was in early 1998 after Booth had taken over from Chisholm. Then he and Wakeling had met Leaver for breakfast at the Lanesborough. While the Sky men had a full English breakfast, Leaver stuck to yoghurt and a glass of water and for the first time he heard Sky's plans for pay-per-view. There followed other meetings, some quite convivial, including drinks at the downstairs bar of the Hempel designed by Anouska Hempel, and they soon involved Richard Dunn and Mark Oliver, television advisers to the Premier League. Leaver recalls:

'They wanted to experiment with pay-per-view. I said let us see a proposal. I think Mark had been told before he became chief executive that Sky had a good relationship with the Premier League. They were very close to Rick and their feeling was that they would say, "Peter Leaver pay-per-view", and it would be waved through without any debate. I think Vic saw there would be a need to make a proper presentation to the clubs. Their original proposal was that all 320 matches which they did not televise [Sky show 60 of the 380 Premiership games every season] would be on pay-per-view. There was a meeting of the clubs in March 1998, the quarterly meeting, and they said they wanted a decision by then. I said I don't think it is feasible in that sort of timeframe. Then they came back and said they would like just under 120 matches a season on pay-per-view. We had numerous meetings between Richard, Mark Oliver, myself, Vic and Trevor. On our side Mark Oliver and Richard Dunn were very unconvinced by the project – very unimpressed by the way it was developed. What troubled us was that there did not appear to be any real research on the sort of audience they might have expected or when the matches were going to be played. It was just they were going to do it. I did not think it was possible. I spoke to the police and the supporters and it was clear it would not be popular. Richard Dunn and Mark Oliver came to me and said they could not recommend it to the clubs and we needed to carry on and discuss it to see if we could have a better proposal.'

The Premier League were due to hold their summer meeting at Stapleford Park, a luxurious hotel set in rolling countryside near Melton Mowbray in Leicestershire, in early June 1998, and Leaver decided to put pay-per-view on the agenda.

'Sky were very keen to make a presentation at the summer meeting. I said I don't think there is any point in you coming. Clubs have to decide on principle and then we can have the detailed presentation. I don't think they were pleased, they were so used to getting their own way.'

So the Premier League discussed a proposal, that from the 1998–99 season, four matches be moved from their Saturday slot to Sunday and put on pay-per-view television. If the experiment worked then more matches could be put on pay-per-view. Manchester United, supported by Aston Villa, were quite keen to have the experiment but the other clubs were not so sure and it was clear that there was no majority in favour of the experiment. Sky had offered £15 million for the experiment, which many chairmen felt was nowhere near enough to disrupt the traditional football Saturday.

After the decision was taken, both the chairmen and Sky were anxious to prove that there had been no battle, let alone that Sky had been beaten. The chairmen publicly advertised their rejection of the Sky pay-per-view experiment as a victory for the fans. The fans had always accused the chairmen of being greedy and always keen to grab every money-making scheme that was presented to them, paying no heed to the needs of the fans and the eternal values of the game. Now the chairmen said they were just as fond of the traditions of the game as the fans and had decided not to accept the experiment as it interfered with the ancient Saturday sanctity of English football.

Sky had a more difficult presentational exercise.

Like any Murdoch organisation they were not accustomed to being beaten, and now that they had suffered this first and unexpected defeat at the hands of the Premier League chairmen, they tried to distance themselves from the whole thing and worked hard to convince the world that the proposal the Premier League chairmen had turned down was not a Sky plan at all.

It suited both the League and Sky to indulge in such semantics, but the fact remained that several clubs were keen on pay-per-view and saw it as the new frontier of money. United was one of them and had been more than a little miffed by the way Leaver had dealt with the Sky proposal for an experiment. They were already beginning to have problems with Leaver; they had recently clashed with him over the issue of perimeter board advertisements and the way he had handled the pay-per-view issue added to their irritation. Despite the rejection, United were convinced that some experiment with pay-per-view would come before the end of the season.

As Peter Kenyon, the deputy chief executive put it: 'If you look at the contracts, there is provision for trials on pay-per-view and I think our view initially was, "Why don't we take this opportunity of trying it in a period of time which is a controlled environment? Let's not go in whole hog, but there is a provision in the contract and there was an understanding we would have a trial during this period." There were wild discrepancies on reports concerning pay-per-view. How do you know unless you try it?'

As Edwards, who normally likes to take the train, flew down with Watkins to London, the pair mulled over what Booth might now propose on pay-per-view. How could Booth get this experiment going again?

United's relationship with Sky had come a long way since that day in June 1992 when Sky had beaten ITV for the right to televise the games of the newly formed Premier League. At that crucial meeting in London's Royal Lancaster Hotel, Edwards and Manchester United had voted against Sky and in favour of ITV, and for some time after that, Edwards had been critical of Sky innovations such as Monday night football.

But since then Sky had worked so well and closely with the Premier League that not only had United been won over, but it had formed a particularly close relationship with Sky. The television company were United's partners in a three-way deal with Granada for United's own television channel, MUTV, the very first for a football club and which was just about to be launched.

Edwards and Watkins were driven to the only building in Sky's Isleworth complex that catches the eye: Athena Court. Its elegant design and the wide foyer of the entrance marks a striking contrast to the hangar-like buildings that surround it and to the desolate landscape that is the hinterland of Sky's headquarters. Typical of a Murdoch media operation, it looks like a cross between a factory and an army camp. If Wapping, where Murdoch's newspapers are based, is the classic example of this, then Isleworth is just as sparse and, apart from Athena Court and the 1930s Gillette building on the A4 main road that runs past the Sky headquarters, nothing takes the eye or relieves the dreary monotony. There is also nowhere to go to eat or entertain. Once employees drive in past the security guards into the 'plant' or 'factory', as they call their offices, they never leave until it is time to go home. What food they need comes from the cafeteria where, under strict Murdoch orders, no alcoholic drinks are ever served.

However, for special guests, the cafeteria can prepare more than the

6

standard canteen food it normally serves the Sky employees. On this occasion Booth had asked the cafeteria to come up with a three-course lunch which was a bit special and more like something to be found in a reasonable restaurant.

Booth had also invited Ian West, another Sky official, to the lunch. He was also chairman of MUTV and well known to both Edwards and Watkins. Edwards and Watkins felt sure that at some stage during the lunch talk would turn to this new channel, details of which were due to be given at the Edinburgh International Television Festival at the end of August.

This was a shrewd move on Booth's part, as neither Edwards nor Watkins knew Booth all that well. He had taken over from Sam Chisholm, the previous chief executive, in August 1997, but was yet to make his mark on the wider world as Chisholm had done.

Edwards and Watkins were shown into Booth's offices and, soon after the pleasantries were over, Booth led them to the boardroom adjoining his office where the canteen had laid out a three-course lunch with a smoked salmon starter and a main course of chicken and rice. It was as the first drinks were consumed and the four men tucked into the smoked salmon that Booth dropped his bombshell.

'Look, Martin,' he said, 'I have got you here under false pretences. When I rang you to invite you for this lunch I said I would like to talk about pay-per-view, but I have a bigger agenda which I didn't want to say over the phone.'

Edwards and Watkins looked at each other not knowing what to say. The silence was filled by Booth.

'What I really wanted to talk about is Sky buying Manchester United. We have looked at it and we would like to make an offer to buy your company.'

Edwards would later joke with friends that he nearly fell off his chair, but whatever the inner turmoil Booth's devastating words produced, outwardly Edwards remained calm. Watkins says, 'Probably we dug our forks a bit harder into the rice and the chicken but otherwise we did not react.'

Booth could see that both Edwards and Watkins were taken totally by surprise. A takeover could mean they might have to leave United. Booth quickly moved to reassure them.

'This is the way all sports were going to go over time and if that assumption was correct then it makes sense to take what we feel is the top entrepreneurial company and combine it with, unquestionably, the biggest club in football. I can assure you the only way we would like to do it was on a friendly basis. The great attraction of this deal is the management you have built up at Old Trafford, Martin. It is superb. You have an extraordinary sports franchise and an extraordinary business. That is a key part of what we are proposing. The only way we want to do it is if you are equally enthusiastic so I would ask you to think about it.'

Sky had often thought of owning a football club in England and even considered buying United. But Sam Chisholm, who had transformed Sky from a loss-making company into a highly profitable one, had always rejected it. He had felt the regulators would not allow such a merger. And whenever the subject had come up Chisholm had dismissed it, saying that if he wanted to buy anything in Manchester it would not be its best-known football club but its best-known soap opera: *Coronation Street*.

Booth saw things differently and this was partly a reflection in the very different ways the two men saw Sky and where it should go now. And partly because of the new dangers facing Sky.

The biggest of them came from the Office of Fair Trading, which had taken Sky, the Premier League and the BBC to the Restrictive Practices Court, alleging that the way the Premier League had entered into the contract with Sky and the BBC was anti-competitive and against the public interest. The OFT's target was the collective way the Premier League had negotiated these rights on behalf of the 20 clubs. The OFT argued that such collective power was illegal and that individual clubs should have the right to negotiate their own television deals. They also argued that Sky, or any broadcaster, should *not* be given the right to sign exclusive contracts.

Booth had been assured by lawyers that Sky would win the case, but there could be no guarantee, and Sky knew if the Restrictive Practices Court found in the OFT's favour then Sky's hold on English domestic football would be in grave danger.

Booth himself had been thinking about making such an offer since February. It was then that he had asked Kevin Kinsella, the Zimbabwean head of the business development unit of BSkyB, to come up with options for Sky. As an American, Booth had grown up with the idea of media companies owning sports clubs (or, as he called them, 'franchises', that being the term used in America). Media ownership of baseball, American football and basketball teams was very common and Murdoch had just bought the Los Angeles Dodgers. In the UK, however, it was unknown. Not that companies did not get involved with football clubs, but historically they had generally been local brewery companies holding shares in their hometown clubs. And in most cases they were very passive investors.

Kinsella, recalls Booth, 'drew up a list of clubs Sky could take over. Arsenal and Liverpool were considered, but top of his recommendation was Manchester United. He did not think the others made much sense.'

Kinsella argued that, should the Restrictive Practices Court declare collective selling illegal, it would benefit top clubs like Manchester United, who could then use their muscle to get the best television deal. That was the way some of the continental clubs were thinking and many of them were pressing for an end to the collective selling of television rights.

United would provide Sky with a solid UK base around which a competitive soccer package could be built in almost all conceivable scenarios. With its very large fan base the club was likely to be a major beneficiary of pay-per-view when that was launched. By buying United, Sky would have tremendous leverage over both domestic and European rights.

Kinsella's argument for buying United was that not only would it mean Sky had a seat at the domestic football table, but it could also provide the broadcaster with a seat at a European Super League, plans for which were in the air and which always included Manchester United as the major English representative.

The European dimension was crucial. Sky had no European club football rights – the major ones being all owned by ITV – but if Sky bought United then, as Murdoch's buying of 20th Century Fox in the US had helped him influence movie negotiations, Sky could shape the development of the European Super League to its advantage.

Booth says, 'The reaction to what the OFT was doing was a factor in our thinking. But the fact is we invest a lot of money in football. Whenever you have a part of this business and invest and continue to invest, it is a natural thing to consider. The more we looked at, and the more we thought, the opportunity to buy United was a very interesting one. That really centred on the fact that if you looked round the world the combination between media companies and sports organisations was a trend that was growing. The value to the sports organisation, be it a football team or a baseball team, was greater if it was part of a larger organisation. It seemed to us that was something that was going to happen along these lines. In that case we wanted to be first in line rather than maybe at the back of the line.'

Booth was also keen to move away from the pattern set by

Chisholm. It had made Sky very successful, but he now wanted to chart a new course. Booth's need to put a stamp on Sky that was different from Chisholm's was understandable.

When Chisholm left Sky, after nearly a decade of unparalleled success he had wanted his deputy David Chance to succeed. But for various reasons it did not happen and Murdoch had brought in Booth.

Chisholm had himself introduced Booth to Murdoch when, after working for Robert Maxwell, he arrived in Australia and found all roads in television in the UK led to Sam Chisholm. Booth got on well with Murdoch and his children and one reason given for his appointment was that he could work with Elizabeth Murdoch, Murdoch's daughter, who is seen as a future head of Murdoch's television operations in the UK.

The whole handover was arranged at a dinner in The Dorchester on the night of 13 June 1997 attended by Murdoch, Chisholm, Booth and Lord Tim Bell, the media guru who had been an influential adviser to Margaret Thatcher.

Lord Bell says: 'There wasn't a power struggle when Chisholm left but a strategy struggle, if you like, in the sense that Sam ran the company one way and Mark was determined to run it a different way. I think Sam – this is a large over-simplification – had positioned Sky as the first and the exclusive, which sort of bullied people into having to buy dishes and subscriptions, because if they didn't, they couldn't get something. So, if you like, it was a sort of negative relationship. People bought Sky subscriptions because they wanted to watch the sport they couldn't watch anywhere else, so they had to.

'I think Mark took the view that people should do things because they wanted to, not because they had no choice. At the same time he didn't want to lose the strength of the exclusivities and the strength of being first and so on. It's a tonal thing more than anything else. It is perhaps reflected in the two people. Sam was a very abrasive, aggressive individual – took no prisoners, very robust, went all the way, was quite prepared to see a deal fall away if it couldn't be agreed on his terms. Mark is a much more charming, sophisticated person, elegant in his manner and very pleasant and pleasing in his demeanour. He's nonetheless very tough – just as tough as Sam – but it's an iron fist in a velvet glove, if you like, rather than an iron fist punching you in the face.'

Bell believes that the key to Booth's thinking, which turned him in the direction of Manchester United, 'was that what Sky sell is television. Television is probably the most popular thing that people do in this country. It's actually more popular than football, which is worth remembering. Given that they sell more of and – what he and I would think is – better television than anybody else, then Sky ought to be more admired. They ought to be thought of by people as the best suppliers and held in the same kind of affection that Tesco or Sainsbury is held by their customers. The duty of the provider is to provide the widest range of choice at affordable levels if it's technically possible and let people make decisions.'

On that basis it was natural, says Bell, to think about buying Manchester United. 'Why Manchester United? Because it is the most famous club in the world and if you are going to buy a football club, why buy a second-rate one? But the first pressure was to change, if you like, the tone or voice of the thing. Part of that, Mark felt quite strongly, was to demonstrate that you were putting something into football; that you weren't just paying for it and sticking it on your screens. Now, of course, it's absolutely true that Sky have been putting something into football ever since they had the Premier League contract. In fact, they invented the Premier League; they invented the coverage of it; they made the matches exciting; they had girls dancing round, music – they entertained the crowd; they entertained the journalists; they entertained the players; they've made it into an enthusiastic, exciting event.

'I think Booth took the view that, although he knows nothing about football – he has no personal interest in it – that it was part of the repositioning of Sky to take an interest in the things they were doing. He took this view right at the very beginning. While he was understudying Sam he was already thinking how he would do things differently, not for the sake of it but because he genuinely believed it was not necessary for Sky to have this very negative image. He set about the process and talked to Vic and Vic in any case had always been keen on putting something back into the game. He was enthusiastic about this idea of being much more positive.'

For the next hour and a half, while Booth, West, Edwards and Watkins finished the three-course lunch the Sky canteen had rustled up, Booth outlined the broad philosophical idea of Sky buying United. Booth did not tell Edwards how much he might pay for United and Edwards did not ask. Booth was very keen to keep this as a 'conceptual' meeting. He wanted to see how Edwards would react; he had to get to know the man and see if he could work with him in a Sky-owned Manchester United. The time to work out a price would come later.

Edwards and Watkins emerged into the sunshine of Isleworth not knowing what to say or do. This was not the first time someone had come knocking at Edwards' door wanting to buy United. In 1989, over a similar lunch – except on that occasion Edwards had hosted it at Old Trafford – Michael Knighton had made an offer for United, and in the summer of 1996, VCI, the video and publishing company, had made an approach for the club. However, Sky was something much bigger and very different.

When Edwards had agreed to sell to Knighton, he had done the deal and then told the Board. But then United was a private company and Edwards owned more than 50%. Now it was a public one with City institutions owning more than 60% and Edwards owning just 14% and Watkins 2%. The Board would have to consider it, but not yet. What Booth had proposed was so revolutionary and wide-reaching that Edwards could not take it to the Board right away. In any case no price had been mentioned, so there was nothing to take to the Board but an idea. However, there was one man who had to know about it straight away.

Before he left the lunch Edwards had told Booth that he would like to widen it out and talk to one other man. Booth understood. Now Edwards and Watkins decided to jump into a car and drive across London to Upper Thames Street – coincidentally a mile up the road from Wapping, where Murdoch's print media of the *Sun*, *Times* and *News of the World* was produced – to see that man.

That man was Sir Roland Smith, who was a consultant to the merchant banking arm of Hong Kong & Shanghai Bank and had an office there. Smith was chairman of Manchester United plc and the man to whom in strict theory Edwards, as chief executive, reported. Although the back pages referred to Edwards as chairman of United, he was only chairman of the football company, which was a wholly owned subsidiary of the plc. It was Smith who as chairman was technically the highest officer, albeit non-executive, of Manchester United.

Smith, who had been chairman since 1991, just before United had been floated on the stock market, was just reaching 70 and had been a legendary figure in British boardrooms for more than four decades. Among his various chairmanships had been that of British Aerospace and of the House of Fraser, where he had successfully stopped Tiny Rowland of Lonhro from getting his hands on the company and its flagship store Harrods. In the midst of this epic battle, in a memorable exchange with Rowland, Smith had said, 'Get your tanks off my lawn,

Tiny.' Rowland had been forced to do that and never succeeded in owning the store he so coveted. Over the decades, Smith had developed an aura about himself, helped by such personal idiosyncracies as never carrying any money on him, which meant that his chaffeur was always having to provide change for small purchases.

Manchester United was one of many executive directorships Smith had, but it was the one that had the most appeal and was closest to his heart. Smith, a former professor of management at the University of Manchester, which had given him the widely used nickname of Prof, had long been a supporter of United and saw his job as chairman of the plc as combining his love for his favourite club with his skill as a company doctor.

As Smith, Edwards and Watkins mulled over Booth's approach, it seemed to Smith that just then United was in need of a business doctor. Booth's approach could not have been better timed if it was designed to exploit United's vulnerability. Kinsella may have felt United was a great buy, but just then United felt more than a little nervous about the future. The season that had ended had been a dreadfully barren one for United. Since the start of the 90s, when Alex Ferguson had won his first trophy, the FA Cup, United had rarely gone through a season without adding to the trophy collection at Old Trafford. So prolific had United been in hunting trophies that in the eight years since the start of the decade United had done the double of the Premiership and the FA Cup twice, won the League Cup and also a European trophy, the Cup Winners Cup.

Only once before, in 1995, when they had lost their talismanic player Eric Cantona, had United finished a season with nothing. But while that season had been just as bleak as 1998, the failure to win anything in 1998 seemed more worrying. In 1995 United had lost the championship by a point to Blackburn and the FA Cup to Everton by a single goal. Neither club, in particular Blackburn, seemed capable of challenging United's dominance of English domestic football.

However, in 1998, the challenger seemed on a different level. Arsenal, who had started the year 12 points adrift of United, had come from behind so splendidly that United, who had appeared impregnable at the turn of the year, had won nothing and Arsenal had done the double. They were a big club, well funded and well run, with an astute manager in Arsène Wenger, and had the potential to match United. United had so badly lost its way after March that they were dumped out of the cup by Barnsley and then went out of the Champions League to Monaco.

Football supporters, even at the boardroom level, always live with fear and the dread of future failure and Smith, in particular, was haunted by the thought that United's golden run may have come to an end.

There was also another fear. Would United's barren 1998 be followed by a stock market collapse? On 8 June the FT All Share Index had reached a peak of 2868, but by 23 June it had fallen to 2708 and, although it recovered, within days of Booth's approach the market started a decline, which by mid-August would see the All Share Index fall to 2539. (Between 30 June 1998 and 30 September 1998 the FT 100 index of leading shares fell by 13.2% from 5832.50 to 5064.40.)

Everywhere Smith looked there seemed to be economic disasters looming. Russia was in crisis; Asian economies, once seen as tiger economies which could show the way to the West, were now on the brink of collapse. There were also fears that the UK would soon be in recession, if it was not already so, but the greatest worry was about the US. For six years since Clinton had come to power, the US had enjoyed unprecedented growth and prosperity and Wall Street had soared. But now there was talk of US growth slowing and of Alan Greenspan, the head of the US Federal Reserve, the central bank, putting up interest rates. The first feeling of a chill in the air had come with the collapse of the hedge firm based in Connecticut, Long Term Credit Management. Its sudden demise had shaken the stability of the markets and, as so often in such circumstances, history books were consulted to see if all this meant another 1929-style Wall Street crash.

To add to the fears, there was growing talk of Clinton being impeached. Clinton would soon be forced to testify before a grand jury about his affair with Monica Lewinsky and nobody could predict how the markets might react if he was forced out of office. In a curious way, like the football fan, the stock market trader likes to think market movements are based on solid fundamentals, but when things start going wrong they have nothing to turn to but hope and prayer.

So that summer day, as Edwards, Smith and Watkins looked out of Smith's office and over the Thames to County Hall, and what was once the headquarters of the GLC, they wondered if the economic winds of change blowing against United might not make merging with the biggest and most entrepreneurial media company in the world the best option.

Smith's office was opposite that of Keith Harris, then chief executive of HSBC's investment banking arm, and Edwards, in the strictest confidence, informed Harris of Booth's approach. Harris could see that Roland Smith was drawn to the offer. 'Roland was very gloomy. He felt United's great run was coming to an end. He was gloomy about the markets. Roland had also turned 70 and he changed at 70.'

Harris had long been an Edwards confidant and even longer a Manchester United fan. Brought up in Manchester, he was taken by his father to Stockport County on Friday nights and United on Saturday and he still recalls his first match just before Munich against Ipswich at home.

The Harris and Edwards families had old ties. Keith's father knew Louis Edwards and had done business with him. He was in the confectionery business and manufactured panyan pickles which he supplied to the butcher shops owned by Louis Edwards. The sons had renewed this business relationship more than 30 years later when, following United's float, Glen Cooper, the merchant banker who had organised the float, took a group of City investors to Old Trafford. The 1991 float had not gone well: the Maxwells had dumped their United shares on the market forcing the price south so dramatically that having floated at 385p it was down to 250p. Cooper knew he had to do something to revive interest in the City and decided a match-day visit by City investors to the theatre of dreams was the answer.

Although the match Harris and the City investors watched, a 0–0 draw with Liverpool in October 1991, was less than enthralling and notable only for the fact that Mark Hughes for United and Gary Ablet for Liverpool were sent off, what made his day was lunch in the boardroom with Sir Matt Busby. For a United fan this was like meeting the creator. The friendship with Edwards that was formed as a result of this visit blossomed and Edwards found that he had much in common with Harris. Like him, Harris was a man with wide sporting interest, not for him the modern tribal love of only one club. He could appreciate other clubs and also took an interest in other sports, avidly following Lancashire cricket during the summer.

It was Harris who had been the conduit for the approach VCI had made to United in the summer of 1996. VCI already had a relationship with United, producing its videos. VCI was also a client of HSBC, which had helped float the company, and was looking to expand. Euro 96 was about to happen, football was fashionable, but a look at the share price showed that the market did not value clubs all that highly. Although United was challenging on two fronts and was about to do the double, the United share price had been around £1.50 for a long time and it seemed this might be a good time to buy the club.

Harris recalls: 'Michael Grade [the chairman] and Steve Ayers [the chief executive] came to me and said they were looking to expand in the sports world. They had a good relationship with the club and they felt it was undervalued. Effectively it would have been a reverse takeover. Our guys in the corporate finance division were confident they could do it.'

On 11 May 1996 United beat Liverpool 1–0 in the FA Cup Final to become the first team to do the double double, to win the League and the Cup in the same season twice. In 1961, when Tottenham had become the first club to do the double in the 20th century, it had seemed an impossible dream, but now United had gone where no club had ever gone before. Having done their first double in 1994 they had now followed it with their second. However, the share price moved hardly a jolt and the following Monday Harris took Ayers to Old Trafford to see Edwards, where Ayers presented his proposal for a takeover of United with VCI looking to pay round about £2 a share.

Edwards listened intently and then promised to consider it and come back. Soon a letter followed from Grade to Edwards. But before Edwards or the Board could consider it, events intervened. Soon after, the Premier League met for its summer meeting in a hotel near Coventry and Sky, led by Sam Chisholm, beat off rivals organised by Lord Hollick's United News and Media Group and a consortium orchestrated by Kelvin Mackenzie and Michael Green's Carlton for the Premier League contract.

The first Sky contract in 1992 was worth £190 million over five years (the contract has often been written off as worth £304 million but that included overseas, highlights and projections for marketing and was a notional figure that was never reached). Now Sky, for just the rights to televise 60 live games, was prepared to pay £670 million for *four years*. It was undreamt-of riches and the share price, unmoved by Ferguson's achievements on the field, took off. VCI's approach did not even turn into a formal offer.

However, if VCI had been seen off by the jump in the share price, Edwards had now begun to worry that others might start thinking of buying United. What if they made an unfriendly approach? So he turned to Harris and wondered if HSBC might be willing to act as United's merchant bankers and advise them on such situations.

Harris was keen: 'I wanted to combine business with pleasure. Also I wanted to go into the leisure business. I knew it was taking off. If we had Manchester United it was a great calling card. You could go to Barcelona and say we represent Manchester United, they are the best in the UK and we would like to advise you. But my colleagues in corporate finance were not convinced. They said what will United bring? I could see their point. United were not going to take over companies which generate work for corporate finance. But I said, "You watch: there will be a bid for United." '

Normally when companies hire merchant bankers there is what the City calls a 'beauty parade': presentations by several merchant bankers explaining what they have to offer. Harris wooed the United directors and finally did a deal. HSBC would prepare a defence document for United which would work out a strategy for coping with anyone else who might want to buy the club in return for being appointed merchant bankers without a beauty parade. It seemed a fair exchange. Normally a merchant bank would charge £150,000 for such a defence document; United were getting it free and HSBC getting United business without a presentation. While Harris had got the business it was Rupert Faure Walker, managing director of corporate finance, and David Blake, a director of corporate finance, who would be in day-to-day charge.

Harris and his two colleagues had a bet about who might bid for Manchester United. 'David said Sky, Rupert said Granada and I agreed with Rupert,' recalls Harris.

Edwards had other links with HSBC and also knew Rupert Faure Walker. This was through Edwards and his family's meat distribution business in Manchester, Louis C Edwards. Louis C Edwards was a shell company which was used by James Gulliver in 1978 to form Argyll Foods, which subsequently became the Safeway Group. It was an enormous success and the shares went up about 60-fold after Gulliver arrived. HSBC had acted for Gulliver in all those deals and Rupert Faure Walker had got to know Edwards very well.

So it is no surprise that when Booth made the offer to Edwards one of the people he turned to was Harris. They discussed the many problems even a club as successful and well run as United faced.

Edwards was well aware that United needed to spend money to buy players. One reason for United's barren season had been their failure to find a replacement for Roy Keane, the captain and influential midfield player, whose injury in September 1997 had played a major part in United's decline, something Ferguson acknowledged. Ferguson had already drawn up a shopping list. United had bought one player on that list – Japp Stam, the Dutch defender, for £10 million – but there were others on Ferguson's list including Dwight Yorke and Patrick Kluivert. Then there was the cost of increasing the capacity at Old Trafford, which would mean an investment of upwards of £30 million.

Costs were always going up. Players' wages were rising inexorably, and even as Booth was making his approach, Edwards had to deal with another wage rise. Brian Kidd, the number two to Ferguson, had received an attractive offer from Everton to manage the ailing Merseyside club. Kidd had always wanted to be number one, and was tempted and, although his contract had another two years to run, United was so keen to keep him that it had given him a new contract at a much higher salary.

Edwards was not gullible enough to believe that letting Sky buy United would mean millions for his club. He knew business did not work that way. However, it would mean being part of a much bigger organisation with vast resources that could come in handy should times get tough.

There was also the personal consideration. If Sky could be persuaded to pay 215p then Edwards' 14% would bring in just under £80 million, a handy sum. Ever since United had floated, Edwards had been selling shares and in the process had his cake and had eaten it too. He had made £38 million but also retained control, a fact that made the other Premier League chairmen extremely envious of him.

Now he could sell his entire stake but still run United for Sky.

The next day Edwards called Booth and told him that he had spoken to Roland Smith and a couple of other people. And while he was not yet sure whether it made sense or not, he was prepared to discuss it further.

For Edwards there was one problem. On 6 July the Manchester United plc Board was due to have a whole-day meeting at Old Trafford to discuss strategy. The idea was to review the bleak season that had just gone and discuss where the club was going and how it should plan for the millennium.

The Board could hardly discuss future strategy without being told of Booth's approach, but Edwards felt it was too early to share this information with the rest of his Board. Edwards was very keen to keep it in a tight circle of himself, Smith, Watkins and Harris, until it had developed into something like a firm offer or there was some idea of how much Sky might be prepared to pay. So it was decided that while the Board would meet, the strategy session would be cancelled.

The United Board met as planned on the morning of 6 July. Most of the Board members were present including Greg Dyke, a non-executive director and also chairman of Pearson Television. Dyke, although born in west London, had been a United supporter since childhood, except for a brief period when he switched allegiance to Brentford when his brother was in the youth team there. He had been invited on to the

Board by Edwards in September 1997 to provide some television expertise and it seemed a shrewd appointment. He had held various positions in ITV, including at one time head of ITV sport when he had lost the rights to televise football for the new Premier League to Chisholm. Dyke had then decided to complain about the deal to the Office of Fair Trading, alleging it was anti-competitive. It was this complaint that had led to the OFT investigation, and ironically, now a bid for United.

Dyke had a bluntness of manner that many found appealing and some disconcerting. Back in the 80s the football world was seeking to prove that there was a cartel between BBC and ITV over televised football, something both the BBC and ITV always denied. But then at a dinner of leading clubs that Edwards had attended, when the clubs asked Dyke whether there was a cartel he, to the amazement of the chairman, instantly replied yes.

Now on 6 July the directors found a rather strange United Board meeting, although the strangeness struck them only afterwards. As one director says: 'Roland Smith opened the meeting and then, when we came to the strategy part, he said he had to go and we did not get on to it. We later learnt it was because of the takeover. It is perfectly legitimate for a chairman and chief executive to have a discussion about takeover without telling the rest of the Board until you get closer to the real nitty gritty. I don't have a problem with that. I have no problem with the way Roland behaved.'

The next meeting was not due until 8 August and by then Edwards hoped things would have progressed for him to tell the Board. For the moment his secret was safe with Smith and Watkins.

This also meant that two other people at Old Trafford knew nothing about the approach from Booth. They were Peter Kenyon, Edwards' deputy, and David Gill, the finance director. Both these men, in particular Kenyon, were heavily involved in another secret negotiation.

Edwards felt it was best they work on this extremely sensitive project and not be dragged into a possible takeover by Sky that might or might not lead to an actual offer.

Edwards says, 'When the bid came in only myself, Sir Roland and Maurice were privy to it at first. Not even Peter Kenyon or David Gill. We advised the Board, the non-executives and Peter and David at the appropriate moment, once we realised how serious it was. We had to first of all consider how serious it was. Once we determined all that you open it up.'

And while Edwards was considering how to open it, something else was opening up for Manchester United that was potentially just as explosive and could have meant that by the time the season began, United might not even be playing in the Premier League and the whole face of European football could be changed forever.

2

A DRINK IN THE BASEMENT BAR

Peter Kenyon was Edwards' chosen successor, the man whose appointment had led to sudden ructions within the Old Trafford management team and the departure of the then commercial supremo Edward Freedman. He was already in London on that July day and, before Edwards and Watkins had gone to Sky, the three had discussed what United's position would be with regard to pay-per-view football on TV.

The next day, 2 July, Kenyon was due at a meeting not far from where Edwards had briefed Sir Roland Smith on Booth's offer. The meeting was at the offices of the highly paid City lawyers Slaughter & May. While Edwards and Watkins had gone to lunch with Booth under false pretences, little suspecting what they would be told, Kenyon knew very well the subject he would discuss at Slaughter & May and how explosive it might prove to be.

For nearly two months he and United had been privy to the plans, ever since a meeting in a bar in São Paolo. The plans were for a European Super League bringing together United and the major clubs of Europe and offering vastly more money than that which the clubs got from UEFA, European football's governing body. But while the opportunity was glittering they carried enormous risks and could end up by tearing apart the European competitions built up by UEFA over the last 40 years.

When Kenyon had first been presented with the plans in the bar of the International Continental Hotel in São Paolo in early May his instinctive reaction was, 'If this is so real, why are we looking at it in a bar?'

The plans had come as a total surprise. Kenyon had gone to Brazil with little thought that he was about to be made an offer he could not possibly refuse. His trip to Brazil, which had taken him to the São

Paolo bar, had come at the invitation of Pele. United, partly through Bobby Charlton, had long been associated with Pele, and Kenyon himself, in his previous job in Umbro, the sports manufacturer, had had a very warm relationship with Pele going back ten years.

The relationship was so close and intimate that when, in April 1998, United opened their Museum in Old Trafford's North Stand, renovated at a cost of £4 million, it was decided to get Pele over to Manchester to inaugurate it. United sent Ken Merrett, the Club Secretary, over to Brazil to collect Pele's World Cup medals, his shirts and various other things such as a replica of the Jules Rimet Trophy – Brazil having been given the trophy when they won it for the third time in Mexico in 1970. United also laid on an exhibition on Pele at their Museum.

Pele arrived in Manchester on 10 April and spent a weekend there opening the Museum and talking about his own plans for Brazil. Kenyon recalls: 'Pele, who was then the Brazilian Sports Minister, was very involved in the restructuring of Brazilian football and, as a consequence of that, when he came to Manchester he asked if I would go over and do a conference in São Paolo on the implications of what was being introduced as the Pele Law, which was meant to help restructure the game there. The amazing thing about Brazilian football is that whilst all the raw talent is there in Brazil, the infrastructure and organisation is a complete nightmare. Pele wanted to look at role models within the Premier League and in particular Manchester United as a football club. We readily agreed to go to Pele's conference and I asked Maurice to come over and be a part of that programme.

'Part of the Pele Law was to consider the opportunities for deriving additional revenues, clubs going public, etc., etc. As a club we've got a good relationship with Glen [Cooper of merchant bankers Apax]; he was involved in our flotation, so I thought it was relevant and asked him to join us.'

One evening during this two-day conference in São Paolo, on 12–13 May 1998, in between finishing sessions at the conference and going to one of the official dinners, Kenyon was having an early-evening drink with Watkins and Cooper in the low-ceilinged bar of the Intercontinental. The three made a distinctive English group sitting in the middle of the bar, all bald or nearly bald, middle-aged and, in Cooper's case, sporting a satisfying middle-age spread which spoke of both authority and affluence.

Kenyon and Watkins had just started on their beers, whilst Cooper, having decided to order a beer, had seen the sun go down, and, reminded of the old colonial adage that at sunset you had your first peg of whisky, had switched to Scotch, when this very English group was approached by two Italians and a Swede. The Italians were well known to Kenyon, being Andrea Locatelli and Paolo Taveggia; the Swede, whom he was to get to know over the next few months, was Peter Ecelund. What they had brought to the bar in the São Paolo Intercontinental were the plans for a European Super League.

Cooper recalls: 'Peter Ecelund, who I later learnt was a Swedish gentleman and got to know quite well, introduced himself to the rest of us and immediately went into this pitch about a European Super League. I must say my initial reaction was rather sniffy and British. It raised my hackles that here we were sitting in the middle of a bar, not a discreet environment at all, and we were talking about this quite revolutionary plan. If you have world-shattering news, then a bar in the basement of the Intercontinental in São Paolo is not the place to discuss them.'

Kenyon says, 'Ecelund told us there was a document they'd like us to have a look at. It was a new concept for a European football competition and it would derive significant revenues and give owner-ship back to the clubs. They'd done an awful lot of work on it. They gave us a booklet, which we took away and packed in our bags as we left Brazil for the UK.'

After Ecelund had gone, and Cooper had got over his British reserve about how such things should be handled, he had a look at the document Ecelund had given and concluded, 'It seemed to be thoughtfully put together and quite clever.'

The clever idea was codenamed Project Parsifal, named after Wagner's last opera, first performed in 1882 at Wagner's own theatre, Festspielhaus at Bayreuth, with the set featuring the temple of the Holy Grail. The Holy Grail proposed by Media Partners was a midweek league of 24 or 32 teams whose membership would partly be determined by merit and partly by status such as previous record in Europe and the size of the club, etc. The most radical part of the plan was that there would be a group of founder members that would enjoy a permanent membership of the league because of their size and wealth.

Peter Ecelund, Andrea Locatelli and Paolo Taveggia were all partners in a company called Media Partners. Kenyon knew the Italians quite well, in particular Paolo Taveggia, a former Italian Foreign Office official. He had been at Crystal Palace on the night in January 1995 when Eric Cantona had made a kung-fu attack on a Palace supporter. Taveggia, who was then general manager of Inter Milan, had come over to try to buy Cantona and, in the aftermath of the incident, come quite close to returning to Milan with the French player.

Some months later, after the world learnt of the plans for a European Super League, there would be intense speculation about Media Partners. Who was the Mr Big behind these men, the virtually unknown boys from the Milan tennis club, as they were derisively dubbed by some at UEFA? Not all of them were from Milan but seven members of their management team were Italians, their President Rodolfo Hecht was an AC Milan supporter, while Locatelli had played for AC Milan. It was this Milan connection, and the fact that Hecht and Taveggia had worked for Silvio Berlusconi, the former Italian Prime Minister and owner of AC Milan, that led to intense speculation that they were really front men for Berlusconi. Newspapers freely said this. Media Partners successfully denied this, saying they were nobody's puppets and, while many of their partners had worked for Berlusconi, they were the sole owners of their company, one with a good track record in sports rights, having put together football's first pay-per-view television contract for Italian television.

What they shared with Berlusconi was the vision that one day there would be a European Super League bringing together the best clubs in Europe and producing the sort of money not available in the current UEFA competitions. The Berlusconi view was, 'There will be a league formed outside UEFA with a team from each country sponsored by that country's biggest company . . . a super professional football league like American football, which will attract millions of viewers.'

Berlusconi's men were also keen to make sure that Media Partners' message reached the right sources. Two days after the meeting in the basement bar of the São Paolo Intercontinental, and as Kenyon, Watkins and Cooper flew back to the UK, Patrick Harverson of the *Financial Times* first broke the story of Media Partners and how its plans for a new European League could be a threat to UEFA.

Harverson had been put on to the story at the prompting of Adriano Galliani, the general manager of AC Milan, whose clean-shaven head makes him a dead ringer for Kojak played by the American film star Telly Savalas. A few weeks before Kenyon travelled to Brazil, Harverson, along with a group of five English journalists, had been flown to Milan to watch a match between Milan and Bologna. Bologna were then thinking of floating on the London stock market and were keen to make themselves known. During a party hosted by Bologna President Guiseppe Gazzoni, Galliani came up to Harverson, and using Gazzoni as interpreter, whispered to Harverson that while he was in

Milan he should speak to Rodolfo Hecht. Harverson did and Hecht told him, 'The way the Champions League is formatted today it is an underperforming asset. We believe we can do better.'

Galliani was not the only one whispering about Media Partners' plans. At the other end of the newspaper spectrum from the *Financial Times*, the *News of the World* heard the whispers too. On 3 May 1998 Alex Montgomery of the *News of the World* ran a back-page lead headlined, 'Super League Sensation', which went on to say that Arsenal, Manchester United and Liverpool were to be involved in a breakaway Super League. That Sunday Arsenal were playing Everton at home; victory would give them the championship and the first part of the Premier League and Cup double.

Montgomery says: 'Late in the week on Thursday or Friday I received a tip-off from two sources. One was someone from Northern Europe and one from Italy. The first guy, the Italian, said things are going on about a Super League. My immediate reaction was, "It is boring, we have heard it so often, nothing seems to materialise". My contact persisted, "There have been meetings in your country. Your clubs have held meetings and are doing it in utmost secrecy." My contacts told me the set-up. I didn't know how I could confirm it. But first I had to convince my office. This took some doing, but in the end they decided to run it. I checked it out with Peter Leaver, who dismissed it out of hand. "Are you telling me people I know, friends of mine, are telling me lies?" I said, "I don't know about that but they are capable of telling you lies." The question was: was it yea or nay and he said nay. We ran a back-page lead.'

Montgomery did not know that Media Partners were involved and he pictured Berlusconi as the prime mover behind it all. But he did have some of the elements of the Media Partners plans, and accurately predicted the names of the top English and European clubs who eventually did get involved and that it was meant to start in two years' time.

However, as Montgomery rather ruefully says, 'It was dismissed out of hand principally because it emerged in a tabloid newspaper. I then found I could not develop the story further and I walked away from it.' Neither Montgomery's story nor that of Harverson, which followed two weeks later, had legs, as they say in journalism, and for the moment Media Partners' secret remained safe.

Media Partners would later claim that they had been working on this project for years, but it was in the spring of 1998 that they began contacting clubs, and the first ones, given the origins of their company, were the Italian ones. Arsenal, about to complete the double, was clearly their first port of call in England but Manchester United and Liverpool were also on the list, although Montgomery's contacts were a bit premature in saying all three of them had been in talks at that stage. Soon Media Partners had visited all three clubs although it was with Arsenal that they initially developed the closest links.

Before Harverson wrote his story he checked with Martin Edwards, who assured him that United had not been approached and even if they were to be they would prefer any restructuring of European competitions to be through UEFA, not in opposition to it.

At this stage, of course, Edwards was not even aware of Media Partners; Kenyon and Watkins had barely got back from Brazil. In any case, neither Kenyon nor Watkins had any reason to believe that this proposal was any different from the umpteen ones that float across the desks of United and other top clubs offering them ideas that say: HOW WE CAN MAKE YOU MORE MONEY. Unlike Kenyon, Watkins had not even taken the material Ecelund had given them. The case the OFT had brought against the Premier League, Sky and the BBC had reached what lawyers call 'the discovery stage', when everything relevant has to be disclosed to the other side. Watkins was a witness and might have been required to yield up documents regarding Media Partners and decided not to take them.

However, a few days after their return, the initial scepticism of Kenyon and United about Project Parsifal gave way to guarded enthusiasm.

Kenyon says: 'It was intriguing from two points of view. First and foremost, the quality of the advisers that had been involved with the project. It was obvious from the outset that this wasn't something that had been put together the week before. There'd been significant research done on competition formats, TV revenues, club ownership and rights.'

Kenyon was now getting increasing evidence of the enormous potential of this project, a potential that was underlined two weeks after Kenyon and Watkins return from Brazil when Real Madrid won the Champions League for the first time since 1966. For United the Champions League was the Holy Grail. They had won it for the only time in 1968 and Real's victory, after 30 years, merely made the hunger for this ultimate goal all the greater at Old Trafford. But as the fans yearned for the glory, the money men asked: If United won, what would it mean in hard cash?

UEFA made mucho of the fact that Real would now bank some £8.5 million; United as beaten quarter-finalists had got £5.37 million.

Media Partners' figures, which Kenyon had in front of him, not only promised each club four times as much money but Media Partners also made much of the fact that UEFA gave the clubs a raw deal. Only 55% of UEFA's total income of £155 million came back to the clubs; UEFA themselves kept nearly £30 million and Team Marketing, the company that did the deals for UEFA, got nearly 12.5% of the gross take. Media Partners' plans promised a complete break from all this and to top it all Media Partners promised that the European Super League meant the top clubs themselves, not UEFA, would own the Super League. This was immensely attractive.

Outside the boardrooms and conference chambers the World Cup in France riveted the world of football and it was here in Paris that a little-noticed decision was taken which further spurred Media Partners and the top clubs. For the 1998–99 season AC Milan, five times winners of the Champions League, had failed to qualify for Europe. This was the second year Milan was out of Europe and as Hecht had told Harverson, 'It's a tragedy. The question is how do you deal with that? I think sport in Europe is ready to be privatised.'

Milan had proposed to UEFA that in such situations clubs like Milan with an established pedigree in Europe should be given a wild card in much the same way tennis players who do not qualify on their form for tournaments can get in on their past record. The UEFA executive discussed this proposal at their meeting in Paris on 25 June, during the World Cup, and decided that football was not tennis. Media Partners made much of this UEFA decision, emphasising that in their proposal the original founding clubs who formed part of the Super League would have a guarantee that they would remain part of the League irrespective of form or lack of it.

By late June United were drawn into the net and, after some informal discussions, Media Partners called their first formal meeting at the offices of Slaughter & May on 2 July. United decided that not only would Kenyon go to the meeting but so would David Gill.

They arrived to find an interesting collection of clubs: the two Milan clubs AC and Inter, Juventus, Ajax from Holland, Marseille and Paris St Germain from France, Borussia Dortmund from Germany, but nobody from Spain. This meeting was followed by a second on 14 July, which saw Arsenal present.

Kenyon would have expected to see David Dein, vice-chairman of Arsenal. He is not only full-time at Arsenal with an office in Highbury, but one of the few men in English soccer with a well-developed European interest. Instead Ken Friar, their then chief executive, and

Danny Fiszman, the immensely wealthy director who owns the largest block of shares in the club, and has cross shareholdings with Dein, came to Slaughter & May to represent Arsenal. Soon the mystery was solved.

There had been a split in the Arsenal Board between Dein on the one hand and Fiszman, Friar, the Carrs and Peter Hill-Wood, the chairman, on the other. Dein was a member of the UEFA Competitions Committee, the one that ran all the European competitions, including the Champions League now threatened by Media Partners' Super League. The fact that he was on this UEFA committee was a testimony to his own personal skills. Normally national associations nominate representatives to UEFA and FIFA. In Dein's case, however, the FA had not recommended him but UEFA President Lennart Johansson had personally put Dein there. Not surprisingly, an approach by Media Partners to Arsenal to take part in a breakaway league put Dein in an impossible position. However, the Arsenal Board led by Peter Hill-Wood was quite keen to at least listen; so keen that they had met Media Partners, who had made a presentation of their plans at Highbury, and it was decided that while Dein could not go, Fiszman and Friar would be there to represent the English champions.

The 14 July meeting also saw Franz Beckenbauer and Karl Heinz Rummenigge there representing Bayern Munich. Rick Parry, chief executive of Liverpool came, the only meeting Liverpool attended in a setting that clearly made them distinctly uncomfortable. Soon other clubs joined in including Galatasaray from Turkey. Despite the rift in its Board, Arsenal did not miss a meeting and was as involved as United. United saw Liverpool's fleeting visit as the sign of the eternal fence sitter or, as the saying in football went, 'letting others do the dirty work, arriving late and then drinking all the champagne'.

Kenyon had not been sure what to expect when he went for the first meeting. But as the meetings went on and more clubs joined he was pleasantly surprised: 'I think it is fair to say there was a surprise in the number of clubs that had attended and the quality of the attendees at the meetings.'

United, once involved, now began to take a very active part. They quickly saw ways where the Media Partners plans could be modified and improved on. Kenyon, Gill and increasingly Watkins, contributing his sharp legal mind to the issues, now began to play a major part in not only participating but shaping and directing the Media Partners plans.

Kenyon says: 'We looked at the Media Partners proposals again and, whilst there had been a huge amount of work done, it was obvious they hadn't taken into account some of the regional and local country issues with regard to sports structures. For example, the impact on players' transfers. What it did to players' contracts if there was, in fact, a breakaway league? Did that mean all players were then out of contract? There was also the whole FIFA–UEFA relationship. We worked on the plans in lots of ways, none of them dramatic, but again, looking at it from inside the sport as opposed to outside the sport.'

Gill was soon part of a finance sub-committee and here again he was impressed with the quality of the people who came to the meetings, in particular Sibel Erkman of Galatasaray, a female Turkish lawyer with an excellent command of the English language, Guy d'Arbonneau from Olympique Marseille and representatives of AC Milan and Bayern Munich, also attended these meetings.

Gill was also taken by the fact that Media Partners had spent some two years working on this project and had invested a lot of their own money in developing the concept. Hiring lawyers Slaughter & May was not cheap and they had done a lot of work researching competition law and meeting Karel van Miert, then the European Union's competitions commissioner.

The American banker JPMorgan was willing to finance the project for the first three seasons to the tune of £2 billion, a sum it planned to recover through the sale of television rights. However, as Gill and his sub-committee probed into the financing, they discovered the first flaws in the Media Partners plans. What if the television income did not match what the Media Partners were offering the clubs, then how would JPMorgan get its money back? Would the clubs have to pay money back to JPMorgan? Gill says: 'In essence it was sold to the clubs on the basis that there would be no recourse to the clubs if income did not match expectations. But when we reviewed the documentation it was not as clear as that. Reality was that when we saw the documentation there was recourse. As regards what JPMorgan were putting in relation to the forecast revenue, I don't think the guarantee or commitment was overly high. But there was a question mark we all had about the financing which struck me as somewhat strange. I was involved in lengthy negotiations with JPMorgan. We had presentations from the media analysts of JPMorgan and we satisfied ourselves the numbers had some credibility. It was not quite the football equivalent of the junk bond deals. But it all came down to the recourse: what would happen if the future income was not as high as was predicted?'

The fact was there was a hole in the financing and Media Partners were well aware of that. Even before they began their formal meetings with the clubs they had begun to look for ways to raise money and turned to a contact they had found through United.

Sometime in June, just before the meetings with the clubs started in earnest at the offices of Slaughter & May, Peter Ecelund rang Glen Cooper and the two men met for lunch. Cooper by now was no longer feeling quite as sniffy about the way Ecelund had introduced the whole thing back in the Intercontinental São Paolo bar. However, the more he looked at the plan the less he was impressed by the financial arrangements Media Partners had made.

'Ecelund approached me because Media Partners were interested in getting some equity investors in the vehicle that was the Super League. JPMorgan were the provider of the guarantee. JPMorgan guaranteed more than $2.3 billion and that guaranteed the clubs an income for three years. It was an esoteric banking deal. Lots of wrinkles, novel, complicated arrangement. In the unsophisticated world of football the JPMorgan gurantee was very alluring. But the Media Partners vehicle needed seed money of $30 to $40 million. Slaughter & May's fees were between $3 to $5 million. JPMorgan was charging $2 million in fees. As they say, "Nowt for nowt and nothing for half a crown".'

The lunch with Ecelund led to further meetings and Cooper, who had heard stories of the Berlusconi connection, decided to check them out and concluded that there was no current connection. In June he flew to Milan to meet Hecht and the other Media Partners men.

'We went a long way down the road to invest in Media Partners. We were quite keen to invest, we would have invested ourselves. Having been dismissive and snotty about them in the bar in São Paolo, I found them thoughtful and energetic.'

United by now were becoming quite enthusiastic about the idea. Gill had not long been involved in football and did not know the politics of the game or how the authorities might react but, as regards the advantages for United, he had no doubts. 'It was a very sensible, well-thought-out project. It was the will of the clubs. It was certainly worth us doing. It would certainly have been of benefit to us. From our perspective, clearly playing in Europe was important to us. Our wages are mainly fixed. You have to look at ways to maximise revenue. But nevertheless from my point of view I felt Media Partners was a long shot.'

At this stage in mid-July, Media Partners and the clubs had successfully kept their involvement secret. Talk of a Super League had swirled around UEFA for years and from time to time clubs would tell Gerhard Aigner, chief executive of UEFA, of the plots being hatched.

At the UEFA Congress in Dublin in April, UEFA officials had warned clubs in general about breaking away to form their own Super League. But this was a general warning; there was no specific knowledge of Media Partners' plans. Even when Montgomery's story was followed by Harverson's, UEFA did not wake up and their stories went the way of all old newspaper stories, into the cuttings file, and were forgotten.

There was, though, one impact of Harverson's. It made Media Partners change their code name from Parsifal to Gandalf, the wizard from JRR Tolkien's *Lord of the Rings* and *The Hobbit*. Gandalf could be seen as an Alex Ferguson-style wizard who has wisdom, experience and in *The Hobbit* organises the Hobbit and dwarfs, much like Ferguson does with his players, and sets them on the way to find treasures.

All this changed in mid-July due to what two journalists in Hamburg thought was the rather curious behaviour of the secretaries at Bayern Munich. The journalists were Bodo Mueller, in charge of sports at *Bild am Sonntag*, the nationwide Sunday paper, and his colleague Helmut Uhl. On Monday 13 July they were trying to get hold of two Bayern Munich officials, Uli Hoeness, the manager, and Karl Heinz Rummenigge, the vice-president. Mueller wanted to know something routine about the contract of Lothar Matthaus, the veteran German player. But Hoeness' secretary, normally so helpful, appeared to be extremely nervous and told Mueller that there was no way he could speak to Hoeness that week. He would not be available until the following Monday, which, given Mueller was working on an article for that Sunday, was useless. Mueller put the phone down wondering what had made the secretary so nervous. He mentioned it to his colleague, Uhl, who looked at him and said, 'Funny, that is exactly how the secretary of Rummenigge reacted. Why should two secretaries react so nervously to a routine inquiry to talk to their bosses? What is going on at Bayern that the top officials are not available for a week and their secretaries are so nervous? And the season has not even begun.'

The next day, says Mueller, 'I got a call from a contact telling me that Rummenigge and Hoeness were in London having secret talks with top European clubs about what we in Germany call the Wild League [this was the meeting on 14 July when Bayern attended for the first time]. I had never heard of Media Partners or anything. I needed somebody in London and I thought if I can get in touch with a Sunday paper then we can work in collaboration with them. But I did not know anybody in London. *Springer News*, which is part of our group, have an office in London and they gave me the number of the *Sunday*

Telegraph. I rang and spoke to someone on their desk. He was not the boss and he did not seem very interested. He said maybe there is a story here. I asked for the boss, Colin Gibson. I was told by this guy, Colin is too busy to talk to me but he said he would give Colin Gibson the message. Some hours later Gibson, who I have never met, rang and he was very excited. He must have spoken to someone, maybe Liverpool and he said, "Do you know, Bodo, we are writing football history".'

Gibson, a former football correspondent of the *Daily Telegraph*, then sports editor of the *Sunday Telegraph*, had indeed made calls to Liverpool, Manchester United and Peter Leaver.

'Peter Leaver went ballistic and dropped the phone. United refused to comment, and when I rang Liverpool, there was a long pause, then the person said, "There is nothing I can say".'

That answer told Gibson all he needed to know. This feeling that he was on to a great story was confirmed when Arsenal asked him to fax the questions – always a defensive measure when someone does not want to talk – and then replied, 'We don't want to comment on this.' However, says Gibson, 'David Dein let us know through another party that he was very anti. The reaction of the clubs convinced us that we were on the right tracks. It was an amazing story to break. Whenever we rang you could hear people draw breath and literally the sound of feet running from the telephone.'

Gibson worked in close collaboration with Mueller, with Mueller faxing his story to the *Telegraph* on Friday and Gibson doing the same. The *Telegraph*'s story was written by Steve Curry, the veteran soccer reporter. Under his by-line, and an 'exclusive' tag, the story was headlined, 'United in Breakaway Talks', and described how United were having secret talks with Europe's other leading clubs. They were discussing a 16-club league with midweek matches, no promotion or relegation, which would involve playing as many as 19 European matches in a season. Curry's piece reflected the heavy German input, with quotes from what Franz Beckenbauer had said during the World Cup in France, when he predicted that clubs would now become more important than national teams. Gibson says that while the *Sunday Telegraph* had heard of Media Partners it was not sure who they were and at this stage did not know of the involvement of Slaughter & May.

Mueller's story was more detailed and, in some ways, less England-centred, being headlined, 'Football Revolution – New European League'. Mueller also detailed the two groups into which the 16 clubs might be split. Group I would be Juventus, Milan, Barcelona, Liverpool, Paris St Germain, Ajax, Borussia Dortmund and Roma or

Glasgow Rangers; and in another group, Real Madrid, Inter Milan, Manchester United, Bayern Munich, Monaco, Antwerp, Arsenal and Sporting Lisbon or Benefica.

This was the third time the Super League story had run in the English press, ten weeks after Alex Montgomery had first written of a Super League, and just over two months after Harverson's story. In a sense the *Sunday Telegraph* had fused the two halves of the *News of the World* and the *Financial Times* stories. Montgomery had the names of the clubs which might be part of a breakaway league, Harverson had Media Partners but no links with clubs, the *Sunday Telegraph* had both. What is more, both Montgomery and Harverson were a bit premature, while the *Telegraph* had, like a lucky general, got its tip at just the right time. Bodo Mueller's phone call had come just as the second formal meeting between Media Partners and the clubs was taking place at the offices of Slaughter & May. Montgomery's tip in early May had come from Italian sources when there had been informal contacts between Media Partners and the clubs. Now in mid-July there were formal meetings less than a mile from the *Sunday Telegraph*'s offices and they made the running in the way that neither Montgomery nor Harverson could. But even here the English papers lagged behind Europe and it was some weeks before the dailies took up the running.

The story was the first of many that Curry would write about the Super League and won his newspaper a journalistic award the following year. Mueller won no awards but Guido Tognoni, head of UEFA's National Teams Department, would console him by saying, 'UEFA ought to give you a medal for waking UEFA up.' Mueller now thinks that the contact who tipped him off wanted the story to break so that UEFA would react and make the changes that the clubs sought.

Gibson had taken a risk with his first story. 'We knew Arsenal and Liverpool were involved but decided not to mention them, to keep something for a follow-up. My fear was the dailies would get to the story but they did not. And then when we ran the first story we were contacted by somebody from Slaughter & May who began to leak. He went under the name of Smith. That was clearly not his name. He did not give us a number, he would ring us up, never asked for money and said he was acting in the best interests of the game. Then he disappeared and we never heard from him again. Media Partners and Slaughter & May became so paranoid that they got the clubs to come to their offices through secret entrances; meetings were held in basements of the buildings in windowless offices so nobody could photograph people and everyone had to go through security checks.'

United were totally unprepared for the story breaking. They had agreed a confidentiality clause in their discussions with Media Partners. In the strict policy of compartmentalisation that Edwards followed, few people at United outside those in the boardroom knew about Media Partners. So on the Sunday morning of 19 July, when other newspapers tried to follow the *Sunday Telegraph* story and rang Ken Ramsden, the assistant secretary, who also handled press relations, he denied it. Ramsden said, 'There is no truth in this at all. It is pure speculation. We are getting fed up with stories linking us with a European Super League.' Over the previous two years Ramsden had often been asked questions about such speculation and had always been assured it was just speculation. Now, without checking with Watkins or Kenyon, he felt safe to issue the standard denial he had issued in the past.

Stuck with that denial, the whole episode revealed a tremendous lacuna in United's press relations. Ramsden, as assistant secretary, was a good public relations man for the needs of a football club. However, this was not a conventional football story but a corporate story. Ramsden, unfortunately, had to bear the brunt of media hostility and Kenyon says 'that denial caused problems but we learnt from that and now realise the need to be proactive'. United's failure to have in-house public relations people who could deal with such stories meant that a blanket denial had been issued which clearly could not be sustained. This proved to be a noose to hang United. Worse still for United, as the story developed, the confidentiality agreement with Media Partners meant they could do nothing to correct the first fatal impression that had been created. This made United easy meat for the tabloids led by the *Daily Mail*.

On 1 August, by which time the *Sunday Telegraph* had had two weeks of exclusives, the *Mail* devoted its back page and two other pages inside to denouncing United. Kenyon was portrayed as 'the man with soccer's future in his hands' and, using a quote from Watkins when he refused to confirm if United were involved in talks, the *Mail* thundered, 'So the country's highest profile club continues to leave its supporters, shareholders and Premiership rivals in the dark with a stoic refusal to deny its clear involvement in the rebel league plotting'.

The point of the *Mail* stiletto jammed into United when a 16-point sub-heading screamed: 'Fans Kept in Dark as United Backtrack'.

This was, of course, popular journalism of the kind now so familiar, the tabloid paper fighting for the fans, although in this case what made it curious was that even as the *Mail* accused United of not telling the truth, it was hardly setting a great example itself. For not only did it not give any credit to the *Sunday Telegraph*, or poor Harverson or Montgomery, let alone Mueller, the *Mail* brazenly claimed that it had broken the story.

The reason for all this excitement was a comment by Maurice Watkins, who was described as trying to repair the damage of previous no-comments by saying, 'The club considers it has a responsibility to examine the proposal for a new European competition for the benefit of supporters, shareholders and football generally.'

All this emphasised that the newspapers were at last taking seriously the Super League story. If the publicity did not show United in a good light it also exposed the tricky PR problems faced by Media Partners. They had employed Brunswick, a City PR firm. But while Brunswick were used to the ways of the City journalists, the football journalist was a new animal. As the publicity mounted, according to Gibson, 'Brunswick started ringing us on Saturday afternoon. Andrew Honor and Craig Breheny would telephone to check what we were printing.'

PR for an organisation like Media Partners would have proved tricky for anyone. The very nature of what they were planning meant secretive meetings and they could not come out in the open until they were ready. Brunswick could never confirm the names of the clubs Media Partners were holding discussions with and when I first rang Honor he started lecturing me on how off the record worked and only stopped when I told him I had been a journalist for 25 years and knew something of off the record briefings. In addition it faced two particular problems. One was to convince everyone Media Partners was not Berlusconi's creation and the other was Media Partners' relationship with UEFA. The press, unable to find out much about Media Partners, and unwilling to believe that they were truly independent, kept suggesting it was all Berlusconi's work. Brunswick worked hard on this and, to an extent, succeeded. But as for Media Partners' relationship with UEFA, even if Brunswick had been familiar with football, it would have struggled because the message it had to publicise was so confused.

Media Partners' plan was to make more money for the top clubs; this was what attracted the top European clubs to their discussions. Yet, in order to curry favour with the fans, they now wanted to strike a populist pose and stress how this would generate money for the grassroots.

Kenyon realised quickly enough the confusion at the heart of the project: 'The amazing thing is, and probably one of the biggest issues they got wrong, was the PR strategy. I think there are several aspects to it. It was not the sole intention that three or four League clubs would get more money, although this was undoubtedly true. But having said that, under the plan, there were huge football funds meant to be going back to football at the grassroots. None of the clubs wanted the Scottish model. We didn't want to play Aston Villa or Arsenal four times. It doesn't work. It's not in anybody's interest to limit that. Our prime consideration is the domestic league and we wanted to help the domestic league. We would like fewer clubs in the domestic league, to be honest, but we'd like a stronger European competition.'

In order to get round fans, who by this stage, not only in this country but around Europe, were denouncing the plans, Media Partners hired MORI to poll opinion and reported that, after a survey of 1,061 fans in 159 sampling points across Britain, 70% of them favoured replacing UEFA competitions with a midweek European league. However, such surveys always depend on how the questions are framed, and this 70% approval came after asking whether fans would like to see more clubs from this country in Europe, more games on free TV, more money for amateur and youth football, no conflicts between club games and national leagues and Cups. It was only after listing such virtues of the Super League that the question was put: Do you approve of the Super League or not? The surprise was only 70% approved; it was a bit like voting for motherhood and against sin.

However important public opinion was, it was UEFA that would make or break Media Partners. A Super League clearly meant going against UEFA, yet Media Partners kept insisting that they wanted to work with UEFA.

Kenyon had always understood this: 'There was always the intention there was a place for UEFA in it. Whilst the model that Media Partners constructed showed that it would generate the monies for the Super League outside of UEFA, from day one every club that had the initial conversation with Media Partners said UEFA has to be involved in this project. We all said UEFA must run this competition. That's different from what the commercial contracts said, but from a game infrastructure, from a regulatory point of view, absolutely there was never a question that UEFA must be involved.'

Media Partners made much of the fact that the clubs would own the Super League, but Gill was not entirely convinced about this: 'That was perhaps over-played.' A competition owned by the clubs raised questions about the part, if any, UEFA would play and here the more Gill talked with Media Partners, the more he seemed to sense an uncertainty at the heart of the project. 'They had gone to see Karel van Miert at the European Union and they had looked at it from a legal perspective. At some of the meetings they stressed UEFA could get involved, but the way they were approaching the project tended to suggest to us that it was unlikely. I think they did not get their presentation right. I am inclined to agree with Peter Leaver when he said that Media Partners had not played the PR side right. They should have said UEFA is part of our set-up as a regulator from the beginning.'

But how could they when they had sought to lobby Karel van Miert and get him to investigate UEFA? As UEFA began to strike back against Media Partners, Brunswick went round distributing articles from the Spanish and other European papers critical of UEFA and describing how Miert was to inquire whether UEFA's monopoly control of European football violated European Union Laws.

Privately, Media Partners were singing a different tune and had sought to put out feelers to UEFA.

Sometime in the middle of August, Peter Ecelund and a colleague went to see Lennart Johansson, the UEFA President, at his holiday home near Stockholm. 'They sent,' says Gerhard Aigner, the German-born UEFA chief executive, 'two people to see Lennart Johansson without telling him what it was about. They did it in a way so that he couldn't know what it was about. Somebody that Lennart knew, who was a former ice hockey player and who is a son of a friend of his, approached Lennart. They said they had an interesting proposal. Lennart was unaware what it was about. Lennart said speak to the general secretary. So they rang me up.'

By this time not only had several clubs told Aigner what was happening, but Aigner and his colleagues had begun their football shuttle diplomacy to the various capitals of Europe to make sure the organisation that had been built up over four decades did not vanish with a puff from Media Partners.

UEFA knew that their most important task was to establish a dialogue with the clubs. For years the big clubs had moaned that they could never talk directly to UEFA; they always had to go via their national associations. The national association in any country is generally dominated by the amateur side of the game, while the clubs are professional. It riled the clubs that they bought the money that sustained the amateur side, yet they had no direct voice at UEFA.

UEFA did have a committee called the Committee for Non-Amateur Football, but its name betrayed how the professional game was viewed. Just as Media Partners began their plotting, UEFA had replaced this with the Committee for Professional Football. But now it needed to do a lot more if the clubs were not to break away. By the weekend of 15 August, Aigner had started a whirlwind tour of major European football capitals to lobby the clubs. That weekend he met Real Madrid and then saw officials of Benefica; Markus Studer, his deputy, went to see Ajax in Amsterdam. On Tuesday 18 August, both Aigner and Studer flew to Manchester to meet United, Liverpool and Arsenal.

It was decided that it would be too risky to meet at Old Trafford and so the meeting was arranged at a conference room in Watkins' law firm, James Chapman & Co, in the centre of Manchester. As well as Watkins and Kenyon, Peter Robinson and Rick Parry came from Liverpool and Ken Friar and Danny Fiszman came from Arsenal. Aigner's message was simple: stick with UEFA. We are ready to change, completely revolutionise the European competitions if necessary and it will bring you more money.

Aigner was willing to consider a Champions League where the top five European countries, including England, could have as many as four teams each, double the existing allocation, a much larger qualifying competition so the champions of Eastern Europe and other European minnows would be eliminated early, a merger of the UEFA and Cup Winners Cups into one competition and even the ultimate heresy, perhaps a wild card system as desired by AC Milan. Most importantly, a bigger share-out of television money with some games on satellite television to generate more money.

Interestingly, despite United's deep involvement with Media Partners, Watkins, Kenyon and Gill listened to Aigner with great interest and gave the impression that they could work with UEFA.

The next day Aigner travelled to Milan to meet the Italian and German clubs: AC and Inter Milan, Juventus, Bayern Munich and Borussia Dortmund.

Now he was ready to meet Media Partners. On Friday 21 August, Aigner met the Media Partners in the Noga Hilton in Geneva. Aigner says: 'We had a legal letter from Geneva on their behalf claiming that we had their documents which we were distributing and which were their property. That was not the case. I first had to tell them that you must withdraw your legal threats before we sit at the table. I am not going to sit down with you if you at the same time threaten us with legal actions.'

They did, and four from Media Partners – Peter Ecelund, Rodolfo

Hecht, a lawyer from Slaughter & May, and a banker from JPMorgan – came to see Aigner. Aigner had with him Markus Studer and two other UEFA officials, Thomas Kurt and Guido Tognoni. Aigner recalls: 'They made a presentation. They wanted to hand over a document. They said it is highly confidential. I said if it is highly confidential you better keep it. We didn't take it. My feeling was the clubs were not going to accept their plans. They had given the clubs the deadline of 31 July, it had passed, the clubs had not signed and they called a meeting with us because the clubs would not sign.'

The following Tuesday Aigner held a meeting of the Committee for Professional Football at the Intercontinental Hotel in Geneva and it was agreed to form a Task Force that would radically restructure European football along the lines Aigner had outlined to the clubs in Watkins' office. Tognoni even went on to publicly talk about the heresy that Aigner had mentioned to Watkins and co. in Manchester. UEFA would still insist that a club could only enter on merit but it might be prepared to look at the definition of sporting merit: 'This could mean entry into European competitions on the basis of the last five years' record and not just last season.' UEFA was coming close to what Milan had proposed and UEFA itself had rejected back in June.

The Geneva meeting had been attended by Peter Leaver, representing the Premier League. Leaver, who played a big part in helping set up the Committee for Professional Football, was now on the Task Force and had come a long way since that May morning and the call from Montgomery. Now he knew exactly which clubs were doing what with Media Partners and as a result his relations with United, never the greatest, had been further strained.

Leaver had had a number of clashes with United ever since he had taken over as chief executive of the Premier League in the summer of 1997, but the Media Partners situation was the most explosive. It did not please him that he had learnt about it through the media, and as he established the truth of the media reports, he found himself in a curious situation. Liverpool had been to one meeting and were the most detached. United's position in essence was that this was a very interesting project; they had to look at it; but in any case this had nothing to do with the Premier League. Arsenal, on the other hand, were hopelessly split and that, in some ways, provided Leaver with the best opportunity of monitoring what was going on.

'David Dein was telling me what was happening. He was in a minority of one on his board. Carr, Fiszman, Hill-Wood, Friar were all for Media Partners. Media Partners had given the clubs a deadline by which time they had to sign. This was 31 July and I was being rung up by David Dein, who was in contact with me on a daily basis, to start proceedings. He said people are about to sign. I was being egged on by Dein to do something. But I could not start proceedings before I sent them a letter before action. So just before I went away on holiday on 31 July, I sent a letter to the three clubs warning them that if they were planning to sign with Media Partners, they would face consequences which could include expulsions from the Premier League.'

The letter incensed United. They felt a letter like that coming out of the blue without any conversation let alone warning beforehand was, as Kenyon says, outrageous, 'and to send it to one of the founder members of the Premier League is ridiculous, particularly in light of the OFT enquiry.'

Leaver returned from his holiday in Portugal, the day before the season started, and as his plane touched down and he switched on his mobile phone he had Ken Bates, chairman of Chelsea, on the line. Media Partners had now started reaching out to the second round of clubs. Bates had been contacted by Media Partners and a meeting had been arranged. However, the meeting had been postponed and Bates, keen to keep Leaver involved, was ringing to tell him that. He was soon to tell Media Partners that he wanted nothing to do with their plans.

If Leaver's letter had made United furious it had put Arsenal in the most curious position. Dein may have egged Leaver to send the letter, but now Dein's Arsenal colleagues Fiszman and Friar came to see Leaver and asked him if he would like to meet Media Partners. In the meeting that followed with Fiszman and Peter Ecelund there, Leaver had an almost surreal conversation with a banker from JPMorgan when discussing the financial guarantees JPMorgan had provided.

The banker told Leaver: 'We have written a highly confidential letter.'

'What does it mean?' asked Leaver.

'It is highly confidential, it cannot be revealed.'

'I have been doing banking for 30 years and I have never heard of a highly confidential letter as a security document. If there is such a thing I better ring my chambers and ask them to throw away my banking law books.'

In the end the conversation petered out and it was agreed that Media Partners would emerge into the light and, instead of having secret meetings with clubs, would make a formal presentation to all 20 Premiership clubs on 20 August. However, sometime after this, Media Partners requested a change in dates and it was put back two weeks to 3 September.

It was to prove a crucial day both for the Media Partners and, as we shall see, for Manchester United.

Leaver also arranged for Gerhard Aigner to make a formal presentation on behalf of UEFA. For Leaver this was a big coup. UEFA had never before spoken in such a fashion to any gathering of clubs anywhere in Europe. Leaver could say that, here again, the Premier League was leading the way, and reflect with some satisfaction how much things had changed since the previous September when he had proposed a voice for the professional leagues. Then UEFA had reacted with the sort of horror that the Media Partners plans had evoked.

It was very nearly a year since Leaver had suggested to the other professional leagues that they should set up their own organisations. It seemed to him that there was a tremendous gap here. This resulted in a meeting in London in September 1997 to which representatives of the Italian, Spanish, Portuguese and other leagues came. Leaver also invited two clubs, Arsenal and Manchester United. It was made clear this gathering was not a threat to UEFA but UEFA, recalls Leaver, 'went ballistic and called it an illegal meeting'.

Before the next meeting in November 1997, to which professional leagues from Scotland and Greece were also invited as well, Leaver had a breakfast meeting with Aigner at White's hotel, next to the FA headquarters in Lancaster Gate. Aigner said that UEFA was not thinking of talking to his gathering. However, a dialogue had now started and in January 1998 UEFA was invited to a further meeting where it was agreed that UEFA would form the Professional Football Committee to replace the Non-Amateur one it had. But it was clear that this was still Aigner and UEFA in charge, reluctantly doling out crumbs to the professional leagues and clubs. Now on the morning of 3 September 1998 a very different Aigner came to the offices of the Premier League. Media Partners had so shaken UEFA up that the very survival of UEFA and its competitions was at stake. Manchester United and other clubs had now to be wooed and Aigner came in a very conciliatory mood, almost like a supplicant at the court of a major power.

Leaver had so organised the day that Media Partners were to make their presentation followed by Aigner. Media Partners prepared long and hard and, in the days leading up to it, they held meetings with United and other clubs discussing what they should say. Their plans had changed considerably since they first met Kenyon and co. in the bar in São Paolo. Now their Super League would have 36 teams in three divisions of 12 each. Four English clubs would be in the Super League, three of them – Manchester United, Liverpool and Arsenal – as part of the magic group of 18 founder members who would be guaranteed qualification for the first three years. Eighteen others would be selected on their performance in the previous season, one of them English.

In addition there would be a ProCup, a knock-out tournament of 96 teams which would include six English teams. In other words, half the Premier League could play in Europe. And the money was more than any English club had ever earned in Europe. The Super League would give the four English clubs a total of £43 million a year; the ProCup would give the six English clubs £28 million a year.

But impressive as these figures were, and the clubs were much taken by the idea that a Premier League club had only to finish tenth to have a chance of some of this European money, even before the Media Partners began their presentation they had run into problems. On the morning of the presentation, Hecht was due to be interviewed on Radio 4's *Today* programme but pulled out because he had a migraine.

He did make it to the Premier League and was part of the team that made the slide presentation. But at the Premier League there was literally a problem of space. Media Partners had come with 11 people and there was no room for all of them to sit in the League's boardroom; most of them had to stand. United were upset by what they saw as gratuitous discourtesy on the part of Leaver and they felt this was directed at them. But Leaver felt justified for he had told Media Partners space was limited – 'Do not come mob-handed' – and had expected no more than four of them.

The bigger issue was money and how they would work with UEFA. Not all the clubs were convinced of the financial basis of the figures and when Keith Wiseman, chairman of the FA, asked, 'When did you approach the FA of England?', and they answered, 'Never', he branded Media Partners as rebels.

In contrast, Aigner's pitch, made without the help of slides, was in the more familiar mould of football with much talk of the football family, UEFA solidarity and how together they had achieved much and could achieve much more.

In the discussions that followed the two presentations, United soon found themselves on the defensive. This was the first time the clubs had met since the Media Partners story broke and many of them made it clear that they saw the way United had acted as indefensible. Although Arsenal had been just as active with Media Partners, if not more, it was

United who got much of the heat. Ken Bates, who has always felt that everything should be done through the League, was one of the most vocal and clashed with Watkins suggesting that if United did not want to be part of the Premier League they could piss off.

Watkins and United's argument was that they were committed to the Premier League, that it was their bread and butter, but Media Partners was a project they had to look at. Moreover, what they did in Europe was no concern of the Premier League; they were a public company and had to consider projects that were interesting.

At the end of the discussion, all the clubs agreed that there should be no more such freelance activity by United or any of the clubs. The clubs were asked to promise that they would not deal individually with Media Partners. If there was to be contact it must be through the Premier League. Leaver knew Arsenal and Manchester United would have to have one further meeting with Media Partners if only to explain they could not meet again. But after that it would have to be through him.

The clubs sit round in alphabetical fashion at Premier League meetings and as the chairman, Sir John Quinton went round they agreed to give this pledge. When he got to M and Manchester United, Watkins and Kenyon looked at Edwards and to their horror he agreed that all future contact would be through Leaver. Watkins and Kenyon knew this had put United in a very difficult situation and as soon as the clubs broke for lunch there was a hurried United confab.

As Kenyon recalls, 'After the Premier League meeting we had already committed to two things really: (1) to have a meeting with Media Partners and (2) I was due to go to a meeting with Karel van Miert on the Monday.'

Edwards' pledge meant United had made a cock-up and it had to be repaired. Watkins offered to do that.

Just as the clubs were due to restart after lunch he went up to Leaver and said, 'I must have a word with you.'

'Maurice,' said Leaver, 'the meeting is about to start.'

'Martin should never have said what he did about not meeting Media Partners and we need to discuss that.'

It was agreed that Watkins and Kenyon would meet Leaver the next day. When they came the next morning Watkins told Leaver, 'Martin made a bit of a cock-up yesterday. He should never have said all future contact will be through the Premier League. You see, Peter has a meeting with Karel van Miert on Monday and there is a meeting of the clubs at Slaughter & May on Tuesday.'

'But Maurice,' said Leaver, 'the resolution all the clubs agreed was clear enough, all future contact must be through the Premier League.'

The previous day's meeting represented a triumph for Leaver and he was not about to relinquish it. Not only had all the clubs agreed he must be the point of contact, but the press briefings he had given suggested that the clubs had decided to stick with UEFA and reject Media Partners, a view not endorsed by all the clubs, not least Liverpool, who felt the consensus of the clubs was that they wanted to talk to both UEFA and Media Partners, perhaps use Media Partners to get better terms from UEFA.

For some time the three men discussed the situation and then Leaver offered them a compromise: they could continue meeting Media Partners provided they did so as representatives of the Premier League. So Kenyon could meet Karel van Miert on behalf of the Premier League and report back to Leaver.

Kenyon and Watkins found this impossible and as they left Leaver they felt angry, unhappy and in a dilemma. However, no sooner had they got to the offices of Slaughter & May, than the mobile phone rang and everything changed.

It was Gill: 'Where are you?'

'We are at the offices of Slaughter & May.'

'Well what are you doing there? You are supposed to be at HSBC; we are waiting here for you.'

'Right, we are on our way.'

Gill's impatience was due to the fact that United's other great secret, the offer from Sky, had now come a long way since a conceptual one made just over a month ago at the lunch between Edwards, Watkins and Booth. It was now a firm bid with a definite price. United had accepted it but some Board members were having second thoughts and that weekend hard decisions had to be taken.

Within hours Kenyon was to learn that he could not have gone to the meeting with Karel van Miert in any case irrespective of whether he wore his United or Premier League hat. A much bigger issue had intervened.

3

KEEPING THE SECRET

Through July 1998, as Kenyon, Gill and increasingly Watkins busied themselves with Media Partners, Edwards kept his counsel about the takeover and his talks with Booth and Sky. He only spoke to Watkins, Roland Smith and Keith Harris.

Sky was not the only company which was sniffing round United. Frank Lowe was another old Manchester boy and United fan who had done well. He had sold his advertising company Lowe-Howard-Spink to a large multinational American-controlled company, Interpublic, and Lowe appears to have had some thoughts that Interpublic could buy United. I use the word 'appears' because Lowe refuses to speak on this and, while Edwards confirms that there was another approach, he will not say who made it. It may be that Lowe went to see Edwards and talked of a possible bid. This was a very preliminary conversation and no formal bid was ever made, not even an approach like the one VCI had made two years earlier. It seems Lowe spoke to Edwards as a preliminary to a bid, but nothing materialised. But the approach convinced Edwards that more than one multinational was looking to bid for his club. If so who should he go with?

Sometime in early July Edwards rang Booth and told him, 'We are definitely interested. We should spend more time together to see that it makes sense for us.'

Booth recalls: 'We did not talk money at first but we spent a lot more time together to make sure it made sense for both of us. I was persuaded of combining the business side of Sky with Manchester United. The question was: Are we going to be able to work together really well? Martin was in a very different business. We are a television industry. They are a football group. The most important football group. For me the question was would Martin continue with United after we bought them? If Martin wasn't going to play an ongoing role it would change our interest level. It was important he carries on and it was important we got along. So from my point of view, while conceptually it was a very powerful idea, the question was could I rely on this person to continue doing the right things? Martin's point of view was: Would these guys interfere and create more problems than solve? I had to understand his principles about running the business and where he thought it was going.'

The two men could not be more contrasting. Edwards – from middle England, public-school-educated, nearly 15 years older than Booth – had the sort of personality that seems to match his complexion. Like his natural blond colouring, which gives the impression it is reluctant to emerge, Edwards always seems loath to play the identikit football chairman: loud, boastful, ever keen to take the limelight away from their players and particularly their manager. Football club chairmen want the world to know that the club is their personal fiefdom: they own the club, the players, the managers, perhaps even the fans. Many of them like to portray themselves as superfans, anoraks in the boardrooms. Edwards could not be more different and emphasises that he manages a business where many others play their part.

If Edwards came over as the reluctant chairman, then Booth, the man from middle America, was the untypical American. Booth laughs when he is reminded of his characteristic greeting, 'Hey, Big Guy'. 'Do I really say that?' he asks innocently. For an American he has an appealing sense of irony, detachment and even cynicism.

Soon after his initial discussions with Edwards, Booth had turned to Martin Stewart, his 35-year-old chief finance officer, to work out the money that would be required to buy United. Stewart, unlike Booth, knew and loved his football, he was a lapsed Tottenham supporter, and had a sharp and instant appreciation of how big and complicated a task Booth had taken on. Booth's decision to buy Manchester United had come as no surprise to Stewart. For some two years there had been much talk in the corridors of Isleworth about buying Manchester United and then, in the spring, had come Kevin Kinsella's proposal for the takeover of the club.

Now that Booth had made a formal approach, it was necessary to find out how much Sky would have to pay for United. On the evening of 28 July Stewart and Kinsella drove to the Royal Lancaster Hotel to meet Maurice Watkins. It was little over ten days since news of United's involvement with Media Partners had been revealed in the media and both sides were paranoid about any plans for Sky buying United leaking to the press.

So instead of meeting in the first-floor lounge of the Royal Lancaster, which is the normal meeting place in the hotel and a very handy one, with a bar in one corner and the carvery down the hallway, they sat in Watkins' room and for two hours, between half past six and half past eight, and discussed how Sky might go about buying United. Both Stewart and Watkins knew this was a very preliminary discussion, but what Stewart wanted to know was what was the ballpark figure Sky would have to pay to get United. How much, asked Stewart, did United expect Sky to pay for the club?

Watkins pulled out a piece of hotel stationery, did some sums on it and said 290p, which was 130p more than the price the United shares had closed that evening on the London stock market. If Booth's offer to buy United at the lunch on 1 July had shocked Edwards and Watkins, now the price, so quickly worked out by Watkins, took Stewart's breath away. It would mean United would be valued at nearly £750 million, far beyond anything Sky was prepared to pay.

The next morning Stewart went back to Isleworth and told Booth that if United was serious about asking for 290p then Sky should forget about the whole thing. Booth and Edwards had got on, they felt they would work together, but the price Watkins had tossed out on the Royal Lancaster Hotel stationery was so way over anything Sky was hoping to pay that it did not seem there could be any deal.

However, surprised as Stewart was about the price Watkins wanted, Stewart instinctively felt that this was just an opening gambit. Watkins, the canny lawyer, was putting a stake in the ground claiming a piece of territory, rather like frontier men in the wild west of America, aware that while they may not get all the land they claimed, it would be a useful counter when the real sharing out of the land began. In that sense, of course, Watkins was fulfilling his historic role for United.

It might have come as a surprise to the outside world to know that Edwards had not told Kenyon or Gill, his fellow executive directors, about the bid but had involved Watkins, who was, after all, a non-executive director. But then Watkins was much more than a mere non-executive director. In many ways he was something of a super director and by the time Sky came knocking at United's door in the summer of 1998, he had been United's legal adviser for some 22 years and had played a pivotal role in almost every major decision affecting the club. Even more than Edwards, it was Watkins who acted as the spokesman for the club and was often its most prominent public face.

He was also trustee of the shares Edwards held in trust for his children, and in the near quarter of a century he had been involved with United, Edwards had almost invariably turned to him in moments of crisis or grave importance.

Watkins was in many ways the classic Manchester United supporter. The son of a mother who was a teacher and a father who was a solicitor's clerk, he came from the sort of aspiring middle-class background where Manchester Grammar was the obvious school – his son Peter was head boy there in 1999/2000 – and the morning paper was likely to be the *Manchester Guardian* (its name changed to the *Guardian* in 1959 when it moved to London) and the evening paper the *Manchester Evening News*.

Like many Lancastrians of his generation Watkins grew up as a sports lover, not merely a tribal fan who could not see beyond a single football club, taking as much interest in cricket as football and playing football himself, for Old Mancunians in the Lancashire amateur league, which meant he missed many of the great games at Old Trafford in which George Best played. Watkins still insists that while he is a good supporter he is not a fan – 'It is a useful distinction; if we lose, I can sleep at night' – and when Watkins finally got on to the Board, on the same day as Sir Bobby Charlton, he quite surprised his fellow directors after United had drawn a game by saying, 'The Old Mancunians would have been happy with the result.'

United came into his life professionally, quite unexpectedly, one evening in 1976, when Bill Royle, a fellow partner in James Chapman & Co. suddenly died at a meeting at the Law Society. That night the Manchester United file was brought round to Watkins' home and he was asked to attend a meeting the next day at Old Trafford.

His first big task came when, following the 1977 FA Cup Final victory, United decided to sack its manager Tommy Docherty because of his affair with the wife of the United physio. Louis Edwards, Martin's father, had been close to Docherty. The whole thing dragged on and Watkins was summoned to Louis Edwards' home in Alderley Edge to sort out the mess that resulted.

After that he had become, almost invariably, the first port of call when the Manchester United Board ran into problems or had new issues to confront. Not long after the Docherty sacking the United Board was embroiled in the rights issue. Matt Busby opposed it; John Fletcher, a local businessman, sought an injunction trying to prevent it; and the very morning after Fletcher started his action, Martin

Edwards and others filed into Watkins' office to prepare affidavits on the basis of which Watkins helped the United Board defeat Fletcher.

Through the 80s his workload for United increased. In 1984, as United signed Gordon Strachan from Aberdeen, Watkins had found himself at three in the morning on the floor of the Intercontinental Hotel in Paris with Chris Anderson, the Aberdeen vice-chairman, sorting out the mess Strachan had made of his contract. Strachan had, without telling his Aberdeen manager Alex Ferguson, signed a pre-contract with the German club Cologne. When United came in for him, this caused enormous complications. Watkins had to go to UEFA and then FIFA before, in the end, Cologne decided that it was hardly worthwhile pursuing a player who did not want to play for it. The whole affair also brought Watkins in close contact with Ferguson. This proved very useful when two years later United returned to Aberdeen to hire Ferguson himself and Watkins flew out with Edwards to Aberdeen to talk to Ferguson.

Ferguson, in his book, which is highly critical of Edwards, goes out of his way to praise Watkins, saying, 'He has consistently earned my respect during my time at the club', and particularly praises the way he got United and Clayton Blackmore out of a very difficult situation when the club were on a tour of Bermuda during the 1986–87 close season. Blackmore had been to a nightclub in Hamilton, Bermuda's capital, and returned to his hotel only to find that a woman had accused him of rape. Late that night police had come to the Elbow Beach Hotel, where United was staying, and taken Blackmore away.

Watkins, informed of the situation, first ascertained that the charge was baseless, with Blackmore maintaining it was a set-up. Watkins quickly realised that he had to prevent Blackmore getting charged. He knew if Blackmore was charged, he would face at least ten months in jail even before the case came up. After Watkins had prevented any charges being laid, he flew Blackmore back to England via Boston to avoid the British press, which by this time had gathered in force in Bermuda.

His two most high-profile moments of being the voice of reason for United, as the *Manchester Evening News* called him, was when he dealt with fall-out from the Eric Cantona kung-fu incident and the transfer of Andrei Kanchelskis. One was the most high-profile case of common assault, the other, involving a transfer of a player from Eastern Europe, suggested that lives may be in danger.

Watkins, while present at Selhurst Park, on the night Cantona launched at the Crystal Palace fan, did not actually see the incident. But the moment it happened he went to the dressing-room to be on hand should Cantona be charged with assault. He found Cantona sitting very quietly in the dressing-room, but over the next few weeks as the crisis developed neither Cantona nor the world was silent about this most amazing episode in English football.

United could have got rid of Cantona by selling him to Inter Milan, whose then general manager, Paulo Taveggia, was at Crystal Palace that night watching Cantona. A few days before, he had rung Edwards inquiring about Cantona, but his approach had been rebuffed. However, if Inter had offered more money Cantona might have gone – as it was, Inter came back later to buy Paul Ince. United, realising the seriousness of the incident, was torn about retaining Cantona and when the following night Watkins met Edwards, Roland Smith and Ferguson at the Edge Hotel in Alderley, there was no consensus as to what should be done about the Frenchman. In the end it was decided that Cantona would be suspended until the end of the season and this was a classic lawyer's decision. United was seen to be doing something and in taking the decision before the FA had acted United felt it would stop the FA doing anything even worse.

However, when things did not work out quite that way, Watkins was involved in damage limitation both on behalf of Cantona, who was being represented by his firm, and United. Watkins himself has always seen his involvement in the Cantona affair as the high point of his association with United. There was the moment at the FA hearing when, sitting next to Cantona, Watkins heard Cantona, after apologising to the FA, his fans, his team mates and the club, say, 'And I want to apologise to the prostitute who shared my bed last evening'. Graham Kelly, then chief executive, who was in the room, says, 'Maurice turned, his mouth dropped open and he almost fell off his chair.' Gordon McKeag, who was one of the three man FA tribunal hearing the Cantona case, misheard and turned to Geoff Thomson, the chaiman, and said, 'What did he say? "He prostrates himself before the FA"?'

'Yes' said Thomson, eager to get away from the subject.

Later that day, the FA decided that United's suspension was not enough and Cantona had to be banned until 30 September. Two members of the FA commission, Thomson and McKeag, wanted a longer ban, but the third member, Ian Stott, persuaded them to limit it to 30 September. It was now Watkins' turn to get angry when he felt that the press release the FA was issuing would seriously prejudice the criminal trial Cantona was facing.

Watkins' most notable moment with Cantona came following the trial. Cantona was originally sent out to serve a prison sentence; Watkins appealed and got him out on bail and then on appeal it was reduced to community service. At the end of it, Watkins decided that there had to be a press conference. Cantona agreed but only if he was allowed to speak. Just before the press conference began, Cantona came to Watkins' hotel room and taking a piece of paper started to write.

He asked Watkins, 'What is the name of the big boat when they catch fish?' Watkins told him it was called a trawler. Then Cantona asked, 'What is the name of the big seabird?' Watkins replied, 'A seagull.'

Having had a Watkins tutorial, Cantona then went to the press conference and uttered his by now immortal lines about, 'When seagulls follow the trawler it is because they think sardines will be thrown into the sea.' Watkins, not sure he should allow Cantona to speak, pretended he did not know what Cantona was on about – the exact meaning of his words is still debated on the sports pages – but it had helped bring the whole affair to a close.

In many ways it was Watkins' involvement in the Kanchelskis affair which reveals how he fits into the modern Manchester United and why, despite the fact that his full-time job is somewhere else, he is often at the centre of things at Old Trafford.

Kanchelskis was transferred from the Ukrainian club Shakter Donetsk to United on 24 March 1991. Watkins, along with Edwards and Ferguson, negotiated a deal which also involved the Norwegian agent Rune Hauge. James Chapman negotiated the contract which provided for a fee of £650,000 plus further payments totalling £550,000 depending on how many matches he played and other events. United also paid £35,000 for Hauge's services.

At that time under football rules, the use of Hauge as an agent was illegal. But it was a common practice in English football and when the Premier League bungs inquiry looked into the transfer, it cleared United of any illegal payments while acknowledging that it had, like many other football clubs, broken football rules.

However, the Kanchelskis story did not end there. On the evening of 22 August 1994, United returned to Old Trafford after a 1–1 match at the Nottingham Forest ground. They arrived back at Old Trafford at one in the morning and Watkins asked Ferguson for a lift to the Four

Seasons Hotel where, like many of the United players and officials, he had left his car. As Ferguson was about to leave the car park Grigory Essaoulenko, a Russian agent who was part of the advisory team around Andrei Kanchelskis, stopped Ferguson and said he had a gift for him. Late as the hour was, he told Ferguson he had to give him the gift that night and asked him to come to the Excelsior Hotel, which is near Manchester airport. When Ferguson got there he found a handsomely wrapped box. He threw it in the back of the car and drove home.

There he unwrapped it, expecting it to be a samovar. It turned out to be stuffed with cash, £40,000 of it.

The next morning he took it back to Old Trafford, where he went to the offices of Ken Merrett, the secretary, and emptied it in front of him. Inevitably Watkins was the first one to be called and he advised that the money should be lodged in the Old Trafford safe and that Ferguson should document what had happened with the United lawyers and his own solicitor.

The money stayed in the safe for a year, when Kanchelskis wanted a move to Everton. Essaoulenko then returned to Old Trafford because Kanchelskis' move to Everton was proving complicated due to clauses in his contract which gave Kanchelskis a third of the transfer fee. United had thought this amount would be waived and done a deal with Everton, then realised it had to be paid to Kanchelskis, which meant United was not going to get anything like the money it thought it was going to get. It was this that caused the problem.

This gave United the opportunity to talk about the money in the safe and Ferguson told Essaoulenko he could not accept the money. It required the intervention of Edwards to persuade the Russian, who was claiming it was a 'thank you' to Ferguson, to take it back. Ferguson says he was bemused as to why the Russian should thank him this way since he had done nothing he would not have ordinarily done. The discussions about the Kanchelskis transfer got so heated that in the course of this Essaoulenko threatened Edwards with physical harm. When Watkins was asked for his opinion, his response was simple: sell the player.

But in order to work out the deal with Everton, Watkins had to fly out to Kiev to try to deal with Shakter Donetsk. Watkins had been warned there might be trouble and took with him Ned Kelly, head of United's security, who had also acted as Cantona's minder. In Kiev Watkins was introduced to a man who was described as a lawyer. But when he left the meeting he got into a Mercedes with three armed policemen and with a police escort which made Kelly and Watkins doubt if he was a lawyer. Some time after, as the whole thing was being sorted out, and Kanchelskis had not yet moved to Everton, Shakter's president Alexander Bragin was assassinated in a remote-controlled bomb explosion as he walked to his reserved seat at the start of a match. Watkins was relieved to read later it was not linked to his own negotiations with Shakter but connected with the growing links between the Russian mafia and sport.

What is truly significant about this story is how very differently Watkins and Edwards dealt with the story. Watkins, while nervous about the Kiev experience, readily talked about it; Edwards even now, several years later, can barely talk about it. When I asked him about the death threats from Essaoulenko, he said: 'There were veiled threats, definitely. I got threats because they wanted Kanchelskis to move on, I believe. I mean . . . I think we have to be very careful what we say . . . We have to be careful. We have to be careful. I wouldn't want you to play too much on that . . .'

It is this difference in attitude, and how they deal with the world, which had led to the situation that, although Edwards as chief executive of the plc and holding 12% shares was the most important man at United, it was often Watkins who took the lead in many matters, as he was doing now in the deal with Sky.

Booth had told Stewart and Deanna Bates, Sky's legal counsel, to put a team together for the bid. At this stage it was still a very tight team so that, for instance, John Sykes of the Sky Sports legal team, a fervent Manchester United fan, did not know about the bid since it was a corporate matter and Booth and Stewart did not want Sky Sports involved just yet.

Booth also asked Stewart to choose his banker for the deal. Stewart turned to Goldman Sachs and Richard Campbell-Breeden. Stewart and Bates now pulled the papers together and did the financial valuations. They had to consider how they would present the mechanics of the offer, the financing, the share issues and a million other details that the offer involved.

Booth had already mentioned to John Thornton what he was proposing to do. Thornton, the chief operating officer at Goldman Sachs and a member of the executive that managed the bank's global operation, had been a director of BSkyB since 1994. Goldman's had intimate links with Murdoch. Whatever price BSkyB eventually paid for United, the deal would have to be recommended by Goldman's.

Booth planned to borrow some £623 million for the deal, hoping to subsequently refund 50% with equity. Companies like Sky don't carry huge cash banks. They borrow at commercial rates – often well below commercial rates – and they fund their investments through such borrowings. The component parts of the transaction were to be the responsibility of Goldman's.

It was not Thornton who got intimately involved but Richard Campbell-Breeden, managing director of Goldman's investment banking division, and the team that he ran. Campbell-Breeden was an old United fan, having lived in Manchester from the age of four until 13, and had first seen them in the 1974 season when they had been relegated to the old Second Division. Ironically that was also the season when a great many supporters who would soon see Sky as their deadly enemy had first fallen in love with United.

Campbell-Breeden was well aware of the contradictions produced by modern football. A close friend says, 'It is quite funny really. His father is an enthusiastic West Ham fan but is part of the generation that refuses to pay to watch football on TV. He is part of the generation who watched football for free on television. So whenever there is a match on Sky he comes round to Richard's house. And when Manchester United played the epic semi-final replay against Arsenal, winning it with that wonder goal from Ryan Giggs, Richard's father was there watching it on Sky at Richard's house.'

Goldman's had been advising Sky on football for some time. Early in 1998, there had been discussions about the formation of a European Super League and then, as Kinsella made his recommendations to Booth about United, several of Campbell-Breeden's staff had discussed its implications with him. Kinsella and his team had done a lot of internal analysis and Campbell-Breeden's staff examined them. Soon after Booth approved Kinsella's plans. Goldman's, in the style of such City takeovers, gave the project a code name: Moore and Best.

The M of Manchester United became Moore, the B of BSkyB, became Best. Moore is the only English captain to lift the World Cup; Best is one of United's greatest heroes. But Moore had never played for United, yet now his name stood for the club, while Best represented the company that wanted to take it over. As it happens both Moore and Best did play together, long after their prime, for a totally different club – Fulham. The code names were meant to ensure that even if some of the paperwork fell into the wrong hands nobody would know the identity of the two companies. However, as often happens, security was not always watertight and occasionally letters would be addressed to Moore plc, Busby Way, Old Trafford, Manchester, which would not have taken a genius to work out.

Campbell-Breeden himself got involved only in mid-July when he got back from a wedding in Spain. Then he looked at the papers Kinsella had prepared and held talks with Booth, Stewart, and Deanna Bates.

As takeovers went, this was for Campbell-Breeden and his Goldman's team pretty small fry. At best Sky would be paying round £600 million, which was the sort of takeover that ordinarily does not excite much interest at the investment bank. But this was not a standard takeover; apart from the emotive factors involved, valuing a football club was not the normal thing merchant bankers did and Goldman's had to start from scratch.

Goldman's soon worked out a range which would give Booth enough room to negotiate with Edwards. The range was between 210p and 225p per share, which was about 40p more than United's then market price. If Sky paid 225p, which was Goldman's upper limit, then United would be worth £570 million, not a significant takeover in City terms but would make United the most expensive football club in the world. One source says, 'We had struggled hard to show more and more value. We told Mark where he should get to and we told him where he should start. We were comfortable with 217p.'

The problem for Booth was that Edwards, 'wanted more than we could do. He wanted something like 225p–229p. I did not want to go much over £2, so we had quite a bit of spread'.

The United Board meeting was due to be held on 6 August. In the early evening of 4 August, Edwards and Watkins met Mark Booth, Ian West, Mark Kinsella and Martin Stewart for a formal meeting in a conference room at the Royal Lancaster Hotel. United had booked the suite and such was the paranoia about secrecy that when a waiter walked in with coffee, everyone froze and the hubbub of conversation ceased instantly. On the table were papers marked Sky and Manchester United and the immediate fear was that the waiter might see them and sense something was going on. But the waiter, unnerved by the total silence that greeted him, stopped in mid-stride. Then someone said, 'Oh, coffee, fine, fine, just leave it there', and the waiter almost dropped it on the nearest table and hurried out not sure whether he had come to the wrong room.

Had the waiter managed to eavesdrop, then what he would have heard is Sky insisting that it needed to get some reality into the discussion about the price: 290p was just not realistic.

United was arguing that the higher price was justified on the grounds that the Super League could happen. But neither Booth nor Stewart thought this was realistic, and even if it happened, it would not bring in the money United thought it might.

The 290p was soon knocked out as utopian and it was agreed that a realistic price would be somewhere around 200p. Sky's starting price was 190p, which was 30% above what the United share price was then. Sky knew it would have to go a bit north beyond 200p, but it wanted to make sure it would be just a little over 200p rather than going over the 250p mark.

Edwards and Watkins soon accepted the logic of this and as the talks developed Sky got the distinct impression that Edwards, who had already consulted Keith Harris informally, was much the more practical, pragmatic one, with Watkins trying to drive a hard bargain. He was trying to get as much as possible. However, by the end of the evening, both Edwards and Watkins had realised that if they wanted the deal they had to accept that much as Sky wanted United there was a limit to what it would pay for the club.

By the time the meeting ended an agreement had been struck. It was decided that the price would be 217.5p and, happy with the result, Edwards and Booth went off for a meal in the Thai restaurant to further develop what both felt was a very good personal chemistry. Meanwhile Martin Stewart and Ian West and Kevin Kinsella took Watkins to the bar of the Royal Lancaster where over beer they discussed what made Manchester United so fascinating and appealing to Sky.

Sky knew it was getting into a new business, the football business, and wanted to know more about the actual mechanics of it. There was none better than Watkins to provide a tutorial. The Sky people were keen to understand the dynamics of the business. Manchester United's strength was the size of its fan base and the remarkable fact that the club had kept its costs as a percentage of the revenue very low. This was due to United's success on the field and the fact that it had had a current crop of home-grown players which meant it had not paid much in big transfer money – although this would change even as the talks were going on. But what if in the future United had to buy players – how would United do it? Could the club still keep costs down and enjoy the same success?

By the time their Thai meal had finished Edwards assured Booth that he would go to the Board and recommend the offer at that price. Edwards also agreed to sell his own 14% stake to Sky, an irrevocable undertaking, at that price.

Booth drove away from the Royal Lancaster feeling not a little pleased with himself and confident the deal was now done. He had agreed it with Edwards and that was that. However, later that evening, when Booth rang Campbell-Breeden at home, told him the news and then asked, 'What happens now?' Campbell-Breeden's response surprised him.

'This is ridiculous,' responded Campbell-Breeden. 'He takes it to the Board. The Board appoints advisers and they do due diligence. Then they come back and say that they cannot recommend it. That's the point where they will try and screw us for more.'

Campbell-Breeden was to prove prophetic; the auction for United had just begun.

The United Board met on the morning of 6 August. An hour before the meeting Sky, having formalised the offer, faxed it to Old Trafford. Campbell-Breeden, who was sitting in Booth's office, wanted to go back to his offices, the old *Telegraph* offices in Fleet Street, but Booth, facing his first major takeover, wanted him to stay. So Campbell-Breeden had to hang round Booth's offices where Booth hoped he would soon get a call from Edwards saying United had said yes to Sky.

All the United directors were present. Kenyon had just come back from holiday in Sicily; Gill, who had turned 41 the previous day, celebrating it with a private dinner, was about to go away for two weeks to Kos. The three non-executive directors, Watkins, Dyke and Amir Midani, who had missed the July meeting, were also present. Apart from Edwards, Roland Smith and Watkins, all of them had come to the meeting not aware of the momentous announcement awaiting them. This was meant to be a routine pre-season Board meeting, three days before the Charity Shield, and nobody knew what was to hit them. The strategy discussion that had been adjourned in July was still on the agenda and some of the directors hoped there would be time to think of the plans for the future.

Then, as everyone settled down, Roland Smith said that before he turned to the agenda he had something to say.

Now Smith revealed the secret he had carried for over a month. Sky had made a bid for United, offering to pay 217.5p in cash and shares, and 212p if it was cash only. Edwards told the Board that, not only had he negotiated the price with Sky and recommended it, but that he had done a personal deal with Booth to sell Sky his shares. Roland Smith made it clear he was in favour of the deal.

Gill could not contain his surprise. 'I was taken by surprise even though I knew as a public company we could be taken over. My initial thoughts were, why do we need to tie up with someone? What is Sky going to bring to the party? What are they going to add over and above things you could do yourself? Those were the thoughts that came to mind immediately.'

Dyke echoed Gill's sentiments and felt more work needed to be done. Why was it necessary to sell to Sky or anybody else? And if there had to be a sale, how much was United worth? This would obviously depend on future income and revenues and things like that. So clearly there was need to commission specialists to examine the subject.

Dyke, of course, was an old foe of Murdoch and Sky, who did not have any faith in Murdoch. Back in 1992 Dyke had turned down an approach from Chisholm to do a joint bid with Sky and ITV for the Premier League rights. In retrospect, he told Mathew Horsman, author of *Sky High*, he should have done a deal with Sky but he feared it would have ended up in tears: 'Anyone who does a deal [with Murdoch] ends up being shafted in the end.'

Now, while totally unconvinced United should sell to Sky, Dyke concentrated on the price, which he felt was too low. United should be worth much, much more.

Kenyon was perhaps the least surprised. 'I was supportive of the bid. I was not agnostic. I always thought a bid would come from a media company if only because of what has happened. Media companies are after content. Sports bodies are content and if you look at the American model, what happens over there happens here sooner or later.'

Soon what Campbell-Breeden had told Booth the previous night came to pass. United were not going to say the quick yes that Booth had hoped for. As Gill pictured it: 'From a fan's perspective you ask why should you need to sell, but once you get over that what you have to look at is the price, right? We did some quick and dirty analysis on that in the boardroom and then we decided to get HSBC and Spectrum, a firm of media consultants, who Greg Dyke put us on to. He had done work with them in the past; they had quite a good reputation and we briefed them the following week. I briefed HSBC and got them modelling on how much United might be worth. Then I went away on two weeks' holiday to Kos; it was a pre-arranged holiday but mobile phones kept ringing and lots of faxes kept flying about between Manchester, London, Kos and Greece.'

Spectrum was asked to do an analysis of the business and what the television bits would add up to. HSBC was asked to do the basic financial analysis of what the takeover would mean and what the price should be.

In mid-afternoon, Edwards rang Booth and told him that United had decided to get HSBC involved. And only after HSBC had looked at the bid would the United Board be able to respond to the offer.

What this meant was that it would now take some weeks and during this period, as one Sky source says, 'Martin had decided that Sky was his favourite partner; what they could have done together was fantastic for the club and for football in the UK. But the involvement of merchant bankers meant a delay and the price kept going up. Everybody on the Manchester United Board now wanted more money.'

So far Rupert Murdoch had played little or no part in the discussions. Booth had not cleared it with him before making the offer. He did not need to, although he had discussed it with him and a couple of other Board members, including then BSkyB chairman Jerome Seydoux.

But now it was decided to brief Murdoch and later that Thursday Murdoch, who was on his boat somewhere off Sardinia, was rung up and told how the United Board had reacted to the offer. Murdoch was to get a first-hand report in the second week of August when Booth took a few days off and joined him on his boat.

'I was on the boat with him in mid-August. This was off the coast of Sardinia. We discussed it. His reaction was, if we could make the deal and it made sense then it was fine. We also discussed the reaction to the bid and the Murdoch factor. We felt it would be a hot topic and, like everybody else, we were conscious of it.'

By this time Booth had also decided that it was time to widen the circle of people who knew.

On 10 August, four days after the United Board meeting, he summoned Tim Allan, former deputy to Alistair Campbell, Tony Blair's press officer at Number 10, who had joined Sky in June of that year, to his office and told him. Allan, who is a keen sports fan (he plays cricket and is a member of the Number 10 football team), was taken aback, and recognised it would be a huge story with massive repercussions.

Booth also rang Tim Bell, who was himself on holiday on a boat off Sardinia.

Bell recalls: 'He rang me when I was on holiday in Sardinia in the first week of August and he told me that it looked possible and would I start thinking about it. I was sitting on a boat in the Calle de Volpe Bay off Sardinia with Robert Sangster. Robert had chartered the boat and invited me to stay on it, together with six or eight other people. Mark rang me on the boat and told me about it. At that point Mark didn't know when the deal might go through. He thought it might be a few weeks, a couple of months. He wasn't sure. He really just wanted to get us all talking about it, thinking about the issues that were raised. I was in a slightly awkward position because I couldn't discuss it with anybody, so I was sitting there with this wonderful piece of information, which I would have loved to have talked about with the people there. One was a top insurance broker, one was a famous racehorse owner, people whose views I could have been interested in, to see how they reacted to it. I couldn't, because it was highly confidential, so I didn't, and I couldn't ring anybody because I was nervous of using all those mobile phones, so I just sat on it. I did discuss it with my wife, because I trust her with everything. Not that she's a great Manchester United fan or, indeed, a football fan. Mark asked me to speak to Tim Allan. I spoke to Tim. We just talked about the rough outline of the whole thing. So I didn't really get involved in it until I came back from holiday, which was a couple of weeks later. I then got involved in conversations internally with Tim and Mark. It was a very small group of people who knew about it: Tim Allan, Vic Wakeling, Elisabeth Murdoch, Martin Stewart, Deanna Bates, and Mark, of course.'

Yet small as this group was it is interesting to note that United played it much more secretively. Nobody apart from the plc Board were told, not even the members of the football Board, which included Bobby Charlton. Booth had told his PR advisers but Edwards did not tell John Bick, his financial PR. And at this stage he had no intention of bringing Alex Ferguson into the loop.

Even at this stage United did not tell HSBC, its merchant banker, that it had had an offer from Sky. Gill had rung Rupert Faure Walker and on 10 August Faure Walker, accompanied by David Blake, travelled up to Manchester to meet Gill and Edwards. They met in Gill's office and were told that United had had an approach and wanted HSBC to prepare a valuation of Manchester United and determine at what price, says Faure Walker, 'we felt an offer could be accepted'.

At this first meeting Manchester United did not tell HSBC *who* had made the approach, let alone that the price was 217.5p. Edwards was very keen to keep this confidential, still fearful it might leak. On the way back from Manchester, Faure Walker and Blake talked about their bet and Blake was sure it was Sky, while Faure Walker stuck to Granada. 'On balance I thought it would be Granada, but when it was Sky I wasn't surprised, because David is the expert on football clubs and UK corporate finance and knows more about the industry than I do.'

Blake was a United fan, having been to university in Manchester. He had stood on the Stretford End, followed Tommy Docherty's team, and taken to the club not long after Campbell-Breeden and many of the supporters who would soon see both of them as mortal enemies.

It is one of the many ironies of the United story that the merchant bankers doing the United–Sky deal and the fans who would fight them had all been attracted to the same United team Docherty had built up, a man whose name is still chanted by the fans and who is still loved for the type of football he produced at Old Trafford. They were all United children of the 70s, drawn to the same theatre of dreams, but now on opposing sides as far as ownership of their beloved club was concerned. Gill's call had not surprised either Faure Walker or Blake. Faure Walker says: 'It had always been our view that if anyone was going to bid for Manchester United they would attempt to do it on a friendly basis. Martin still retained a sizeable stake in the company and Maurice Watkins has 2%. Between them they have about 16%, so any bidder would want to get them on their side. I think we'd always had a view that at some point in time sports clubs would become the targets for media companies. We could see the UK market moving towards the American model and in some respects the European and continental market as well. It was only a matter of time before a media group itself came in to buy United. There's a long list of media organisations who could be potentially interested in sport and News Corp was obviously one of them.'

Over the next two weeks, while Gill was kept glued to his mobile phone in Kos, HSBC prepared their report. 'We made,' recalls Faure Walker, 'several visits to Manchester and must have been there for about ten days in all to see everything and everyone. It was basically to gather information, latest projections, TV, sponsorship, transfer fees – that's a big thing these days – and Manchester United's views of the future. Those sorts of things.' This included Media Partners' plans and projections about income from Europe.

HSBC only learnt that BSkyB was the bidder when Faure Walker and Blake went up to Old Trafford on 23 August. This time they met Edwards, Gill and Roland Smith. HSBC had come up with a valuation, but both Faure Walker and Blake were impatient to know who the bidder was and what they were offering. They asked to be told and Roland Smith now informed them it was BSkyB and that there might be another bidder but its identity was never disclosed. They were also told the offer was 217.5p.

The implication of Sky's offer of 217.5p in cash was that it was as far as they were prepared to go. United shares were trading at around 160p and the Sky offer was a 40% premium on the market price. Normally a 30–40% premium on the market price is an offer which a merchant banker will support and, as Faure Walker confesses, 'it was giving us some difficulty, that figure of 217.5p. We had some contact with Goldman's at that stage. Goldman's were very keen to get on with things, but very little happened until about the end of August.'

Goldman's was getting fed up with how slowly things were going and the time HSBC was taking to review the business. When Edwards had told Booth that they had called in HSBC, Campbell-Breeden asked, 'How long is this going to take? That was when we found out that Gill was going on holiday, and that HSBC were not going to start working until they had sat down with Gill to review the financial forecasts. We wasted a week at a time when there was a real risk of a leak.'

What Goldman's did not know was the enormous waves of anguish and disquiet Sky's offer was causing in the Old Trafford Board. Dyke had not shaken off his reservations about the deal and sometime during this period he spoke to Mark Booth. Booth was not surprised to hear that Dyke felt the price was too low, but what considerably surprised him was that Dyke told him the deal would not go through. It would face competition arguments. All Booth's legal advice from Herbert Smith's, and his own in-house lawyers, had been, yes, the deal might be referred to the Monopolies and Mergers Commission but in the end it would go through. United was in football, Sky was in television – surely there could not be conflict on competition grounds here.

No, argued Dyke, those who say that do not know how television works. Here was a monopoly supplier of television sports buying the biggest football club in the country, if not the world – it would raise competition arguments.

The United Board was due to meet on Friday 28 August and on 25 August Edwards came down to London and met Booth at the Royal Lancaster Hotel. Harris was back from holiday and he had arranged to have dinner with him. Harris also came along to meet Booth. The three met in the first-floor tea room just outside the carvery. As far as the deal was concerned Edwards exuded confidence. The share price was 157p, Sky was offering 217.5p. What more could anybody ask? At some stage during the conversation, Edwards excused himself and went up to his room to get ready for dinner. As he did so, Booth told Harris of the wonders of Sky digital and promised to get him a flat screen, which was ideal for digital television.

Edwards and Harris then went off to dinner at the Nobu restaurant in the Metropole Hotel. The City was still in deep gloom; August had been a month of misery on the stock market; and while United looked like they would qualify for the Champions League proper – they had taken a 2–0 lead over LKS Lodz in the first leg of their qualifying match – Arsenal had thumped them 3–0 in the Charity Shield, which did little to lift the depression that had descended on Old Trafford after Arsenal had done the double the previous season. An alliance with Sky now looked even more appealing and Edwards and Harris felt the details could now be left to the merchant bankers on either side.

The same day Faure Walker had met Campbell-Breeden to discuss the details. On 26 August, Campbell-Breeden wrote to Faure Walker confirming that Sky's 217.5p offer was a cash and share alternative.

On Friday 28 August, the United Board met again at Old Trafford. Harris had told Edwards the price of 217.5p was a good price. Faure Walker told Gill and Dyke that they now had a duty to shareholders to accept the price and recommend it to shareholders. Neither Gill nor Dyke was truly convinced but by the end of the Board meeting, with HSBC recommending it, the Board agreed that United would accept the Sky offer of 217.5p. This was the best they could get.

However, there was one thing they could do to improve the offer. The United Board were quite keen there should be a full cash alternative. Sky's offer of a mixture of cash and shares meant that every United shareholder accepting the offer would get 109p in cash and 108.5p in Sky shares, with a mix-and-match alternative so people could have either more cash or more shares but they could not have it all in cash. They had to accept some Sky shares. But what if they did not want to own Sky shares? There were many small shareholders who had bought the shares merely because they were fans and did not care for the stock market. For them an all-cash alternative might be more tempting.

It was to Sky's advantage for it to be both a share and cash deal to limit the financing it would have to arrange through Goldman's. United's request for a cash alternative meant more discussions between Faure Walker and Campbell-Breeden, which took some part of the following week. By Friday 4 September, Campbell-Breeden was able to write to Faure Walker and say Sky was prepared to offer a complete cash alternative at 217.5p. But just then, as Sky discovered, United was about to move the goalposts.

* * *

By now it was nearly two months since Edwards' lunch with Booth and very nearly four weeks since a much wider circle of people, numbering a couple of hundred or more, knew about the bid. There were fears that it might leak. Indeed the day after the United Board meeting, which also marked the start of the August bank holiday weekend, one reporter came within an ace of breaking the story.

Tim Allan had decided to take a holiday that week and had motored up the East Coast of Scotland with his great friend James Purnell. Purnell dealt with sports in the Downing Street Policy Unit and Allan knew should the deal be agreed it would land on Purnell's desk. But he could not tell his friend. However, he also knew that the deal could be announced any time and he would have to hurry back to London, so he told Purnell that a big story might break and he would have to return but refused to tell him what the big story might be.

On the morning of 25 August, while they were at the Boat of Garteri near Inverness, Purnell came to his room and said, 'I know what the big story is that might break.'

Allan's colour drained and he asked in a barely audible whisper, 'What?'

'Sky is bidding for Tottenham.'

'Definitely, not true,' said Allan with great relief.

'How do you know?' asked Purnell.

'I know,' said Allan, trying hard to conceal his delight over the close shave and refused to discuss it further.

Purnell's source that day was the *Guardian*, which had picked up some City rumours about a bid and, in the classic style, added two and two and come to nine. Tottenham was for sale. The season had just started and Tottenham was the crisis club. It had just managed to avoid relegation the previous season; its Swiss manager Christian Gross was finding life at the Lane impossible; and the chairman Alan Sugar, after being told by fans following two successive defeats to get his wallet out – common advice by fans for all chairmen – had decided, for the second time in four years, to sell. ENIC, the investment company, had made an offer, which Sugar turned down; and later the journalist Richard Littlejohn, a Tottenham supporter, got a consortium together to bid for the company. Two weeks earlier Sam Chisholm had joined the Tottenham Board as non-executive director. The *Guardian* had clearly picked up some rumours of a Sky bid for a club, mixed it in with various bits and pieces, and concluded Sky was after Tottenham. Interestingly, it quoted a spokesman for the Tottenham Independent

Supporters Association saying, 'It's good news for the supporters because at least it means that someone will be investing in the club to ensure that we have a team that can compete with the best in Europe.' This would be very different from the response Manchester United fans made when they heard of the real club Sky was seeking to buy, and while some of it expressed the deep frustration felt by Tottenham fans for their team's performance over many years, it also underlined the real gulf in class and supporter expectations that was developing between United and the rest of English football.

However, within days, another reporter picked up the right scent. By the Saturday of that August bank holiday Allan was in Edinburgh at the Edinburgh Television Festival. It was a time of some activity for both Sky and Manchester United. Elisabeth Murdoch was speaking at the Edinburgh Television Festival and Paul Ridley, former editor of the *Sun* – he has since gone back to his old job – and then managing director of MUTV was also there to talk about the new television channel that United was going to launch. Maurice Watkins was also there. Allan took a break from his holiday to be in Edinburgh to help out and he was approached by Christine Harper of Bloomberg News Services, an agency that specialises in business news.

'News is coming through that you are buying Manchester United,' said Harper.

Allan, still learning his job as press officer, was not sure if he could lie brazenly and tried to hedge it by saying, 'Spurs last week, Manchester United now,' and shrugged his shoulders as if to say, what next?

'So you are not buying?'

'Look, we can't run around issuing denials everytime there is a silly rumour about a football club,' replied Allan, trying hard not to give any hint of how close Harper was to the truth.

Allan felt that under lobby terms Harper had the story but she took it as denial and did not run it. What had saved Sky and Allan was that Bloomberg, being an American company, seeks to research its stories very thoroughly and have them verified by many sources, many more than a comparable British news organisation would require before it decided to run a story. In this case, having failed to source it well, they decided not to run it.

There was a Manchester United exclusive that weekend. It was on the front page of the *Sun* that Saturday and on pages 4 and 5 and it was not about the takeover but the antics of Dwight Yorke. Headlined 'Orgy Video Shame of £12m Yorke', the exclusive story by Andrew Parker said: 'Soccer star Dwight Yorke made a shameful secret video of a drunken orgy at his home. The goal ace, who has just joined Manchester United for £12.6 million, filmed the hour-long romp with a hidden camera. It shows him, his former Aston Villa team-mate Mark Bosnich and a third man dressed in women's clothes and frolicking with four girls. None of the girls knew they were being taped – and we are protecting their identities.

'Yorke, 26, is seen as having wild sex with one on a double bed. And goalkeeper Bosnich, also 26, was filmed being spanked with leather belts by two of the girls – and having his toes sucked by the others.'

Pages 4 and 5 had more, including two of the girls kneeling at the end of the bed sucking each of Bosnich's feet. While Bosnich and Yorke were clearly identifiable, the girls' faces were blanked out with tape.

This was, of course, a classic tabloid story and it meant the real secret was safe. However, fears that the Sky story might leak had by now begun to haunt the merchant bankers and Faure Walker was amazed that with nearly a month gone nothing had surfaced. 'What amazed us was that there were no leaks for four weeks. Frankly, it amazed us. This thing was so hot and sensitive and for four weeks beforehand there were no leaks. Everyone was very security conscious.'

On Sky's behalf, Tim Bell was planning how to deal with leaks if they came. Bell had been working on this ever since he had got back from Robert Sangster's boat. 'When I got back from holiday in the middle of August we had spent three weeks discussing a leak strategy with Goldman Sachs, because it seemed to me that as the process was going on, so many people would get involved and it would eventually leak. My view was, if it leaked we should put the whole story out straight away and not go through all this nonsense of, "We confirm that we are in talks with a third party", and all that kind of stuff. It seemed to me that, if we drafted something that did that and put it to the Manchester United advisers, we would find out how committed they were. Well, this would have been in the last week of August and the first few days of September. We did a range of options and they ranged from simple one-liners that said, "Sky confirms that it is the third party mentioned in the Manchester United press release", through to, "Sky announces it is making a bid for Manchester United, which has the unanimous support of the Board and has agreed at a price of XXX", and so on and so forth. Of course what happens in these deals is both sides are dancing with each other. Our fear was that Manchester United would leak it into the market place to get the price up, because they would leak it at a higher price which means we'd then have to go to the higher price because the share price would move to it. Their fear was that we would leak it at the lower price so the share price would go to the lower price. In financial transactions, whatever the rules may be, all this goes on. We became more and more concerned it would leak.'

By Friday 4 September, the story had not leaked. Now it seemed it only required the details to be worked out for the deal to be done and it could go public. That day, as we have seen, Campbell-Breeden wrote to Faure Walker, saying Sky were now prepared to provide a full cash alternative, thus meeting all of the United Board's requests. But now a new City adviser, or rather an old United adviser, came on the scene and threatened to change everything.

It was the turn of United's brokers, Merrill Lynch.

Curiously at this stage Merrill Lynch had not yet been involved. It was only after the 26 August Board meeting that it was briefed by Gill, and on that September Friday, Merrill Lynch produced a preliminary assessment. In stark contrast to what HSBC were saying, Merrill Lynch made it very clear that it thought 217.5p was too low a price.

For Dyke this was the signal he needed. The moment he heard, he got on the phone to Roland Smith at his offices in HSBC and told him that the Board decision of 26 August, agreeing to 217.5p, would have to be changed. Merrill Lynch had produced new information and the 26 August decision could not stand. That day Gill and the main players in the United Board – Edwards, Watkins, Kenyon – were due to meet at HSBC with Roland Smith, Faure Walker and Blake. Gill agreed with Dyke and it was clear that Kenyon and Watkins must consider this new information. It was this that had prompted Gill's call to them, catching them on the mobile phone at the offices of Slaughter & May.

Soon all the principal United Board members, barring Dyke, who remained at his offices at Pearson Television near Tottenham Court Road, were at HSBC discussing what Merrill Lynch was saying United was worth. But how could they get Sky to offer more? The mood seemed to be that United would now reject the deal until Sky were prepared to pay more.

Faure Walker felt, 'Sky had said that [217.5p] was the highest offer they could make and on that Friday night David and I talked to each other and assumed that the Board would not accept the offer and therefore we assumed the deal would not take place. So I think we said to ourselves, "This thing probably won't happen and the feeling of David and myself, yes, that there would be no deal and the price wouldn't be agreed".'

But things were not quite as pessimistic as they seemed. Edwards was constantly speaking to Booth and had made it clear that if Sky were prepared to push the price up to 226p, or at least 225p, then he might swing the Board behind him.

If this was not quite what Booth wanted to hear, his advisers reacted with some fury to the news that United's price kept going up. Goldman's, fed up with the delay, was now getting increasingly angry about what it saw as the constant demand for more money from United's directors. Booth had another problem. He knew that if it went up beyond 225p he would have to clear it with Murdoch.

Booth had previously told Murdoch that 225p was the absolute ceiling, but now Edwards was telling him they may have to find more and Murdoch had to be involved. He decided to ring Murdoch on his yacht and made the call in the presence of Campbell-Breeden and Martin Stewart. After Booth had informed him of what United wanted Murdoch said, 'It's your deal, Mark. Do you want to do it, Mark?'

'Yeah,' said Booth.

'Fine,' responded Murdoch, and then, in that mock humble pose he can adopt so successfully, added, 'I am just a Board member.'

Booth was confident that, despite the haggling over the price, the deal would go through. It was decided that Sky would offer 226p and Booth decided to call a formal Board meeting of BSkyB on Tuesday 8 September, the first time the Board would meet to consider the deal.

Booth spoke to Bell and they agreed that Booth would travel to Manchester on the evening of Sunday 6 September, meet Alex Ferguson for the first time and take him out for dinner.

Ferguson fascinated Sky. They knew that to help sell the deal to the fans it would be essential to have him and Bobby Charlton on board. Before Booth made the offer to buy United, the feeling in Sky was that the Edwards–Ferguson partnership was a strong one with mutual respect and understanding. The first inkling that this might not be so, and an insight into how Edwards felt about Ferguson, had come in the third week of August when Edwards and Kenyon came to Sky and had lunch with Booth and Allan. The idea was to discuss how they would handle the media when the story broke. During the lunch the conversation turned to Ferguson. Edwards made it clear he did not appreciate Ferguson's political leanings. 'He has got very close to New Labour and to Number 10,' said Edwards. 'He is very friendly with Alistair Campbell. He is a socialist, you know. Very strange. And all this friendship with New Labour and Campbell I do not understand.'

Booth and Allan listened with some wonder, for Edwards was clearly unaware of Allan's links with Number 10 or the fact that Allan still saw Campbell as one of his great friends. At that stage Edwards' view of Ferguson's socialism seemed to be the sort of view rich football chairmen may have for their employees. It would assume more significance two weeks later as Bell prepared to manage the publicity when the deal was announced and get Ferguson on board.

'My job was to look at it from a public relations point of view. It was clear to me that it would be greeted very hostilely by the anti-Murdoch press, or the non-Murdoch press, and would be very limp-wristedly supported by the Murdoch press, because that's what they do in order to avoid accusations of being dictated to by Murdoch. It would be greeted badly by the BBC because it's commercialism and they don't understand commercialism. It would be greeted badly by ITV and Channel 4 or 5 because they're competitors. Whatever you say, the fact is that if you are a competitor you find yourself being negative about things. It would be greeted badly by the fans because Murdoch has been demonised. It would be greeted badly by the opinion-formers of the game, because they can't stand change. They are just automatically negative. The problem with British people is, if you put an idea in front of them, they say, "What's wrong with this . . . ?" They never say, "What a good idea!" Americans are very optimistic. They say, "What a good idea! That'll work." Even if they do later on say, "It's a lousy idea and it doesn't work", they will at least give it a chance before they kill it. The sports commentators would greet it very badly because they don't understand it. I don't mean that rudely but they've never been in that world.'

Bell was also aware 'that Martin Edwards and his Board were very unpopular with the fans anyway; that the club itself actually had got a mixed reputation. On the one hand it's loved by people and on the other people hate it and fear it, because it's too successful. It would raise questions about the European Super League because Manchester United had been in the van of that. It was nothing to do with properly thought-through things. It was all knee-jerk reactions.'

But, 'the biggest issue for us was Alex Ferguson. Our view was that this welter of bad publicity that we would get, there was only one way to diminish it, to minimise it. That was we'd announce it in our own time, without a leak, and that Alex Ferguson would come out on the same day and say he was in favour of it in some way, shape or form. Clearly my view was, at the very least, we must make sure he didn't come out and say he was opposed to it and was leaving the club. That would cause us great difficulties. My expectation was that he would say, "This is not for me, it's for the Board." That's the safest ground to take. He has lots of close advisers, notably Alistair Campbell from Number 10, who would give him that advice, because these are experts in knowing how to kick things into touch.'

Bell and Sky took the view that before a formal announcement was made Booth must see Ferguson. It was this that had led to the dinner idea between the two men.

So on the afternoon of 4 September Bell went to the offices of HSBC to talk to Edwards, Kenyon and Roland Smith about how Sky wanted to handle the publicity and also bring Ferguson into the loop.

Bell recalls: 'We had a meeting with the Manchester United Board on the afternoon of Friday September 4 at HSBC, where it was agreed we'd all go to Manchester on that Sunday. We were going to go up and talk with their Board about how to announce it and how it would take place, look at the stadium, see where it would be done and so on. We wanted to do the announcement in London in the morning and in Manchester in the afternoon. It was agreed that that Sunday evening, Mark would have supper with Alex Ferguson and see him for the first time. I was asked by Mark to convince the Manchester United Board that this meeting should take place. I had a meeting with Martin Edwards, Peter Kenyon and Roland Smith at HSBC. At the beginning of the meeting I asked if I could do so privately. Edwards and Roland Smith came and they brought Peter Kenyon with them. I said to them, "The one possibility of stemming the flow of entirely hostile and negative media would be if the most important person (as I saw it), namely Alex Ferguson, would come out in favour." The Board's view was that if we told him the announcement it would leak and that was dangerous. My answer was, I'd rather have a leak with Alex Ferguson knowing than one without him knowing.'

It was finally decided that Edwards was to ring Ferguson on that Sunday morning. Edwards told Bell, 'I'll ring him on the Sunday morning, because if I ring him in advance, he'll start ringing everybody up to find out why I want to see him.'

'It was quite clear to me,' says Bell, 'that they did not have a great relationship.'

However, according to a source present at this meeting, and who does not wish to be identified, the relationship, far from being great, was quite bad. When Bell had suggested to Edwards that Booth wanted to have dinner with Ferguson and bring him in the loop, Edwards had reacted with horror saying, 'Christ, no! You don't want to see him. He's a troublemaker. If you tell him, he'll leak everything. He's totally hostile and I've just written him a letter warning him.' The source says, 'It was a nightmare. When Sky inquired was there any way we could involve Ferguson in the transaction and make him benefit from it, Edwards said, "Don't give him money for Christ's sake. The man's useless." Unbelievable! It is like when you find a journalist on the paper that seems to be the top writer. Then you meet the proprietor and he says, "I hate the bastard. He never co-operates" and so on. Clearly Ferguson was not friendly with Edwards and Edwards was not friendly with Ferguson. They'd had a bad time during the summer. They'd obviously had a huge disagreement about [which, as we shall see had led Ferguson to threaten to leave Old Trafford] Dwight Yorke and they'd obviously had a disagreement about other things as well. I think it was to do with money. I'm not so sure it wasn't also that Edwards wanted him to buy other players and he had failed to do so.'

The Edwards–Ferguson relationship is a fascinating one and goes to the heart of this great club. We shall have more to say about that later. But at that particular moment, the anger Edwards felt towards Ferguson was caused both because of the purchase of Yorke and by the clever way he had undermined the sale that Edwards had planned.

Edwards and the Board had just paid £12.5 million to buy Dwight Yorke from Aston Villa. This had caused a surfeit of strikers and Ferguson clearly could not play them all. The purchase of Yorke had taken United's spending to over £28 million on three players and the Board was told Ferguson would have to sell a surplus striker. Gunnar Solskjaer was the obvious choice.

Tottenham came in for him and Edwards discussed a deal. When Alan Sugar sent a fax offering £5.5 million he signed. Now Tottenham had to agree terms with the player. Then Ferguson stepped in.

David Pleat, Tottenham's director of football, was acting on the deal for Tottenham. 'The boy went to see Alex. He told him you are still in my plans. I still rate you. Alex says to him you don't have to go, we are not under financial pressure. The boy's wife was about to start a course at Manchester University. Solskjaer being a nice boy says he'd stay here. His agent Rune Hauge came to see us and we discussed the transfer. If we at Tottenham had been hard-nosed, we could have made life difficult for Manchester United about it.'

Ferguson quickly began to play Solskjaer in his team, and although he never commanded a regular place, he often came on very effectively as substitute – never more so than against Bayern Munich to score the winner in Barcelona in injury time and win United the Champions League. The way Ferguson played the transfer showed the power a manager can exercise. In strict theory he had done nothing. A transfer had been agreed but the player did not go. However, Ferguson helped the player decide not to go.

The tabloid press, particularly the *Daily Mail*, heaped abuse on Tottenham and the *Mail* claimed quite wrongly that Tottenham had signed Solskjaer and was not telling fans. Tottenham's laywers contacted the *Mail* and they had to print a retraction. Tottenham made much of the *Mail's* apology. Bell's conversation with Edwards came within days of this and explains Edwards' fury. Chairmen of football clubs know that, when it comes to back-page manipulation, they can never compete with their managers, and now that he faced the biggest deal of his career, Edwards did not want to take any chances and see Ferguson ruin it.

Sky were also keen to get Bobby Charlton, one of Old Trafford's greatest names, on the side of the bid. Bell says, 'The second thing we talked about at some length was Bobby Charlton, as to whether or not we should tell him. I, in my simplistic way, argued that as Charlton was clearly under contract to Sky – because he does that *Bobby Charlton Memories* programme – why couldn't Vic give him a ring and tell him? Anyway, we discovered that he was in Thailand, going over for the Commonwealth Games in Malaysia and so on, so that couldn't be done.'

Bell also had a raft of other ideas he wanted to do: 'We talked about the fact that we wanted to mail all the Manchester United fans on the first day of the announcement – have a mailshot into their homes to tell them about it, to put our point of view. There was to be a jointly signed letter from Mark Booth and Martin Edwards. We wanted to take ads in the local newspapers, putting our point of view. We had a complete programme. I did explain to everybody at Sky that I thought the takeover panel would ban us from doing any of these things, but nevertheless you have to go down these roads.'

Despite the way Edwards had reacted to the idea of recruiting Ferguson, the meeting that Friday between Bell and the United Board went well. 'Roland Smith was very positive – I've known him for years. We worked together on Harrods, so we've been through the media fire before. Kenyon was very co-operative and persuasive; Maurice Watkins was fine. The finance director [David Gill] was very hostile throughout the entire conversations, but I suspect that was because he didn't have a deal worked out at the time. Our view of their Board was that from the outside it was not 100% accurate on the relationships inside, if you see what I mean. It was a perfectly civilised meeting and I have to tell you the meeting discussed press releases, leak announcements, how to announce it, so there was no question of it not being done. It was quite clear this transaction was going ahead. They had to have a final Board meeting and Sky had to have a final Board meeting.'

There was still a lot of what Bell calls 'argy-bargy about which went first. Does Sky have to get the Board to agree to doing things or does Manchester United have to get its Board to agree? It was a very complicated process. The bankers met and worked out a detailed timetable and we all participated in the whole process.'

Bell left HSBC confident the deal was going through.

And Booth was so confident that he decided to call a Board meeting. If Edwards had kept the initial offer of Booth to a very closed group, then Booth, having worked on the deal for months, was only now prepared to present it formally to his Board. His Board had many other broadcasters and he was always wary of discussing it too early in a formal meeting. Now confident that 226p would get United, he called a Board meeting.

'We had,' says Booth, 'people from Granada. They could have been rivals. I played it by not talking to everybody on the Board, but talking to a number I felt I could with confidence, so then I could speak to Martin and United on behalf of the Board. That was a correct deduction. I did not need to call a Board meeting.'

As Booth sent out the notices for the meeting, he made it clear that any Board member who felt he might have a conflict of interest should not attend. Granada decided not to attend.

Campbell-Breeden says, 'Graham Parrott from Granada is on the Sky Board. We thought that Granada as the Manchester-based ITV company would be the most likely competitor to us. But the day after we announced the deal they could not believe the price we were paying. Sky didn't call a Board meeting until the last minute. We called the Board meeting with the minimum amount of time, 48 hours, and they kept the other non-executives informed without calling a Board meeting. We did not inform Chisholm and Chance [non-executive directors] until quite late.'

The United Board were not quite as confident that the deal was in the bag as Sky, but clearly a decision would be made the following week. What everybody was relieved about was that the news had not leaked.

There seemed nothing to worry about now. The PR men relaxed, confident that they had control of the publicity agenda, and Richard Campbell-Breeden went off for a weekend to Sweden.

It was meant to be a classic Swedish crayfish party of a friend on the archipelago outside Stockholm. He had a meeting all day on Friday 4 September preparing for the BSkyB Board. His wife and kid were already in Stockholm but he stayed in London on the Saturday, worried there might be a leak. On Saturday evening, having been reassured there was no leak, he took the last flight to Stockholm and switched off his mobile. He would be just in time for dinner.

The English sporting world had enough to worry about that weekend. That Saturday evening England were in Stockholm, playing the first match of the qualifying campaign for Euro 2000 against Sweden. England had bowed out of the World Cup against Argentina feeling distinctly unlucky. They were immediately seen as favourites for Euro 2000. But then had come the ill-advised *World Cup Diary* by England coach Glen Hoddle, which revealed dressing-room secrets and upset the players, and there were dark mutterings in the English camp as they travelled to Sweden. David Beckham, sent off against Argentina, was missing, and although England took an early lead, the Swedes bounced back. By the time Campbell-Breeden's plane touched down in Stockholm, England were well beaten.

As he landed in Stockholm he switched his mobile phone back on. Almost instantly it rang. It was one of Campbell-Breeden's team, Mark Sorrell, whose father Martin Sorrell is head of the giant media company WPP. Mark's message for Campbell-Breeden was so disturbing that he spent most of the dinner holding conference calls on his mobile phone with Booth, Stewart, Bell, Allan and other Sky advisers.

The message was that the takeover cover had been blown. It would be in a Sunday paper the following morning.

4

THE LEAK

The call that Mark Sorrell had made to Campbell-Breeden was one of many whizzing between Manchester United, BSkyB and their advisers on that Saturday evening and reflected the utter panic that had gripped them as they realised that their secret had been rumbled.

The man who had finally nailed the story and was prepared to go where Christine Harper couldn't was Neil Bennett. On Thursday 4 September, just as Merrill Lynch were looking at the Sky bid, Neil Bennett, City editor of the *Daily* and *Sunday Telegraph*, got a call. 'The call said that BSkyB was planning to bid for United. The caller knew they were talking. In the past this contact had given me some good stories and some bum steers. This was a good one.'

Bennett was not surprised. It was coming up to a year since he had made a prediction that BSkyB would make a bid for United. The occasion was the annual visit of Dominic Lawson, editor of the *Sunday Telegraph* to the City offices. The *Sunday Telegraph*'s City offices are not in Canary Wharf, where the main offices of the Telegraph group are, but in Fore Street in the City of London, the reason being that Canary Wharf is felt to be too far away for reporters to get to City meetings.

As Lawson walked round the City offices, he noticed that Bennett's screen was showing the Manchester United website. Bennett told Lawson, 'Dominic, someday BSkyB will buy Manchester United.' It was, says Bennett, 'a combination of intuition, their link-up with MUTV; I knew Murdoch's passion for concentration of businesses. Call it a flash of inspiration.'

A year later, on that Thursday evening, Bennett called Lawson at his home. 'I could not risk calling Dominic on his mobile; he had not changed to the digital, which cannot be scrambled. I said to him that I had the story of BSkyB bidding for Manchester United. Internally I kept it very tight. I spoke to Dominic and Ron Embler, the chief sub. Dominic was superb. It is difficult in newspapers when you have a great story not to talk, but he did not talk. We were worried that if we widened the circle of people who knew, and it leaked, then BSkyB and United would have to issue a statement to the stock exchange. So we had to keep it very tight until the markets closed on Friday evening. Then Dominic told Chris Andersen, executive editor, and Mathew d'Ancona, deputy editor.'

It was decided the *Sunday Telegraph* would have a spoof first edition, where the lead stories would be different from the one about Sky buying United. Lawson had decided to give the story a lot of prominence and back up the front-page splash with background features on Martin Edwards on the focus pages and a big City-page feature explaining how Sky had shaped the Premier League and English football. All these stories would be printed only in the second and subsequent editions, so there had to be stories to take their place in the spoof first edition.

Bennett spent the Saturday morning doing this spoof first edition, which had a feature by Alan Walters, the former economics adviser to Mrs Margaret Thatcher, and a lead story in the business section on talks going on between the Futures Market and the London Clearing Houses.

The spoof edition was necessary because, if the *Sunday Telegraph* ran the story in the first edition, it would be available to their competitors by 9.00pm on Saturday and they would have enough time to change their pages for their own second and later editions and destroy the exclusivity the *Sunday Telegraph* wanted. Such spoof editions are usual for tabloids but are virtually unknown among the broadsheets. Indeed the City editors of the Sunday broadsheets have an agreement to exchange their first edition late on Saturday night so that if there is something interesting in another paper they lift it after due credit. 'The broadsheets,' says Bennett, 'are run in a gentlemanly atmosphere. We don't play those sort of games. Those are games played by the tabloids.'

Bennett was haunted by what had happened to him when he broke the Archer story. 'When in was on the *Times*, I had worked on the story of Jeffrey Archer's insider dealing with Anglia shares, buying them when his wife Mary was director. We had worked very hard for days. Late in the afternoon, before publication, we told the political staff and they told their colleagues and the next day all the papers had it. I vowed to myself then that if I ever have a story of similar magnitude then I will not lose my grip on it. We wanted to make sure the story remained secure. We wanted to claim full ownership. It was very difficult to do that.'

The spoof edition would make sure very few people outside the *Telegraph* would know about the story. But Lawson and Bennett also decided to make sure very few people within the *Sunday Telegraph* knew about the story. So, says Bennett, 'one writer was told to write a feature about Manchester United, the history and the background of the club, but wasn't told why we wanted such a story.' Colin Gibson was told about the story at Saturday lunchtime and, at the same time, Bennett took his deputy Mary Fagan to a pub and told her about it. He then returned to the office and told the rest of the City staff who had spent most of that Saturday morning wondering why Bennett was behaving in a quite extraordinary fashion and being so furtive.

Normally, when a paper has a great story, a buzz goes round the office. But even now information was tightly controlled. In addition to providing sporting bits for Bennett's front-page story, Gibson was also writing a feature. When at 7.00pm he gave it to the sub, he did not tell him what it was about. Only when the sub read it did he realise with a shock that the story he had been asked to sub, which he had thought was a routine sports story, was actually the remarkable exclusive on Sky bidding for Manchester United.

However, having got everything ready, Bennett had a problem. It was now about four in the afternoon and he needed one more check call to make sure his contact had not given him a bum steer. 'My biggest problem was I couldn't go to print without some confirmation of the story. The obvious thing would be to ring either United or BSkyB. But if I rang BSkyB and they knew I had got the story then they could release it to the Murdoch papers and my exclusive control of the story would be lost. I got hold of someone who knew somebody who called back and said the story was broadly correct.'

Bennett, understandably, will not say who he rang. He rang Pearson Television. With Dyke wearing two hats, one as chairman of Pearson and the other of Manchester United, Bennett knew that even if he got a 'no comment' that would confirm the story. The head of PR at Pearson contacted Dyke at his country home in Hampshire and asked, 'I suppose you want me to deny it as complete rubbish?'

'No,' said Dyke, 'you better not do that. I don't think you better get back to them at all.'

Dyke then got on the phone to Gill and to Mark Booth telling them that this 'thing', as he called it, was out and that Neil Bennett of the *Sunday Telegraph* would be running the story the next day.

Gill immediately got on the phone and rang Edwards, Faure Walker and David Blake.

Faure Walker was in his garden at home (out in Essex) clearing up a large pile of rubbish. 'It was about 4.30. Suddenly I heard three people had telephoned me. My children came up to see me and straightaway I knew there was a leak. When you suddenly get three calls like that – bang, bang, bang – within ten minutes you know there's a leak. The three people who tried to call me were Martin Edwards, David Gill and David Blake. I went back into the house and called them back. They had heard that the *Telegraph* were inquiring into the details and nobody at Manchester United had spoken to them. We took the view that it was much better not to call the *Sunday Telegraph*. You know what it is with press leaks. You don't know if it's someone trying to fly a kite or not. If you call them back you get yourselves in a very embarrassing position, so we took the view not to call them back at that stage.'

As Faure Walker was clearing out his garden, Keith Harris was with Roland Smith at Lord's to see their beloved Lancashire play the NatWest Final against Derbyshire. It was a filthy day, with rain preventing play until 4.30pm – the only consolation for them was that Lancashire won in a canter by nine wickets. Just as play was about to start Roland Smith got a call on his mobile.

'Roland and I went outside the box in the Mound Stand at Lord's at the back of the stand and we discussed the fact that the next day's *Sunday Telegraph* would have the story', Harris explains.

But since the *Sunday Telegraph* had not contacted Manchester United there was nothing for Manchester United to do, just let the story unfold.

In one of these curious twists Booth had misheard Dyke, mixing up two Neils. When he rang Tim Bell he said, 'It's a guy called Neil Collins.'

Bell felt reassured by this and said, 'Well, he's the *Daily Telegraph* [Neil Collins is the City editor of the *Daily Telegraph*]. So we won't have the leak tomorrow, it'll be on Monday. So at least we can get all the meetings in Manchester done on the Sunday before it comes out. We also might consider whether we should put it out on the Sunday, ahead of any leak.'

However, after he had put the phone down, 'I thought to myself, "You know, it's Saturday afternoon. It can't be Neil Collins, because he doesn't work on Saturdays – or, if he does, I'm most surprised. He usually works on Sundays." So I rang Mark back and said, "Are you sure it wasn't Neil Bennett?" He said, "I don't know. I don't remember people's names." Anyway, we checked back with the bankers and they said, "Yes, it is Neil Bennett." So I said, "Oh my God. It's Sunday. We're already in the shit." '

Bell's theory was that Booth had got the name right at one point and maybe someone had said another name to him and that had confused him.

'Anyway it emerged that our best bet was that it was Neil Bennett. Then I got a phone call from the *Mail on Sunday* who said, "We understand the *Sunday Telegraph*'s got a big story and is boxing out the second edition. They're putting a spoof story in the first edition, printing the second edition late and putting that big story on the front page of the second edition. The *Express* have heard the same thing." So I thought to myself, "Well, this has got to be *it*." '

Bell rang his colleague, David Beck, who is the managing director of Bell's financial PR and knows Neil Bennett very well. 'I said to David, "Ring Neil Bennett and find out what he's got. Just plead with him to give us a clue. Just say to him we don't all want our weekends ruined, spending the whole night on the bloody telephone, making calls and all the rest of it." '

Bell didn't want to risk anything by making the call himself, because that would have elevated it into a much heavier atmosphere.

Meanwhile Tim Allan was also trying to find out what the *Sunday Telegraph* had. He had a more than unusually stressful day. James Purnell, who had split up with his girlfriend, was staying at his flat in Islington. That morning he had been working on possible questions and answers Booth might face when he held the press conference to announce the bid and it had gone horribly wrong.

He had sent a fax to Beck. Although neither Manchester United nor BSkyB were named, the code names Moore and Best being used, the fax failed to arrive and Allan was fearful it would have landed on some news desk.

Then at 4.30pm Booth rang to tell him of his conversation with Dyke. 'My immediate reaction was Greg Dyke had leaked the story on the basis that the person who is contacted about the leak is the source of the leak.'

Allan drove up to Booth's house in Belgravia and initially, like Bell, Allan was relaxed about the leak. Booth had said it was Neil Collins, so that meant they had another 24 hours to deal with the leak, not just a couple of hours. But then Booth said Neil Collins of the *Sunday Telegraph* and Allan decided it must be the *Sunday Telegraph* and he started making calls.

He rang the news desk of the *Sunday Telegraph*, pretending he was responding to a call from the *Sunday Telegraph* about Sky, but they did not fall for that. He then rang Graham Webb, deputy political editor, who said, 'I'll go and find out; I'll call you back in two minutes,' and Allan to this day has not heard from him again. All this convinced Allan that the *Sunday Telegraph* had the story.

At the *Sunday Telegraph* excitement was growing. 'We were about to close the ring,' says Bennett. 'I had already written about 80% of the story. How much information did I have? I have written a lot of deals in my life. From limited information you can develop a lot.'

The limited information Bennett had was quite crucial. Bennett knew BSkyB was prepared to pay 225p, valuing United at £575 million. Given his informant had rung on Thursday, and that was about the day Merrill's involvement began to move the price up from 217.5p, this indicates that Bennett's source was very well informed. Bennett also pictured Roland Smith as the architect of the deal and particularly for getting the price to 225p. If Bennett was being a bit premature in saying Booth had already secured Granada's backing – at this stage they did not even know about it – it was a remarkably accurate story. Interestingly, the story was written in the style of political journalists who are briefed on a lobby basis. There were no quotes or comments on the story from Sky or United, creating the impression, as in such political stories, that Bennett had received a leak from a very high-powered source.

Bennett knew, 'as deals go it was not a big deal. That week there were bigger deals going on. But it was a big story. Colin Gibson added some sporting bits about United. Then at about 8 o'clock or so, just as we were putting the edition to bed, I had a call. It was from David Beck.'

'Neil, what are you doing?' he asked.

There was a long pause.

Then Bennett said, 'You know full well what we are doing.'

That was enough to tell Beck that the *Sunday Telegraph* had got the story. Even now Booth could have thrown a spanner in Bennett's carefully laid plans; he could have rung the *Sunday Times* and the *News of the World*. But says Bennett, 'To Mark Booth's credit he did not tell the *Sunday Times* or the *News of the World*. They did not get it until midnight when our second edition hit the streets.'

As soon as Bell heard from Beck he rang Booth and Richard Campbell-Breeden and set about organising a conference call. 'There was a farce over the conference call. It took about an hour-and-a-half to get the bloody thing together. But we eventually all got on it and I told them what I knew. We had Richard Campbell-Breeden, David Beck, the lawyers – Deanna Bates, the in-house lawyer at Sky and Tim Belles of Herbert Smith – Martin Stewart, the finance director and Tim Allan, of course. We discussed whether to put it out, what to do, and it was agreed that we would put out the minimal holding statement – the "We are in talks with a third party" one. It wasn't up to us to say anything, anyway. It was up to Manchester United to say something. Only if we were mentioned in the story should we put something out. Of course, we were going to be mentioned in the story, so we were prepared to do that. Then until midnight I got another 15 calls from other papers to find out what was going. At about half-past midnight someone rang me up and read me the story, which I'd already heard anyway, because David had told me roughly what was in it. People exchanged phone calls and there was general wittering about what to do. The *Sunday Telegraph* did not ring Sky for confirmation so we didn't put out a general statement. Of course, what happened was the *Mail on Sunday*, the *Express* and one or two others held their second editions to wait for the *Sunday Telegraph*. Or they put on an extra third edition. I'm not sure.'

By then every editor in Fleet Street knew something was happening at the *Sunday Telegraph*. Bennett says: 'News that we had something began to be suspected because we had ordered extra copies for Manchester and the circulation people who gossip put the word around that we had something special going. This alerted the other papers, and when our man went at about 10 o'clock to King's Cross, he saw a huge knot of journalists waiting for the first edition of the *Sunday Telegraph*. There is a convention amongst the Sunday broadsheets that they send each other their first editions which come out at about 8.00pm or so. However, the tabloids, who are always trying to keep their rivals guessing, have no such convention, so journalists gather round the newsagent at King's Cross round about 10.00pm or so for the first editions of all the papers they can get. On Saturday the tradition in the *Sunday Telegraph*'s City office is that the reporters can wear whatever they like and not the normal tie and jacket they would wear on other days. That day, the late man whose job was to collect the papers was Simon English, deputy personal finance editor. He was wearing jeans and T-shirt. One of the tabloid journalists, a woman, approached him and said, "I hear your paper has got something special." He said, "I don't know anything." She looked him up and down, taking in his jeans and T-shirt, and said now they are sending drivers to pick up papers. She could not believe a reporter could be there not wearing a suit and he got through unmolested.'

As the other papers finally learnt what the *Sunday Telegraph* exclusive was, panic broke out in the newsrooms. One sports journalist rang up Paul Ridley and asked him for Martin Edwards' home telephone number. Joe Melling, football editor at the *Mail on Sunday*, rang Trevor East, deputy to Vic Wakeling at Sky. John Jay, City editor of the *Sunday Times*, was hauled out of bed at one in the morning to write a special feature for the *Sunday Times*, just before he was due to go on holiday. Jay spoke at length to Allan and was not best pleased that one part of the Murdoch empire did not know what the other was doing.

Through the night Allan's bleeper kept going off every few minutes and he slept for about 15 minutes. It was for him one of the most horrible nights he had endured. Among the things he had to do was call the *News of the World* and placate Murdoch's best-selling UK paper as best as he could. The *News of the World* tried to make the best of it for its final edition and, true to style, even put an exclusive on its story.

One Sky source says that while Booth did not tell the Murdoch papers, Murdoch, not best pleased that his papers were being scooped on their own story, did so himself late on that Saturday night to rectify matters. 'In the middle of all this a problem occurred, which is that the man who owns the large majority of the shares in Sky also owns two other famous national newspapers, who were about to be scooped by a competitor. Now, I've been a long time in the game and know what happens in these situations, which is, of course, everybody rings everybody else, "I didn't do anything". But the fact of the matter is the story appeared in the *News of the World* and the *Sunday Times*, and it appeared before the *Sunday Telegraph* was on the bookstalls, or before the ordinary punter could have got a copy of it. So it seems quite clear to me that somebody in News Corp or News International gave the story to the *News of the World* and the *Sunday Times*. Because . . . how can a man . . . how can people who run a collection of newspapers, who know about a massive story that a competitor has – how can they just sit there and not tell their own newspapers. I think it was Rupert who rang, or possibly Les Hinton, the chairman of News International. Probably Hinton did it on the back of a phone call with Rupert. "Shall I do it, or shan't I?" I can't prove any of these things. I just draw a list of very probable conclusions.'

Mark Booth was also surprised at the dimensions of the story: 'Saturday surprised me. That is when I realised the emotion of it. Then on Sunday I saw the papers come out and after that there were no more surprises. I knew this was a very big story.'

Booth by now had also been warned that the deal might not go through. 'When Greg Dyke rang me on Saturday he told me the bid would not be allowed through on competition grounds. I said nonsense and we had a bet that if he was right I would buy him lunch, if I was right he would buy me lunch.'

5

THE STORM BREAKS

The *Sunday Telegraph* story had put the deal in jeopardy. 'It put the whole thing at great risk,' says Mark Booth. 'It was an unwelcome moment with the deal a couple of days away. What it meant was that we had lost control. It is in the public domain and it put a dimension of risk that you would not have to deal with ordinarily. Ordinarily you have an agreement, then you announce it. So it was unhelpful.'

What particularly concerned Booth was that, now that it was in the public domain, 'you have the risk of a new entrant coming in. If Gerry Robinson [chief executive of Granada] wanted to, if he was thinking about making a bid, then this created a potential situation where he could come in.' Granada had figured large in Booth's thoughts. It was part owner of BSkyB and had a member on the Board. 'We had people from Granada. They could have been rivals.'

But now that it was in the public domain, as the notices for the meeting went out, Booth made it clear that any Board member who felt he might have a conflict of interest should not attend. Granada decided not to attend.

The other worry for Sky was the price United would now want for their club.

Campbell-Breeden briefed John Thornton from Sweden and he decided that he should call Faure Walker at home. The earlier calls had found him in the garden but now he was in the shower and had to come out to take it. After they discussed the leak the conversation moved to what the United Board might do now. Faure Walker 'believed the Board would reject 217.5p, that it wasn't enough. So the seeds were sown. Until then Sky had said 217.5p was the maximum. I couldn't say that the Board had rejected it. All I could say was that I believed, and that I would recommend, that the Board would reject it. That was all before the Board meeting.'

Of course Edwards had been telling Booth the same thing since Friday and Thornton knew about the conversations. But his chat with Faure Walker reinforced the impression that with the bid having leaked, Sky would have to pay a lot more if they wanted to get United.

The Sunday morning saw a series of telephone calls between United directors and Faure Walker and Blake. It was decided to have an impromptu United Board meeting via a telephone conference. As often happens in such situations, the United Board decided to gather at Maurice Watkins' home. In time of stress he was the rock, the lawyer who always worked out things, round whom they clustered.

Faure Walker recalls: 'David arranged a conference call on Sunday morning at 11 – David was at home, I was at home, Maurice Watkins, Martin Edwards and David Gill and Roland Smith all went to Maurice Watkins' house in Manchester. Greg Dyke was also on the phone from his home. There were two people who were not present – Peter Kenyon, because he was travelling back from Germany, and Amir Midani, who was in Spain.'

The leak had transformed the mood of the United Board. Faure Walker says: 'Until Friday, Sky had said they were offering 217.5p and were not prepared to increase it. We didn't have any leverage to make them pay more. As of the Friday there was no indication whatever that Sky would pay more than 217.5p and our view at that stage was they wouldn't necessarily do that and therefore there would be no transaction. The expectation on the Friday night was that no deal would happen. The Sunday did, I think, change things immensely because one saw the newspaper article and then we were on the front foot. I would say we were on the back foot re Sky until the Sunday when the newspaper article appeared. Then we were very much on the front foot with Sky.'

The United Board quickly saw how they could use the *Sunday Telegraph* story to their own advantage. 'When the newspaper article appeared, one rapidly realised that if terms couldn't be agreed, then Manchester United could put out a statement which would basically say that they had had a number of constructive and friendly talks with Sky, but that Sky hadn't made a proposal which they, Manchester United, felt they could recommend to their shareholders. In that way there wouldn't be much egg on Manchester United's face. There was obviously far more downside after that on Sky than on Manchester United and that very much helped us.'

Campbell-Breeden is convinced that the leak was part of HSBC's strategy: 'We couldn't believe the leak; the story had far too much detail and the timing put us on the back foot. Everyone in the Sky team had been paranoid about secrecy. We knew that the deal was going to need significant PR spin and, with the confines of the takeover code, the only way we could get our story across was with a proper announcement. The leak had to have come from the United camp.'

However, Faure Walker refuses to accept that this means that somebody from United leaked the story. 'I don't accept that because nobody from Manchester United spoke to the *Telegraph*. Also, if you read the article, lots of information was given about the bid and the negotiations which, frankly, Manchester United were not aware of. So I don't accept that someone from Manchester United leaked the story. I don't accept that at all. On the Friday evening I didn't think – and David Blake didn't think, and a number of Manchester United directors didn't think – the deal would happen, so the last thing in the world that anyone at Manchester United would want is to leak the story, with lots of publicity and things like that, about a potential deal that didn't happen. So, apart from anything else, if the deal didn't happen, and you'd told the whole world about this story, that you'd turned down 217.5p, a number of shareholders could well have criticised it. So there was no incentive for anybody from Manchester United to leak that story whatsoever.'

For an hour on Sunday, the United Board discussed these and other issues. It was then agreed that the Board would unanimously decline the offer of 217.5p.

Faure Walker emphasises that it was a rejection not in principle but in price. However, he says, 'if someone said to you, "Would you like that sandwich?" and you said, "No", I don't know whether it's because you've had enough or because you don't like what's in it or the bread or something. The fact is, you say, "No". It's not very relevant, really.'

Faure Walker now rang Richard Campbell-Breeden, 'to tell him we had decided we would reject the offer.'

Everyone knew the rejection did not mean the deal was dead; it only meant United wanted more money and this was now going to be part of the haggling that would go on. Publicly, United had to say something to the mounting media interest and, by 4.00pm, Ken Ramsden had confirmed they were in talks with a third party.

Sky was still in a state of shock, worsened by the fact that its PR men were firmly held on a leash by the bankers and the lawyers. Bell, Allan and the others were feeling very frustrated at their inability to tell their side of the story.

Bell had driven up to Isleworth, early on Sunday morning, from his country home in Sussex, and such was his speed that at 6.45am that Sunday morning he got a speeding ticket.

'Ridiculous! We all went to Isleworth at seven o'clock in the morning and worked all day Sunday. We spent the whole of Sunday farting around. Eventually Manchester United put their holding statement out at about four o'clock in the afternoon, at which point we were able to confirm it. So Tim Allan and I and David Beck sat after four o'clock in the room with a loudspeaker phone and a merchant banker watching us, vetting what we were saying. We spoke to most of the newspapers and told them exactly what was in the Manchester United statement and confirmed that we were the third party in talks with them. That's it. We put no spin on it. We weren't able to put any arguments behind it. We weren't allowed to use the case we had for making a bid for Manchester United.'

Tim Allan felt particularly frustrated. Allan had not had much sleep on Saturday night having been woken up at two in the morning by the Press Association which, to add to his worries, then quoted him by name when he expected it merely to attribute statements to a press spokesman.

Allan had spent some time on Saturday night trying to prise out from the editor of *Breakfast with Frost* who he may have on his programme. Allan felt Frost might have a minister, but the editor had got suspicious and asked: Now that Allan was no longer in Number 10, why did he want to know? Frost got Tony Banks, the sports minister, on the telephone, who made it clear he was opposed to the bid.

Allan had by now told his political friends, unburdening himself of this secret he had carried for so long. On Saturday night he told his flatmate James Purnell, whose reaction was, 'Yes, it is a big story.' On Sunday morning Allan rang Alistair Campbell. Campbell was instinctively against the bid and felt it could all end in tears.

When Allan told Peter Mandelson, who had just taken over as the minister in charge of the Department of Trade and Industry, Mandelson's first reaction was, 'Oh my God, what have you done now?' Mandelson knew the bid, if it went through, would soon land on his desk and he would have to decide whether to refer it to the Monopolies and Mergers Commission. Mandelson's friendship with Elisabeth Murdoch was well known and he knew that questions would soon be asked as to whether he was sufficiently detached from the Murdochs to take a view.

The lawyers were telling Sky that whatever happened Mandelson could not possibly block the bid on competition grounds and they were determined to control Sky's press reactions. At this stage on Sunday afternoon, with the stock market not yet officially told, they would only allow Allan to issue the barest minimum statement on the bid. The press team felt that merely saying Sky was in talks with Manchester United, and that it may or may not lead to an offer, was useless. The bankers' advice was that they couldn't even confirm Sky was buying the club.

One source in the press team says: 'There was a complete and utter failure to realise the power of the press. There were so many bankers and lawyers involved who were used to dealing with takeovers being covered in the business press. But this one led the news pages and we should have put people up to explain our side of the story. We proposed it and the news team were adamant that we put people up. But the bankers and lawyers said take the heat off the press, they are not going to turn it down.'

'We were put in an impossible position,' says Campbell-Breeden. 'It was obvious that the two Tims were right: we had to get our story out and couldn't let the negative sentiment build momentum. We had to get a broad cross-section of interested parties: United fans, other clubs, politicians and Sky Sports subscribers. But the rules governing communication with the least important group from a PR aspect – Manchester United shareholders – meant that we had both hands tied behind our back. Whereas everybody else had a free-for-all.'

Allan did talk to Roland Watson, the deputy political editor of the *Times*, and after much badgering he gave one little titbit to the *Sun*, that, if the takeover went ahead, season-ticket prices at Old Trafford would be frozen. This led the *Sun* to trumpet the deal as 'Gold Trafford' which did not please Allan or the Sky press team. 'Gold Trafford,' says an insider, 'added to the Murdoch world-domination thesis. We were not best pleased by that. What people on the outside don't realise is that we at Sky do not see ourselves as part of News International, who are minority shareholders in Sky. Sky always gets a hammering even at times from the Murdoch papers and our attitude is often: fuck them.'

However, at this point, it was the outside world that was doing that to Sky. Faure Walker may have felt that the leak had put United on the front foot in the negotiations with Sky, but as far as the wider public were concerned, both United and Sky were firmly on the defensive, looking like men in an isolated fortress besieged by an angry army.

The angry army had begun to muster almost as soon as the news broke.

And in a sense there had been an army in waiting for just such a day to rise and march.

That army had begun to form several years previously and had originally come together on a very different issue. On 15 April 1995 the Independent Manchester United Supporters Association was set up. The catalyst for this had been the attempt by Manchester United to get people to sit down during matches. This may seem trivial but it added to the feeling that had been growing for some time amongst some of the fans, that the United Board did not care about the genuine fans and was only interested in making money.

The whole thing boiled over on 22 March 1995, when Arsenal came to visit Old Trafford. Despite the 3–0 victory over Arsenal, fans were not appeased and with stewards constantly telling them to sit down some of them decided to form an organisation which would channel their views.

It was a fraught time for United fans, one of great tension and heartache. Their great hero Eric Cantona had been banned from football for the rest of the season and faced a possible jail sentence for his kung-fu kick at a Crystal Palace supporter. If love and reverence for Cantona was a common bond linking these fans then so was an elemental, almost visceral hatred of the United Board and, in particular, Martin Edwards.

Some of the supporters had been meeting for some time at the Gorse Hill pub on Chester Road, near the Stretford End, discussing the setting up of a group that would reflect supporters' views. This was known as the 'Dirty Dozen' and included Peter Boyle, Richard Kurt and one man, who soon came to be seen as the principal voice of the group, Andy Walsh.

All three had been intimately involved in promoting a Cantona single – Boyle had made it, Kurt had produced it and Walsh had publicised it, going on the *Big Breakfast* show on the day that Cantona's hearing regarding his kung-fu assault took place at the Croydon Magistrates Court.

Walsh, an information technology consultant – he tests computer software – is well versed in organising protest movements. He had been active in Militant and chaired the Greater Manchester Poll Tax Federation, his opposition to which saw him jailed for 14 days in

Congleton, while Boyle, also opposed to the poll tax, was jailed in Walsall. They all knew how to organise and appreciated how important it was to get the media right.

The Arsenal match crystalised matters. It was decided to hold an initial meeting to gauge reactions and the stage had to be something grander than Gorse Hill pub. The Free Trade Hall in Manchester, site of the Peterloo massacre, was chosen. Three hundred people turned up and it was decided to set up a formal organisation called the Independent Manchester United Supporters Associations, which inevitably became known as IMUSA.

The inaugural meeting was held in the Lancashire Cricket Club where between 500 and 600 people turned up to elect officials, with Boyle, Kurt and Walsh in charge. At this meeting Walsh and his colleagues also invited Kevin Myles of the Newcastle Independent Supporters Association. Nothing could be more provocative given the rivalry between the two supporters. But Myles' message showed how shrewd Walsh and his colleagues had been.

Myles said, 'I don't like you, you don't like me. But we have more in common than we have with the likes of Hall [Sir John and his son Douglas, major shareowners of Newcastle] and Edwards.' That was to be the creed on which the organisation was to be founded.

If Cantona was God and Edwards was the devil then one other figure was beyond criticism: Alex Ferguson. Some time after, Kurt, who was the original press officer, made what he thought were some private comments about Ferguson to a journalist. United was having one of its relatively not so successful spells and the gist of his remarks was that Ferguson had lost the plot and ought to go. This was reported and it was Kurt who went.

By September 1997 IMUSA, says Walsh, was established in the minds of the Manchester United fans. Walsh and his colleagues were watching the stock market trying to follow market rumours of a possible bid for the club. In early January 1998 the organisation was put on what Walsh calls a 'professional footing', with specific tasks given to members. The most important of these tasks was media work; people were trained in media work, issuing press releases, how to handle journalist questions. There were more and more demands from the media and Walsh started taking colleagues along when he gave interviews to show how the press should be handled. 'We were establishing ourselves,' says Walsh, 'as the first port of call.'

The world called on the morning of 6 September, when at 6.15am, on the Sunday morning, Walsh was woken up by the Press Association and asked to comment on the *Sunday Telegraph* story.

'I asked who had written the story. We had heard many rumours and false stories before. When I heard it was the *Sunday Telegraph*, I gave a holding reply, and since we are a democratic body with elected officers I began to contact my elected officials.'

By ten that morning Walsh had gone to the ground, as had many United supporters. The feeling in that gathering was mixed, many were bemused, some indifferent and a small minority opposed. Walsh and IMUSA's task was to make sure that this voice of opposition came through loud and clear on the media. By midday, with some 200 supporters gathered outside Old Trafford and IMUSA having talked to the press, Walsh and his colleagues decided to leave so as to allow, he says, supporters other than IMUSA to have their say.

So while Sky's PR advisers fumed, as the bankers and lawyers told them they could not say anything, IMUSA made its opposition to the bid very clear and made sure its message was being heard round the world.

It was clear there had to be a campaign. For some weeks after that the campaign was run from Walsh's front room, where he had three phones lines plus a mobile line, which crashed on the Monday and had to be replaced. Even then he could not cope with the number of calls from journalists and others in the media.

If IMUSA was the army already organised and ready to strike at the Board, then the announcement of the deal led to the birth of another equally potent army.

Michael Crick, a writer and broadcaster – he works on a freelance basis for BBC's *Newsnight* – had spent the summer preparing a proposal to write a book on Murdoch (it has since been published). The deal was announced just as he finished his book proposal, so he was well up on the Murdoch lore. He has written well-researched and well-received books on Jeffrey Archer and Michael Heseltine. Interestingly, one of his first books had been on Militant, researching and exposing the former colleagues of Walsh. Crick says, 'Andy is working-class, political, Militant. I wrote all those books exposing the Militant, but they were before Andy joined the Militant. I was a member of IMUSA but did not know Andy. Now I keep telling Andy that he has moved to the right so much so that I am to the left of him.'

However, on that Sunday morning, such political differences did not matter. As far as United and their views on Martin Edwards and the Board were concerned, they were of like mind. Back in 1990 Crick, with co-author David Smith, had written *Manchester United: The Betrayal of a Legend*, excoriating Edwards and describing the Manchester United Board as 'ruled by the Edwards clan. Businessmen who put profits above all else'. As with Walsh, for Crick news of Sky bidding for United was ultimate proof that all Edwards cared for was money.

On that Sunday Crick got a call from the *Evening Standard* to write a piece about the bid. He used the platform provided to denounce the bid and of course Edwards, and what he saw as his greed and drive for more and more money.

On Monday Crick returned to *Newsnight* after his long ten-week sabbatical researching the book proposal on Murdoch and offered to do a piece on the bid. He discovered that the United Board were meeting at the offices of HSBC and got shots of them through a window.

It was clear Crick was going to present a personal view and the introduction was meant to reflect this. But he did not write or see it. *Newsnight* missed out this warning and gave the impression that it was a BBC view which, not surprisingly, attracted criticism from Sky for being biased.

Richard Hytner, who runs Publicist, an advertising agency, was one of the millions who saw Crick on *Newsnight*. Hytner was an old school friend from Manchester Grammar with whom Crick had only re-established links in the last year. Both Crick and Hytner were shareholders in United and it was quickly decided to set up an organisation of shareholders opposed to the deal. Hytner came up with the name Shareholders United Against Murdoch.

SUAM was born and had joined IMUSA in the battle to stop the bid.

By setting up another organisation, Crick and Hytner knew they were not duplicating IMUSA but getting two strikes against the deal. Also both IMUSA and SUAM took a major strategical decision that was to prove very crucial. From the beginning they decided that they would present this as a Murdoch deal. As we have seen at this stage Murdoch had played little or no personal part in the deal, but both IMUSA and SUAM knew they had to present this as a Murdoch deal. Booth was an unknown and it would be difficult to generate any passion against him. It would also not be easy to present Sky as the devil. Murdoch was already considered by some an evil incarnate, known and hated, and by focusing on Murdoch both Crick and Walsh could easily plug into the non-Murdoch press.

If United were behind in the publicity battle, then within the Premier League the initial reaction to the deal was also quite hostile. On the Sunday morning Andrew Neill, who presented a morning show on Radio Five Live, had rung up Peter Leaver to get his reaction.

'I was rung up about 7.15 on the Sunday morning and asked to comment. My reaction was, "I don't know very much about it." My view was they are big boys, they are on the stock exchange. If you have shares quoted on the stock market, then you can have a bid, and I could see no reason why BSkyB could not acquire Manchester United. But I could also see there could be competition issues. There could be all sorts of problems in television negotiations. Then I phoned all the clubs. Most of them were pretty hostile. I rang Rick Parry, whose view was that they should be thrown out of the League. Ken Bates was for booting them out. Blackburn were very hostile and said they should be thrown out of the League if the deal went ahead. On the other hand David Dein was cautious; he said let's wait and see and that was also the attitude of Alan Sugar. David probably wanted to get on the phone to Michael Green at Carlton and see what he could get.'

Dein and Arsenal were in talks with Carlton about a possible involvement there and Sugar, who had been mulling over an offer from ENIC for Tottenham of £70 million, decided that if United was worth £570 million, he should get at least half that.

Leaver urged the clubs to 'just calm down and play it a bit more cautiously. There was no real Premier League view on this and although there was talk of holding a Premier League meeting, there was no real drive to hold one.'

6

THE DONE DEAL?

Monday 7 September and Tuesday 8 September 1998 were two of the most crucial days in the recent history of Manchester United. They began with the Board still not sure it could accept the Sky offer; they ended with acceptance of the offer which meant United were no longer an independent company.

It was this decision that, late on the night of 8 September, prompted Howard Davies, head of the Securities and Financial Authority and a passionate Manchester City fan, to say in some exultation: 'I am so glad it is happening. I have hated Manchester United all my life. Manchester United was born in Munich and will die with Murdoch.'

In the morning both United and Sky had put out a statement at the stock exchange confirming they were in discussions about a possible merger.

Sky was keen to fly to Manchester to meet the United Board and settle the bid so that it could present a completed deal to the Sky Board. But the United Board chose not to meet in Manchester but in London instead. Sky got the impression it was Faure Walker and HSBC stalling and playing for time.

As the United Board met on Monday, the decision it had to ratify was the telephone conversation of the Executive of the Board on the Sunday which, as we have seen, had basically rejected Sky's offer of 217.5p. Martin Edwards knew this was very far from the end of the story.

He was only too aware of the many phone calls he had made to Mark Booth each time asking for more money. He knew he would have to go back for more and, while he did not like being the supplicant, he remained convinced that the deal was a good one for the club and could see no other way of carrying the Board and, in particular, Greg Dyke.

It would be tough and Keith Harris appreciated that Roland Smith would have to sell Manchester United to Sky. Sometime on Monday morning, after he had digested the Sunday and Monday papers, Harris strolled across his room to that of Roland Smith's and said: 'Roland, you have got to think of the time 20 years ago when you were battling Tiny Rowland. You have got to believe you are 20 years younger and fight for Manchester United as you fought for Harrods.' The irony was inescapable. Then, he was fighting to keep Harrods independent; now, he was seeking to end United's history as an independent company.

By mid-morning on Monday most of the Board members barring Midani, who could not be there but was in touch by telephone, were on their way to London, Kenyon having long abandoned his plan to go to Brussels to meet with Karel van Miert in the company of Media Partners.

Edwards, as he generally prefers, chose the train to get to London, only to find on arrival at Euston that, as he got off the train, he was faced by a swarm of media microphones and tape-recorders and jostled by photographers. Moreover, from the fringes of the crowd gathered round him, he could hear cries of Judas from some of the supporters opposed to the bid. It made him look hunted and besieged and it was the picture that inevitably made the front pages of the next day's papers. But he had faced such attacks so often before that he was inured to them. His greater concern was to make sure the Board was united as it discussed the Sky bid.

His first priority though, like that of the other directors, was to avoid more media hassle as he tried to get to the offices of HSBC where the Board meeting was due to start at 5.30 in the afternoon.

From fairly early that morning television camera crews had arrived outside the offices of HSBC in Vintners Place in Upper Thames Street and, even as Edwards left Euston, he knew he could not just drive up to the entrance as he normally did. His driver had to pull up across the road outside Thames Exchange, the building which houses the HSBC Securities business. At the reception he walked down to the basement and then through the tunnel, which linked Thames Exchange with the building across the road, to get to the investment banking building and the Tower Room where the meeting was due to be held.

By 5.30pm all the United directors had safely negotiated this detour through the tunnel to the Tower Room and none of them had been caught on camera.

The Tower Room was one of many such meeting rooms overlooking the Thames that HSBC had. HSBC staff had organised the room in the style common for all such City meeting rooms. Before every United director was a small notepad with a dark green leather cover filled with HSBC letterheaded paper and next to it a pencil. At the centre of the long rectangular table were bottles of mineral water and large plates of sandwiches made of white and brown bread and various fillings. On an adjoining table were pots of coffee and tea.

Just as the meeting started a messenger came in to say that there was a call for Roland Smith and Rupert Faure Walker. 'Mark Booth was on the phone. It was a conference call, which we took in another office, between Roland Smith, Martin Edwards and myself with, I think, Richard Campbell-Breeden and Mark Booth on the other end. They knew the Board meeting was about to start and, rather than have the Board meeting reject their proposal, they decided to increase their bid. They initially increased their bid to 230p in shares and 220p in cash. We had a conversation on this new offer and the long and the short of it was that we said, "No, that couldn't be recommended." Then they increased it to 230p in cash as well. So both the shares and the cash would be the same value.'

Faure Walker, Smith and Edwards went back to the Tower Room and Faure Walker informed the Board of Sky's new offer. As he spoke he glanced at his watch. It was six o'clock; with luck it should be over in good time for dinner. And then they could have more than mere sandwiches.

But that was not taking into account Greg Dyke.

Dyke had come to the meeting having pondered long and hard about his position. Although the *Sunday Telegraph* had not named him, it had clearly identified him as the one dissident director on the Manchester United Board. It seemed that there were two perspectives on the bid. It may be right for the shareholders but did that make it right for the club? The way IMUSA and SUAM were developing their case against the bid, these were presented as mutually contradictory positions. The interests of the club, they argued, were not the same as those of the shareholder. Dyke was not convinced the gap was unbridgeable. He would rather a bid not take place, but if there was one, then a good deal for a shareholder might also be a good one for the club.

What he needed was his own legal advice. What was his fiduciary responsibility towards shareholders? Some time on that Monday he had rung a lawyer from Slaughter & May who he had met through the takeover of London Weekend. The advice was that if the bid reached a position where he felt the price was in the range where it had to be put to shareholders, then he had a duty to put it to shareholders. The lawyer had warned him that he should not get into a situation where he was the only director who stopped the bid from being put to shareholders. In that case he could be accused of violating his fiduciary responsibilities. It was possible to get a very good deal for the shareholders which was also a good deal for the club.

Initially, as the discussions started on whether 230p was an acceptable price, Dyke seemed happy with it. Indeed, on hearing the news, Dyke had called Booth and told him, 'You've got a great deal.' But that was before Merrill Lynch made its report. At that Monday's Board meeting for the first time Merrill Lynch's report was available. It had also spoken to some of the major institutional shareholders who had indicated they thought United was worth more; 230p was way below what they thought was an acceptable price. Merrill had worked out a range and 240p was the very bottom of the range and, in its opinion, the very least Sky should pay for Manchester United.

HSBC had not been particularly happy about Merrill Lynch arriving on the scene. It seemed like HSBC was being second-guessed by another, in some ways more powerful, organisation. What made it worse was that like Goldman Sachs, Merrill Lynch was American.

There was also an added complication in that Dyke and HSBC had what is called 'previous'. HSBC had first come across Dyke when they had acted for London Weekend Television. Granada were bidding for them and Dyke, then head of LWT, had not hit it off with HSBC. HSBC thought Dyke was a bit chippy; Dyke thought HSBC were not very good. Now with Dyke championing Merrill, the old resentments resurfaced and were reinforced. So the more Dyke and Merrill talked the United price up, the more HSBC felt Dyke was questioning its competence, the work it had done on the bid and the valuation it had put on Manchester United.

On 28 August Faure Walker had told Dyke and Gill that it was their duty as directors to accept a price of 217.5p. Now Sky had gone up to 230p and Faure Walker was even more convinced this was the right price. 'First of all in terms of current profits, in terms of profits this year or even next year, 230p was a very, very generous price. It was 60p more than the market price. The shares had never been higher than their all-time high, which was 183p. And it was trading – before Sky came in – at 160p. For about a couple of years there'd been a lot of press speculation that one day someone would buy Manchester United, so I do think there was some discounting in the price.'

As Dyke used Merrill Lynch to argue against 230p, Faure Walker and David Blake pulled out what they thought was their trump card: the note that Merrill Lynch, as Manchester United's broker, had prepared on 2 September, two days before they were called in to value the club. At that stage Merrill did not know about the bid and had recommended United to its clients as a long-term buy. The price was 157p and Merrill felt that if within 12 months the price went up to 185p that would be a reasonable objective.

The note forecast profits for the year to July 1998 of £14 million – that was after transfer fees – and suggested earnings per share at 3.8p. Merrill Lynch had also forecast profits of £26 million for the year to July 1999, but that was on the basis of transfer expenditure of £2.5 million, an assumption that had already been made to look ridiculous by United spending £12.5 million on Dwight Yorke alone.

It was with some relish that HSBC flourished this note from United's own broker to defend its view that Sky was paying well over the odds in offering 230p and that the Board would be mad to ask for more. Before Sky had come in, on the basis of the 1997 figures, Merrill calculated that United was on a PE of 21.2. Based on the 1998 figures, Merrill worked out a PE of 41.3, prepared on the basis of a United share price of 157p. The price of 240p, which Merrill now said was the bottom of their range, would give United a PE of 60.

Dyke retorted by speaking of future earnings, particularly from television where his expertise lay and the likely earnings from pay-per-view. The argument was a classic one. Faure Walker and Blake were taking the standard merchant banking position. Given the current share price of United and likely future earnings, 230p was more than Sky should be paying and United should grab it. But could it be that Dyke was seeing it beyond conventional City terms but in the more specialised world of television rights?

In buying United Sky were getting Manchester United's television rights in perpetuity, for ever and a day. In little over a decade Dyke had seen the amazing rise in the television value of soccer. Before 1988 the television rights of English football brought in £5 million a year to the then 92 clubs of the Football League. That year Dyke, as head of ITV sport, had started the inflation by snatching the exclusive rights, paying £20 million a year. Then in 1992 the formation of the Premier League had seen Dyke himself guzumped by Sky, who beat Dyke's ITV by paying nearly £40 million a year. And the season about to start was to see a new four-year Sky deal under which it would be paying more than

£160 million a year. So between 1988 and 1998 football's yearly income from television had gone from £5 million a year to £160 million a year. Who could say what the next couple of years, let alone decade, might bring? And against such a tremendous growth could 230p be the right price? With Merrill providing the City backing, Dyke was more than ever convinced that Sky was getting it very cheap.

But Dyke's television arguments, far from convincing HSBC, only led into a long involved discussion about what might or might not happen with future television rights. The past decade had seen the formation of the Premier League and then Sky's use of televised football to become a major television channel. Could Media Partners and the OFT case against the Premier League–Sky television agreement do the same trick in the next?

Could the Board assume that there would be a breakaway European League of super clubs along the Media Partners proposal, whereby the super clubs – the Manchester Uniteds, Arsenals, Liverpools – could get more revenue than they did by remaining with UEFA?

Fair enough said Faure Walker and Blake. The projections of what future television income might be was very alluring. When HSBC were asked to do valuation work on United at the beginning of August, it still seemed possible there could be a breakaway Super League. But look, they said, at what happened last Thursday when Media Partners made its presentation to the Premier League, the very day that, at Dyke's insistence, Merrill Lynch had been called in. After the meeting, prospects of a Super League looked pretty gloomy. The meeting had decided that no club in the Premier League would be allowed to continue discussions with the European Super League. Manchester United were not even allowed to continue talking to Media Partners.

Surely, argued Faure Walker and Blake, the breakdown in Media Partners talks reduced the expectations of the sort of money the Super League might bring?

'I mean,' says Faure Walker, 'it really looked pretty remote, the chance of this huge income from the Super League. We'd always been a little bit doubtful about it. As far as the OFT case against the Premier League and Sky was concerned, we obviously had endless debates about this. Even if we assumed that the OFT won and there was a free-for-all, did it mean a huge share of revenue going to Manchester United? One could assume that the rich clubs get richer and the poor get poorer. But in our assessment of value we never assumed it would be a complete free-for-all or that Manchester United would keep all the future TV revenue. We assumed there'd be some compromise and some sharing of revenue basically to help the poor clubs.'

Faure Walker felt that 'in the arguments about pay TV and things like that, some of the enthusiasts in the business have got very, very bullish projections for pay TV, very very bullish projections. If you assume the European Super League would happen; if you assume the whole of the Premier League negotiating rights would break down, with winner takes all; if you assume both of those things, then you can see that 230p was possibly not such a wonderful price. It wouldn't be worth doing it.'

As Dyke kept insisting that 230p was too low and he had to go for 240p, or even more, Faure Walker tried to sketch out what he saw as the fantastic scenario whereby Manchester United might be worth a lot more: 'If we assume the complete European Super League happens, you assume a complete breakdown of negotiating rights over television. In other words, a free-for-all, so that Manchester United gets the lion's share of that. You also assume pay TV comes in and that the high street on Saturday afternoons in the UK is deserted, because everybody's at home paying £6 a throw to watch pay TV Premier League every Saturday of the year. You assume all that – then you can come to valuations of £700 to £800 million for Manchester United. That's in four years' time. You can come to these figures, but I think, to be realistic, that won't happen.'

In late evening the Board adjourned, just to provide a break to the directors.

Dyke, unconvinced by Faure Walker and HSBC, had set about making his own enquiries. He went into a separate room and started ringing up the various persons at Merrill Lynch who had made the valuations. He wanted to know how they had worked out the figures, the assumptions they had made. By now most of them had left Merrill's office in the City. Some of them he found in their homes, others he had to drag out from their hotel rooms where they were on business. Dyke spent a good part of the evening on the phone talking to them and trying to get City backing for his view that at 230p Manchester United was a steal for Sky.

He returned to the Tower Room to say that having spoken to Merrill at some length he could not accept 230p. The minimum, very minimum, was 240p.

Until this point Edwards had kept his cool. But now as Dyke spoke he lost his temper and shouted, 'Greg, if we lose this deal because of you then I shall sue you.' The remark was uncharacteristic and showed the tremendous strain Edwards was under. Dyke's eyes lit up and, looking across at Edwards, he said, 'That is a good one for the book, eh, Martin?' With that, Dyke laughed in that full-throated, mischievous way of his. But nobody in the Tower Room joined Dyke in the laughter. Dyke was on his own in opposing 230p.

The Tower Room was tense and across the Thames the lights could be seen shining brightly on the South Bank and the old London County Council headquarters. It was well past dinner time, sandwiches were all there was to eat, and the unanimous Board agreement that Roland Smith was so keen to get seemed nowhere in sight.

Roland Smith had made it clear that he wanted the directors to make a unanimous recommendation. Even a bid unanimously recommended might be difficult to sell to the fans, but if there was one director who was dissenting it would make life hellishly complicated. Not only would he be a focus for fans unhappy with the bid, but as a dissenting director he would, under company law, have to be given all the facilities at United's expense to make his case to the shareholders. It would greatly add to the costs and also open up to the world the divisions within the Board. Roland Smith was determined to avoid that.

As the evening wore on the meeting got livelier and by half-past one in the morning the Board was no nearer agreement. It was decided to adjourn until the next morning.

The TV cameras had gone but unfortunately, for Faure Walker, 'they had a camera on the bridge there with a long telephoto lens into our rooms and, although we had the blinds down, they could see through it. They saw Martin leave when he went home, at half-past one, and they saw all of us as we left at about the same time.'

On Tuesday morning the United Board met again at HSBC, this time in the Thames Room. But this was a replay of the Tower Room: another room with little HSBC notepads, pencils, mineral water and sandwiches, and with Dyke again refusing to agree to 230p. The discussions had been going on for very nearly 24 hours and there seemed no conclusion to this situation of Dyke against the rest of the United Board supported by HSBC.

Dyke, having got back home well past 2.00am on Tuesday, was up at six and living, as his partner said, on adrenalin. During the course of the day his resolve was to be further strengthened when he heard that at the Sky Board meeting, which was going on at the same time, Murdoch had spoken of him as a traditional enemy of BSkyB and a man United should watch out for.

By two in the afternoon there was still no agreement, says Faure Walker; 'There was a conversation with Mark Booth and Roland Smith and then it was either Roland Smith or Martin Edwards – it wasn't me – floated the idea that the Board were having problems accepting 230p and it hadn't been resolved yet, but they would accept 240p. This was put to Sky, but it was aggressively rejected by Sky. They made it quite clear they were prepared to pay 230p and not a penny more. Early in the afternoon they sent us a fax and telephoned as well, basically saying that unless we agreed 230p by five o'clock on Tuesday, the deal was off.' The fax also had a sting that would have a devastating impact on one United director.

Sky had sent the fax just before the Sky Board had gathered across London in Isleworth at 2.30 that Tuesday afternoon. But if Edwards and his Board trooped into the Thames Room, tired and weary after their long meeting on Monday, the Sky Board was full of spirit as the directors walked into an office down the corridor from Mark Booth's office where the lunch Booth had had with Edwards and Watkins on 1 July had started the whole saga. The United Board may have had its fill of discussing the offer, but this was the first time the Sky Board was meeting to discuss the deal: many of the Sky Board members had only learnt about it when they had received their Board papers the previous day.

Originally Booth had not expected Murdoch to attend the Board meeting. But he was in London for Sir David English's funeral and came to the meeting.

Everyone was there apart from David DeVoe, Arthur Siskind, David Chance and Sam Chisholm who was in the south of France. Graham Parrott of Granada had excused himself on the grounds that there might be a conflict of interest, should Granada decide to bid for United. It was a high-powered Board and showed Murdoch's touch in constructing such boards. Despite Murdoch's close links with Mrs Thatcher, it included Lord St John of Fawsley, the former Norman St John Stevas and a Tory wet, who as Leader of the House under Mrs Thatcher had earned her wrath by first alluding to her bossy tendencies and describing her as 'she who must be obeyed'. He was one of the first Tory wets to be sacked from her cabinet.

After Booth made his presentation, explaining why he wanted to buy United, there was some discussion as to whether this was indeed the right deal. Not the idea of buying a football club but whether Manchester United was the right club. At 230p, Sky was paying £600 million for Manchester United, a billion dollars. That was a lot of money, felt some directors.

Dennis Stevenson, chairman of Pearson and Dyke's ultimate, if nominal, boss, wondered if it would not be a better idea for Sky to buy Arsenal. The real centre of population was not Manchester but London. 'Dennis Stevenson,' recalls Booth, 'posed this as: Why is this a smarter thing to do than buying Arsenal?' This led to quite a lively discussion between Stevenson and Thornton, with others joining in.

Booth, Stewart and Campbell-Breeden pointed out that they were dealing with football, which was not quite like any other business. You could not buy fans. Fans created the value of the club because fans pay for the merchandising and fans create the demand for TV. However much money you spend on a football club, you don't necessarily create a club bigger than Manchester United. There were plenty of examples of that. Blackburn was the classic one. It might buy a championship through Jack Walker's money, as it had done in 1995, but it could not create a club that could truly rival Manchester United.

It was explained that as far as Arsenal was concerned, there were problems with Highbury. Its capacity was only 38,000 compared with United's 55,000. United could grow and had plans to do so. Arsenal could not do much more to Highbury, and even if it moved to a bigger stadium at King's Cross, that would be at least five years away and by no means certain.

After some discussion it was agreed that United was the right choice, that this was a great deal and Booth should go ahead and do it.

The Board meeting had been going for some time and Campbell-Breeden was just making his presentation about values when a secretary walked in to say there was a phone call for Mark Booth from Martin Edwards and Roland Smith. Campbell-Breeden suggested he had better take the call as United was having its Board meeting as well and it could be important.

So Booth, Thornton and Campbell-Breeden went to Booth's office to talk to Edwards. Edwards told Booth, 'I am sorry, Mark, but I can't do it. I can't deliver. It is Greg Dyke. Would you be prepared to do it without the full Board because everybody else has recommended it?'

'No,' said Booth.

'Well if you want the entire Board, then I can only get them if you are prepared to go to 240p.'

There was a pause.

'I'll have to think about it,' said Booth.

Booth went back to the boardroom and told the Board, 'Edwards is telling us it is 240p.'

The silence that greeted the announcement was quickly followed by howls of protest. This is like being salami-sliced, said one Board member. They had been told they had a deal at 217p, then last Friday before the leak it was 225p, then it inched up to 226p, on the basis of which Board papers were prepared at the weekend. On Monday it was 230p. Now on Tuesday it was 240p. And Murdoch was not best pleased that it was Dyke who was manning the roadblock. He is an old enemy of Sky, warned Murdoch. He fought against us for the Premier League rights, then tried to take us to court, and then complained against the Sky deal to the OFT, which triggered the case in the Restrictive Practices Court and, in many ways, the bid for Manchester United.

The Board turned to Booth who said, 'If you take everything in and with a following wind, it is just about a good price.'

Finally Murdoch looked at Booth and said, 'Mark, it's up to you. I'm sure the Board will support you. What is your recommendation?'

'This is ridiculous,' said Booth. 'If we say yes at 240p they will come back asking for £3. At 240p it's beginning not to make sense.'

'I was,' reflects Booth, 'playing pretty tough. I was prepared to be tough and say, fine, we couldn't agree terms. I had a feeling that during the day it might come to that. I think you can be mucked about so many times. At some point you have to say we have reached agreement and if the ball keeps moving you have to draw a line somewhere. The ball kept moving and we were getting frustrated. I think we didn't have to have it at any cost. It was not vital. It was a very good thing for both companies. If it was done it was one of those things that was very smart for both companies.'

For Booth the ball had moved about far too much since he had tea with Edwards at the Royal Lancaster on 4 August and agreed the price of 217.5p. However, he liked Edwards and had a lot of sympathy for his inability to control this constantly moving offer-price ball: 'Martin was having problems carrying his Board. But that is not unusual. It is not surprising. On the other hand you have got to say this is how we are going to do it.'

Booth, Murdoch, Stewart, Campbell-Breeden and Thornton went into Booth's office. Booth called Edwards and asked for Roland Smith. Murdoch wanted to speak to him.

Murdoch was polite but direct: 'I want to know why you think your club is worth so much, Sir Roland.' Smith, trying to follow Harris' advice of the previous day and imagining himself 20 years younger, launched into his well-rehearsed spiel about United's global brand, its achievements as a football club and both the size of its fan base and their fantastic loyalty to United.

Murdoch was, initially, not much impressed and made it clear that he did not want to pay a penny more than the 230p that had been offered. As Murdoch saw it, that was the price everybody bar Dyke was prepared to accept, so why not cast Dyke aside. 'We don't care,' said Murdoch, 'we'll do the deal at 230p and let Dyke vote against you. Let there be a director who doesn't agree with you.' But for Roland Smith the issue of the unanimity of the Manchester United Board was crucial and Smith said, 'I'm not prepared to do this deal unless there is unanimity. The only price I can get you unanimity is 240p. We're not doing it except unanimously and that has to be at 240p.'

In the Sky boardroom the debate continued as to whether Sky could pay 240p. Then one News Corp director said 240p 'means paying £623 million for Manchester United. Shit, that is a lot of money. But we are ready to approve the deal at 230p and that is another 10p, only another £26 million. We are agreed, are we not, that this is a good deal? So I say let's go and do it. It is a great brand. Sky is moving from distribution to real content, real sports content.'

Now as Booth, Murdoch and the others were about to leave Booth's office to get back to the boardroom and say it was a deal, a call came which was, perhaps, the most extraordinary of this extraordinary day. It was from Edwards for Booth and it related to the fax Sky had sent to United earlier in the day.

Booth, in trying to help his friend Martin stop the ball moving and Dyke blocking the deal had, says Booth, 'sent a letter to Manchester United saying that we would be prepared to accept a less than unanimous recommendation. We didn't want one person to knock over the deal. It was that simple.'

The director it was meant to isolate was Dyke. However, as can so often happen, the fax had a devastating effect on somebody else that nobody could have anticipated and hardly anyone in Sky had given much thought to. The fax had mentioned the names of the directors whose approval would satisfy Sky. The way Sky saw it, if the directors who had significant shares, Edwards, Watkins and Midani – between them they had 17% – voted in favour, then Sky could go to the City and say the major director shareholders supported the deal. Dyke had few shares and his name was missing and so was that of Gill, who had share options but hardly any shares.

Sky had picked up that Gill was not very enthusiastic; Bell had reported back from his Friday encounter how hostile he was. But Gill was not uppermost in Sky's mind when it wrote the letter. Booth says, 'We did not know Gill was not in favour of it.' But because unlike Edwards, Watkins and Midani, he was not a major shareholder they omitted his name as they did of Kenyon.

However, as the Sky letter came over the HSBC fax machine, all hell broke loose in the Thames Room. The Manchester United Board read the fax and were in uproar.

As one United insider says: 'Everybody went nuts. The letter showed us they knew what was happening in our Board meetings. You get a letter which says we will take all these votes without yours. You are vulnerable. You need protection. We had to protect David and negotiate a deal for him. In any case a few other persons were negotiating their own positions. Maurice was negotiating from the beginning to end. The Board said we need to protect Gill.'

It was agreed that Roland Smith would phone Booth, and now with the clock well past five o'clock and the deadline imposed by Sky, the call came. Roland Smith told Booth that Gill could not vote for the offer unless he was sure that he would be protected and would not be out on his ear if Sky took over.

According to a Sky insider this caused a great deal of annoyance not least to Booth. He told Roland Smith, 'Get Gill on the phone right now. I want to hear this from his own lips that he won't vote for it unless he gets this.'

Gill came on the phone. He was put on the speaker phone so that Rupert Murdoch and others in Booth's office heard Gill say, 'I want this change in my service contract. I have just started the job and moved my family up here and want this increase in my service contract.' As he did so, John Thornton whispered to Booth, 'Ask him will he not vote for Sky if he does not get a new contract.' Booth did and Gill said, 'Yes. I will not vote for this unless I get an increase in my personal contract.'

Booth recalls, 'I had a conversation with Martin and he asked me to speak to David. And I did. David felt a bit insecure.'

The United boardroom source is adamant that Gill had no part in this, but that Roland Smith negotiated the new service contract. A source there says: 'Did Gill ring Sky? Gill did not ring them. Roland Smith rang them on behalf of the Board and did the deal. We also instructed Martin to get Sky to withdraw the letter. He spoke to Booth and the letter was withdrawn.' The discrepancies in recollection are not as significant as they seem. Roland Smith did make the call but Gill did speak to Booth.

Whatever the minutiae of this, the fact is that when the offer document was issued, this showed that Gill did get a deal which ensured he would continue to work for Manchester United after the merger and if any time before 30 June 2000 his contract was terminated he would be paid 200% of the aggregate of his current salary, the average of his bonuses for each of the two financial years preceding and the value of his benefits excluding share options. The offer document also had details of the arrangement Watkins had negotiated, to continue as non-executive director for another three years after the takeover at his current remuneration.

With this drama over, Booth now instructed Stewart and Deanna Bates to tell the Board that the deal was done and Sky was ready to roll and was going ahead with the takeover.

However, Sky and its advisers were no longer prepared to accept Faure Walker's words, or for that matter that of anybody from United. The feeling against the United Board was now running quite high at Isleworth. Already Booth had told the Board that if Sky accepted 240p now, then United would come back and ask for 300p, and then where would Sky draw the line? In the last few weeks Sky had had a number of verbal assurances and they had all turned to dust. One Sky source says, 'We were feeling pretty pissed off. We thought we had agreed a deal with Edwards at 217p and then at 226p, and then they came back and scored us for 230p. Now it was 240p. For most people their word is their bond. For these people it was not the case. We didn't trust them. They had agreed so many times before. We now said we wanted all the directors to send us a written fax to Sky saying they would recommend a deal at 240p.'

Campbell-Breeden rang Faure Walker and dictated to him what Sky wanted them to sign.

Faure Walker recalls: 'They asked me to confirm that to them so I went back to the Board and reported my conversation to them. I said, "Look, can I just confirm that we will support 240p in cash? We at HSBC would certainly recommend the Board to accept that." The Board unanimously agreed that they would support 240p in cash. So I then sent a fax back to Campbell-Breeden at Sky from myself. The fax – which wasn't actually sent off until about six o'clock because there were one or two other details we had to go through – confirmed that we would unanimously recommend 240p in cash. The fax was signed by all the directors including Dyke, except Midani who was actually overseas in Spain.'

To at least one Manchester United director the way the deal was concluded was a bit like a goal that comes in injury time from nowhere and decides the result – not dissimilar to the Ryan Giggs goal that won United the FA Cup semi-final against Arsenal or the two from Sheringham and Solskjaer that won the club the Champions League. 'If you had asked at 3 o'clock,' says this director, 'we felt the deal was not going to happen. Suddenly the deal was done at 5 o'clock.'

But by this time, and long before Sky received the written confirmation, Murdoch had decided that the deal was done. The moment the conversations in Booth's room had finished, he returned to the boardroom, finished some non-bid Board business he had with Booth, and announced that he was going to take the Concorde back to New York.

Murdoch waited for the fax to arrive confirming agreement at 240p. Then, as he prepared to leave, he calmly said, 'I want this story in my newspapers. The *Telegraph* got the first. This time I want to make sure my papers get it tomorrow. I'll call the editors from the car on my way to the airport.'

Nothing revealed more clearly the classic journalistic instincts of Murdoch, or was more calculated to alarm the Board members and particularly the bankers and lawyers, who pleaded with him not to do that. Whilst the Manchester United Board had agreed to the price, the deal was very far from done. But Murdoch, as they soon realised, ignored their advice. Sometime during the drive between Isleworth and Terminal 4 he rang his editors.

The Sky and United Boards now made their way to the offices of Freshfields, where all the United directors, barring Midani, signed their undertakings.

It was only now that Edwards felt able to tell Alex Ferguson. He rang him on his mobile phone as he was on his way to a match, Port Vale at home. Bobby Charlton, away in Thailand, where he was helping England's bid to get the 2006 World Cup, learnt about it first from the radio and immediately rang Edwards. While the timing of these calls was forced on Edwards by the way the story broke – and he could do little about the leak – Sky were not best pleased with the fact that Ferguson and Charlton had not been brought into the loop earlier.

Tim Bell says: 'Ferguson was all right. He wasn't great, but he was all right. They spoke to Bobby Charlton, who was in Thailand, and he was furious that he hadn't known about it. They both were important to the bid. We had said all along they would be, especially Bobby and Alex. We had no intentions of these people not knowing about it before it was announced. Yes, we intended to leave it to the last minute, as you have to. After all, you are breaking rules when you do this. You don't break rules lightly. You have to be able to defend yourself when you are up in front of the takeover panel as to why you have done this. You can defend doing it at the last minute because they need to know and so on, but you can't defend telling them weeks in advance. Then a bloody leak takes place and you have to list all the people who knew about it and they all become part of the leak enquiry.'

Two days later, ITV screened their long-planned documentary about Ferguson and he granted interviews in advance of the programme to various newspapers. In the *Times* he kept his feelings about the bid close to himself. He was only an employee, it had nothing to do with him: 'I am just trying to do my job. I know the fans are concerned, I understand that. The supporters are very important to this club; they have this incredible loyalty. But we can't know how it will pan out and affect everyone. We will just have to wait and see how things develop.'

However, a day earlier, interviewed by the *Sun*, again as pre-publicity for the programme, Ferguson was presented as more upbeat, praising Sky for the fantastic job it had done. The *Sun* may have talked up the praise, enabling it to put the headline, 'Sky's Good for Game, by Ferguson', but it indicated how cleverly Ferguson played the media, even two different papers owned by the same man.

With the Sky team having to travel from west London it took them longer to get to Freshfields and when they did they found the United team had already started on the drinks. This was the first time the two Boards were meeting and the United directors made it clear that had Sky not gone to 240p there would have been no deal.

As City deals went, £623 million was not a very big one; that week BP and Amoco were involved in a deal worth ten times that figure. But, as the high-priced Sky team of lawyers and bankers was realising, this was an infinitely more complicated deal. One insider in the deal says: 'You had so many different agendas. It made the United Board very hard to deal with. The problem was everyone on the Board had their own agenda. Martin would have done the deal at 217p. Edwards, despite what everyone says, cares about the club and recognises the deal was good business. He knew they needed money for players. He had to develop two ends of the stadium. If they wanted to spend another £28 million on players it would be tough. That is one reason why Sky would be useful. They would not have the same capital requirements. Also a lot of benefits for Manchester United in their distribution abroad, particularly the Far East, and just greater general awareness of United. Edwards was not that concerned about the price. He was much more concerned about the way Sky was going to manage the club. Watkins, a long-term Manchester United person, realised the worth but he was also out to get the highest price. Gill, a new boy, was looking after himself and wanted to get a service contract. Roland Smith, as chairman, had to think about his duty to shareholders. Greg Dyke had his own agenda. Some of his projections were ridiculous. Greg Dyke kept saying pay-per-view was worth billions. Dyke was fundamentally opposed. He did not care. And then there was United's merchant bankers, HSBC. For them it was a big deal and very high-profile.'

If Dyke was the one who stood as the dissident in the United boardroom there is just a hint one or two other United directors may have been ambivalent. At Freshfields, as Dyke signed the undertaking, Watkins came up to him and said, 'We might have stopped that if you had stuck out a bit longer.'

'Who is the "we", Maurice?' asked an astonished Dyke. 'Where were you?'

However, the next day, some of Watkins' ambivalence would seep through into the press: the *Guardian* reported he and Dyke were opposed, and then a day later, John Cassey writing in the *Express* pictured him, along with Dyke, as the two dissidents: 'Despite United's insistence that the deal was voted through unanimously, two directors, Greg Dyke and Maurice Watkins, were adamant that the club was worth more and that there was no need to sell now.' The *Express* article also criticised Gill, saying he was being 'blamed by insiders for failing to take a stronger line in negotiations'.

Dyke had signed but he was determined to give away the money he was making. That night he had a Shelter dinner and, as he left for it, suggested to Edwards that he might want to give away the £80 million he was going to make to charity. Dyke proposed giving all his profits to charity and sent a letter to Roland Smith saying that while he had agreed with the price he was determined to donate the profits. Initially this did not produce any reaction. The next day, when Dyke got ready to issue a press release, HSBC objected. Just before he issued it to the media he had sent HSBC a copy, who then rang to say he could not do that. Dyke's response was that he had checked it with his lawyers. Dyke's intentions were clear: he wanted to broadcast that, while he had agreed to the deal, he did not like it very much, but that his lawyers had advised that his fiduciary duty was to let shareholders decide. His lawyers had told him that as a director his fiduciary duty under the law was to represent the interests of the shareholders and nobody else. The *Express*, under the banner headline, 'Dyke Tells Directors: Give Away Your Ill-Gotten Gains', wrote: 'A close friend of Dyke said: "You can infer from this that he doesn't want anything to do with it. He does not want to be seen profiting personally from the sale. He has been a supporter since he was a kid, despite the fact he comes from London. He took a job on the Manchester United Board with absolute delight, not because it was another directorship but because they are so close to his heart. He's fanatical about them"'.'

When the deal fell through Dyke still gave Shelter £10,000 and another £20,000 to another charity, which meant the abortive bid cost him £30,000.

Even now at Freshfields neither United nor Sky could relax. The due diligence to check through the various contracts and make sure Sky was not taking on a company which had any hidden traps still had to be completed. Normally in a deal this can take days; now it had to be done in a night. Freshfields ordered a Chinese takeaway as the bankers, lawyers, PR and media spin doctors gathered in various rooms doing what Bell calls 'lots of housekeeping and all those things in the course of the night'.

At this stage no announcement had yet been made and as far as the official world knew no deal had yet been struck. But pressure to make sure all the housekeeping was finished by the morning increased at around 11.00pm when someone brought the first edition of the *Sun*. Covering most of its front page were the words: 'It's a Deal', with the subheading, 'Sky Buys Man Utd for £625 million'. The *Sun* in its editorial said, 'The deal is done. BSkyB is buying Manchester United. And football is the winner – from top to bottom.'

Murdoch had briefed the *Sun* well. He had spoken personally to David Yelland, although after the deal was done there had been briefings from Allan as well. The *Sun* had all the important details apart from the right price. For some reason, perhaps deliberately, the *Sun* got it wrong, adding another £2 million to the deal, and the other newspapers, thinking the Murdoch paper could not get it wrong, copied the mistake. The *Sunday Telegraph* had led with the story of the offer; now the *Sun* had led with the story of the deal and the others tried to follow. But since neither Sky nor United made any official announcements that night they had to rely on sources and there were some comical errors. The *Guardian* said the deal was being signed in Roland Smith's home; the *Mirror* said that the deal had not yet been formally approved by the United Board.

If the *Sun* glowed about it then just as predictably the rest of the press not owned by Murdoch could see little merit in the deal. The *Mirror* led the way with a front-page headline: 'Sold to the Red Devil'. Underneath was a picture of Murdoch painted red and horns sticking out from each side of his head and another two over each ear. The *Mirror*'s editorial said: 'This is a sad day for soccer. The day when money talked louder than the roar of the fans. The day when control of Manchester United was grabbed from the people who love the club and the game.'

If Murdoch was the devil on the front page then on the back page the target was also a familiar one. 'Traitor', it screamed above a photograph of Edwards with a sub-heading: 'Edwards is Facing Fans' Backlash After Cave-in to Murdoch'. 'Martin Edwards is facing a massive Old Trafford revolt after he last night caved in to Rupert Murdoch's millions' ran the intro.

The *Mirror*'s reaction, it being the main rival to the *Sun*, was understandable, but the rest of the non-Murdoch press also took a similar line. This meant that despite all the efforts of Sky and Manchester United, the deal was pictured as one personally directed and controlled by Murdoch. Reports of Murdoch's phone call with Roland Smith soon appeared, and with spin doctors picturing it as crucial, this strengthened the perception that Murdoch had played a leading role in the bid. It helped crystalise the opposition to the bid and made it easier for its opponents to present it as a personal fight against world domination by Rupert Murdoch.

Privately, however, even papers presenting it as the hour of the Red Devil were saying something very different. On the Monday, Piers Morgan, editor of the *Mirror*, had personally rung Tim Bell and Tim Allan to, as Bell recalls, 'tell us that he thought the deal was fabulous. It was a great deal and brilliant for Manchester United; brilliant for football; brilliant for us. But, of course, his newspaper had to attack it because they were worried about the circulation figures in Manchester. If the *Sun* got all the news stories, then the *Mirror*'s circulation would take a dive in the North and therefore he would try and stop it, because it was a matter of circulation. Most of the press who attacked it rang us up to say they didn't really mean it. They were just doing it because that's what you do. You attack Murdoch. We're used to that kind of thing.'

This has made them develop, as one Sky source says, 'a second skin'. 'If you work at Sky you develop a "what-the-fuck" attitude because you get a fucking in the press all the time, even at times from the Murdoch press. If we could have announced that as a result of the deal we are buying Ronaldo, that would have been different, but we could not.'

This may explain why there was a touch of fatalism, almost Oriental acceptance, that the world would kick against this bid whatever Sky did as Allan and co. prepared for the publicity. The press conference, the first time Sky and United could explain their case, should have seen Sky's PR advisers, freed from the shackles imposed on them since the weekend by the bankers and lawyers, set the agenda. But it did not turn quite like that, particularly for Booth.

There had been some debate as to whether Booth should be at the press conference and Booth himself was not that keen, preferring either Allan or Vic Wakeling to do it. But with Edwards representing Manchester United it was clear Booth had to be there, the two chief executives explaining why this was a great deal for both companies.

The plan was to have a London press conference at 11.00am aimed mainly at the City, then fly up to Manchester and hold another one at Old Trafford aimed mainly at the fans. That evening United was at home to newly promoted Charlton.

Bell recalls: 'We were a bit nervous about whether a bunch of fans would turn up at the City press conference. But it was Michael Crick who turned up and asked an utterly stupid question. "How much money are you going to give the club to spend on players?" "Whatever it takes," said Mark Booth. "How much is that?" "Well, we clearly don't know, that's why I said 'Whatever it takes'." "You see, he's not prepared to put a figure on it."'

Crick's memory of that press conference is a very different one. 'I did not follow my own rule: never ask a complicated or stupid question. I followed up my question about how much new money there may be for players with one to Edwards where I asked, "Ten years ago when you sold to Michael Knighton it was £10 million for the Stretford End and £10 million for the players. What is it now?" I knew the moment I asked the question I had made a mistake, for it provided Martin Edwards to jump in and say, "Look what happened to Michael Knighton", which got a huge laugh and made me look a chump. Given that Edwards had not had much sleep in the previous 48 hours it was a pretty smart answer.'

But then Edwards had over the years developed a pretty thick skin and had handled these barbs before. Also, as far as United was concerned, the media interest, while great, was nothing compared with some previous United occasions. In contrast, Faure Walker and the merchant bankers who did much bigger deals, but barely got a mention in the City pages, found the media interest awesome.

On the Wednesday morning, as Faure Walker arrived at the press conference and saw all the TV cameras, he turned to Maurice Watkins and said, 'I've never seen 15 different TV cameras like this covering one transaction before.' Watkins looked at him with a face which suggested he had not lived with Manchester United as long as Watkins had done and said, 'When Cantona faced court action there was double the TV and media interest compared to Manchester United being sold.' Faure Walker says, 'I found this extraordinary.'

But if United coped with the publicity, even the negative publicity, it was Booth and Sky, the men from the media, who could not quite manage it. To add to their agony, their moment of humiliation, which provided further grist to the anti-Murdoch press, came just as they thought their ordeal was over. Booth had prepared himself meticulously for the press conference. He had left Freshfields at midnight, leaving Edwards and most of the United Board there, and gone over the Q&A Tim Allan had prepared.

He knew the London conference would have a heavy City influence and after the London press conference Booth and his team flew to Manchester. Sky had rented a plane from City airport, which flew out containing Booth, Campbell-Breeden, Stewart, Allan, with Edwards, Kenyon, Gill and Watkins getting a lift home. David Blake from HSBC also came along.

As they got on the plane, the party discussed the uproar Crick had caused and how on Monday, when Edwards arrived in London from Manchester, he had had to push and shove his way through journalists and photographers to get to his car. Suddenly Edwards looked out across the tarmac and said, 'If this plane goes down there will be a lot of happy fans.' The laughter this produced relieved some of the tension and by the time Booth arrived in Manchester he was feeling quite relaxed.

The press conference seemed to be going well. He had answered nearly all the questions. There had been tons of other interviews, the so-called one-to-ones with individual radio and television journalists. The day was nearly done. Time for two more questions, said Edwards, and a woman put up her hand. Looking at Booth she asked, 'Mr Booth, who plays left back for Manchester United?'

Booth had worked out a plan to deal with football questions. He had never seen Manchester United play; football to him meant American football and it had been agreed that if there was a football question then Vic Wakeling would answer it. So when the woman asked the question Booth said, 'I'll pass on that. The football side and naming of players is not my area of expertise.' He turned to Wakeling, who knew Dennis Irwin did, but thinking the question was who would play left back that night against Charlton said, 'The only person who can name the team is Alex Ferguson.' He was keen to emphasise that he would not interfere with Ferguson. But it backfired.

The press conference dissolved into laughter. Even Booth joined in and 'thought it was funny, everybody had a lot of fun with it. But the fact is from a PR point of view it was not a very good outcome.'

In fact it was a disaster and a godsend for the *Mirror*. The next day's front page had a picture of Booth, looking like a cuddly but clueless executive, under a headline:

'Who plays left back for Manchester United?
Answer:
Pass. Football is not my area of expertise.'

The *Mirror* rubbed it in, 'The *Mirror* can help out Rupert Murdoch's henchmen – United's regular left back is Irish international Dennis Irwin.'

As it happened, in its first editions, the *Mirror* itself needed help as it identified Irwin as being from Northern Ireland but corrected it to the Republic later. The *Mirror* could do that; poor Booth had no such opportunity.

To an extent Booth's *faux pas* set the pattern for publicity on the deal. Bell and Allan had planned all sorts of ways they could publicise the deal – leaflets to fans, pledge cards and a mailshot to all Manchester United fans on the first day of the announcement to explain why Sky was buying their club. There was also to be a jointly signed letter from

Mark Booth and Martin Edwards. Sky also wanted to take ads in the local newspapers putting its point of view.

But the takeover panel ruled out most of these plans, and when Bell and Allan fretted about the fact that opponents of the bid were free to publicise their cause, the lawyers and bankers, who through the Sunday and Monday had prevented them from presenting their case to the press, reassured them that all the publicity the opponents of the bid were getting would make no difference.

Both Sky's lawyers Herbert Smith and United's lawyers Freshfields were confident that, even if the bid was referred to the Monopolies and Mergers Commission, there were no competition grounds on which the bid could be blocked. So, said the lawyers, the anti-Murdoch press and supporters may win the media battle but Sky would win the war and carry off Manchester United. The marriage had been announced and there was nobody who could prevent it from being consummated.

But the anti-Murdoch supporters were just getting their act together. On the morning of the Charlton match, as United and Sky were having their press conference in London, IMUSA held a press conference in the Stretford Trades and Labour Club, which some 70 journalists attended. It had called for demonstrations at the Charlton match in the, by now standard, form of football protest, with fans during the match shouting 'Stand up if you hate Murdoch'. This did get some response and the Stretford End unfurled a banner which read, 'Sold Out. No Surrender to the Plc'. As United failed to score in the first half-hour and Charlton scored the first goal after 32 minutes, chants of 'There's only one greedy bastard', a chant reserved in the past for Alan Shearer, were hurled at Martin Edwards. But then, as Yorke showed how well he had integrated with the team and United won 4–1, all the boardroom talk vanished. The *Independent* noted that no mass demonstration outside the club had taken place.

Paul Hayward wrote, 'The expected torrent of rage failed to descend. It was left to Charlton supporters to sing "Sack the Board". In the end most fans don't give a stuff who owns the club as long as they run it properly. If United continue to dazzle in the way they did after going a goal down, the dissenters will have a red devil of a job fomenting insurrection.'

The dissenters had not quite given up, although at this stage they were short of money and had yet to organise themselves properly. Just after the Charlton match Walsh was interviewed on *Newsnight* and, like Crick's appearance on *Newsnight*, this triggered a response. IMUSA were debating whether they should hold a rally. But Bridgewater Hall would cost £6,000 to hire and IMUSA just did not have that sort of money. Following *Newsnight*, Walsh got a call from Phil Symes, who told him someone in the music industry was willing to help. How much would they need for their rally? Walsh immediately said £10,000, knowing that IMUSA could do with the extra money. Symes said he would call back.

The man who rang back was Roger Taylor, drummer of Queen. His son was a United fan; he had written an anti-Murdoch song; he wanted, he said, to support ordinary people standing up to Murdoch and he was ready to finance the costs of Bridgewater.

By this time Walsh had also got a call from Yasmin Waljee of the law firm Lovells. This firm did a lot of *pro bono* legal work and was willing to help IMUSA deal with the Office of Fair Trading. Since the Sky bid was more than £70 million, the OFT was under the law required to deal with it. Lovells was keen to help IMUSA prepare a submission on behalf of the dissenters. Lovells could not do *pro bono* work for the shareholders since, potentially, they had money, but IMUSA, an organisation that depended on donations, was different.

Waljee says: 'I am the *pro bono* officer and I am responsible for bringing in cases where the firm can use its expertise. I do enjoy football. I play mixed football in Islington, a team made of people from law firms on Sunday mornings. I originally saw it in the *Guardian* and I thought it might be something that our competition law department might find useful. The reason we do *pro bono* is partly to highlight our profile but because people in the firm like to do it. It gives a lot of satisfaction, gives a good feel. It is a great experience.'

On Wednesday 16 September, Manchester United were playing Barcelona in the first group match of the Champions League, having qualified for the competition proper through victories over the Polish champions LKS Lodz. IMUSA decided that on Tuesday night it would hold a meeting at Bridgewater Hall. Fans and journalists would be gathering for the match the following day and it seemed the ideal time. There had been a great deal of discussions about whether it should be a meeting or a rally, before Walsh and his colleagues decided it would be a meeting. The hall could accommodate a thousand, maybe many more. Walsh and his colleagues were worried about how many they might attract and the upper balconies were closed off and lighting adjusted. It was not quite full but between 500 and 600 turned up. Walsh and his colleagues were keen that the meeting should convey that this was more than a sectarian Manchester United gathering and got Jimmy Wagg, a sports presenter for local BBC radio, but more significantly a Manchester City fan, to chair the meeting.

The meeting was carefully structured. It was not just an IMUSA meeting. Crick, who was also an IMUSA member, was invited to talk about what shareholders amongst the fans could do to stop Murdoch; Walsh would speak for what he calls the 'raggy-arsed supporters'; and Jim White of the *Guardian* would do the comic knockabout turn sending up Murdoch and the Board through gales of laughter.

White, who like Crick, had gone to Manchester Grammar, and who is a man from a middle-class background who had been attracted to United as a teenager because of the 70s reputation of United fans for hooliganism, says: 'I was playing football on that Sunday morning when the news broke and came back to find ten messages on my answerphone. Why was I against it? You have to ask the question why did Murdoch want Manchester United? To ensure he would be in pole position for the negotiations of television rights. For his own commercial interests. When you have an emotional investment you do not want Rupert Murdoch. Martin Edwards was bad enough. Murdoch was worse. At least Edwards was the devil we knew. At least Edwards turned up for matches.'

Crick's involvement meant Bridgewater Hall became in effect a joint meeting of IMUSA and SUAM, although at that stage the organisation had barely been born. White says: 'Before the public meeting there was a private meeting between Andy Walsh, myself, Michael Crick and a few others from IMUSA. All of us decided to stay focused and concentrate on the first attainable objective, which was to get a referral to the Monopolies and Mergers Commission. Basically it was decided that Michael would go for the middle class and Andy would go for the grassroots, although it was not quite put in those terms. Andy organised the fans who went in on the David Mellor-style phone-in. The strategy was to work the system. We decided to focus on Rupert Murdoch. At every point we mentioned it was a bid by Rupert Murdoch. We spoke about the *Sun*'s comments following Hillsborough [when it angered Liverpool fans by suggesting that many of the Liverpool dead were drunk and that this contributed to the tragedy].

'Our protest was never going to be a gathering of fans outside the ground on a Saturday saying, "Sack the Board". It was a carefully thought-out strategy. Broadly speaking it had two prongs: one was an appeal to the middle-class supporters and the other was to the working-class supporters. Andy Walsh orchestrated the working-class fans' appeal making sure fans got on to every available phone-in programme. The middle-class and City supporters and shareholders was handled by Michael Crick. My job was to do some publicity in the media.'

The Bridgewater meeting, however, did not get much publicity and while the following evening the Barcelona game also saw some shouts of 'Stand up if you hate Murdoch', the antis never gained any great momentum. United, in one of its most pulsating displays, took a 2–0 lead and with memories fresh of the humiliations Barcelona had inflicted on United in recent seasons, few fans were worried about who owned United. Soon the scattered shouts of 'Stand up if you hate Murdoch' were replaced by one in which all parts of the stadium joined in.

United had tried and failed to sign Patrick Kluviert. He had eventually signed for Barcelona but too late to play in the match. He travelled to Old Trafford and sat in the stand. As first Giggs and then Scholes scored to put Manchester United 2–0 up the fans sang, 'You can stick your Kluviert up your arse'. The laughter which rolled round the stadium saw some in the directors' box also join in. It indicated that for all the passion and energy Walsh, Crick, White and others were putting into the campaign, at the end of the day, the fans wanted to win and did not really care that much if Murdoch or his companies owned the club.

The next morning I sensed that Crick shared that view. We were both travelling back to London and I bought a copy of his book, *Manchester United: The Betrayal of a Legend*. It was out of print and Crick charged me £5.00, a penny more than its original paperback sale price back in 1990, which given it was out of print and hard to get was not unreasonable.

Crick was in a sombre mood. With disarming honesty he readily confessed that he had not enjoyed writing the book. It had been a collaboration with another author and the conclusions of the book, written just after the Knighton bid failed, had been proved wrong in almost all aspects. In the decade since then United, far from being eclipsed by Liverpool, as Crick had written, had won so many honours, including the double twice, that it was Liverpool fans who felt they had been betrayed.

I asked Crick what he saw as his aims. 'My plan is to make sure that at least 10% of the shareholders do not accept Sky's offer. If they do not get 90% of acceptances, then Sky will under the law have to preserve the separate identity of Manchester United. They will have to publish separate accounts, hold annual general meetings and we will still be able to make our views known. If they get more than 90%, then Manchester United will be absorbed in Murdoch's vast empire and our independence will be completely lost, even the nuisance value.'

If that answer showed that Crick already thought the deal would go through, then the anecdote he narrated about Maurice Watkins revealed the very special nature of the battle over the deal.

At the London press conference Crick had encountered Watkins and was asked, 'Have you contributed to the school appeal?'

The school Watkins referred to was their *alma mater*, Manchester Grammar. Watkins was not only on the appeal committee but his son was soon to become head boy. Crick, a bit taken aback, said, 'If I am forced to sell my shares [as he would be if Sky got 90% acceptance] then I shall donate a quarter of my profits to the school appeal.'

As he told me the story Crick said, 'It was some cheek on Watkins' part to ask me if I had contributed to the school appeal. I did not have the presence of mind to say to him, "In that case will you agree to donate a quarter of your profits, and if you do, the appeal fund will have reached its objective and nobody else will have to pay".'

Crick did later write to the High Master suggesting that Watkins be approached with this proposal. The High Master did not respond, but the whole episode emphasised that this battle over the Sky deal was in some ways a family quarrel. Crick, Watkins, White and Hytner were all part of Manchester Grammar, and while Walsh and his colleagues did not go to Manchester Grammar, and Edwards had gone to a public school, they were all from Manchester, as was Keith Harris. It was just that they were on different wings of the same family.

The Edwards, Watkins and Harris wing believed the takeover was good. They were outraged that anybody could doubt their love for Manchester United. However, Crick, White, Walsh and the others, like estranged members of a once united family who had since been cast away, could not credit them with any goodness and doubted everything they did. Yet both wings passionately believed that what they were doing was for the good of the club. They both claimed to represent this unique inheritance called Manchester United.

So what was this inheritance, and who had built it?

PART TWO

THE NEW RED DEVILS
The Men Who Have Remade
Manchester United

7

THE HEAVY BURDEN OF GLORY

The Manchester United inheritance is summed up in one name: Matt Busby. Before he arrived at Old Trafford the club was nothing; after him it was set on the path to glory which others, who have come in his wake, have struggled to emulate.

The way the story is told, there was darkness before Busby came and then he said let there be light and Old Trafford has been bathed in glory ever since. This is how the believers of the Old Trafford testament see it and even in official histories of Manchester United the period between 1878 and 1945, when Busby arrived, can at times be dismissed in a single paragraph or not even mentioned at all. Martin Edwards makes it a point of emphasising that he is carrying on Busby's tradition.

But for all believers there are also dissenters who say that the light Busby shed on Old Trafford has been tarnished by the greed and avarice of the money men led by Edwards; and the dissenters' campaign, as Crick and Smith made clear in their book, is to restore the Busby philosophy. These dissidents acknowledge that Alex Ferguson is creating his own halo and while it may come close to that of Busby, it would never quite match it. The target of the dissenters is the Edwards family, who are held to have usurped the Busby legacy and ruined it.

Like many myths the Busby myth is only partly true. United had started life as Newton Heath Lancashire and Yorkshire Railway Company Cricket and Football Club, (known as Newton Heath LYR) in 1878; the name was changed to Manchester United in 1902 and the club moved to Old Trafford in 1910. It had a pretty ordinary and undistinguished life for much of its existence before Busby arrived. In the opinion of Eamon Dunphy, a biographer of Busby, the club was a pre-WWII music hall joke. The club had not been one of the 12 founders of the Football League, although six of the 12 clubs were from Lancashire: Preston North End, Burnley, Accrington, Blackburn Rovers, Bolton Wanderers and Everton – but not Newton Heath. Like all such football clubs in those days, Newton Heath had originated as part of the need for recreation for working men and it had been founded as the football team of the Lancashire and Yorkshire Dining Room Committee. Even after the initials dropped out, and Newton Heath changed its name to Manchester United and moved to Old Trafford, its fortunes did not change much.

There were isolated moments of glory. United won the League Championship in 1908 and 1911 and the FA Cup in 1909. In between, on Saturday 19 February 1910, United moved to Old Trafford, a ground whose lush green carpet received rave notices of being a classic in the press and the first game against Liverpool saw 50,000 paying customers inside and another 5,000 getting in without paying. The *Manchester Guardian* reported that such scenes had never before been seen.

But this was fleeting fame and, even as United fans celebrated, they lost the man who had made the success possible. Ernest Mangnall, the manager who had brought the Championships and Cup, soon moved across the city to Manchester City. The club had exhausted its resources in building Old Trafford and, worse still, there was the scandal of match fixing.

On Good Friday, 2 April 1915, facing relegation, United played Liverpool, who were in mid-table security. Two days before the game some players met in Manchester's Dog and Partridge pub and decided that Liverpool would lose the match 2–0. The match, played in driving rain, saw just such a result as an apathetic Liverpool allowed United to score two goals. However, the fans were incensed and a bookie, smelling a rat, refused to pay. The FA investigated and Jackie Sheldon of Liverpool confessed. Nine players were suspended including several from United. United's Enoch 'Knocker' West did not have his suspension lifted until 1945 when he was 62. The others had their bans lifted more speedily and went off to fight in the First World War. One of them, Sandy Turnbull, was killed.

The inter-War years were to see the club relegated three times to the Second Division and in 1934 just miss relegation to the Third when, against the odds, United unexpectedly won the last match of the season at Millwall. Even a draw for Millwall would have consigned United to the Third Division North, as the Third Division was regionalised in those days. In the inter-War period the club spent as much time in the Second as the First Division.

In the early 1900s the club had been saved from bankruptcy by JH

Davies. Davies, a rich Manchester businessman, behaved in an autocratic fashion that would be unthinkable today. He changed the name, changed the colours and moved the club to Old Trafford but there was no protest. Ninety years later, United fans opposed to Sky would freely allege that Murdoch had the same plans as Davies without appreciating the irony of their claims. But his death in October 1927 plunged it into such a crisis that for a time it seemed the very existence of the club might be in jeopardy.

In the 1930s it seemed nobody could save United. By November 1930 United had not won a single league point after a run of 12 consecutive defeats and 49 goals conceded since the start of the season. The previous month had seen a revolt by the fans when 3,000 of them met at Hulme town hall and voted a motion of no confidence in the Board, the first recorded cry of the now familiar 'Sack the Board' chant. The meeting also called for fans to boycott the game the following day against FA Cup holders Arsenal. Twenty-three thousand turned up when 50,000 had been expected, but that may have partly been due to the fact that it had been a day of rain in Manchester.

The following year, with United in Division Two, the prospects were if anything grimmer and on Friday 18 December, when Walter Crickmer, the secretary, went to collect the players' wages from the National Provincial Bank in Spring Gardens, he was refused by the bank as the club was in debt to the tune of £30,000, a vast sum in those days. It was then that wealthy local businessman James W Gibson, a director of a major clothing company, Biggs, Jones & Gibson Ltd, came to the rescue to save United. He paid the players' wages and gave a further £2,000. The existing directors resigned, new shares were issued, a public appeal was made for £20,000 and Albert Hughes, the chairman of Manchester City, which was the leading Manchester club in the inter-War period and far more successful than United, joined in the efforts to save United. At City's Annual Hot-Pot and Social at the Stock Exchange Restaurant held on 20 January 1932, he urged his guests to do what they could to support Manchester United's appeal.

United bounced back into the First Division, was relegated again, but as the Second World War loomed, Gibson, the benevolent owner, and Crickmer, the efficient secretary, provided some stability and far-sighted management. In 1938, the Manchester United Junior Athletics Club was set up to produce young players and was the forerunner of the famous United nursery which was to serve Busby so well.

The War put a stop to all football but not to United's misery. On 11 March 1941 the Luftwaffe bombed Old Trafford and now United were homeless and forced to play at Maine Road, the home of Manchester City. Not only had City dominated football before the War, now they were United's landlords.

However, the light was about to descend. Louis Rocca, a legendary scout and a man with a reputation for finding the right men – it was he who had found Gibson in 1931 and helped save United; he even claimed to have come up with the name Manchester United – now sought out a manager. On 15 December 1944 he wrote to Matt Busby, then an instructor in the Army Training Corps. Before the War Busby had played for City, bringing back the FA Cup in 1934. He had then gone to Liverpool. Rocca had timed his letter brilliantly. Busby was looking for opportunities when the War ended. Liverpool had offered him a coaching job and other clubs north and south of the border were interested. But Rocca, whose letter only spoke of 'a great job if you are willing to take it on', tempted him. Rocca, like Busby, was a Catholic and their connection went back a long way. In February 1945 Busby, on leave from the army, met Gibson at the Cornbrook Cold Storage, one of his companies, a mile from Old Trafford.

On 19 February 1945 Company Sergeant-Major Instructor Matt Busby was made manager of Manchester United. The War would rage on for another three months in Europe, another six in the Far East, but the Busby era had begun and with it the legend of Manchester United.

Much has been written about the Busby era and there is little point duplicating it. Busby was a man of vision who remade British football. He also began the cult of the manager with which we are now so familiar. Before him there had been notable managers – Herbert Chapman, who had led Huddersfield and Arsenal to the Championship in the 30s and whose success made Arsenal the team of the 30s, was the most legendary – but the concept of a manager as understood in modern English football was totally unknown. In many clubs the secretary also acted as the manager and team selection was often done by the directors. Since 1937 Crickmer had acted as secretary and part-time manager and, until 1947, two years into the Busby reign, the first item on the Manchester United Board agenda was team selection. Busby would leave the meeting after this had been done. It is only then that the directors would move on to other matters, including the financial health of the club.

But in this, as in many other areas, Busby set about changing things and moulding it in his fashion. Busby was no tactician, not for him 4–4–2 or the sweeper system of defence. When he signed Noel Cantwell and the big Irish defender asked what kind of system he liked playing in defence, Busby was nonplussed. He had bought a good defender, he expected him to play. Cantwell is not the only player to suggest that Busby was an off-the-cuff man although Wilf McGuiness, who succeeded him as manager, has said this is myth. Busby talked tactics, had a blackboard with magnetised discs to represent players, and every Friday would go through the opposition individually pointing out weakness and strengths. McGuiness' argument is that, because just before a match Busby would tell a player, 'Go out and enjoy yourselves, go and entertain', they didn't remember him for all his tactical talk.

However, he was not quite a tactical innovator in the way that one of the other great English managers of the period was. Bill Nicholson at Tottenham became the first manager in the 20th century to do the double in 1961 and the following season Tottenham, in their only season in the European Cup, got to the semi-finals. On the way they beat Dukla Prague and Nicholson surprised everyone by playing a sweeper, Tony Marchi. It was an innovation that was extraordinary from an English coach but typical of Nicholson. Busby's gifts lay in other directions.

Players like Bobby Charlton emphasise that for coaching skills and detailed tactical knowledge they looked to Jimmy Murphy, who like Busby was a Catholic, whose job it was to coach the reserves. But he knew how to get the best out of people and always had the right person for the right job. When in 1950 Rocca died, Busby appointed Joe Armstrong, who, helped by Bob Bishop and Bob Harper in Northern Ireland and Billy Behan in Dublin, found United a whole host of talented young players whom Busby could groom into stars. The youth scheme that was discontinued in 1941 was restarted and slowly the Busby babes began to stun the world of football.

United had won the FA Cup in 1948; in 1952 they won the Championship; there were further Championship wins in 1956 and 1957. By this time Busby had in effect created two winning teams during his ten years at Old Trafford. The 1948 team was a very experienced one, containing as it did pre-War players like Jimmy Carey, Jimmy Delaney and Charlie Mitten. By 1954 the Busby babes, in the shape of Roger Byrne, Duncan Edwards and Dennis Violett, were coming through. There would be a third Busby team, but its creation was forced on Busby through tragedy in Europe.

Busby's leadership was most evident when the debate about whether English clubs should enter Europe started. England may have created the game of football, or more accurately codified the laws of the game, but when it came to international competitions, England, true to the little-island mentality, had stayed away. Before the Second World War, the Football Association had dropped out of FIFA, the organisation formed to run world football, and had not taken part in the first three World Cups. It was only in 1950, the fourth World Cup, that England finally sent a team for the first time. By the mid-50s this English superiority had been badly dented. In 1953 the Hungarians had destroyed the myth of Wembley's invincibility, winning 6–3 in a scintillating display, and then repeated the triumph even more emphatically in Budapest the following year, winning 7–1. English football was now forced to concede it was not the best in the world.

In 1955 the French sports daily *L'Equipe* had started the competition where the champions of Europe played each other on a home-and-away basis to decide the best club side in Europe. The trophy was called the European Cup and Chelsea, champions in 1955, were invited. But the Football League, always resistant to change, stopped Chelsea from taking part.

However, Busby realised that Europe and international competitions were where the future lay and the United Board decided to take part. Although the League tried to stop United, Busby would not give up and, in September 1956, Manchester United played their first match against the Belgian champions Anderlecht. With no floodlights at Old Trafford, and with fears that a Wednesday afternoon kick-off would meet objections from local employers, Busby persuaded City to let them hire Maine Road, which had floodlights. The City chairman did not think this European idea would work, did not expect more than 30,000 and asked for £300 or 15% of the gate. On the night 43,635 turned up and saw United beat Anderlecht 10–0. The European idea, thanks to Busby, had been born.

The following match against the German champions Borussia Dortmund saw 75,598 turn up, again at Maine road, to see a 3–2 victory. That season United got to the semi-finals, where they lost to the eventual champions Real Madrid, who were to win the European Cup in its first five seasons.

In 1957–58 United were again in Europe and again reached the semi-final, this time beating Red Star Belgrade. What Busby and Manchester United did not know as they boarded the flight to return to England after the match was that was the last game his brilliant team would ever play. On 6 February 1958, the Manchester United team and officials left Belgrade in their chartered Elizabethan aircraft *Lord Burghley*. The 1,500-mile journey could only be completed by a stopover in Munich. The flying conditions were bad and, as the aircraft tried to take off from Munich airport for the third time, two attempts having failed, it hit a house at the end of the runway and crashed.

Disasters there have been many, plane disasters too, but this one touched the heart of the nation and the world. Twenty-three people were killed, including eight journalists and the flower of Busby's remarkable side. Roger Byrne, David Pegg, Tommy Taylor, Eddie Colman, Mark Jones, Billy Wheelan and Geoff Bent. If all these players were wonderfully gifted – they had won two successive championships, one of them by 11 points – then the eighth player who died, after fighting desperately for his life for two weeks, was the greatest of them all and, arguably, the greatest English player ever: Duncan Edwards. He was only 21 but already an England legend.

Walter Crickmer had also died and Busby himself was badly injured and given the last rites. But he survived and returned to build another winning side.

Munich changed everything. As Eamon Dunphy has written: 'Many planes have crashed, costing many more lives since that day almost 34 years ago. [He was writing in 1992.] Yet the Munich Disaster lives poignantly in memory. On an afternoon like the one on which President Kennedy was assassinated, a shadow fell across the world, when something was lost never to be replaced. Those who saw them claim this was the greatest team ever to grace the English League. The average age of that Busby side was 21. Mere boys, they had won two successive First Division Championships, one of them by 11 points.'

Manchester United were a well-known, well-respected club before Munich, but the air crash elevated them on to a different level. The glory had been touched with tragedy and one in which young lives which seemed destined for greatness had been destroyed and the whole nation was drawn to Old Trafford. As with Kennedy's death, people as diverse as Jimmy Savile and the novelist HE Bates remembered precisely where they were when they heard the news. Bates was driving home from London, Savile had been preparing for that night's Manchester Press Ball at the Plaza. It was cancelled and they put the radio in the middle of the floor and tried to follow the news. From now on United became everyone's second team and millions willed them to win for the sake of the boys who had died in Munich. That year in the most dramatic of circumstances the team, managed by Murphy, while Busby recovered, got to Wembley for the FA Cup Final but, despite the entire nation urging them on, could not quite win.

Just over ten years later, however, Busby did fulfil his European dream, which by now had become the Holy Grail of Old Trafford. In 1968 his rebuilt Manchester United team, having won two League Championships in 1965 and 1967, went on to win the European Cup in a memorable night at Wembley, the first English club to do so, and redeem the young men who had died in Munich. United has carefully preserved the memory of Munich. The photograph on the reception as you enter the building shows Busby in a track suit – itself an innovation – talking to Edwards and Byrne and, outside on the clock, is a reminder of Munich and the date.

Yet the Busby legacy is not all dreams and the tragedy of Munich. Busby could be a smart street operator. As a working-class Scottish Catholic, he was well aware of sectarian prejudice. He suffered from it in his playing days at Manchester City, which had a reputation of being controlled by Masons, and in his life he worked the Manchester Catholic mafia to his advantage. Great and far-sighted as he was as a football manager, he had all the prejudices and failings of a man of his generation and background.

Busby was also very much part of the United system that gave backhanders to parents to persuade young talent to come to United. No subject, probably, raises more heat in football than the means used by clubs to sign young talent. Under football rules it is illegal to pay schoolboys or their parents to persuade them to sign for the club. But all clubs, faced by the irresistible prospect of signing the next great star player, at some stage or the other make such payments in some form or another, although they all deny making them. United under Busby was no exception.

In 1979 Granada's *World in Action* programme began investigating this, and other activities at United, and found a wealth of evidence to show that Busby was actively involved in United's scheme of paying for young talent.

In a signed affidavit John Aston, who had been with United for 32 years and had succeeded Joe Armstrong as chief scout, described how a young player called Bernard Marshall was signed from Liverpool for £1,000 at a meeting which took place in a small room off the Old Trafford boardroom where Aston, Armstrong, Busby and Murphy were present, the money being paid by either Murphy or Busby.

Aston's affidavit also said: 'Some of these boys were induced to sign because United offered them or their parents backhand payments. In some cases I was personally involved in obtaining cash from Les Olive, the United club secretary, and later handing it to the families of the boys.'

Aston also told Granada's researcher: 'It was not until I became a full-time scout for United in the mid-60s, that I found out how money was raised for such payments. It involved a system of fictitious expenses by which cash was raised and put into a "number two account" administered by Les Olive.'

In some ways United was forced to pay because other clubs were doing the same, and when it became known that United were interested, the size of the backhander increased.

Aston would fill in false claims on the same blue form as he did for his legitimate expenses. 'I remember seeing Joe Armstrong filling in an expense form one day and telling me it was for the number two account. He then explained the system to me. From then onwards, I would hand Mr Olive an expenses claim for anything from £5 to £43 at varying intervals, sometimes every week, sometimes only once a month. For instance, I would claim, falsely, that I had been to Scotland on a scouting trip. I would claim travel, subsistence and hospitality payments. But I did not receive money back for these claims as I did for my legitimate expenses.'

According to Aston, a boy's father may be put on a scouting job and paid between £3 and £4 a week for a year or two, although it was well known that he did not know anything about football.

Of the many young players and their parents Aston listed as having received money in a statement that ran to 17 pages, two stand out: Brian Greenhoff and Peter Lorimer. In the case of Greenhoff, Manchester United knew Leeds were interested, other clubs were willing to pay and that £500 would swing the deal. 'It was,' said Aston 'like buying a commodity.' Aston, who had paid at least six visits to the Greenhoff home, told Murphy, who told Busby, and then Aston himself spoke to Busby. 'He said, "fair enough", or words like that.'

Aston then went to Les Olive's office and received money in an envelope which Olive took out from a file kept in the drawer of a filing cabinet. Aston drove with his wife to Barnsley. She counted the money in the car and Aston gave it to Greenhoff senior, an unemployed miner. As they were talking they heard young Brian come in and Greenhoff senior hid the envelope under a cushion. Aston never knew whether Brian Greenhoff was aware that his parents had received the money.

The case of Lorimer is fascinating. According to Aston, Lorimer had already signed undated schoolboy forms for Leeds. Armstrong had gone to see Lorimer's parents in Dundee and paid Mrs Lorimer £2,500. But he then developed cold feet and worried it might upset the friendship between Busby and Don Revie, the then Leeds manager. It then turned out Leeds had registered Lorimer with the League and, with Armstrong feeling twitchy, Aston and he went up by train to Dundee to get the money back from Mrs Lorimer.

Mrs Lorimer would tell Granada's researchers that Lorimer had wanted to play for United and was due to play for Scotland schoolboys against England schoolboys at Wembley. Busby was supposed to be there but had to fly to Italy to sign Dennis Law and did not turn up. This upset Lorimer and he decided he would rather sign for Leeds. When Aston and Armstrong turned up in Dundee, Mrs Lorimer, sensing they were worried about the money, handed it back.

Mrs Lorimer denied Leeds paid the Lorimers but said the then Leeds chairman Harry Reynolds had promised Mrs Lorimer a house if she decided to come and live in Leeds. She did not take up the invitation.

Aston went on to emphasise that while Busby was against such payments he was aware of them.

It could be argued that Aston was a disgruntled employee who was bitter about the way he was sacked in Christmas 1972, the same day that Frank O'Farrell was sacked as manager. Aston was convinced that one reason for his sacking was that he had been critical of Jimmy Mathie, Busby's half-brother, who was employed by United as a scout in Scotland.

But the wealth of detail Aston provided was stunning and neither Olive nor Busby made any efforts to rebut them. Les Olive when contacted by Granada researchers felt that, as company secretary, he could not discuss confidential company policy with them.

The researchers had met Busby on 19 January 1979, some seven months before Aston gave his statement. But at the time, they were inquiring into the rights issue, a subject we will look at shortly. Busby was not very forthcoming. By November 1979, as Granada wanted to probe further and this time into payments to schoolboys, Busby refused to meet with them at all, cancelled one meeting on 2 November 1979, and then there followed correspondence between John Gorna, senior partner of a solicitor's firm of that name, and Granada. In the course of the correspondence, which became quite acrimonious, Gorna wanted Granada to 'refrain from intruding on the privacy of Sir Matt Busby'. However, Busby could not avoid the League and after Granada's programme went out, he was admonished by the League and according to Graham Kelly 'lay himself at the mercy of the Management Committee, saying he had always done his best for the game.' The League decided not to pursue it further.

More than a decade after the Granada programme, when Crick and

Smith came to write their book claiming Busby's legend had been betrayed by the Edwards family, they made little of the enormous and detailed research on how United recruited schoolboys just as Busby was creating his great teams. In writing about payments to young schoolboys, they have one paragraph which reads:

'As other clubs began to copy United, there were stories of boys' parents being offered illegal payments to clinch their signatures. Five hundred pounds or £1,000 might be handed over in banknotes. Alternatively, the father of a promising young player might be employed as a part-time scout, though of course he was not expected to do anything for this. But such inducements were rarely the deciding factor in joining United. The club's growing prestige was more important.'

Dunphy is nearer the mark when he says: 'Year by year Matt Busby had found himself sucked into this moral quagmire. A few quid in an envelope to the father of a talented youngster for scouting, no bribe intended.'

The reason why Crick and Smith see none of this moral quagmire into which Busby found himself was because they already had a villain ready at hand and one unearthed by the same Granada researchers who had documented the payments to the schoolboys that Busby condoned. That villain was Louis Edwards, Martin's father. Granada's research into United went beyond payments to schoolboys into the business practices of Louis Edwards and the way he had acquired control of Manchester United. It was a damning programme and Crick and Smith, building on this, but supplemented by their own research, have presented a detailed picture of Louis which makes it very clear that in the Manchester United story he is the great villain. So detailed and damning is Crick and Smith's book that others writing on Manchester United have not felt the need to question it. In the modern history of Manchester United, Louis Edwards and the Edwards family have been demonised as the usurpers who stole Busby's heritage. But as Eamon Dunphy says:

'Louis was no villain. He was a nice man, a classic, "Billy" in the argot of the dressing room. Billy Bunters, Punters, there were good ones and pains in the arse. Louis was OK. He was a bit *gauche* and physically clumsy [he had a stammer], but Louis was generous, bought the lads a drink, and he wasn't a snob . . . most importantly he was not Harold Hardman [who had succeeded Gibson as chairman in the early years of the Busby era]. Hardman, Busby's chairman, was one of the Gibsonian school of directors. Straight as a die, bright as a button, tough as they make them. Hardman never succumbed to Matt's charm.

He respected his manager but expected respect in return. Hardman unsettled Busby . . . Harold Hardman had been a player and that was a problem in Busby's view. He had an opinion. The worst kind of director was the man who thought he knew. Louis Edwards came along at the right time . . . Louis Edwards did as he was told . . . Louis Edwards tipped the boardroom balance in Matt's favour.'

Louis Edwards originated from Italian silversmiths on his mother's side. He had inherited a family business of food and grocery and, after the War, built it into a formidable one in the meat trade that centred round butcher jobs in and around Manchester, supplying meat to local authorities and running meat counters in Woolworth's stores and shops owned by Littlewoods. In 1962, when the business went public, it had more than 80 retail outlets and a turnover of £5 million.

Edwards, who was known as 'Champagne Louis' for his liking for cigars and champagne, had a family connection with Busby's great friend Louis Rocca (Rocca's cousin having married Edwards's sister). This developed into personal friendship with Busby in 1950 when Tommy Appleby, a leading theatre manager in the north whose parties were legendary, introduced them.

Louis Edwards was drawn into the Busby circle and it no doubt helped that, like Busby, he was a Catholic as well. He was on the *QE* in 1952 when United, having just won the Championship, travelled to New York to play Tottenham, who had won the Championship the previous year. Tottenham won 10–1 in an exhibition match. On the trip Edwards entertained, and for the first time came to the notice of, the players.

That was when Jackie Blanchflower, who was injured in the Munich crash, first recalled meeting Edwards. Twenty-five years later he would provide Paul Greengrass, the producer of the Granada programme, with a vivid picture of how players saw life at United in the 50s and 60s. Talking of how United had been mean to the victims of the crash, Blanchflower told Greengrass: 'The survivors had been given a payment of £5,000 with the club getting the other £5,000 [this was the result of a block insurance policy which paid £10,000], but losing £5,600 of this in tax. Players who were able to play again received no money. Tommy Taylor's mother only received £1,800 because he was one of a large family, and she was not a dependant.'

Blanchflower thought it was an example of the club's meanness that they didn't provide any of the widows with pensions, Greengrass noted. 'I asked what had happened after the crash. He had come back to Manchester to live in the club house and had rung Les Olive to see how he was fixed. He was disappointed to hear Les Olive say they had to leave the house within the next month or two. The same had happened to Johnny and Hazel Berry. Blanchflower felt that this was particularly heartless in view of the appalling injuries from which Berry had hardly yet begun to recover. Later the club had taken away Blanchflower's season tickets, saying that he didn't use them, and that if he rang up a few days before a big game they would try to fix him up. On the odd occasions that Blanchflower had taken them up on this offer he was made to feel unwelcome. At the centenary dinner, he felt that injured survivors had been equally shabbily treated. Harry Gregg [the goalkeeper injured in the crash] had been particularly hurt at not being invited. Blanchflower said he couldn't understand Gregg then taking up a post with the club a few months later. The ex-internationals were invited to the centenary match against Real Madrid, but had been shunted off into a back room and weren't allowed to go into the boardroom. The bar was free, although he noticed that the till was being rung up, an old trick to get round licensing regulations. At 11.00pm sharp, Les Olive had come in and got them all out, whilst Busby and the hangers-on like Paddy McGrath [a great friend of Busby] had gone into the boardroom. Jimmy Delaney, who had travelled from Scotland at his own expense, was left standing at the top of Warwick Road trying to hail a cab.'

Blanchflower said that the first time he met Louis Edwards was on a trip to the United States in 1952. To his knowledge Edwards had never been in the forefront of people likely to get on to the Board. Busby fought Hardman all the time, and with all the directors getting old, Busby set about to pick his own. Blanchflower thought a man called Willie Satinoff, who died in the crash, was being groomed by Busby for the Board. The fact that Satinoff, and not Edwards, went to Belgrade, indicated how well-in Satinoff was compared with Edwards. Soon after the crash Edwards had offered Blanchflower a job for £14 per week loading pork pies at six in the morning.

The day after the crash Edwards joined the Board. The United Board met at the home of Alan Gibson, son of James. They had originally gathered to mourn the death of George Whittaker, who it is said had opposed Edwards' appointment to the Board, which was the reason he had missed the trip to Belgrade. He had died the previous Saturday, just before United played Arsenal, winning 5–4, in the last game the Busby babes played in England. Now the Board had to cope with a much greater tragedy and appointed Les Olive to replace Walter Crickmer and unanimously appointed Edwards as director.

That date marks the beginning of what is seen by Crick and Smith, and those who accept their thesis, as the start of Edwards' villainy. And like all good villains, Edwards first started by being very nice and useful. Soon he was the most active United director, going to all the Munich funerals including that of Duncan Edwards, attending to the insurance policy claims post-Munich and transfers like that of Dennis Law from Torino.

All this was a prelude to a takeover of the club which he mounted in 1962. Working with a 1962 share register, he started approaching United shareholders and buying their shares. Soon after his election he was given ten shares. Now, four years later, he wanted to increase his shareholding.

Manchester United was a private company. There was no market in the shares and they were held by a diverse collection of people. Many of them had inherited them from people associated with the club in the past and who looked on the shares as if they were a special kind of trinket, something to be kept in a locker as having immense senti-mental value but no monetary value whatsoever. Now Louis Edwards came along and started offering unheard of money for these pieces of paper.

Initially he offered the money using the Conservative councillor Frank Farrington who, Crick and Smith say, was corrupt. Farrington knocked on the doors of the unsuspecting shareholders and made an offer they could not refuse. Soon Edwards decided it would be simpler to write personal letters. By January 1964, Edwards had bought 54% of the club, having paid, calculate Crick and Smith, between £31,000 and £41,000 for it. 'In return for that money he had bought control of one of Britain's wealthiest and most popular clubs.' In December 1964, Edwards became vice chairman and in June 1965, when Hardman died, Edwards became chairman.

This is the first charge of villainy, that Edwards bullied his share-holders into selling and bought United too cheaply. But did he? The bullying charge seems overdone. He certainly badgered them but then they held what was in effect worthless shares with which they were going to do nothing. In one case, one observer close to the scene feels there may be some merit in the charge that Edwards did bully.

This is the case of Alan Gibson. Had Alan Gibson been a strong man of good health then the Edwards saga at United might never have happened. But Alan Gibson was not quite like his father, James, who had saved United. His health had been so poor that he had never really worked and he had not felt he could take the pressure of being chairman of United. In any case, he was not a man of football, although United had given him many happy moments. This observer says, 'Louis Edwards badgered Alan Gibson, who was not in good health, until he sold. There is no doubt he hounded the poor man and it was not pleasant. Poor Alan, not well at all, just gave in.'

It was the deal with Gibson in September 1963, when Louis Edwards acquired 500 of his shares, paying £25 each for a total consideration of £12,500, that really made sure Edwards would be the majority holder. Gibson never made public any misgivings, although when, on 7 January and 17 January 1979, Granada researchers came calling at his house, Gibson gave some inkling of his feelings. Gibson by then had sold his last packet of shares to Martin Edwards, which would eventually help him, personally, to become the majority owner.

In the notes made after the visit, one of the Granada researchers noted: 'He and his wife discussed very carefully the decision to sell their holding this year. Felt that Martin Edwards was the sort of person they could trust not to abuse their shares. By implication, they had not fancied selling to Louis Edwards. Alan Gibson mentioned that they were worried that their shareholding might end up in the hands of the owner of the Bunny Club, which may be a reference to a bid to obtain these shares by Paddy McGrath, Busby's close friend.'

But even if Louis Edwards was hard with Alan Gibson and exploited what he saw as an opportunity, this hardly amounts to villainy. The larger question was: Did he pay too little for United? In 1964 football clubs were effectively closed companies. The directors who controlled them could decide whether to register a share sale or not. This condition existed in Tottenham until 1980 when Irving Scholar, through legal advice, got round it. They were also essentially feudal places where a man once in position could not be removed – and it was always a man. They were dreadfully sexist and racist, and no woman was allowed into the boardroom – there are clubs even now in the Second and Third Divisions where, as Delia Smith, who is a director of Norwich, has found out, this still applies. And there are clubs in the Premier League, which boasts of being the greatest league in the world, where a wife of a visiting director will be told she cannot go into the main boardroom but has to sit in an annexe looking, as one director put it, 'like high-priced hookers in a glass cage'.

Edwards had to employ the methods he used to get the shares because there was no other way and there was nothing remotely illegal or shady in what he did. What is more, all the evidence suggests Edwards paid the going price if not a bit more. If Edwards paid

£41,000 for his 54% of United, then the entire club was valued at just about £70,000, and that was about the going rate for a club of United's standing. In 1963 the biggest club in the land was Tottenham, whose income was £328,849 with a profit of £125,044, compared with United's income of £271,181 and a loss of £51,429. That year Tottenham had become the first British club to win a European title, the Cup Winners Cup. Everton was the next in size with a revenue of £313,165 but a profit of only £19,659. That year Everton's shares (there were only 2,500 of them) were valued at about £30 each, which gave the club a total valuation of £75,000, £5,000 more than what United was worth. Of course these were notional values.

Most clubs were owned by small-town businessmen, but the Everton ownership was different. The majority shareholder in Everton was John Moores, whose family owned the Littlewoods group, itself another private company. As it happened the Moores family also owned Liverpool in contravention of League regulations, which forbid one family owning two clubs (although Alan Hardaker, the League's secretary, occasionally made noises about it, nothing was done).

The Moores had a neat division within the family to distinguish their ownership of the two clubs. John Moores was interested in Everton. His brother Cecil, who ran the pools side of Littlewoods, was interested in Liverpool. But since it was considered bad form if as a pools operator he owned shares, the Liverpool shares were held through a nominee company. The two Merseyside clubs remained in the Moores family until the 1990s, when David Moores, son of Cecil, became the majority owner of Liverpool and Everton was sold by another branch of his family to Peter Johnson.

This was the strange world of football ownership that Louis Edwards had decided to enter. The idea that in 1963 or '64 he saw the £31,000 or £41,000, or whatever he had spent, as an investment is nonsense. Nobody at that stage thought of football clubs as an investment. The maximum dividend Edwards could earn was £100 a year, and television, which has made football into a business, had barely started. Nineteen sixty-four was the first year the BBC began broadcasting recorded highlights in a programme on BBC2 called *Match of the Day*, and for these highlights the BBC paid the Football League £5,000. Manchester United's share was £50 a year.

Louis Edwards would have had to be a genius greater than Einstein to even daydream in 1964 that, 45 years later, Manchester United's annual income from television would be £10 million a year and that even this would be considered too little compared with what Barcelona could get.

Even critics like Crick and Smith have to concede, albeit grudgingly, that Edwards started the stadium redevelopment which would see United get two World Cup games in 1966 and which would end 30 years later with the greatest club stadium in the country. United was also one of the first club grounds in the country to have executive boxes.

The more serious charge of villainy laid against Louis Edwards is the rights issue in 1978, which saw United raise £1 million. It allowed every United shareholder to buy 208 new shares for £1 each.

In essence, the charge is that by this time Edwards' meat business was doing very badly; it had started making losses and the Edwards family, which by now owned 74% of Manchester United, had at last realised that United was a business to be exploited. The grand strategy was, say the critics, that now that meat was going nowhere they would move into football.

The fact is that United desperately needed money. In 1978 United had made a loss of £132,000. What was even more worrying, the income, having crossed the £2 million mark the previous year, had fallen *below* the magic £2 million mark to £1.77 million.

Nineteen seventy-eight was also a crucial year for English football. Although in the history of the modern game 1961 is seen as the turning point, the year the maximum wage of £20 a week was abolished and Johnny Haynes suddenly became a £100-a-week player, the economics of the game and the modern wage inflation for players really started in 1978, more than 17 years later. That is when the retain-and-transfer system was finally abolished. Under this system, a player whose contract had expired with a club was not free to move. His old club could offer him a new contract at a lower wage and still hold on to his registration, without which the player could not sign for another club. The players had challenged this in 1963, but it was only in 1978 that it was finally abolished, indicating the glacial pace of change in England. In Belgium the system remained in place until Marc Bosman challenged it, winning his landmark case in the European court in 1995 and revolutionising the transfer system.

If the 1978 change was not as far-reaching as Bosman in 1995, the change was dramatic enough for the English game and, as Stefan Szymanski and Tim Kuypers in their book, *Winners and Losers*, indicate, it was the advent of free agency in 1978 that led to a wage explosion and wage expenditure over the next five years. It was also to lead to a huge rise in transfer costs and, within two years, we had the first £1 million player in Trevor Francis.

The Edwards knew money would be needed and identified that Manchester United desperately needed more capital. With double-digit inflation and bank interest rates high, they were not willing to borrow from the bank and burden the club with debt. They felt the best way would be a rights issue where existing shareholders put money into the club.

However, the plan met with opposition from both within and outside the club. Busby, who had gone to early meetings at the merchant banker Kleinworth Benson – the first meeting took place in 1976 – did not like it; Les Olive sketched out potential problems; and from outside John Fletcher, a rich businessman and supporter for 40 years, started an action group and launched a court battle to stop it.

The merchant bankers patiently explained that the alternatives Fletcher proposed had no validity. The Edwards family were under-writing the issue, itself an indication that no merchant bank would underwrite it, and this was the cheapest way to put money into the club.

Martin Edwards took a lead part in making the case for the rights issue, presenting an affidavit in the case. Martin Edwards himself had to borrow money to finance his take-up of the rights, which was agreed on 18 December 1978.

Edwards, in trying to justify the need for money, had mentioned that it would help United get a goalkeeper. In the end Gary Bailey came cheap – according to Crick and Smith no more than a £5,000 donation to the football club at De Witts University in South Africa. But United had to pay £700,000 in August 1979 for Ray Wilkins from Chelsea. The reason for the sale showed the dangers of clubs not getting their money right.

Chelsea had begun the 70s in great style, winning their first ever FA Cup and then the European Cup Winners Cup. The team was exciting and it looked like Chelsea might match Tottenham and Arsenal. But then the Mears family, which owned the club, decided to build a new stand; they lost control of the costs and, by the time Ray Wilkins was sold, Chelsea was in a parlous financial state. In 1982, with the club effectively bankrupt, it was sold to Ken Bates, who had been at Oldham and Wigan before that, for £1. He also had to take on the running costs and it was nearly two decades and with not a little help from a rich businessman, Mathew Harding, that Bates was to turn Chelsea round and make it one of the top clubs in the land. The experience of Chelsea showed how easily clubs could get into trouble when the directors lost control and did not exercise good management. Edwards was determined that that would not happen at United.

However, such is the sheer hatred that the Edwards family generates that Crick and Smith even criticise him for doing a good deal with Chelsea, which saw United drive down the price of Wilkins from £825,000 to £700,000.

The most amazing charge made against the Edwards family was that they were financing the rights issue in order to increase the number of shares so they could pay themselves more in dividends. If that was the intention, then it did not work out very well, as over the next 12 years up to 1990, the year before Manchester United floated, the club made pre-tax losses in six of them and therefore there was no profit to divide.

The rights issue did, however, have serious consequences for Edwards. It led to a further chill in the relations between Edwards and the Busby families. Louis and Matt had an agreement that both their sons Martin and Sandy would go on the Board. Martin had done so in 1970 but Sandy Busby had been in the bookmaking business and could not get on the Board. When Sandy was no longer in it, Busby brought the subject up. But Louis Edwards proposed that his younger son Roger should get on.

Eamon Dunphy describes a scene in a villa in Majorca where the club was on holiday and Busby turned to Louis: 'Sir Matt turned to him and said: "I want this in the minutes of the next Board meeting". Then he turned back to his lap-dog, "We had an agreement, you and I, that Sandy would go on the Board". Louis told him it would be discussed at the next Board meeting. The Board supported Louis. Sir Matt and Lady Jean went round to Sandy's house that night to break the news. "My mam was sick," Sandy recalls. Sir Matt was too. Sandy told them not to worry, he would not be on a Board with people like that.'

The Busbys still had the shop. In August 1967 United had opened a small souvenir shop by the entrance, the Board lending £1,000 to get it going. It had been given to Busby in September 1968 for £2,000 to run on a 21-year lease, at a rental of £5 per week. Busby remained on the Board and eventually became president but never chairman.

The controversy of the rights issue brought Granada's *World in Action* programme to United's door and it was screened in January 1980. It dealt with payments to schoolboys, how the Edwards family had bought their way into United, and Edwards' business practices. The programme also showed how over many years Edwards had used bribes to first get and then maintain his meat contracts. Corruption in local government and provincial business was hardly new, but linked to the man who had bought Manchester United it made the news.

A month after the programme was aired, Louis Edwards suffered a massive heart attack in his bath and died. Martin Edwards has always believed the programme killed him although Crick and Smith suggest he was overweight and had a history of heart trouble.

On Saturday 22 March 1980, just before United played Manchester City at Old Trafford, the Board met to elect a new chairman. Busby had been urged by Paddy Crerand and Paddy McGrath to go for the chairmanship, but he did not have the votes and Martin Edwards was elected chairman. Busby was elected president, a post that had been vacant since the death of James Gibson in 1951. It was his son Alan who proposed Martin Edwards' name as chairman.

Edwards was the second youngest chairman in the league, after Elton John, but the events of the last few years, and *World in Action*'s airing of them, had created a millstone round his neck and he has never been quite able to escape that.

Paul Greengrass, the man who made the Granada programme, says, 'There was a faction fight for the control of the United boardroom, both Catholics, and the Edwards faction beat the Busby faction and that is how it was seen.'

David Meek, who reported United for 40 years for the *Manchester Evening News*, emphasises that it was Busby who brought in Edwards, because he saw the need for people of business to be involved and knew that he had no feel for business, which was not his speciality.

But for the fans this meant, as Jim White says, 'The fight for the control of United between Busby and Edwards which Busby lost; the feeling was that the man of football lost out.'

Martin Edwards, in the eyes of many United fans, was pictured as the son of the interloper who had taken over the club that rightfully belonged to Matt.

If Busby had left a great and glorious inheritance then it was also a heavy burden and not easy for his successors to carry.

8

EDWARDS' LUCKY ESCAPE

Martin Edwards is a difficult man to provoke. He rarely loses his temper but one thing always raises his hackles. This is any suggestion that he inherited Manchester United from his father Louis. Mention to Edwards he inherited the business and he bristles, 'Why do you say inherited? I was on the Board and I became chairman when my father died. But my father gave me only 16% of the shares, exactly the same as my brother. I bought the rest, which took me to just over 50%.'

He did so partly through taking up his rights and then by buying more shares, all of which meant Edwards had saddled himself with huge debts. Edwards says: 'Contrary to the nonsense Crick writes, I put in a lot of money to acquire the club. I put in £400,000 of my own money in the rights issue in 1978, which was a hell of a lot of money in those days. Subsequently I bought the vice chairman's shares and I paid £200,000 for some shares off Alan Gibson before that and, of course, interest was running up on those two amounts – that's £600,000 – the interest was running up and at one stage I was about £1 million in debt to the bank for years.'

It is interesting to note that the amount of money Martin Edwards had paid for his shares was, if anything, slightly more than the going rate for clubs. In 1982 Doug Ellis, for instance, bought back control at Aston Villa, paying £600,000, and the following year David Dein paid just under £300,000 for his 16% share in Arsenal.

Despite what critics of the rights issue had said, there was no market in United shares and no way Edwards could realise his holding unless he sold United. However, in 1983, another option presented itself for the first time in English football.

Tottenham, their glory days long gone, had run into financial problems in the usual way all English football clubs do: trying to build a new stand, in their case the West Stand. Unlike their Italian counterparts, local authorities do not fund grounds in England and the intense tribalism of fans means a Tottenham fan could not dream of sharing a ground with an Arsenal fan in the way Milan fans, both AC and Inter, share the San Siro.

Irving Scholar, who had made his money in property, realised that the old Board had mismanaged the construction of the West Stand and offered to help. His letters were not even acknowledged and Scholar decided to look into the ownership of the club. He found Tottenham, a bit like United before the arrival of Louis Edwards, a closed shop where the old directors could not be displaced. The directors had the right to decide whether they would register a new shareholder. A barrister, Robin Potts, devised a clever scheme whereby he bought the shares, did not try to register it in his name, but got an irrevocable proxy from the person he was buying it from to appoint Scholar as his nominee. In other words, while the shares remained in the old shareholders' name, Scholar had the complete power to use them as he thought fit, if necessary to vote against the Board. By the time the Board realised what was up Scholar had won control.

However, once he had done so, he found the problems even worse than he had imagined. By now he had a partner, Paul Bobroff, who ran a publicly listed property company, and the question was how could Tottenham raise money and wipe off its debts? The fate of Chelsea haunted every club. It was then that the idea came: why not float on the stock market? No football club had ever floated but at a stroke this seemed the most democratic and fruitful idea. Fans could buy shares, the shares could be freely traded without any feudal Victorian restrictions, and Tottenham could get enough money to wipe out its debts.

In October 1983 Tottenham made its debut on the stock exchange – then in pre-Big Bang days there was still a stock-exchange floor – and it raised £3.8 million plus another £1.1 million in new shares underwritten by Scholar and Bobroff. Initially the share price did quite well, although it soon fell from the £1 it had been floated at and drifted below the issue price for a long time.

Martin Edwards had met Scholar during the summer of 1983 when both Manchester United and Tottenham travelled to Swaziland to play in a series of friendly matches. Scholar was an enthusiastic player and a match was arranged between the two teams of bosses. Peter Shreeves, Tottenham's assistant manager, kitted Scholar and his team in the Spurs kit, while Manchester United came out in an odd assortment of

T-shirts and swimming costumes. When Edwards saw this he immediately ordered the United staff to wear the first-team kit as he did not want, even in this kick-about match, Tottenham to look smarter. As it happened, Tottenham not only looked smarter but played much better and Scholar's team beat Edwards' by eight goals to four, with Scholar getting three goals.

But could United follow Tottenham's lead and float on the market? Sometime in late 1983, Scholar got a call from Edwards and they arranged to have dinner at Harry's Bar.

'Martin came with his accountant and he wanted to talk about the flotation. He listened to what we had done and then said he did not think Manchester United would be able to afford the dividends which would have to be paid if the club was floated. My feeling was that a number of clubs would have to go public. The problem had been that, since the War, very little money had come into football. Just after the War, there had been a huge boom in football with gates of 50,000 and 60,000 common. With construction costs low and players' wages fixed, that was the time to rebuild our old Victorian grounds. But that had not been done, thanks to the Inland Revenue, who refused to allow tax relief on new stands, as Burnley found to their cost. Now in the 1980s we were faced with massive expenditure and there was no new source of income. In 1983 Tottenham and Manchester United got £25,000 each a year from television, just the same as Rochdale. When we had met in Swaziland, we had discovered that we had similar problems and had to tackle similar issues. The only thing was, United got gates of 50,000 while we got between 30,000 and 40,000, but Martin said you can charge a lot more in London. "Our 50,000 is equivalent to your 27,000 because we cannot charge as much."'

So if flotation was out what could Edwards do?

Not long after the dinner at Harry's Bar, Edwards was visited by an intermediary who told him that a bid of £10 million was on its way. According to Crick and Smith the intermediary was Andrew McHutchon, a businessman based in Yorkshire, who was later banned by the Football League because of his association with Anton Johnson, another man on football's 'not wanted' list. The bid was from Robert Maxwell.

Edwards recalls: 'He rang me one day and said he wanted to buy the club and talk about it and all the rest of it. We arranged a meeting ten days hence. I said, "Look, I don't want any publicity on this. We must keep this quiet." Of course, next day, it was all over every single newspaper and I think we know where that came from. Then, of course, we had ten days of hell before we were actually due to meet.'

The hell of the ten days was a combination of the opposition of some fans and rival bidders wanting to buy the club. Maxwell then owned Oxford and was not much liked by even his own football fans. The rival bid was led by Peter Raymond, who worked for an American chemicals company. Maxwell used Roland Smith, who had advised United on the rights issue, as his adviser and he was there when Edwards and Maurice Watkins arrived at Maxwell House near Liverpool Street for their lunch. Before they went for the lunch Edwards and Watkins had met James Gulliver, the Scottish business-man who had bought Louis Edwards' business, then bought shares in United itself and also got on the Board of the club. Then they went to see Kleinworth Benson and, after ascertaining how much the club might be worth, they headed for Maxwell House. Edwards and Watkins were under the impression it would be a private lunch with Maxwell.

But as Watkins recalls: 'It was like a circus with PR men, advisers. That day the Soviet leader Andropov had died and Maxwell was getting calls from everywhere and always interrupting the lunch, so there was no real discussion.'

In any case, by then Edwards and Watkins had decided that a sale was not on. That seemed the end of this curious saga. But unknown to Edwards, Maxwell acquired shares in United and the way he sold these shares would ultimately have a devastating effect on the club.

Edwards still looked at the possibility of floating and talked to Kleinworth's. But soon all these discussions were to prove academic. English football was about to enter its most desperate decade when, for a time, it seemed it would become a sport fit only for hooligans.

A few months after the meeting with Maxwell, the 1984–85 season began and it was to prove one of the most traumatic in English soccer history. The hooliganism that had been a part of English football for much of the 70s and early 80s – in the 70s Manchester United fans had been some of the early pioneers of this new English disease – now took on a more vicious note. The season was to see Millwall fans behave as if they were a medieval army on the pillage when their team played Luton in the FA Cup. They not only rioted on the pitch but in the town and their antics involved the by now usual damage to houses, cars and also a train, which was wrecked. Forty-seven people, including 31 policemen, were injured.

The riot on the Luton ground was shown live on television and Mrs Thatcher was so appalled she called the football chiefs to Downing Street. They came on 1 April and Ted Crocker, the FA secretary, in what has now gone down as an infamous comment, said, 'These people are society's problems. We don't want your hooligans at our sport.'

Luton banned away supporters and Ken Bates, chairman of Chelsea, erected an electrified fence to prevent pitch invasions and talked of introducing ID cards. As it happened the electrified fence fell foul of the then Greater London Council.

The wisdom of not having fences, let alone electrified fences, was demonstrated at the end of the 1984–85 season when the tragedy at Bradford would have been even worse had there been such fences. Bradford were playing their last league match of the season and looking forward to celebrating their promotion from the old Third Division. Just before half-time a fire started in the old wooden main stand. Many escaped by jumping on the pitch, but 56 could not in one of the worst sporting disasters in England.

This also demonstrated how antiquated and dangerous English football stadiums were and bore out Scholar's lament of the lack of investments in grounds since the War.

Two weeks later the hooligans demonstrated how wretched their attitude was. This was when the nadir for English football violence was reached on 24 May 1985, just before the European Cup final between Juventus and Liverpool, at the Heysel Stadium in Brussels. For more than a decade English football had been journeying down this path, inflicting carnage and violence often on bystanders, almost always in a foreign city or stadium. But in the litany of grotesque acts by English football fans, few have plumbed the depths of the events of the Heysel Stadium in Brussels.

In previous years Liverpool's triumphs in Europe had given warning signs of the trouble that might come. In 1981 they beat Real Madrid in the European Cup Final at the Parc des Princes in Paris. Fans threw missiles at police outside the stadium and then faced a baton charge.

Then in 1984 Liverpool travelled to Rome to play Roma for the European Cup. They won but incurred the wrath of the Roman supporters. Some of them ambushed Liverpool fans, which led to a comical aftermath where two English football journalists, Hugh McIlvaney and Colin Mallam, were rounded up by the Roman police for their own protection along with two thoroughly bemused Americans.

According to some Liverpool fans the ambush created a burning hatred for the Italians amongst the Liverpool fans and shaped their attitude towards them.

Heysel was a run-down antiquated stadium and should probably never have been chosen. But this in no way excuses what happened. The Liverpool fans were very drunk and security and policing was virtually non-existent. Liverpool fans inside could easily hand their tickets over the wire to those outside; some just crawled under the fence.

The police, not anticipating violence, made no attempts to search spectators or take any notice of fans bringing more alcohol into the ground. The result was that fans, already drunk, could drink even more and, what is worse, many of them were armed with sticks, bottles and iron bats.

Liverpool fans were in the X and Y sections. The Z section was supposed to be neutral, but some Juventus fans got in there. The corner of Z terrace was a death trap with the two adjacent walls at one end providing no safe exit.

At 6.30pm the first charge came from the Liverpool fans following the by now traditional bout of taunts and insults between the two sets of supporters. As they charged from the X and Y sections into the Z section, eight policemen looked on. It was the third charge, at about 7.00pm, that was to prove the most deadly. Many of the Liverpool fans were drunk and used flagpoles and metal torn from safety barriers as weapons.

The police, in trying to control the situation, made matters worse. The Italian fans trying to escape were trapped by an old wall which collapsed and, in the panic, Italian fans fell over each other and some were crushed to death.

By the time the horrific evening was over 38 people had died (one more died in hospital later, making 39 in all) and 600 were injured. Of the dead piled high in two tents outside the main gates of the stadium, there were 32 Juventus supporters and seven Belgians. After the game, the supporters of both sides walked around looking for the wounded and asking whether their friends had survived. Nobody from Liverpool was killed.

The result of the match was academic but Juventus eventually triumphed 1–0 through a dubious penalty – neither team was told before the game that so many had died.

The next day English teams were banned from Belgium and a day later the FA took English clubs out of Europe; they did not return until 1990–1991 season, five years later.

None of the Liverpool fans who was responsible for this carnage suffered any real punishment. In April 1989, 14 of the 24 fans charged were found guilty and sentenced to three years with half the term suspended and to £1,000 fines. They were given two weeks to appeal and in the end they did not serve their sentences. The Liverpool fans maintain to this day that it was all the fault of the Belgians, their rotten stadium and their rotten police.

Blame was also put on the National Front. John Smith, the then Liverpool chairman, claimed to have evidence of such infiltration, saying that he and Bob Paisley, the former Liverpool manager, had been confronted in the VIP area of the stadium by right-wing elements from England. Six members of the Chelsea National Front had boasted to him of their part in provoking the violence. Paisley said he was forced to leave the directors' box at the start of the game as dozens of fans poured over the dividing wall and that the person next to him claimed he was a Chelsea supporter and was wearing a National Front badge. A number of banners decorated with swastikas were recovered after the match, including one marked 'Liverpool Edgehill'. Banners which read 'England for the English' and 'Europe for the English' were visible and contingents of National Front were clearly seen in blocks X and Y. One party leaving Brussels' main station consisted of Londoners wearing Liverpool colours carrying Union flags and sporting National Front swastika tattoos.

Malcolm McDonald, a BBC producer and also a Liverpool fan, who was there, recalls how he arrived at Heysel Stadium to find the approach littered with hundreds of posters from the National Front making a very straightforward racist appeal to the Liverpool fans and blaming blacks for white unemployment.

The fact that there were National Front agitators at Heysel should have come as no surprise.

The NF had long targeted football. Liverpool fans, coming from an area of high unemployment, would have been an obvious choice. The climate was right for the National Front to operate. However, Mr Justice Popplewell, who examined the evidence, did not conclude that the National Front was responsible for Heysel. But the whole tragedy illustrated how hooliganism had gripped English football and led to this black day.

To add to the problems, television seemed to give up on football. Indeed, the 1984–85 season had seen a television blackout of football – almost unthinkable these days. In the early 80s, as a result of the abortive attempt by Michael Grade of ITV to have exclusive rights to the edited highlights for football, football on television had alternated between the BBC and ITV each season. In its off year, ITV had discovered that a big movie always drew more viewers than the big match and in 1985, following the failure to negotiate a deal with the BBC and ITV, the season started without any televised highlights. It was only halfway through the season that a deal was done and televised highlights were back.

In the immediate aftermath of Heysel it seemed the English game would be completely revolutionised. Mrs Thatcher called the soccer writers who had been at Heysel to Number 10 and it was soon clear that the government would impose ID cards, which everybody going to football would have to carry. Despite many objections – from within and without the game – Mrs Thatcher persisted and it was only the much greater carnage of Hillsborough and Justice Taylor's report that finally slew this Thatcherite dragon.

Nevertheless there was one immediate consequence of Heysel which remains with us to this day. The Liverpool fans in Heysel had been extraordinarily drunk – on this everyone is agreed – and drink was considered the main cause of hooliganism. So drink was banned from English football grounds (or rather more accurately nobody could drink in sight of the pitch). This led to some rather comical arrangements for those who had executive boxes. In the Thatcherite yuppie 80s, these boxes had emerged on English football grounds with the intention of providing their occupants an opportunity to eat and drink in great comfort – and in great quantity – whilst watching a football match. The boxholders could hardly go without their gin and tonics and the ban meant that they had to be served in an anteroom – a place from where they could not see the pitch – and this could be done only when the game was not on.

The result was that at football grounds with boxes a new phenomenon emerged post-Heysel: a crush in the allotted anteroom before the start of the match and a near stampede to get to the room and the drinks during half-time and at the end of the match. While all this was going on, those in the stands and terraces could not drink. The net result was that it merely reinforced the already strong class distinctions in English football.

As if all this was not bad enough, in April 1989, there was an even greater tragedy at Hillsborough. On a bright, warm day with clear skies and the weather hot enough to wear T-shirts, 54,000 fans from Liverpool and Nottingham Forest travelled up to Hillsborough for an FA Cup semi-final. The Liverpool supporters were at the Leppings End of the ground, the Forest fans at the other East Terrace end. Leppings was the smaller end of the ground and it had 23 turnstiles to try to filter through just under 25,000 people, when at the other end there were 60 turnstiles to filter through just under 30,000 people.

Police had closed 12 turnstiles at the Leppings End because they were close to some Forest fans and they feared a clash between Liverpool and Forest fans. The Hillsborough authorities appear to have assumed that each turnstile at Leppings End would filter through 1,450 people when in most grounds they work on about 400. This, interestingly, is what the turnstiles at the other end filtering through Forest fans were doing.

They also made the fatal assumption that people come through at regular intervals when football crowds normally come in some numbers when the ground is first opened, then the crowd slows to a trickle before growing to a flood in the 15 minutes leading up to the start of the match.

The inevitable result was a crush. Thirty-five minutes before the match a crush had developed and a police officer tried unsuccessfully to open one of the outer gates to relieve the pressure. A police horse showed panic, spectators had begun to scream and children were being held above their parents' heads. Fans close to the edge of the crush climbed up on the turnstiles, some jumping down into the area beyond.

David Duckenfield, the chief superintendent in command of the 1,122 police officers at the ground, accepted there was a difficulty but refused to delay the kick-off.

The terracing at Leppings End was soon showing signs of over-crowding. Divided by iron railings into seven sections, but without any proper signs telling fans where to go, most of the fans converged on to the terrace and crowded into pens 3 and 4 leaving quite a bit of space in the other pens.

The overcrowding outside was even more terrible. Superintendent Roger Marshall asked if exit gates outside either side of the turnstiles could be opened. Duckenfield said no, fearing 'drunken fans' or that those without tickets would get in. After more requests from Marshall, Duckenfield ordered the gates to be opened. The 2,000 who poured in went into pens 3 and 4, crowding it even further and doubling its capacity.

By this time the game had kicked off. Forest won a corner. Two fans who had escaped the crush came on to the pitch and appealed to Bruce Grobbelaar, the Liverpool goalkeeper. He screamed at the police-woman to open the 'fucking gates'. A supporter, who was known to another Liverpool player Steve McMahon, had come on to the pitch and shouted, 'There are people dying.'

At 3.06, a policeman advised the referee to take the players off. The players sat in the players' lounge and watched on television as the tragedy unfolded within yards of where they sat. They could see police still treating this as a possible hooligan problem, with 150 officers lined up in front of the north stand terrace to prevent fans from entering the playing area. The officers thought they were facing a possible pitch invasion. In fact the fans trying to pour on to the ground were just seeking oxygen to breathe and get away from the killing crush.

By now television was already carrying pictures of the fans dying; perimeter advertising boards were being used as emergency stretchers and the gymnasium had been turned into a mortuary.

In the end 96 fans died and the report by Lord Justice Taylor blamed the police for 'a blunder of the first magnitude'. Clearly something drastic had to be done if Hillsborough was not to be repeated and Taylor's final report laid out a blueprint for safe all-seats grounds.

Martin Edwards, like everyone else connected with English football, knew the tragedy of Hillsborough meant English football would have to change. The recommendations of the Taylor Report were to bring in remodelled stadiums. It did away with terracing and the traditional standing and also forced football authorities to accept that fans could not be treated like caged animals.

But where was the money to come from? Initial reports suggested the cost of implementing Taylor might come to £1 billion. In fact by the time all the changes are made come 2006 the total cost may rise even further. As of now Taylor has cost some £600 million, £200 million of which has come from the Football Trust helped by the government cutting the tax levied on football pools. The rest has had to be funded by the clubs, with the Premier League clubs facing the heaviest burden.

It was against this background of a game apparently in terminal decline and a desperate need for money that Edwards was to receive the most intriguing phone call he has ever had.

Just two months after Hillsborough Martin Edwards received a call from Barry Chaytow, a former chairman of Bolton Wanderers. Would he be interested in meeting a man called Michael Knighton? Edwards knew nothing about him, but it was agreed Chaytow would bring him over to Old Trafford to have lunch.

Knighton was 37, a former teacher, who had made his money in property and had retired. 'I'd gone over to the Isle of Man in 1988 to retire basically and write my books. I wanted to get my health and well-being sorted. I think you should put retire in inverted commas! I wanted to indulge in one of my passions, which was professional football; Barry Chaytow knew I was looking to buy a football club and I'd targeted one or two. He phoned and said, "You're one of the few men who would be interested." He said he understood Martin was ready to relinquish his shares. So I made an appointment with Martin and went for lunch.'

It turned out, says Knighton, 'an outstanding lunch. We had melon to start – I had a superb melon to start. Dover sole, which was extremely pleasant, and we had a very good lunch indeed.'

As they lunched on that summer's day Knighton and Edwards looked out over Old Trafford and Knighton gave Edwards a very brief vision of his view of the game. 'We sat and looked at the Stretford End. Martin's dream was to see the oval finished. He said, "Michael, it'll never be done." I smiled and said, "Martin, I assure you that the Stretford End will be developed in my time. Not only that, I can assure you I have the financial wherewithal and the vision to make it happen." Whether he believed that or not is almost irrelevant.'

Edwards could hardly believe what he was hearing. That two months after Hillsborough there was an investor who was not only prepared to buy him out but develop the ground seemed too good to be true. Selling to Knighton seemed to be the best of all possible solutions; the Stretford End would be rebuilt and Edwards would liquidate his debt.

'Michael Knighton knew someone I knew quite well, a chap who used to be chairman of Bolton Wanderers, who was a friend of Mike Edelsen's [a fellow director of Edwards at United]. He rang me up and asked if he could come to lunch and bring a friend. They came to Old Trafford and I didn't know what the topic was going to be. The attraction of the Knighton deal was that Knighton was going to build the Stretford End as part of it. That was going to be his contribution and that was the attraction of the deal. When Michael Knighton approached me, the Stretford End needed replacement. It needed a £10 million expenditure. We hadn't got £10 million in the bank. In fact we had debts in the bank. I hadn't got £10 million. What should I have done? Could I turn round to the supporters and say I have turned down a deal which would mean the Stretford End is going to be completed for nothing?'

There was also a personal pull in the deal: 'When Knighton came I was in debt. It was more than a million because I'd been carrying that debt for years – ten years. It was certainly over £1 million and I'd been putting off the banks for years. My house in Cheshire was mortgaged to the bank. Nobody knew quite how things were going to go in those days. I carried that debt for years and some day I knew I had to become liquid.'

For two people who had never met, Edwards and Knighton struck up an immediate rapport. 'That lunch,' recalls Knighton, 'was excellent in the sense that we did strike up an immediate chemistry and empathy.'

After the deal became public, there was much criticism about how Edwards and Knighton had kept it all secret. But Knighton denies there was excessive secrecy. 'Over the next few weeks Martin and I had meetings and telephone conversations. But it is not true that we didn't tell anyone. Of course we both had professional teams who were briefed and close friends who were party to it. It was a very tight circle, yes, but why announce something which may come to nothing? Maurice Watkins knew pretty quickly, that's my understanding of it.'

But, however vigorously Knighton may now defend himself, as the deal became public he certainly made public statements that were, to say the least, not full and forthcoming and did not enable people to understand what exactly was going on.

Edwards went away on holiday to the Greek islands and then on a Friday evening in July 1989 he flew to Killochan Castle, a castle in Aryshire in southwest Scotland, to discuss the details of the deal with Knighton. And there at midnight the two men shook hands on the deal whereby Edwards would sell his stake to Knighton. But even at this stage, after weeks of talking, nobody had mentioned price. Edwards had not asked and Knighton had not offered.

'I like Martin Edwards. I think Martin Edwards is essentially a decent soul. I like his company socially. I think he's got vast experience of being a chief executive, so I'm not here to run Martin Edwards down. But there's no question, when we struck the deal – and now we come to the Scottish castle and at the stroke of midnight, to make it even more dramatic – we had never, after weeks and weeks of negotiation, mentioned price, which I find quite interesting. We'd never mentioned price until the stroke of midnight, when we shook hands. It's a pretty poignant point, because we knew we'd got a deal, whatever the price was going to be. Call it Martin's public school reticence, call it what you will, the English don't like talking about money. They do now, in football terms, but they didn't in 1989 and I suppose – not that I was a public school boy, but I taught in public schools for a long, long time, so you know the values and mores and how they behave – it was only when we shook hands that we talked about the price. He took a deep draw on his Benson & Hedges cigarette and he said, "You never told me the price".'

The price was £10 million for the 50.2% stake in United that Martin Edwards owned. It meant Knighton was paying £20 a share. Although when the news emerged it would be said Edwards had sold United, what he had done was give an option to Knighton to buy his shares, a distinction that was lost and was crucial. The next morning Edwards, ferried by helicopter to Glasgow, flew back to Manchester and now the United Board began to learn about the deal, among them one of Edwards' close friends Mike Edelson.

Mike Edelson, a Manchester fur trader, had been put on the United Board in 1982. 'I met Martin Edwards in 1971 at a Christmas Eve party. We were invited by some people we both knew. We met and I asked him if he wanted a game of squash. We played reasonably regularly. I was a United supporter, anyway. My first match that I can remember was in 1952–53. My father had taken me to City and my uncle had taken me to United. For whatever reason I became a United supporter. I first started going in 1952–53, when United lost at home to Portsmouth. Jack Rowley scored from an overhead kick. So when I met Martin we were talking about United, as you do, and as time went on he invited me to one or two games. So instead of standing on the Stretford End Paddock, I went in the directors' box. By then I'd progressed to having a season ticket in G Stand. When the rights issue came up in 1979 I took some shares up.'

Following the rights issue, Edwards had sold to Edelson 15,400 shares for £125,000. The agreement with Edelson gave Edwards the option of buying them back at the same price. However, Edelson did not get on the Board at the time of the sale and had to wait for four years. According to Crick and Smith this was because of opposition from Busby. In June 1981 when Edelson's name was proposed Busby had opposed it. But in August 1982 Edelson got on and at the same Board meeting Busby announced he wanted to retire for 'personal and domestic reasons'. Crick and Smith imply it was because he did not approve of Edelson; but Busby was 73 and had suffered a cerebral haemorrhage the year before; also Lady Busby was not well.

Edelson readily confesses that, 'As far as I'm concerned I owe the whole of my Manchester United life to Martin, so I wouldn't ever say I thought he was doing something for United that was wrong. If he was doing something for himself, that's his own business, and I would be supportive.'

However, when he heard about the Knighton deal, he was 'surprised and shocked because I didn't know there was anything brewing. Martin didn't tell us until after the event. His rationale was that Knighton would build the Stretford End. The fact that Martin sold was his personal reasons. The fact that the person also said that he would put £10 million in to do the Stretford End was a major factor, because he could have found somebody else.'

Edelson did not know Knighton but knew Chaytow, with whom he had done business.

Other people were also surprised to hear Edwards was selling to Knighton. Edwards rang Scholar, who says, 'I quickly sensed something was wrong. Michael Knighton was supposed to be in the property business, but I had never heard his name and the property business is a little too small for mysterious strangers with lots of money to appear. I remember asking Martin whether he had proved that the money was available; Martin seemed to get a bit nervous about this and quickly ended the conversation.'

Martin's nervousness was understandable for he did not quite realise what he had let himself in for. Almost from the beginning there was a touch of the comic opera about this proposed sale. At the press conference announcing the deal, Edwards introduced Michael Knighton as Michael Whetton, the name of the catering manager at Old Trafford.

Then came the Knighton juggle with the ball on 24 August, the opening day of the 1989–90 season, as Manchester United played the champions Arsenal. Barely had the Old Trafford faithful been able to take in that they were getting a new owner than he was on the pitch wearing the United kit, juggling with the ball and kicking it into the empty net.

Knighton had told Edwards the previous day that he wanted to get on the pitch before the game in the United kit and Edwards had advised against it. The police had to be involved because there was a security risk and while the fans roared many of the Manchester United Board missed this party act. Edelson says, 'I knew he wanted to do it before the game. He had said so and Martin told him not to do it. As directors, we don't normally go out until the teams are coming out – about ten to three or whatever. Knighton went out on his own before that. I only saw it on the news that night. I heard it obviously, because the ground was abuzz.'

That night Edelson rang Maurice Watkins, who was on holiday in Malta, and said, 'You won't believe what that Michael Knighton did today.' Watkins would have time to savour the Knighton experience when he visited him in his Scottish castle – the only United director to take up the invitation – to find himself in the company of Rod Hull, the man with the Emu, who was also Knighton's guest.

Knighton accepts that in retrospect he did not help matters by juggling with the ball in front of the Stretford End. 'I appreciate you are going to set yourself up as a target. It comes with the territory. You don't just juggle a ball in front of 50,000 people and not accept people are going to sit up and notice – that would be absurd. I can live with that totally. People can criticise it or laugh at it or whatever. I accept that. That was a spontaneous action, a totally spontaneous action. I'd been asked by a photographer who wanted to take a photograph in my Manchester United kit. It was the opening day of the season, visiting champions, Arsenal. I was obliging, as you try to be – I was extremely media-friendly. I'll tell you why I did it. There was this void and gap of mistrust between the fans and the Board. Martin is a good man, I think, but I don't think he is somebody who understands the media. The media requires special skill. You have to have that charm. What I wanted to do, very quickly, the rationale behind this was there was a huge divide between the boardroom and the terraces in 1989. People forget the facts. Gates had fallen to 23,000. Against Wimbledon it was 23,368, Everton it was 26,722. There was this tremendous gulf of feeling and empathy. In fact it was hostile, incredibly hostile. It was absurd and pretty foul. People forget that's where Manchester United was in 1989. It had never done better than break even. Never won the Holy Grail for the previous 20-odd years or whatever it was. Had the brief excursions in the FA Cup. Always finished fourth or fifth and always underachieved. For the size of the institution they had under-achieved and were not fulfilling their potential off the field. That was absolutely certain.'

Knighton thought his ball-juggling act would strike a chord with the fans, but it merely raised more risible questions about Knighton who? However, for one man who saw the ball-juggling that night on television, it solved a puzzling mystery, and he was very thankful that the letter he was planning to write had not gone off, which meant he had saved his company half a million pounds. Two weeks before this

Knighton had met Graham Sharp, who is in charge of publicity for William Hill, and asked what odds he would give about Knighton playing in the first team of a First Division club before the end of the season. Knighton told Sharp he had played for the youth team of a league club but been forced to give up because of injury. His wife was writing a book on dieting and will power and, in order to publicise it, he wanted to get back into league football. The bet was, if he played in a First Division match before the season was out, he would win £500,000. Sharp checked him out and it looked like a safe bet. But Sharp wanted to get some publicity out of it and so he proposed that William Hill would also offer odds on Knighton not playing. Sharp was about to confirm all this in writing when he saw the pictures of Knighton's ball-juggling and realised who the mystery player-to-be was. Then Knighton rang to say, 'Well, the cat's out of the bag now. I suppose it is too late for the bet?'

'Yes,' replied Sharp.

'You've had a lucky escape. I can tell you that if you'd taken the bet, I would have got Alex Ferguson to play me as substitute in an end-of-season game.'

I met Knighton at the Marriott Hotel in Slough on a Friday evening where Knighton, still in track suit, had just come off the coach that had brought his Carlisle team – he was not only owner but also the manager – to play Brentford the next day. It promised to be an intriguing match since Brentford's owner Ron Noades is also the manager, a clash between two owner–managers – although, in the event, because of a waterlogged pitch, the match did not take place. The whole thing showed off the very distinctive Knighton style and it emphasised that the ball-juggling act was both instinctive and part of the essential character of this showman. It marked out the great contrast Knighton would have been as owner, as indeed had his attempted bet with Sharp.

News of the bid made the newspapers try and find out who Knighton was and there followed a media frenzy of stories about him, with intense speculation as to whether he had the money and who his backers were.

Knighton did not help matters by at first suggesting he was acting on his own, for it turned out he was backed by two well-known businessmen, Robert Thornton and Stanley Cohen. Knighton says: 'When I first started to talk to Martin, he never asked me was I doing this by myself, or with a few close friends, or anything. Once we knew we were making progress and a deal could be actually struck, it was at that point that the partners came on. Just after I met Martin, a few weeks later, I had lunch with my next-door neighbour in Scotland, Bob Thornton. Bob and I would often exchange ideas about various things. Bob said, "What are you doing?" and he was taken into my confidence. He said, "I'd love to be involved." We talked about that and the agreement was, as long as I remained the majority share-holder of the shelf company, MK Trafford Holdings – it was a shelf company brought down from the shelf simply to target Manchester United – he said he'd like to take 40%, to which I agreed. He didn't want any publicity or his name exposing at all because, after all, he was retired and had been chairman of Debenhams plc. He was a highly respected and well-known City figure, unlike myself, who was totally unknown. I had every confidence he would bring something to the table. Certainly his merchandising expertise – *Who's Who* had him down as the greatest retailer in the world in his active days – and he's a thoroughly nice man and Rosemary, my wife, and his wife and I get on very well.'

Knighton would tell Crick and Smith that Thornton in turn had made a private arrangement with Cohen, who Knighton had not even met at that stage.

Edwards had been told about Thornton's involvement but the other United directors, such as Edelson, did not know and only discovered it when the *Manchester Evening News* revealed Thornton and Cohen's name. However, Thornton didn't want the publicity, and as the media frenzy grew he and Cohen withdrew. This was just seven days before Knighton was due to confirm the deal and Thornton had also taken him to see his adviser City Corp and lawyer Forsythe Kerman.

This increased the media frenzy and a whole host of stories emerged which suggested that Knighton did not have the money. Knighton has always maintained that the newspapers got it wrong; he always had the money. Here we may be dealing with semantics. When newspapers speculated about whether he had the money, some of them meant in the very literal sense: did he have it in his back pocket? That he didn't. But he had access to finance and could have done the deal. Knighton says, 'The money was there anyway. The money was never not there. This was a total misconception. There were different forms of it. The fact is, the Bank of Scotland had provided a £24 million overdraft which was simply awaiting my signature. I've got faxes urging me to get to their head office in Edinburgh to sign the documentation. Fact. That can be vindicated by many people that you would know, because they were there at the time.'

However, Knighton admits that, 'The point is, there was only a very brief spell in the whole time where we undid one mechanism of financing to another mechanism.'

The undoing of one mechanism for another saw Knighton meet David Murray, owner of Glasgow Rangers, a man he admired. It was Murray who helped Knighton put together the financing deal from the Bank of Scotland. But then Knighton did not seem to like the deal and tried to find other backers. This put him into contact with Eddie Shah, who had taken on the print unions and revolutionised British journalism, and Owen Oyston, then a socialist radio owner, since jailed for rape. Knighton said Oyston approached him first; a spokesman for Oyston denied it. But the two men were spotted together watching Manchester City playing Luton on a day when United were not playing.

Eddie Shah confirmed that his office had got in touch with Knighton to explore financial opportunities, but had no interest in financing United, being a Tottenham supporter. Knighton rang Shah and sent him information about his own finances and a copy of a report on Manchester United prepared by his accountant Robson Rhodes.

Knighton says, 'The Eddie Shah thing was a different story altogether. The facts are there were so many people in on this at the end and trying to hawk it round and sell it and so on. Some of the issues I knew nothing of, I promise you.'

Knighton's decision to send the Robson Rhodes report to Shah would prove a big mistake. It meant confidential information about United was now floating about, some of which could have got into the hands of their rivals Manchester City. The involvement of David Murray meant there was also the extraordinary saga that the chairman of Glasgow Rangers was trying to help sell Manchester United on behalf of a man who did not own it but had the option to buy the majority stake.

By this time there was a group of Manchester United directors who were determined to stop Knighton. They included Edelson, Bobby Charlton, Nigel Burrows, a businessman who had come on the Board the previous year in 1998, and Amir Midani. Midani was the most crucial in the group. Midani's father, Mouaffac Midani, was said to be one of the richest men in the world and Midani's arrival on the United Board was the story of two basketball teams. In 1985 Manchester United had bought the Warrington Vikings Basketball Club. Midani owned the rival Manchester Giants and there was a legal battle between Midani and United. United lost money in basketball and it was resolved and the two basketball teams were to be merged. About this time Midani bought 100,862 shares in United for £700,000, which James Gulliver had sold back to Susan Edwards, Martin's wife. They were purchased through an organisation called the Philen Establishment, based in Lichtenstein, which belongs to Midani's father and which described Amir Midani as its UK representative. In 1987 Midani joined the Manchester United Board.

A week after Edwards had done the deal with Knighton this group had met at Edelson's house. They were confused by what Edwards had done and did not know what to do. As Edelson says, 'I remember we had a meeting at my house in Hale on a Friday evening. This was a week after the Knighton announcement. We were the Board of a plc, not quoted as such, but a plc. None of us had any experience of a public company. We were directors of a plc and there are rules to being a director of a plc, even if it's only a plc in the form we were without a quote on the stock markets. We didn't actually know our rights or duties at that time, so it took us some time to get together and we discovered what we had to do. We had been talking to various people. We were duty-bound to take advice which was separate from Martin. We couldn't do it together. Martin couldn't be at the meeting. The meeting at my house wasn't behind his back. He wasn't allowed to be there by company rules.'

Gareth Hayward of City Corp, one of Knighton's advisers, had suggested that the other directors should take advice and, as so often in such situations, they turned to Maurice Watkins: 'Maurice was a lawyer, a commercial lawyer. Maurice was the one who realised that we needed advice on our duties as directors. We approached merchant bankers in the City but they did not want to know. We were turned down by five, six, seven, eight . . . They didn't want to act for a football club. Too common; too small; not worth the problem and all the rest. They didn't want to do it. Ansbachers ultimately took us on. It was somebody called Mark Phythian-Adams. He was the managing director at Ansbachers at the time and it was he who came in and he bought Knighton off. He did all the fighting.'

Glenn Cooper, who was then at Ansbachers, recalls how the association began: 'Gareth Hayward, one of the people acting on the Knighton side, felt that it was important that Manchester United ought to be properly represented by a merchant bank and they recommended us. We were brought in specifically to deal with the situation which had arisen as a result of Michael Knighton's involvement in 1989. I wasn't involved right at the very beginning, but we went up to Manchester to help them sort out the situation. Martin's situation was very plain at the time. He had been involved with the business for some considerable time, his family even more. Martin eventually bought his shares. This is not widely known. It is always assumed he just inherited his dominant share, but he didn't. He bought it with real money. For the most part he inherited a very small amount and he recognised, in a way that I think not many other people in the football industry had, what was happening. He realised there was going to be a need to develop the stadium and that there was going to be the need for further money to be spent on the team. They hadn't been particularly successful in recent history. And he saw a general ongoing need for ever-increasing amounts of capital. He knew what his own resources were and that he didn't have it. It was really a question of how he was going to deal with that future.

'I think he's been rather castigated, unfortunately, for entering into that Knighton situation, but he wrongly presumed that Knighton had the necessary money and would be able to provide the collateral support. Halfway through the process he recognised – there was the wonderful moment in a TV interview where you could see the first look of recognition of his mistake going across Martin's face – that he was dealing with a man of straw. Knighton's real intention was to go off and raise the necessary money, having secured the option. He's a very charming and rather whimsical character in lots of ways. For instance, he's reported to have seen flying saucers. As I say, a rather Walter Mittyish type of character.'

But, Edwards having given Knighton the option, the other directors had to cope with the consequences and the picture Edelson paints of what happened is fascinating. There was Knighton asserting he had the money to buy United and there was Edelson, Charlton, Burrows and Midani advised by the canny Watkins, and now the man from Ansbachers, seeking to stop him exercise his option.

'We used to be at Old Trafford every day sitting round gorging ourselves on food – it was mostly sitting, but fighting, trying to find out what Knighton was up to. It was a campaign. It went on for two, three months, I can't remember. The story broke in the summer, so I should think August, September, October. So it must have been almost three months. We used to get calls from waiters to say he [Knighton] was in a restaurant with so-and-so. Somebody said Knighton was meeting whoever in the Midland Hotel. So Bobby and I went and sat outside waiting for him to come out, to see who he was with. I don't remember. In fact, I don't think he did come out. He was in there, but he didn't come out. We were all consciously working to find ways to win.'

There is one moment in the campaign that stands out for Edelson: 'I remember Eddie Shah. Knighton had a meeting with Eddie Shah. Eddie Shah was straight upfront and phoned up and offered help. He phoned once about two o'clock in the morning. I remember going to Eddie Shah's house to get something he wanted to give us [this was a copy of the Robson Rhodes report on Manchester United that Knighton had sent him]. Bobby came with me. Eddie Shah has three of those great big dogs – Dobermans – and when we got there these dogs came from nowhere. Bobby was very good because he's got dogs and he just stood there. I dived back in the car and wouldn't get out!'

However, they got the report. Robson Rhodes denied they had any part in the leak and that only three copies had been sent out. The photocopy that Edelson and Charlton got back from Eddie Shah's house had 'No 3' on it.

This was to be the springboard of a legal action that Edwards now filed on behalf of Manchester United to stop Knighton releasing confidential information. The hearing took place in chambers and the judge granted an interim ruling in Edwards' favour.

It was clear that while Knighton may have the money, the deal could not go ahead. Even if he got United, most of his fellow directors would leave. But he still had the option to buy Edwards' stake and he could still insist on exercising it. Edwards had got United into this, he had to get United out of it.

Edelson says: 'In doing the deal with Knighton, Martin had done what he felt was right at the time. We felt it was the wrong thing. In the end Martin felt that it was the wrong thing. In the end, while we were doing all this fighting, Martin, although he couldn't involve himself in it, was obviously in agreement.'

Edwards met Knighton on the evening of 9 October 1989. This time he did not go alone as he had to his Scottish castle in July. He went with Maurice Watkins and to a more humdrum location, the Novotel, on the M63, just on the outskirts of Manchester.

Edwards sees it as his lucky escape and in the modern history of Manchester United it must rank as one of the most important meetings ever held. Edwards recalls: 'Maurice and I were there and we just said, "Look, Michael, originally you came in here to do this deal with two partners. Those two partners [Thornton and Cohen] have fallen away." Don't forget, even after that, Michael Knighton had been walking round with club accounts and things, trying to get other backers. Then it got rather nasty and we took an injunction out, didn't we, to stop him doing that. So we said, "Look, Michael, the publicity you are getting is horrendous." By then the adverse publicity on him was incessant. It had come out about his background and also that he'd tried to give the financial details to Eddie Shah. Eddie Shah had informed the club and brought the papers back. We said, "Look, Michael, even if you do go ahead with this, it's not going to be in the best interests of you or the club in the long term and all the rest of it, really. Let's tear it up and we suggest you come on the Board as a director." '

By now it seemed there were any number of people willing to help Knighton exercise his option and complete the deal. Jack De Lall (Black Jack), a successful property dealer of Iraqi–Jewish extraction in London, was prepared to finance it and there were others. Knighton says: 'Jack or the other three gentlemen from this city who also promised did not need to finance me, because I had the money in place from the Bank of Scotland, and this is the great myth about this whole story, I had the money to do the deal.'

Knighton, however, did share Edwards' concern about the adverse media publicity: 'We both were extremely concerned about the media Frankenstein that had been created and the enormous amount of misinformation.'

There followed, what Knighton describes, as 'a very civilised discussion and I decided to return the contract to Martin'.

Knighton's dream was over and Martin Edwards had had a very lucky escape. Looking back on that night, ten years after, Edwards provides this summary of this most curious night: 'Yes, I pleaded with him to tear up the contract because his backers fell away. Michael Knighton at one stage had backers, Cohen and Thornton. They pulled out and as soon as they pulled out he had the contract but not the money. As soon as he started hawking it around we took action to stop him using confidential financial information to hawk it round with. At that stage we said if his backers had fallen out, not only is he struggling to raise the money to complete the deal, what about the Stretford End? He needed £20 million to do the deal plus the Stretford End. So at that stage it was in our best interest to tear the contract up. Because had he raised the money he could still have gone ahead with the deal, but what else would he had brought to the party? And he wouldn't have delivered on the Stretford End.'

The agreement at the Novotel was ratified on the night of Tuesday 10 October at the Midland Hotel where, with advisers and the other directors present, Knighton gave up his option and in return went on to the Manchester United Board.

But why did Knighton let Edwards escape? Was he perhaps not ruthless enough? 'The point is, at the end of the day – to answer your question about ruthlessness and why didn't I close the deal – the financial consequences were only a tiny part of the gambit of the thing. They were only a tiny part of what I was about. I knew I was going to have great fun, great enjoyment, and it was a fabulous investment. But the investment was never the sole or key tenet of the project and that's where people get confused. I said to Martin and Maurice Watkins at the Novotel: "I don't need to be chairman. I don't need to own the company. But I do want to make a contribution, because it's under-achieving. It could be the greatest force in Planet Football." Those were my exact words. A fortune in fiscal terms, but if I'm being provided with the opportunity to make a valid contribution to its next few years' development, I'm a very happy man. I let Martin go completely. It was the prize salmon. You can let things go and not know why. The extraordinary thing is I knew precisely why. I was emptying my fishing net and I knew precisely what I was letting swim away.'

Knighton blames the media and in particular Robert Maxwell for forcing him to let the prize salmon go: 'Robert Maxwell already had an illegal over-5% stake in a plc, which he should have declared in the accounts. He had tried to buy the company before in 1983–84 and he'd always coveted the great jewel in the crown. He was the existing chairman of Derby County and his son was chairman of Oxford United and clearly he coveted Manchester United. Through his *Daily Mirror* title in particular and with various journalists – and we all know who they are – he set about creating a media circus, front and back page. Now clearly Martin and I never wanted that. We were not sufficiently naive to know there wouldn't be some publicity, but the circus was quite amazing.'

The media are an easy scapegoat and the dead Maxwell, who no doubt had his own agenda, can be blamed for just about everything. The fact is Knighton's actions, including the ball-juggling act and, in particular, the way he organised the financing of the deal, led to the media circus, irrespective of what Robert Maxwell did. It is hard to argue with Crick and Smith's conclusion that Knighton contributed hugely to his own debacle by his statements and would have benefited from more openness.

Ten years on Knighton now consoles himself with the thought that, while he may have let the prize salmon go, he was the one who saw how rich the fishing rights for Manchester United would become, that in business terms he was ten years ahead of his time: 'I had a blueprint to make Manchester United what I believe to be the greatest sporting leisure company. That is what my blueprint was called and every item in it has come to fruition over the last six-and-a-half years. I valued it at £150 to £200 million. You'll find that quote in the *Financial Times*. The blueprint is a written document. Martin Edwards saw the blueprint and so did the Board of directors, but what I'm saying is that at a time when the club was valued at £20 million, I was saying £150 to £200 million in my blueprint. It was the whole global explosion of soccer, which was inevitable, but not only that. This was the greatest brand name. In 1989 I got absolutely slaughtered for even calling Manchester United a brand! This was the greatest brand in the world, which needed to be exploited, not in a pejorative way, but in a positive way to enable the football club to buy any player in the world and to make it profitable, and only profitable companies are successful. Manchester United, from 1979–89, as my report demonstrated, had never done better financially than break even. When I did the interview in the *Financial Times* with Paul Cheeswright on 12 September 1989, I said to him, "I'm buying potential." He had asked me why I was doing it, because they had never made any money and had just announced losses of £1.2 million. I said, "Because I believe" – and it says so in that report – "that it's £150 million in the next 15 years." I was slaughtered and ridiculed and was called a Walter Mitty figure. "There you are, the man is mad. He's just valued the club at £150 million." I got crucified for this. They were right and I was wrong – I was £450 million out! Even I did not anticipate the fabulous football financial juggernaut that it has become.'

And while he may look back and think about how he let the prize salmon of Manchester United go he would not, he says, trade places with Edwards: 'No, not for all the tea in China. Martin now is hugely wealthy – £200 million cash rich – but I don't begrudge him one single halfpenny, I really don't, not one. I never look back, I'm not made that way, I never have been. I've never chased a shilling in my life, never chased a shilling in my life.'

So, Knighton, having claimed to predict the future but missed out on the riches, now takes pride in the fact that he was a witness to the transformation of United: 'What happened was very simple. I went on to the Board in October and I stayed two-and-a-half years. I saw that football club achieve six major trophies: FA Cup, FA League Cup, European Cup Winner Cup, European Super Cup – even the FA Youth

Cup. We'd been to Wembley three or four times and we'd just missed out on the Championship. But more importantly, we'd turned the company around and put in the seeds of all those items in my blueprint. I claim no credit whatever to say it's all down to Michael Knighton etc., because that falls straight into the hands of those people that just think I'm some kind of raging egomaniac. What I do say is that Old Trafford on that sunny August afternoon was the new horizon and was the catalyst that made everything that happened subsequently happen. I was the catalyst. That's absolutely right. I saw it turn around, all the ingredients put in place from my blueprint, I saw the flotation through and I signed some of the most important minutes for that flotation – Maurice, myself and Martin. I remember them in Rotterdam when we had a Board meeting – we were there for the Cup Winners Cup – and we had a Board meeting in the hotel. It was a very important Board meeting to consolidate the way forward. That was the vision, and they were sharing the vision, and were just beginning to see the wood for the trees, of course.'

However, not everybody at Manchester United echoes that view.

Knighton brushes this aside, saying, 'They wouldn't because there were a lot of machinations at the time. Edelson wouldn't echo it, for instance. Edelson was trying to buy it at the same time. Although we've always been perfectly civil to each other. Edelson was with Nigel Burroughs and Bobby Charlton trying to buy it. They were fuming, livid, of course they were. I'd come on the blind side from nowhere. I have signed some of the most important boardroom minutes of that football club's history and I'm extremely proud of that. That was my contribution. I walked into Old Trafford with a huge smile on my face, looking forward to it. Just under three years later I walked out with a huge smile on my face. In 1992, after the season had finished. I stayed on for a year after the flotation. I never even put myself forward to go on the plc, unlike others on that Board who did and didn't get on. All I'm saying is that I didn't put myself forward. Certain details of this whole affair are only known to Martin and myself. Some of the essential points in the whole of this piece of the history of this great institution, many of the misnomers and misinterpretations of what was going on, were in the red tops and have gone down in history, unfortunately, as fact, instead of the pure fiction which is what they were, and are. Martin and I never had a cross word, *ever*.'

Edwards would agree with that but that is about all he would agree with. He does not share the view that Knighton was the catalyst for change. Ask him if the subsequent success of Manchester United is due to the Knighton plan to reinvent Manchester United, Edwards responds: 'In terms of what? I quite like Michael and I get on very well with him, but I don't believe any of the ideas Michael had were adopted by this club. I mean, you know, Michael was very quiet, particularly when all that fell through. He used to come to the Board meetings and he'd sit there and not say too much. I wouldn't have thought anything we'd done since was as a result of Michael Knighton. I'm saying it in the nicest possible way because I don't want to offend him or whatever, but I don't think it's just me speaking like that. I think if you speak to any other member of the Board, they'd say the same thing. Michael is a dreamer. I know he claims he saw the vision. A lot of people saw the vision.'

Yet there is one vision whose memory Knighton will carry and which still consoles him. On the very first day, as he had lunch with Edwards at Old Trafford and tucked into his Dover sole, he had looked out at the old Stretford End and promised to redevelop it, a promise that attracted Edwards. Now, 'on the very last day as I left that football club as a director, the JCBs and bulldozers were driving in to pull the Stretford End down to rebuild it'.

There is something of the little boy in the way Knighton tells the story and it is an appropriate conclusion to what must still be the strangest story in the history of the club.

9

THE STRUGGLE TO FLOAT

The recent history of Manchester United could have been vastly different if in 1989 the then managers of Granada listened to one of their executives, Paul Docherty, the son of a former Manchester City player.

Docherty, then head of sport at Granada, got a tip-off in the summer of 1989 that Manchester United was to be sold. He took a camera crew down to Old Trafford and got there as Edwards was lunching with Knighton. Nobody knew who Knighton was and Docherty went up to several people asking 'are you the gentlemen buying United?' He got a dismissive reaction but when the news of the Knighton bid emerged, he tried to get his bosses at Granada to buy Manchester United. The Premier League, or Super League as it was then called, was a gleam in only a few eyes. Television had not really begun to pay huge sums of money for football and, for Docherty, it seemed to make perfect sense for Granada, very much a Manchester company, to buy its local football club. Such links between local business and football were hardly unknown. Just down the road the local brewers at Oldham held a majority stake there. But although David Plowright, the chief executive was keen, the board was not. United did not even know of this attempt within Granada to buy the club.

So with the Knighton fiasco now behind it, Manchester United had to find some other means to get money. Ansbachers, having fought off Knighton, now began to turn to the issue of what United could do next. Edelson says: 'Once the deal with Knighton was done, when he finished, it was almost as though United was "in play", in stock-exchange terms, and somebody would come along. Ansbachers had been appointed, were there, and the conversations obviously went several ways as to what to do. Ultimately, it became obvious that the float was the best way forward.'

It was at this stage that Glenn Cooper got involved. Cooper was a vastly experienced City man, having started in 1963, the very year Louis Edwards bought control of Manchester United. He had worked for a whole host of blue-chip City stockbrokers, including Greiveson Grant, which would become Kleinworth Benson Greiveson Grant, the firm that had advised the Edwards on the rights issue. He also had experience of the North American investment scene, having worked at Hoare Govett as partner in charge of the firm's North American development, then for the American Investment bank Oppenheimer & Co. and for a short while at EF Hutton. But he had no interest in football and had not really followed the game.

'I'd certainly not been a regular watcher of football until I came into contact with Manchester United in 1990,' says Cooper. Even now, a decade later, and after innumerable visits to the Manchester United boardroom, he can find the passion in the Manchester United box when the news of the defeat of Manchester City comes through quite bewildering.

His first visit to Old Trafford came sometime in early 1990. 'The Knighton thing had disappeared but the issues, however, had not disappeared. There was still going to be the need under the new Football Supporters Act, which had not then been passed but was at the Report Stage then, for the whole ground to be seated and covered. This would require a lot of money, including the redevelopment of the Stretford End. So, although Michael Knighton had gone away, the important issues which had got him involved hadn't. So the real question was how were they going to proceed. As a result of it, I was invited to a Manchester United Board meeting – in 1990 – and asked whether I thought a flotation was possible.'

The Board was Knighton, Edwards, Watkins, Midani, Edelson, Les Olive, Bobby Charlton and Nigel Burrows. That 1989–90 season had been a dreadful one for Manchester United. Alex Ferguson had been there for almost three years, United had got knocked out of the League Cup losing at home to Tottenham 3–0, lost league matches including an awful 5–1 defeat at Maine Road at the hands of Manchester City. United faced the prospect of relegation and only an FA Cup run which saw it win the Cup after a replay kept Ferguson in the job.

Cooper met the Board just before United's FA Cup run began. The meeting, recalls Cooper, was in the old, small, windowless boardroom, which is now a suite, and as they discussed flotation they went round the table and then finally came to Cooper. All the directors looked at him as Edwards asked him: Can we float Manchester United?

'I hesitated for a long time before I gave an answer and then I said just one word: "Just". I thought it was just possible. I was not very confident and I was not very sure it would not all be a ghastly mistake.'

Cooper's doubts about flotation were based on how the City had taken to the only other major football club that had floated: Tottenham. (By the time Manchester United floated, Millwall was also on the stock market, but it was not in Tottenham's or United's league.) The City and the financial press took a very dim view of football clubs on the stock market. Tottenham had been on the stock market since 1983 and by the time Cooper was answering Edwards' question, Tottenham was in serious financial trouble. Ironically the problems of the West Stand had brought Scholar to Tottenham; now the costs of rebuilding the East Stand made a bad financial position dire. By 1989 Tottenham was casting round for a way to raise money, either through a rights issue or some other means, and not long after Cooper went up to meet the Manchester United Board, Tottenham were in such a parlous state that Irving Scholar had to borrow £1.1 million from Robert Maxwell to pay for the balance of the transfer money owed on Gary Lineker to Barcelona, otherwise Lineker would have had to go back to Barcelona. The disclosure of this loan at the start of the 1990–91 season would trigger a chain of reactions that eventually contributed to the departure of Scholar from Tottenham and the sale of the club the following year to Alan Sugar and Terry Venables.

Cooper says: 'At that stage not many City institutions had invested in Spurs. They shied away from football. There was a very substantial body of opinion that said football clubs should not be on the stock market; that they were fundamentally not capable of being commercial and they had no place on the market. The example was given of Spurs, who had made a complete Horlicks of it and then gone over budget on the one hand on their stadium and, on the other, they'd diversified into highly unprofitable activities. They had practically bankrupted themselves. On top of which they behaved in a way which was against the stock-exchange rules and, to make the whole thing worse, Gascoigne broke his leg in the Cup Final, allowing people to say, "There you are. Your most valuable business assets run around on the field and break their legs." So, if you throw all that together, there's a natural antipathy; together with the living example of Spurs, it was a very, very negative environment. In one way or the other financial journalists and institutions had this opinion. It was a fairly widely held opinion. If you read the press at the time it was stridently against clubs floating.'

Cooper's scepticism about flotation was shared by Edwards.

But there were hawks on the Board who wanted to float. During the Knighton saga, both Burrows and Midani had called for flotation. Midani had said, 'Give Manchester United back to its people. I believe it should be owned by a number of shareholders and solid institutions so that its future is safe for eternity.' Midani, who had himself held abortive talks with Edwards about buying him out, had also promised that the club would be floated if he got control.

But Edwards who, alone among the directors had experience of being involved in a public company (albeit his father's Louis Edwards & Co), was not convinced. 'I was the last person to be convinced we should float. There was strong support in that Board to float and I warned if you float this will no longer be a private company; you won't be able to do everything you want. You will have to look after shareholders' interest and pay dividends. And although it will give us what we want in building the Stretford End, there will be restraints about us in the future. Everybody was aware of that. But that was the decision the Board made in 1991.'

Edwards was well aware that, by floating, he could finally clear his debts: 'Don't forget in 1991 I had heavy debts. I had to pay those off. They were certainly seven figures. I had carried the debt since 1978. Indeed my house was in debt to the bank. I was not prepared to carry on for the rest of my life being in debt to the bank. We had a situation where I was the majority shareholder, holding 50%, but how could I liquidate my position? The choice was, instead of selling to an individual go public. Plus the fact that we also wanted to raise money to build the Stretford End.'

In recent years it has become fashionable to take credit for Manchester United floating. Indeed, many have claimed credit. Cooper says: 'Forget who was the author of it or whether there was an author or not. The fact of the matter is for a private business under those circumstances, flotation was an option that had to be considered. Page one of the corporate finance handbook. It's not an act of intuitive genius to reach the conclusion that they ought to consider flotation. The question was, could it be done?'

Cooper set about trying to find out. He now began to prepare for what he calls the well-worn path of preparing for a flotation. 'There's quite a lot to do. First of all we had to create a takeover of the old Manchester United Football Club by a new plc, because the FA has some rather odious rules in the Memorandum of Articles of Association of a football club which aren't accepted on the stock exchange. One of them being, you can't pay dividends. The other is that, in the event of a liquidation, any surplus goes to the players' pension funds – things which were perfectly understandable in the context of a private football club, but not acceptable to a plc.'

So just as Tottenham had done, an off-the-shelf company was bought and a plc created with the football club, which continued to exist with its own Board, becoming a wholly owned subsidiary of this newly created plc.

A company called Voteasset Public Limited, which had been formed on 21 December 1990, was bought off the shelf, and on 25 January 1991, its name was changed to Manchester United plc. The plc's first task was to acquire all the shares of the Manchester United football club. This was done on 27 February 1991 when the company recommended a share-for-share exchange for the whole of the issued share capital of the club. On 22 March 1991 the share-for-share exchange was declared unconditional and during the period to 10 May 1991, the company acquired all the issued share capital of the football club.

In many ways the structural thing of creating a new plc was a fairly standard procedure; more problematic was to get the Board and the management of Manchester United right so that the company could be taken to the stock market. 'The structural hurdle of creating the new company was not a huge hurdle, there were all the other hurdles of a flotation. You've got to have an accountants' report to make sure that you are able to produce a prospectus which is accurate in all respects. You've got to put a Board together which is going to be acceptable in name and in form. That meant a non-executive chairman and a proper finance director and more non-executives than executives on the Board. In a funny way, one of the things I'm quite proud about is the fact that this was done all prior to Cadbury and Greenbury [rules which now determine what sort of directors, particularly non-executive directors, a public company should have] and that the Board required no changes once these rules were introduced, in order to comply with them.'

Roland Smith was brought in as non-executive chairman. Midani, who had 14% of the shares, went on to the plc Board and so did Maurice Watkins. But Edelson, Burrows, Knighton, Bobby Charlton and Les Olive did not make the plc Board, although they all stayed on the football club Board. The people who went on to the plc Board (as elected immediately prior to the flotation) were Roland Smith (chairman), Martin Edwards (chief executive), Robin Launders (finance director – executive), Midani (non-executive) and Maurice Watkins (non-executive).

The directors of United at this stage had intimate business links with the club, which was not unusual for a small private company. Watkins' firm, James Chapman, was United's solicitors and in 1991 received £40,000 in legal fees. Watkins' firm also received a fee for the share-for-share exchange which saw the football club become a wholly owned subsidiary of the plc and for its services in connection with the offer. Charlton was a director and shareholder of Halba Travel Ltd, which in 1991 supplied United with rail and air tickets worth £15,000. Charlton, Edelson and Burrows were all linked in business, being directors of Conrad Continental plc, where Midani had an 11.9% stake. In January 1989 Edelson's textile firm, M Edelson, had gone into receivership and Mike Edelson became executive director of Conrad Continental, then a clothing company chaired by Lord Barnett. At the time of the float, Conrad supplied goods and services to United to the value of £100,000. A subsidiary of Conrad also acted as an agent for two United first-team players in their off-field activities. United, in turn, supplied goods and services and received royalties from Conrad on normal commercial terms to the tune of £60,000.

With Ansbachers the sponsors of the issue, Cooper was the one-man selection committee who had to make the choice and he did not find it easy: 'It was a source of difficulty to select the plc Board. We had to construct a Board to meet the City criterion. There was a lot of manoeuvring from the existing Board of the football club. None of the directors were appropriate to be a non-executive chairman of a public company. I had discussions with Martin and he said I need Maurice Watkins. He had the legal background and was important and essential to the functioning of Manchester United. So he came on the plc Board. Midani, who had a substantial stake, came on the plc Board. That left Edelson, Burrows, Knighton, Charlton and Les Olive. Les Olive was not a contender. Knighton was never a contender and I told him so. I told him, "I don't think you are suitable for the plc Board." He asked whether as an indulgence he could remain on the football club Board through the flotation process and the Board agreed.'

As we have seen, Knighton now consoles himself with the thought that he made an important contribution in the process leading up to the float and talks of a vital Board meeting in Rotterdam during the Cup Winners Cup Final. Cooper says, 'I wasn't at that Board meeting, and since Ansbachers as sponsors were bringing United to the market, it could not have been a very important Board meeting. The only thing I remember about Knighton at Board meetings was he was always taking notes. Whenever I looked over my shoulder I could see him writing, "Glenn Cooper says". I believe he was writing a book; I have not seen it; it should be interesting.'

Edelson and Burrows were also very keen to be on the plc Board. Cooper could not select them: 'With the Tottenham experience, I had to construct the Board that had credibility in the City. Edelson lobbied me hard, really out of an inexperienced belief that he was important. Charlton was the most grumpy. He threatened to resign at one point if he did not go on the plc Board. He realised later that he was much better off sitting where he was on the football club Board rather than on the plc Board. But he didn't feel that at that time.'

The most important decision was that of chairman. Tottenham's troubles were by now well known and Cooper needed a name as chairman who would inspire confidence in the City. Edwards suggested Roland Smith and it was the ideal name. 'Martin came up with Roland Smith's name after I suggested we needed a non-executive chairman who had some standing in the City. Roland was ideal. The City knew him well, he was a Manchester United supporter, a Mancunian and it was very important that Martin as chief executive and Roland as chairman had confidence in each other. He was an old friend of the Edwards family.'

The decision not to put Burrows on the plc Board by Cooper proved prescient. Nigel Burrows had been the co-founder and director of Analysis Financial Services of Harrogate, which was then taken over by the British & Commonwealth Group, a company that subsequently failed and with which Burrows had a service contract. By the time of the float, Burrows was a director of a company called Independent Financial Group plc, the holding company of IFG Financial Services Ltd. This administered United's staff pension scheme and insurances. IFG did not receive a fee but, as is normal in the insurance industry, received a commission from the insurance companies with which it placed United's business.

Edwards came into contact with him as a member of United's executive suite and patron of the club's luncheon club. According to Crick and Smith, the two men had been negotiating a deal for Burrows to buy United shares since 1987. Crick and Smith say that Burrows eventually bought the shares that were originally meant to be sold to Oscar Goldstein, who worked for accountants Price Waterhouse and advised both United and Edwards. At one stage there was talk of Goldstein becoming secretary after Les Olive; but this came to nothing. In September 1985 Goldstein pleaded guilty in a Manchester court to falsifying Inland Revenue forms which brought him an £11,000 fine and expulsion from the Institute of Chartered Accountants. Edwards had to buy Goldstein's shares back and these were then sold to Burrows. Burrows, who was then 34, described himself as a former Stretford Ender and his election to the Board as a 'dream come true'. Edelson says: 'Nigel Burrows was a situation where Martin wanted to dispose of some of his shares. Nigel Burrows was a big supporter, apparently wealthy, and he had a good business in the pensions fund business. He was a really big supporter. He'd spoken to Martin on a number of occasions, just as a supporter, and made suggestions. So Martin agreed some deal and proposed that he should come on the Board.'

Burrows was the one who had felt most unhappy about the Knighton deal, having learnt about it quite accidentally while the team were on tour in Japan. At the breakfast table he overhead a discussion between Watkins and Edwards about Susan Edwards buying a house in the Lake District for a million. Burrows asked Edwards whether he intended to sell and was told in his hotel room at four the next morning but agreed to keep it confidential.

At the time of the float Burrows had 4% in United through IFG. However, sometime after the float, like Goldstein, Burrows ran into trouble with the law. He was jailed and made bankrupt. His shares in United were taken control of by his bank and sold and ended up with the BBC pension fund.

Cooper also had to make sure that the directors sold some of their shares. Edwards sold the biggest chunk as he brought down his stake from just over 50% to 27.8%. His sale of 1,671,882 shares at the offer price of 385p brought him £6.445 million. Midani sold 283,690 on his own and 143,381 of his company Philen Establishment; a total of 427,071, which gave him £1.644 million, leaving him with 7.1% of the floated company. Watkins sold 175,725, which gave him £676,541 and a stake in United of 2.9%.

Edelson sold various chunks: 39,719 in his own name, which gave him £152,918; Edelson and Kanas sold 20,000 which gave them £77,000; and Edelson, Field, Lyons and Burks sold 25,000 which brought in £96,250. Burrows, who held shares through a company called TA Le Sueur and D de Ste Croix, sold 238,007 which gave him £916,327.

Manchester United directors now had a ready outlet for their shares. For Edwards this was very sweet. Finally, after many fruitless years and one humiliating experience with Knighton, he had found the ideal route. The float was going to raise the £7 million necessary to rebuild the Stretford End and he could sell some of his shares, pay off his bank manager, make money, yet retain control. He had at last squared the circle no previous football club chairman had quite managed: build a stand, sell personal shares, make some money and still be in control.

One of Cooper's major tasks was to find a finance director for the new stock-market company. Manchester United had been going for very nearly a century but, says Cooper, 'there wasn't a financial director as such. A secretary did the books. There was a whole department, but there was no financial director in the sense a public company on the stock market would need.'

Broadbeck were appointed as headhunters and some 40 people applied from whom Robin Launders was chosen. He came from Reg Vardy, the car distribution firm in the north: 'I believe Robin had a combination of skills that was very attractive to the Board at the time. Robin Launders was a chartered accountant. He had also qualified as an engineer and that was one of the reasons he was hired for the flotation. They were going into a major construction phase – we didn't realise it at the time that probably the Stretford End construction phase would lead on to other construction work – so it was even bigger than they thought at the time. But nonetheless they were going to be building the Stretford End and this needed handling. Bearing in mind, the only prior history of a publicly quoted football club doing development of its ground was Tottenham and they had a disaster, going five times over budget and four times over time. The City in my view – and it was to some extent my call – took the view that there were certain things that were wrong with the way football clubs were run. One was that they were run in a "spivvy" way and in an irresponsible manner, which called for a proper, credible Board to be put in place. They also felt that they were financially irresponsible, which meant that we had to put on the Board a proper plc-style finance director. Robin had both the project engineering skills and the finance skills.'

But as fellow United Board members were to discover, Launders did not always have the man-management skills that would endear him to his colleagues. However, at this stage in the flotation, any problems were far into the future and his arrival marked the final modernisation of Manchester United. It gave the right impression to the City that was looking for reassurance that Manchester United on the stock market would behave in a responsible financial way.

Launders did this partly through an innovation called the Transfer Fee Reserve Account. The prospectus said: 'At the discretion of the directors this reserve may be increased both from profits after taxation arising from Cup success and from transfer fee receipts, and may be used to the extent available, to offset the effect of transfer fee payments on reported profits in any particular year.'

It was pure accounting fiction. It was created to reassure the City that Manchester United would not use up the money it made to splash out on players and that the dividend policy would be maintained. In fact over the years the reserve was never used, but its existence would feed any number of stories of how much Ferguson had in the kitty to spend on players when the truth was the figure in the reserve was a pure accounting entry. It never represented hard cash and never determined United's ability to deal in the transfer market.

But if getting a Board together that would please the City was not easy, Cooper had a torrid time trying to get a stockbroker to handle the issue: 'I had great difficulty persuading a broker to get involved. I was going round the City pulling strings to get myself a broker. I must have seen six or seven brokers. BZW, Kleinwort Benson, firms like that. I just went round talking to anybody I could. I'm pretty sure it was at least six who turned it down. They were influenced by what had happened to Tottenham. They felt it was going to be very difficult to get it away. They thought sentiment was against football clubs and they didn't want to get involved. Finally I got Smith New Court and I think they were persuaded it was a good idea. It took me about seven weeks to find a broker.'

The next big problem for Cooper was convincing the institutions that it was worth investing in Manchester United: 'Institutions were taken round. There would have been quite a number of them. They were primarily, of course, taken round by the broker, Richard Osmond. I remember Commercial Union were there and Philips & Drew. Richard died, tragically early, I'm afraid.'

Before the institutions went to Old Trafford, they had been fairly dubious about investing. But, says Cooper, 'the moment you got an institution up to Old Trafford and they saw and understood the scale and nature of the business, they turned from being dubious to being quite enthusiastic.'

The only City people Cooper did not have to persuade, and who were all too eager for the float and queuing up outside his door, were the financial PRs. 'It was the one desirable part of the float. In all other respects I had great difficulty with that float. The only difficulty I didn't have was getting a financial PR firm. It showed the PR business was different. Everybody wanted to do it. I think we short-listed six or seven. Brunswick made the best overall presentation, the most convincing.'

Cooper knew the Brunswick founder and main man Alan Parker very well, although the man who handled the account was John Bick, which was ironical. Bick, who still handles the account but has set up his own firm now, is a committed Tottenham fan.

Brunswick's task was not easy. Cooper says: 'It was not going to be an easy assignment and they did a pretty good job. You can't change press view, you can only make sure that it is properly informed as it's required to be. It was very difficult because you had for the first time the crossover between sports journalists and City journalists. The sports journalists were writing for the first time about City matters and the City journalists were writing for the first time about sporting matters. By and large they both made a complete cock-up of it. To some extent we have a little of that still. We still get a lot of very strident sports writers writing about the financial aspects of the business and a lot of rubbish being written by financial journalists about the sport part of the business. It's something we still suffer from. But at the time it was very difficult because there was very little research. Sports journalists had never written about the business aspects of sport or sports rights. And to think now how it has burgeoned.'

Cooper had valued the company at £42 million, £22 million more than Knighton was prepared to pay two years earlier. 'I valued it the same way I value football businesses today. I took core earnings – that's to say what they received from their 40-odd League games (20 matches at home) together with two rounds of each Cup [FA and League]: the core repeatable earnings, pre-transfer. It included no transfer deals. It included sponsorship, merchandising and other commercial income. This core earning came to £4 million, and I then multiplied it by the multiple on the leisure index, which at that time was eleven.' This figure was then discounted to reach £42 million.

Cooper was ready to float in early May 1991, but he decided to wait. Ferguson, having won his first trophy in 1990 after three years at Old

Trafford, was now going for his second. In the 1990–91 season, English clubs had been readmitted to Europe after a gap of five years, and Manchester United were now in the Cup Winners Cup Final. This was always the easiest of the three European competitions to win – but United faced Barcelona and it looked tough.

Cooper decided to wait until the end of the Final to float. 'We decided to hang on. It was my decision. I did it on the basis that if we won the Cup Winners Cup it might help and it wouldn't hurt if we didn't. We delayed the flotation as a gamble. I think in the event these things are always marginal. There's no way of knowing. As you know, they won the Cup Winners Cup in 1991.'

Whether victory in Rotterdam helped with the City is impossible to say. It did, however, show the fine line Cooper had to tread as he brought United to the market and he accepts that in the weeks leading up to the float there were moments of nervousness.

'A flotation is a very long drawn-out process and always pretty torrid affairs. We were having meetings with the Board probably once or twice a week. There was no major crisis. Not really. The issues were always pretty much the same and you always have difficulties when it comes to sign the underwriting element, because you need warranties from the directors and they are always difficult. You are asking directors to assure you of many things and it takes time to get them.'

Manchester United beat Barcelona on 15 May 1991. Flotation day was fixed for 10 June 1991, the day the first dealings in Manchester United shares would take place on the stock market. At two that morning, Cooper and Edwards were driven down from Manchester to Ansbachers headquarters in Mitre Square in the City. 'We had the final negotiations in Manchester, the closing and signing documents, underwriting agreements. We did that in Manchester and Martin and I were driven down. We left at two in the morning and got to my offices at sort of five, maybe a bit later, and there were press conferences and all of that for much of the day. That's when the process started.'

Old Trafford was abuzz with this new dawn. But one man in Old Trafford did not share the excitement – that man was Alex Ferguson. Cooper says: 'I don't think he was particularly interested in the process. He was always around and about but I don't think we had any meetings with him directly, no. I think he found the process a bit alien. Millions of meetings were taking place and so they weren't always sitting round a board table in jackets. They were sleeves rolled up, smoke-filled rooms, and people wandering in and out. Not properly delineated meetings with agendas and beginnings and endings. So Alex was wandering in and out of the boardroom from time to time and we ran into him in the corridors, in restaurants, but I don't recall any occasion when he actually sat at a meeting. There would have been an occasion when I, or a member of my team, explained to all the senior people who hadn't been greatly involved at boardroom level what was going on; what it meant for them; what their rights were; how to apply for shares and so on. We did a certain amount of that, particularly towards the end, and Alex would have been part of that. But he did not show any particular interest.'

Ferguson's indifference was shared by most of the fans.

The share issue was divided between an institutional placement and an open offer to the public, which it was hoped would be supporters of the club. Of the 4.675 million shares offered, 2.077 million were offered in a placing to the institutions, and slightly more, 2.597 million, to the public. Cooper says: 'The institutional quota was fully placed and the public offering was the one that was not completely taken up. Contrary to what most people think, football fans or supporters are not great buyers of shares, not even of their own club. The public not taking it all up meant there was about 5–6% left with the underwriters.'

Cooper insists the issue was not a flop: 'But a lot of the shares were left with the institutions. As an underwriter, we had to swallow the shortfall on public subscription, which we did, because that's what we are paid for.' Ansbachers had charged £300,000 for the flotation and was now left with some 3% of Manchester United.

That would not have mattered had Ansbachers not decided that it was not worth holding on to Manchester United. 'When Henry Ansbacher got taken over by the South Africans, they took the view that the near 3% on the books in London wasn't a very promising investment and sold it only for a profit of £2–3 million. I think if they'd kept it, which is what I wanted to do, they would have made a good deal of money.'

But in the week following 10 June 1991, it would have required rare courage to hold on to Manchester United shares. The share issue might not have been a flop, but the days after that, the share price was a disaster. It seemed all the old fears of Tottenham were being revived if anything in an even more alarming way. And this was because of the actions of that bugbear of Manchester United, the Maxwells.

Crick and Smith, writing their book in 1989, had doubted that the Maxwells had a holding. But they did. They had bought shares years before the float which gave them 505,000 shares, a 4.25% stake in the new plc. And it was a stake that had worried Cooper.

'Prior to the flotation, it must have been in early 1991, I had a conversation with Kevin Maxwell, when I asked him what the Maxwells' intentions were in respect of that holding. He said the Maxwell family was a friend of Manchester United and intended to hold on to the shares and would prove to be no embarrassment on the flotation. In the event the Maxwells dumped the shares on the market within a day or two, and the price fell straight away. I did not want him to sell in the aftermarket. Absolutely not. If I'd thought then the Maxwells would have been a seller in the aftermarket, I would have tied it up at the time. I'd either have placed them or taken them out during the course of the flotation or obliged them to sign a standstill. That is to agree not to sell. The last thing in the world you want is a loose-cannon shareholder in the aftermarket. That's what actually knocked the price down.' It has to be noted of course, that it was Robert Maxwell who had an iron grip over the family and its assets at this time, and it is very probable it was his decision, and his alone, to dump the shares.

On 10 June 1991 the share price was £3.85. The moment Kevin Maxwell sold, the price dropped like a stone and within a week it was down to £2.60. So having been floated at £42 million, Manchester United was suddenly worth £26 million.

However, even as the Manchester United Board watched this fall in frustration, there was a man from Tottenham who, as chance would have it, was on his way to Old Trafford to help it recover its share price and its stock-market standing.

10

THE MAN FROM TOTTENHAM

In the modern history of Manchester United many people can lay claim to have turned the club around, from a club with a vast following but not much money to what is now called a corporate monster. But one man who has more reason than most to make that claim is Edward Freedman. And like all such stories his association with Old Trafford began unusually. Freedman went to Old Trafford to try to get business for another club and ended up joining Manchester United and driving the marketing juggernaut United has become.

In June 1992, when Edward Freedman first visited Old Trafford, he was in charge of merchandising at Tottenham, a club which seemed the natural home for him.

Freedman had been educated in London at a grammar school in Hendon. After he left school he went to the Retail College of Distribution in Charing Cross Road and from there he trained in a company which was then called Times Furnishing, now part of the GUS group. 'I thought at the time retailing for clothing needed to be changed. I thought what was needed was a supermarket style of presenting the product. I was probably the first person to bring it to England and we started and built up a chain of shops. What was needed was a retail environment which was more a supermarket type of retailing. This was about 1965. We built up a chain of retail shops and then sold them. Then we started again.'

Growing up in North London in the 1950s he supported Spurs as a kid and had been going to the ground ever since he was a little boy. However, football support in those days was not quite the intensely tribal thing it has since become. One week he would go to Tottenham and another week to Arsenal. His cousin was an Arsenal supporter so they went on alternate weekends. The result was, as Tottenham were building up their greatest side, the double team, he saw every home match and quite a few of the away ones.

Freedman's move into football happened in the 1980s when he came into contact with Irving Scholar. 'I had a friend, Jan Stoord, who was an accredited football agent in Belgium. He telephoned me just after the Mexico World Cup in 1986. He said that David Pleat [then Tottenham manager] had been looking at one of the players, Nico Classen, and asked me if I knew Irving. I said I did, which was not quite true. I knew of him, of course, but I didn't know him personally then. I contacted Irving and he said he was interested in the player. There were protracted negotiations, and during them, Irving had found out quite a lot about me and that my knowledge was in the retail area and in products and producing. He asked me to have a look at the Tottenham shop – and also the products they were selling. I didn't get a very good impression of what the Tottenham shop was doing. I started doing some work with Irving and Irving asked me if I would go full-time at Tottenham, because I was in between two camps. I thought, well, football is something I love and I saw a big opportunity for Tottenham in marketing. So I went and joined them.'

Freedman's arrival revolutionised Tottenham's marketing and it seemed the partnership would work well. But in the summer of 1991, as a result of other financial pressures, Scholar sold Tottenham and the club was taken over by Alan Sugar and Terry Venables. Venables, who had been a player and manager at Tottenham, had always wanted to own his football club and had advanced the argument that football people knew best how to run football clubs. He had said that he could do the job of running a football club better than people like Ken Bates or Ron Noades or Doug Ellis. This was now his great moment to prove his theory. Although it was Sugar's wealth which made the takeover possible, and the money brought by the sale of Gascoigne to Lazio helped turn Tottenham round, Venables did buy a stake and he was seen as the senior partner in this unique partnership between the man of football and the man of money. His arrival was widely welcomed as the man of football at last getting into the boardroom and the *Times* hailed Venables as the Renaissance man of football, the Leonardo da Vinci capable of doing everything and anything.

Venables became chief executive of Tottenham Hotspur plc and brought with him as his financial adviser a man called Eddie Ashby. Freedman soon found that the Venables regime had a rotten core. He could not work with Venables and, in particular, Ashby who, despite being a bankrupt, had major executive responsibility at Tottenham under Venables. Ashby's business record prior to joining Tottenham as Venables' right-hand man showed that he had been a director of 43 companies, 16 of which were in receiverships, eight in liquidation and 15 were struck off. By 1993, Venables' relations with Sugar were at breaking point due to his refusal to sack Ashby and other disagreements. In May 1993, what had been seen as the dream team of Sugar and Venables, dissolved into a bitter court battle as Sugar sacked Venables amidst much acrimony.

In 1995 the Department of Trade and Industry brought a criminal action against Ashby for his role at Tottenham and another Venables company called Scribes West, a drinking club in Knightsbridge. The DTI, after a long investigation, had found he had violated bankruptcy laws. Ashby had already been disqualified from acting as a director as a result of a previous DTI legal action (arising from his business practices before Venables brought him to Tottenham) with the judge warning that business needed to be protected from him. In October 1997, after a two-month hearing before a jury in the Crown Courts, he was jailed with the judge accusing him of perjuring himself during his evidence. He served three months in jail. Following two BBC *Panorama* progammes officials at the DTI investigated Venables' activities at Tottenham, Scribes West and Edenote, another Venables company, decided to bring a civil case against him, the charges centring round his stewardship at Tottenham, the way he had financed his purchase of the stake, and his activities at Scribes West and Edenote. On 14 January 1998 he was disqualified for seven years from acting as a company director, having admitted to 19 charges of various wrongdoings, which amounted to serious breaches of his obligations and responsibilities as a director. He also agreed to pay the DTI's legal costs estimated to be £500,000.

All this was in the future and although in June 1992, when Freedman went up to Old Trafford, Ashby's and Venables' wrongdoings were not known, despite his unhappiness at Tottenham he had no immediate plans to leave. However, his visit to Old Trafford was to turn out very differently from the one he had imagined when he set off from London; it was to dramatically change Manchester United and Freedman's life. Freedman recalls the moment he went up to Old Trafford: 'Martin Edwards had known about me through Irving and what I'd done at Tottenham. At the time Tottenham were turning over more money through merchandise than Manchester United – by a long way. I would say Tottenham were turning over 50% more than Manchester United at the time. I knew the Manchester United shop wasn't doing very well.

So I went up to see it. I knew they were underperforming. I had an idea we at Tottenham could sell our expertise to other clubs and show them how to be as successful as Tottenham. We were the best in the field and I went up there to have a look. I went to see Danny McGregor, the commercial manager at the time, and gave a presentation in his office.'

As Freedman was making the presentation, Martin Edwards came in and listened for a while, and before Freedman had finished, Edwards said to Freedman: 'Edward, is it possible for you to come up to my office and have a chat with me before you leave?'

When Freedman went to his office he found that Martin Edwards had been so impressed by what he was saying he wanted him to leave Tottenham and come and work full time for Manchester United. Freedman was amazed: 'I was shocked because I'd never worked outside London before. At first I said no and he suggested another meeting. I talked it over with my wife and she said, "You're unhappy at Tottenham and even though it will be difficult, I think you should do it."'

Martin Edwards already knew Freedman, having met him once or twice when he had visited Irving Scholar: 'I'd been to Irving's office a couple of times and met Edward. When Edward came to see Danny McGregor, our commercial manager, what he wanted to do was to open some football franchises within stores. I asked him to join Manchester United because I saw Edward as someone who could drive the merchandising. At the time, of course, he was with Tottenham – although he was unhappy – and he said he would think about it.'

Martin Edwards' decision to appoint Freedman was not quite as much off-the-cuff as this may make it appear. For almost six months before Freedman came to Old Trafford he had been mulling over bringing someone in to do something about United's marketing and, ironically given what would happen between Kenyon and Edwards, it was Kenyon, then in Umbro, who had first suggested Freedman's name.

'In 1990, when I was with Umbro, we were in talks with Manchester United with regard to their new kit contract, which started in 1992. At that stage, kit sales from Manchester United were round about £8 million a year, that is to say sale of replica kits in 1991 were about £8 million. One of the things I talked to Martin Edwards about when we were making the pitch was that the product was not distributed well enough. You could not get it in Scotland and parts of the southeast. United was a nationally known club; probably they and

Liverpool were the two clubs that had national appeal. So we felt there were two issues really: (1) to get national distribution initially and (2) for the club itself to generate significantly more sales than they were currently generating. That was the platform of Umbro's pitch to United.

'During the course of the negotiations I went to Old Trafford where I had several meetings with Martin. I'd met him before, but I really got to know him through the negotiations and made this point to him.'

The deal was done in Christmas 1991 with United deciding to switch from Adidas to Umbro. Some time after that Martin Edwards rang Kenyon and said, 'We've taken on board your views regarding a bigger merchandising set-up.' United had decided to look for someone to run the new set-up and Edwards asked Kenyon who he would suggest. 'I put forward Edward Freedman. We at Umbro had dealt with Tottenham and I had got to know Freedman.'

Freedman, of course, was unaware of all this when he arrived that day at Old Trafford looking for business. But now that Edwards had made his play it did not take long for Freedman to be persuaded that it made sense to leave his beloved Tottenham for Manchester United. Life with Venables and Ashby was getting increasingly difficult and it also helped that, 'Manchester United was always my second team. It wasn't Liverpool because I thought Manchester United played in a style similar to the way Tottenham played.'

Soon Freedman and Edwards got together for a second meeting when terms were decided. Edwards put it to the Board and within months Freedman had transferred in a move that was to have dramatic consequences both for Manchester United and Tottenham.

By the time Freedman came back to Old Trafford as an employee, it was a year since United had floated and the club had barely gone forward in that time. If anything, by the end of the 1991–92 season, many felt that the elusive Championship trophy, which United had sought since Busby last won it in 1967, would never come back to Old Trafford. Part of the reason for the depression was the tremendous expectations raised by the 1991–92 season, the last season of the old unified Football League, 1992–93 seeing the start of the Premier League. For much of 1991–92, Manchester United had made such a spirited challenge for the League that going into the final weeks it seemed almost certain Alex Ferguson would take the title back to Old Trafford and end the hunger that had gnawed at United for 26 long years.

But in the last weeks of the season, United stumbled and a pretty average Leeds side managed by Howard Wilkinson, much to their own surprise, won the title.

Off the field, the share price was going nowhere. The share price after the Maxwell dump had been flat, almost a straight line on the graphs (see appendix) and United's marketing was underperforming Tottenham, a club which had had serious financial difficulties. Why?

'There were,' says Freedman, 'a whole host of reasons. One, the retail environment itself was very, very old-fashioned and backward. The store they had was approximately 12,000 square feet and 500 square feet of that was given over to the lottery. The mail order had just one telephone operator. The product range was very poor and old-fashioned. The product quality was very bad. They were selling their own T-shirts but they had licensed a lot of the products outside – given them away to people who were obviously there to make their own money but not worry about the quality. They did not understand what a brand was, they had never realised they *had* a brand, that Manchester United *was* a brand.'

The first day Freedman got to Old Trafford he found that, for all the hype in marketing terms, Old Trafford just did not compare to White Hart Lane: 'There was no comparison. Tottenham was ahead of it in staff, thinking, product, environment. Tottenham was far, far ahead.'

The other great problem Freedman encountered was an enormous cultural one. Manchester United may have had great support, but when it came to marketing, it still had to understand how to make its name and its considerable reputation into a product that would sell.

'It had never been done before. It was something that traditionally they just carried on in the normal way without asking questions, like should it change or shouldn't it change, and if it should, how? To any idea of change they used the old excuses, "We haven't won the League", or we haven't done this or that.'

During the flotation, Glenn Cooper had already come across this attitude. There was a great deal of internal resistance to change in the way the business was run. 'One of the criticisms that comes out a lot is, "Ee, bah gum, lad, you don't understand. This is about passion, it's not about business."' On one occasion in an interview I heard myself responding, "Yes, but have you tried passion in a cold bedroom with an ugly partner?" You can't actually divorce these things. Clubs sustain incredibly long periods of poor performance without it reflecting amongst their supporters or customers. Look at Manchester

City. Bugger all and now they are on a decline, which in some ways looks almost terminal in most respects, and yet large numbers of people continue to support them as passionately as they ever did when they were in the Premier League. Now, eventually that goes away, but it is very resilient.'

The problem, as Martin Edwards saw it, was structural and that was the reason he had recruited Edward Freedman: 'Don't forget when Edward Freedman came it was basically the shop and there was no wholesale. We had a video agreement with VCI, but that was purely on a royalty basis. In other words, they paid us so much for each video they sold. We didn't actually do the videoing ourselves. A lot of our products were licensed out. Apart from what the shops sold – jackets, T-shirts – a lot of items we got a royalty for what was sold. Anything we sold through our own shop was OK, but the shop was half the size of the one we have now and there is also now a shop at the back as well. What Edward did was to drive the retail, in other words increase the size of the shop, and eventually build a second shop at the back.'

As we have seen, the shop had been given to Sandy, Busby's son. Some time before Freedman joined, the shop had been taken back and United had given it to another businessman to run. When that did not work there was talk while Scholar was at Tottenham of Tottenham running the United shop. Tottenham, who under Scholar, had gone into publishing under the imprint Cockerill Books, had already published a United book, *Red Devils in Europe*, which sold some 12,000 copies. But the talks over the shop had come to nothing.

Freedman's recall is that there were no problems with Sandy Busby over the shop, contrary to stories that circulated round Old Trafford later: 'There was a pay-off. Martin knew we had to get the shop back. The Busby family was still very affectionate towards Manchester United and there was no problem with the family. The shop's lease was coming to an end anyway. And we quickly opened another shop.'

United built a megastore of 5,000 square feet and a superstore of 2,500 square feet at Old Trafford. A third store of 3,000 square feet opened only on match days.

Expanding the stores was only a part of the Freedman marketing revolution. Freedman also, says Martin Edwards, 'started the whole-sale, whereby we brought the products in, sorted it and then sold it to the other retailers. And he also then took the videos back on board ourselves and he started the magazine. We certainly increased the mail order. While Edward was here we did go overseas but not as much as people think. We started a magazine in Thailand and now we've got our wholesale stock in retail stores in Thailand. But there is a lot of overseas expansion still to be done.'

Almost the first thing Freedman did when he got to Old Trafford was stop the licensing on the products and re-sourced the whole product range. He also improved the retail environment. He took on good staff who understood marketing and how to portray Manchester United, not just as a football club but as an environment which would compete in the market with companies like Marks & Spencer, capable of giving customers what they wanted.

Scholar, admittedly a Freedman fan, says, 'Edward's basic task was to cut out the middle man. When he went first to Manchester United, he terminated all agreements and went directly to the manufacturers. He also did wholesale business himself. One of his customers was Birthdays, a big Manchester United fan, the big card shop who was stocking all Manchester United stuff all over the country.'

With merchandising becoming a major business on its own, Freedman persuaded United to set up its own separate merchandising subsidiary. 'I always believe you have to account in your own right for everything. So if there was a club for merchandising, it should be for merchandising, and it shouldn't be lumped in with anything else to do with the club. So I wanted it run as a separate business. Every month we produced management figures and management reports and we knew where we were going profit-and-loss-wise. That had never happened before.'

Perhaps his most significant innovation was the launch of the Manchester United magazine, the first time a club had its own individual magazine. Freedman was keen to get the Manchester United marketing message across, and soon after he arrived, he surveyed the publications available to the supporters: 'At that particular time the major ones were *Shoot!* and *Match*. They were aiming at a very much younger age group and market. I thought there was just a possibility that if we launched our own publication this could succeed because it would: (a) talk to the supporters on a level which I thought they needed to be talked to, not talked down to, but at the correct level. We did a lot of research and some surveys on this; (b) I also wasn't very happy with the Manchester United programme at the time. It was pretty bad and we needed a new look. It was produced in-house and was an old traditional thing which was very hard to get changed. It was done by committee, rather than by understanding where the future of publishing lay.'

The obvious answer was United's own magazine. But Freedman did not find it easy to launch it: 'I approached all sorts of people and no-one was interested.' Then, almost in desperation, Freedman turned to his son, James, and said, 'I really think this idea is going to work. We'll do it on a contract publishing basis. Come up with a whole layout and a scheme, how much its going to cost, etc. I'll present it to the Board.' Freedman declared his interest to Robin Launders, well aware that the decision had to be made with the Board knowing he had an interest.

James had been to Cambridge where he had studied classics and then gone into the film industry. 'I was doing a Masters at the UCLA Film School in America. I had also set up a contract publishing firm through contacts I knew from university and things like that. It was very low-key set-up in our flat in Belsize Park in London, out of our bedrooms with a couple of AppleMacs. We had started in 1992, before United won the Championship. I worked very closely with a friend of mine who was at Cambridge with me and he had a friend who was writing for the *Guardian* and *Observer* called Gavin Hills. He was also a football supporter and I asked him if he'd like to try and write an article about Manchester United for this magazine.'

But if the journalism was relatively easy, the problems for the Freedmans was to convince the retail trade that it was worth stocking the magazine. In 1992, not having won the Championship since 1967, United was seen as a northwestern provincial club, that was interesting but not a winner with a world-wide appeal, as James Freedman quickly found out: 'When my father launched it no-one else wanted to publish it. We went to IPC, Haymarket and companies like that, but no-one was interested. The news trade thought we might sell 20,000 a month, but they weren't convinced it would be a long-term financial proposition. Manchester United was seen as a northwestern provincial club.'

Nevertheless, in November 1992, the magazine was launched and the first issue sold 15,000 copies. James Freedman recalls: 'Inevitably the first issues of the magazine were being done in a rather amateurish way, in a piecemeal fashion. My background wasn't in publishing but I had a lot of friends in media and journalism. The magazine was selling in the low 20,000s and I thought it must have more potential than that. It was quite shoddy at the start, but not disastrous. It was a mish-mash, but I could see that there could be a turnaround if it could be done in a professional manner. It was entrepreneurial in a quaint way but it wasn't slack. After a few months I put forward a proposal that was more attractive to Manchester United. I had found a much better publishing organisa-tion, a much better repro house, much better journalists, and we took the idea back to the Board. Within 18 months it was selling over 100,000 a year and was hugely successful.'

As United started to perform on the field, and Freedman was able to market the brand name of Manchester United, the magazine took off. 'The retailers led by WH Smith liked the magazine, which proved a big seller for them and all the major retailers. It's now the biggest-selling football monthly in the world. It sells now about 80 to 90,000 a month.'

In December 1993, six months after the club had won its first League title since 1967, Manchester United launched a monthly video magazine, which was to prove enormously successful.

This was another proposal made by James Freedman, whose company by then had expanded its work as a contract publishing company and, says James Freedman, 'came up with other ideas like the video magazine, books and all the things that helped to grow Manchester United's merchandising division.' United decided to take in all the video production in-house and at one stage had 2% of the video market in this country. In 1995 James Freedman's company, Zone, was so successful that, no longer run from his bedroom in Belsize Park, it won the Small Publisher of the Year Award. 'What had happened,' says Freedman, 'was that the magazine and the video magazine was successful not only from the brand-building point of view, but also financially.'

In January 1996 United sold the magazine, the publications and the videos to VCI for £6 million, in a ten-year deal that saw the club receive £3.5 million in advanced royalties. But it continued with the retail and wholesale operations Freedman had set up. Now Freedman can look back on the dark days of 1992 and brush away the initial problems, saying, 'I had only been worried before we started.'

In essence what Freedman had done was to tap into a source of support that had never been tapped before. 'I was also to do this revolutionary merchandising because there was a large number of untapped Manchester United supporters, and to my mind, there is still a lot of football clubs that have an untapped potential. We were doing business overseas by mail order and then the magazine started to open the market up. It so happened that someone came from Thailand and said he would like to produce this magazine in Thailand. He had seen the magazine and he produced sports magazines and a major daily sports publication. He had written to every club in the country, saying that football was becoming very big in Thailand and could he come and see them? The only one to answer his letter was me. I invited him to come and see me and he got on a plane the following week.'

Manchester United had been a big club since Busby reinvented it in the 1950s, but its popularity had never been converted into money and profits. Freedman was the first one to mine the gold that lay beneath the surface.

Statistics can often be misleading. But the figures below illustrate how Freedman made a success of building up the brand of Manchester United and how badly United had been underperforming before he arrived despite the club's vast name and glorious history.

No table probably more easily illustrates the contrasting growth patterns of the two clubs Freedman worked for and how things changed after Freedman moved from Tottenham to Manchester United.

Tottenham in 1990 had revenues of £28,018,000. This was, however, a sign of disaster to come rather than success as it was a

(All figures in £)

MANCHESTER UNITED

	Revenue	Wages	Net Transfers	Profit
1991	17,816,000	5,214,000	801,000	5,306,000
1992	12,193,000	5,291,000	2,625,000	80,000
1993	14,064,000	6,182,000	3,986,000	− 145,000
1994	20,852,000	9,002,000	675,000	2,881,000
1995	60,622,000	13,020,000	− 3,733,000	20,014,000
1996	53,316,000	13,275,000	1,300,000	15,399,000
1997	87,939,000	22,552,000	− 293,000	27,577,000

TOTTENHAM

	Revenue	Wages	Net Transfers	Profit
1991	18,713,000	5,259,000	− 335,000	− 1,781,000
1992	19,308,000	5,372,000	1,475,000	3,057,000
1993	25,265,000	6,248,000	910,000	3,361,000
1994	15,061,000	6,207,000	748,000	− 1,535,000
1995	21,296,000	8,358,000	− 578,000	157,000
1996	27,394,000	11,453,000	4,908,000	2,912,000
1997	27,874,000	12,057,000	1,528,000	7,573,000

result of Tottenham diversifying into activities not directly related to football and contributed to the downfall of the Scholar regime. But even after Tottenham had restructured and slimmed down, Manchester United did not surpass Tottenham in revenue terms until 1994, the second year after Freedman's arrival at Old Trafford, and did not begin to become the corporate monster it is routinely described today until 1995.

Of course, by then, United was having tremendous success on the field, having followed the League title in 1993 with a double in 1994, which was fuelling Freedman's marketing drive. But the crucial fact is that Freedman had built the mechanism and the infrastructure that could exploit that success. Freedman had constructed the machinery to exploit the brand name of Manchester United.

Success on the field building upon an historic fan base, even relative success after years of underperformance, can translate into higher revenues. The classic case of this is Newcastle. The northeast, as any number of football experts will testify, is a hotbed of football. The passion for the game is unbelievable. In 1991 Newcastle had done nothing for decades, not having won a domestic trophy since the 50s (it had won the Inter Cities Fairs Cup, a forerunner for the UEFA Cup, in 1970). In 1991 its revenues were £4.418 million; it spent £2.754 million in wages and made losses of £2.541 million.

In 1994, after Kevin Keegan had revitalised Newcastle, revenues had risen to £17.004 million, wages to £6.575 million and profits to £3.766 million, but with no net transfer payments.

In 1995, with Newcastle back in the top division, revenue increased to £24.723 million, wages to £7.105 million, but it made losses of £8.159 million as more was spent on players.

In 1996, with Newcastle challenging Manchester United for the Premiership title and, doing in effect what United had done against Leeds in 1992, letting their long lead slip to finish second, revenues increased to £28.970 million, wages rose to £19.746 million and transfers of £27.596 million meant losses were £23.604 million. By 1997, revenue had gone up again to £41.134 million, wages were £17.487 million, but with more players sold than bought, transfers brought in £1.436 million, the club had profits of £8.302 million.

What these figures emphasise is that Newcastle remained a conventional club. Better performances on the field lead to higher income, but as more money was spent on players the club went into the red. Manchester United from 1994 did something very different. It created that unheard of event in football, a virtuous cycle where whatever the temporary setbacks on the field, the club just kept growing. From 1994 United started bucking the universal trend clubs had suffered from, where instant success brought instant money and sudden failure huge debts. In 1995 United was, at one stage, chasing on three fronts but won nothing. However, the marketing machine went rolling on, as the figures show. From the chance business of football, United had created something quite permanent.

Freedman's impact is best judged if we compare an average take during a league match in three seasons: 1991–92, 1993–94 and 1994–95.

On a league match day in the 1991–92 season, the last one before Freedman arrived at Old Trafford – and a season it is worth recalling when United came closest to winning the League since 1967 – the average league match day income was £500,000 (season tickets £240,000, gate receipts £160,000, executive boxes £20,000, programmes £30,000, shop £22,000 and catering £30,000).

In 1993–94, a year after Freedman had come, a league match day produced on average a total of £760,000 (season tickets £420,000, gate receipts £180,000, executive boxes £20,000, programme £30,000, shop £44,000 and catering £60,000).

By the 1994–95 season, a league match day produced £900,000 (season tickets £500,000, gate receipts £180,000, executive boxes £40,000, programme £20,000, shop £70,000 and catering £80,000).

Before Freedman came to United there had been a huge gap between reality and hype about Manchester United's financial resources. The huge gates United attracted fed this illusion. While the gates were large the money they brought in was often less than London clubs like Arsenal and Tottenham, who had smaller stadiums but could charge more money. Martin Edwards has always been sensitive about ticket pricing and even today United is in the bottom half of the ticket price league headed by London clubs such as Chelsea. The huge support led to the illusion that United had pots of money; the reality came as a big shock to Alex Ferguson as he explains in his autobiography *Managing My Life*.

In the summer of 1987, little more than six months after he had become manager, he went to Martin Edwards and told him he needed to sign eight new players. Ferguson says that, to his surprise, Edwards was 'taken aback' by this demand: 'You could say I was shocked at how shocked he was. It was hardly cheering to hear the chairman say that the club did not have the resources to finance the purchases I knew were necessary. He reminded me that there was no Jack Walker around to reach into an endless store of personal wealth. That conversation might have astonished all the outsiders who, even back then, thought of United as an organisation rich enough to attack the problems with a blitz of cash.' It seems odd that in 1987 Edwards should have been talking about Jack Walker since he did not surface at Blackburn until 1991, but even if Ferguson's recall is slightly confused on this, the essential point of the story, that United was not a rich club, is well made.

Yet for all of Freedman's marketing skills, his innovative idea of the magazine, which was key to driving the Manchester United brand, may never have got off the ground but for the support Martin Edwards gave. In the dark days of 1992, as Freedman struggled to find anyone willing to back his idea of a Manchester United magazine, and with constant warnings ringing in his ear that it was never going to work or stand on its own two feet, he grew a bit apprehensive. 'It was the first time I ever actually went to Martin Edwards. I said, "Martin, I'm very worried about this product. I've been to big publishers and small publishers and no-one wants to touch it. I think overall as a brand builder we need it, but we could lose money on it. They all say they can't see it surviving on its own." He said, "Tell me the upside and the downside." When I did so he said, "If you think you can go with it, go with it."'

Edwards says: 'I appointed Edward [Freedman] because I could see the potential there. I supported Edward with finance to buy the warehouse. I think about £125,000 in 1991, putting all the infra-structure there, staff costs, rebuilding the shops, rebuilding the super-store, building the megastore. What I am saying is, I recognised the potential. I supported Edward a lot in terms of building that business. Which is my duty, one of support. So we do recognise the potential there. Edward did well there. He built up the business to £30 million.'

Freedman readily acknowledges Martin Edwards' vital role in giving him the freedom to do it his way. 'The major thing was Martin Edwards let me get on with it and he didn't interfere. If there was anything major that I wanted to talk to him about, he never actually asked me questions. He let me get on with it. That was a major point.'

Soon after Freedman arrived there were problems with Robin Launders, the finance director. 'Robin Launders started to ask questions about what I was doing and how I was doing it. Three or four months after I was there I actually went to Martin and said, "This guy doesn't understand what I'm doing. If you don't get him off my back, I'm going. Let me get on with it." Martin got him off my back. That's how it was. I was reporting direct to Martin. When I went there I was merchandising manager and I finished up as managing director of the merchandising division.'

Just as Freedman had cut out the middle man in building up the Manchester United brand name, Edwards had cut out the finance director to allow Freedman a free hand in marketing. The result was Freedman reported directly to Edwards and there was only one other Board member he came into contact with and that was, inevitably, Maurice Watkins, so often the linchpin of the modern United: 'Maurice Watkins looked at any legal issues or points which needed looking at. Apart from that, the Board had very little say in the running of anything, as far as I was concerned.'

If Freedman built the structure to drive the Manchester United marketing, then a crucial part in Freedman's merchandising revolution was played by the arrival at United of a Frenchman whose move to the club was even more dramatic. That man was Eric Cantona. Just as Freedman coming to United from Tottenham was a chance then Cantona's transfer from Leeds to United in November 1992 was for United the sort of unexpected move that turns magical and it must be rated as the greatest transfer in the history of English football. No one player has made such a dramatic impact on a club, yet given what he achieved, no player could have been more of a bargain buy.

Cantona arrived at United little over six months after Freedman did and his arrival made Freedman's job of selling United as a brand name all that much easier. Martin Edwards says: 'He came for a fantastically low fee, the bargain of the century, a million.'

The day the deal was done Freedman had lunch with Martin Edwards at Old Trafford. During the meal Edwards asked, 'If there's any player you could pick in this country at the moment who would it be?'

'You couldn't buy him,' said Freedman.

'Why, who is it then?' asked Edwards.

'Eric Cantona,' replied Freedman.

'How much would you pay?' Edwards asked.

'He must be worth at least 4 to 5 million,' said Freedman.

'I can get him for £1.2 million,' said Edwards.

'It can't be true,' said Freedman, thinking Martin Edwards was kidding.

But Edwards knew he could get Cantona for £1.2 million; he eventually got him for a million. Freedman says: 'He hadn't done the deal but he knew he was going to. He had kept me guessing at the lunch. He quite likes that sort of thing.'

Cantona's arrival at Old Trafford did, in a curious way, mirror that of Freedman. Freedman, as we have seen, had arrived at Old Trafford looking for business for Tottenham and deciding to stay. Cantona's arrival was the result of a call from Leeds looking to buy Denis Irwin. Martin Edwards recalls: 'What happened is Bill Fotherby rang me about Denis Irwin and I'd actually heard that Cantona was unsettled. I had a call from Denis Roach. He originally had brought Cantona over to play for Sheffield Wednesday on loan. He rang me to say that Cantona was unsettled. I then get a call from Bill Fotherby about Denis Irwin. I said, "Look, Bill, I'll find out about Denis Irwin. I need to speak to Alex Ferguson. I don't think he would be available. But we would be interested in Cantona." So he said, "Let me come back to you." I'd already rung Alex in between the first call and I said, "If I could get Cantona, would you take him?" Alex said, "I certainly would." So I told him to leave it with me. Fotherby came back and I told him there was no way we'd let Irwin go, but they said they would be prepared to let Cantona go. He asked for £1.6 million. Then I did the deal with Bill Fotherby and rang Alex back to tell him we'd got him.'

Edwards sees it 'as the greatest deal in the history of English football. The one season, in 1994–95, when after the kung-fu kick he didn't have a full season, was the only season we didn't win anything. His first season we won the League [1992–93] and we won the double twice [1993–94 and 1995–96]. I mean, his contribution is absolutely enormous. Unbelievable. He unlocked the door for us.'

At that stage United was not spending a lot of money on transfers. And the general impression in the football world was that the United transfer budget was quite tight. Had Cantona been available at £4 million, United would have baulked at the figure, which is why Freedman had said to Edwards that he could not afford the player. What Manchester United needed to do on the field was convert the promise of the 1992 side into reality and that is exactly what Cantona helped United achieve.

Off the field, Freedman made sure that he made the most of the Cantona factor, and he marketed Cantona like no footballer had ever been marketed before. 'As soon as he joined Manchester United I knew he was massive. I marketed Cantona to the hilt. He was on T-shirts, sweatshirts – whatever I could do with him. We did books, a calendar, magazines. I sent someone over to spend a whole weekend with him in France to take photos. With Cantona I made every product possible available, anything that people wanted, we did everything that was possible to justify Cantona as a marketing product.'

Cantona's arrival, which helped win the League, took United into the Champions League (as the European Cup is now known). While United did not fulfil expectations and win the Champions League, it did have a run, which in Europe further helped sales. But the market in Europe was not quite as big as some experts had predicted, as Freedman soon found out: 'Success in Europe, which we had, helped sales in Europe. But there wasn't a big, big market for Manchester United in Europe. It's more in Asia and Scandinavia is also a very big market.'

By 1995 Cantona's future at United had become uncertain, but the marketing drive was going so well that even without him on the field it went on. The marketing drive was not affected in 1995 when Cantona was banned from the game between January and September 1995 after his kung-fu kick at a Crystal Palace supporter. Nor even in the spring of 1997 when he made known he was going to leave United for good.

Freedman says: 'We didn't really find a dip in sales or anything. There wasn't any drastic dip in circulation or product selling with Cantona away. The ground was still full every week, so what more we could have done with him there I don't really know, but I don't think we found any really big effect. Maybe for a week or two things dipped a bit. Cantona's suspension and eventual departure was good publicity and it was all over the world and everyone was talking about Manchester United. It was on the front covers everywhere. It's the same with the Sky situation [the bid for Manchester United]. I think it will be a big boost to Manchester United. It's in people's minds all the time. Look at the Spice Girls. Everyone was complaining there's too much marketing of the Spice Girls, but you know, they were better off in 1998 when they were on the front pages of the *Sun* and everyone was talking about them. Now it's difficult to get them in the newspapers. They were very much more successful in 1998 when they were everywhere than when they weren't. Overcommercialism has to be looked at carefully. If it's *bad* overcommercialism and if you are giving bad products or you are giving bad value, that's another story. But if you are giving good value and you are giving what the customers want – at the end of the day they are the people who say yes or no and they are the people who buy the tickets. I saw an argument on TV yesterday. Before the guy was interviewed he said, "Has anyone out there got a ticket? I'll pay, £50–£100 for a ticket." He said that on TV. Then you get complaints that you charge £25 for your tickets. Now that's the going rate in the market, so it's not over-commercialism. You are paying a going rate.'

Freedman agrees that there is ground for fans to complain that United has made frequent changes of replica shirts: 'I think there is possibly an argument for that. I've been saying for a long time – but I was outvoted at Manchester United – that a football shirt should be changed once every season. That would be less than what's actually happening in the cycle and the result is there are too many shirts. All there should be is two shirts for sale, and if you need a third shirt because you have to change it if your colours clash, then that third shirt shouldn't be for sale. There should only ever be two shirts, a home shirt and an away shirt. The home shirt should be changed every season because the fans don't mind that being changed every year. The away shirt should only be changed every other year. It is changed too many times. They invent shirts – the European shirt and so on.'

At times United's proliferation of shirts even led to a revolt from the players. In the 1997 season, while playing away at the Dell against Southampton, United's players wore a grey shirt. With United losing 1–0 at half-time, the players decided to throw away the grey shirts. 'It was a grey shirt. Alex had been consulted and he would have been shown the shirts. Alex would be involved all along when we produced a new shirt. We would have a shirt and would say to him, "Alex, this is what we'd like. What do you think about it?" He'd be very good about it. He never said he didn't like a shirt. But on this occasion, Alex got it into his head it was responsible for the bad performance – you know there's a lot of superstition in football – so if the manager can blame anything other than the players for a bad team performance, he will. They had a terrible first half and blamed it on the shirts. They said they couldn't see each other playing in grey shirts.'

United played the second half in white and still lost. But the incident, while trivial, highlighted the whole issue about shirts and their marketing. While Freedman concedes that United change their shirts too often he, not surprisingly, bridles at the suggestion that the marketing revolution he started at United meant the club became too commercial: 'When you say "too commercial", what is "too commercial"? You have a business there which has got lots and lots of money.

Obviously it isn't as Sky think it is because they wouldn't have paid that amount of money if they think they can make it more commercial. I don't think it is that commercial. All they've done is use their assets to the best way by putting on products. In some ways there are certain areas the assets are still underperforming.'

If anything Freedman would argue that United appears so commercial because its rivals have not been as successful in following United's lead: 'I don't think David Dein at Arsenal has done so much actually. The Arsenal shop at Finsbury Park, I don't like it and I don't think it is particularly good. I know him reasonably well and think David doesn't necessarily like the detail. Ken Bates, on the other hand, has thrown his resources into developing his football club.'

Freedman's real criticism is directed at his old club, Tottenham, which once showed Manchester United the way and has now fallen behind. 'The problem is Alan Sugar doesn't understand football. Whatever might be wrong with Bates or Dein or Edwards, they are football people – even Irving Scholar. They mind about football. It's taken Ken Bates a very *long* time to bring the top people to the club, yes. The one thing to talk about Sugar is he has had fantastic football personalities at the club – like Klinsmann and Ginola. What have they done with those products? Like we did with Cantona, Sugar should have done the same with Klinsmann. The minute he joined Tottenham, if I'd still been in Tottenham, I would have done the same as I did with Cantona and marketed every conceivable product I could think of to make the most of Klinsmann. Tottenham did not do that.'

However, one consequence of Freedman's marketing revolution and United's success on the field, was that the club everybody loved and regarded as their second club if they did not already support United, became one of the most hated clubs in the country and even round the world. Whereas Busby had created a club everyone wanted to cherish, the new United of the 1990s and its success was resented by many and the cry 'Stand up if you hate Manchester United' began to be heard round the country. This reached its peak in 1996 when Hunter Davies did a television documentary which castigated United for always looking to make money and losing touch with its supporters.

Apart from criticising United's pursuit of the marketing riches, Hunter Davies made much of the fact that match days at United saw many of the supporters coming from hundreds of miles away, often on long coach trips from the south of England and even overseas from Scandinavia and Ireland. Surely, argued Davies, this was the ultimate evidence of the club losing its soul. It was no longer a community-based football club but had instead transformed itself into a money-making machine, attracting mercenaries from all over the world who had no affinity with the club but were drawn to it by its success.

Even before Freedman had started his marketing revolution in Ireland, a movement had started which had turned from love to hate for United. The Irish broadcaster Des Cahill, who presents the breakfast programme on the pop music station of RTE, the Irish broadcasting service, had formed ABU (Anybody But United). The organisation has since grown and prospered and Cahill calls it 'a state of the mind'.

Cahill, who is himself a West Ham supporter, found his mind filled with anti-United feeling in 1992, when United just lost the old First Division title to Leeds. 'The United supporters started crawling out of the woodwork. Ireland has always had a huge United support. Some 4,000 to 5,000 go to Old Trafford from Ireland for every home game and what got me was, should someone from Cork care so much about what happens to the full back of United?'

Cahill's state of mind soon expanded into a very Irish style evangelical movement delighting in every United defeat as if the club was the devil incarnate. So a T-shirt was produced which listed all the clubs, such as York and Galatasaray, who over the years had inflicted humiliating defeats on United. And the ABU movement also acquired a theme song.

The morning after a United defeat Cahill began to play on his programme the theme tune of 'Zippedee doodah, zippedee day'. 'My post bag is huge from Leeds and Newcastle fans, and in Ireland, it has got to the stage that if you go into a pub you have Manchester United in one corner and ABU in another corner.'

Cahill emphasises that much of this is done tongue in cheek as part of the celebrated Irish sense of fun. However, he feels strongly that what spoils United is not so much their success on the field but their supporters who, he says, exude such an air of arrogance and invincibility that it makes it difficult for supporters of other clubs to like United.

By May 1999, this hatred for United would reach into some very unusual areas. As United travelled again to Wembley for yet another FA Cup Final, searching for its third double and what turned out to be the first ever treble in English football, the hate in some quarters was so intense that David Meek was unable to go to Wembley to watch his beloved club.

At 3.00pm that May afternoon, while Manchester United took the field at Wembley, Meek, who has followed the club's fortunes for the last 40 years, couldn't be there because his brother-in-law, a City fan, so hated Manchester United that he had arranged his wedding to coincide with the match. As the match kicked off at Wembley, in a church in Manchester the priest began the wedding ceremony.

It would be easy to see this as the intensely tribal feeling that exists between City and United fans; there is after all a book entitled *How Manchester United Ruined My Life* written by a City fan. But it is symptomatic of something much larger and extending well beyond derby rivalries into what is now an institutionalised hatred of United.

Meek took over as football reporter of the *Manchester Evening News* following the Munich crash, which saw the death of the then *Evening News* correspondent. Since then, until his retirement a couple of years ago, Meek has written more words about United than any other human being, having chronicled on a daily basis the Old Trafford saga, describing both the great glories and the awful despairs.

James Freedman says, 'There's an arrogance about Manchester United, unquestionably. There's been some incredibly poor handling of the media. Ferguson doesn't want to be liked. He has always enjoyed playing the underdog. He always did, even when he was at Aberdeen, but he had the perfect excuse there. He wasn't part of the Old Firm and he was able to rally the players around this idea of everyone against us. He's tried to do this at Manchester United, but he's not getting a lot of sympathy because they're winning everything. Then you've got Cantona as someone that the fans who do not support Manchester United love to hate. Keane, Ince – these are also characters that supporters of other clubs do not like.'

Edward Freedman argues that the reason Manchester United, once one of the best-loved clubs in the land, is now the most hated is because 'success makes people not like things. In England we don't like success and Manchester United have been remarkably successful. People now haven't grown up with the memory of Munich. If you grew up in the 60s and 70s with the memory of Munich and what Busby did and Duncan Edwards dying in this great northern tragedy, then obviously you are going to feel sympathy for the club. Then you've got people like George Best, who was obviously a massive national hero, together with Denis Law and Bobby Charlton. All three of them have reason to be loved and are very popular figures and they only had limited success on the field. In the 70s and 80s Manchester United wasn't a particularly successful club and went down to the Second Division.'

But however much the sports romantic may regret this hatred of United the sports marketing men, of course, could not get enough of Manchester United and this was to provide Freedman's crowning moment of glory in the summer of 1996 just after, inspired by Cantona, United did its second double. Even as United was chasing this then unique honour, the marketing talk had turned to a new kit sponsorship deal. United was with Umbro; Umbro wanted to retain the contract but its rivals were keen to get in with United.

Freedman recalls: 'It was very interesting. This was a time when we were getting near the point where we were going to negotiate a new kit contract. The way the kit contract had worked in the past was the chairman would come in and say, "What do you think we should get for the kit contract this year?", and you'd say, "£20 million". He'd say, "Why £20 million?" You'd say, "Liverpool got £15 million." That's how the thing worked. But that time I said, "Martin, let me go away and spend two or three months with a couple of my people to go through the whole thing in detail and actually come up with what value this contract is worth." He agreed and I did an exercise. We went through how many shirts are sold, how many tracksuits are sold – how many of whatever product we were involved with was sold. We worked out how much it cost to produce the kit, how much to buy the kit and we came up with three scenarios: (a) the worst-case scenario which saw us get £8 million; (b) possible scenario which meant we could get £15 million; (c) optimistic scenario where we could get £21 million.'

With United having done the double twice, a feat then not matched by any other English club, Nike were keen to sign the Manchester United kit and get it away from Umbro. Nike contacted Martin Edwards. Says Freedman: 'They knew the contract was up for grabs and they contacted Martin. He came to me and said, "Nike want to discuss it and fly us to America." They flew me, Martin and Danny McGregor to the States. We flew from Manchester to Chicago and we went to see Niketown and then on to Portland, where they have their operation. We were there two or three days. We were wined and dined – goods in the room, all that sort of thing. We had very hard negotiations but they wouldn't come to the figures I wanted. It was nowhere near: £5 million was the most they would offer.'

Umbro knew Nike had flown Manchester United to the States and began to get very nervous. Freedman relished the situation Manchester United were in: 'They were very keen to discuss with us. I thought these were the best negotiations I'd ever had in my life, because I felt I'd got them into such a corner. I said to Martin: (1) they can't afford to lose the deal; (2) they can't afford to pay for the deal. We negotiated and it was Peter Kenyon who did the negotiating for Umbro, and it was Martin who said at the eleventh hour, "Do you mind if I give them your report to read?" I said that I didn't and they were going to read it overnight because they brought over a team from America. I thought the following morning they would tear it to shreds and shoot holes all through it. They came in the morning and found very little wrong with it. They agreed a figure that was unbelievable. It was a phenomenal amount of money. I also had something in my mind because I've been in this business a long time. Just because we are selling x amount of shirts today doesn't mean it will go on forever. At the time it was a very high-fashion product, and in my mind, we based it on the highest level we possibly could.'

Kenyon and Umbro had watched United's trip to Niketown with a great deal of anxiety. 'The Umbro deal I had done in 1991 was for six years. We started re-negotiating that in 1996 and that was when Nike got involved. I was worried when I heard they had flown them to Oregon. I think that was a recognition of how big United were and Nike wanting icon teams. Sports manufacturers like icon teams. Umbro got Brazil and then they went to Nike. I was involved in doing the negotiations and it was just like the TV deals. Brazil only won the World Cup when they were with Umbro. We re-signed them in 1990 and they won in 1994. But when they did it with Nike they did not win in France in 1998.'

In August 1996, United signed a new six-year deal with Umbro. While Umbro had never revealed how much it was, it had in fact matched Freedman's second scenario (the 'possible scenario') agreeing to pay £15 million. For Freedman the deal justified everything he had been doing at United and was undoubtedly his high point.

There is one other trait of Manchester United that this deal highlighted – one not usually associated with the sort of hard-nosed, commercial beast United are supposed to have become.

Kenyon says: 'There's a fairly special trait within United and that is they are hard negotiators but they are loyal. Having dealt with lots of different entities within football, Martin Edwards is probably the most direct and honourable chairman to deal with. His word has always been – if he's done the deal, he's done the deal. I think he gets the best deal for United, and if he can do that and retain a relationship through that, that's the preferred route. You've only to look at Sharp, who've been with us for 16 years. I think that demonstrates a real commitment.'

But are we making too much of the Freedman merchandising revolution at United? He certainly pushed up the turnover but how did this feed through to the bottom line, the profits?

Glenn Cooper's view is: 'Freedman was brought in and selected by Martin Edwards because he recognised that the job needed to be done and chose the man to do it and put him in place. I think Freedman thought he'd died and gone to heaven. He was given the opportunity to exploit a brand name in the way he knows how to do. On his own admission he would, I think, tell you that he only scratched the surface of it. He was, understandably, highly successful at developing the merchandising arm of the business. It was very successful. The only equivocation I would possibly make is that it was an easy job and I think he would agree with me in saying that.'

Cooper accepts that there is much merit in Freedman's view that when he went there to make his presentations, with the idea that Spurs would franchise its expertise to other clubs, and ended up working for Manchester United, at that stage United was still a northwestern club and wasn't the mega-club that it has since become. Says Cooper: 'It's quite clear to me that in the long term all these influences are interlinked. In 1990 Manchester United had won very little for a longish time – apart from a couple of Cups – but in the previous 16 or 17 years they hadn't really done a great deal. Then you got the flotation and the resolution of the immediate capital problem; the development of the ground, which began to create more revenue; the development of merchandising. All of that began to flow alongside a more successful team.'

Kenyon sees Freedman's success as part of the wider changes coming to the football industry at that time. Just as the mid-80s were a grim period for English soccer, the tide had begun to turn in the early 90s. 'We'd come through the hooliganism of the 80s, had a very successful England in Italia '90 and, within three weeks of Italia '90, football almost became respectable again. It became a national game. Hooliganism didn't necessarily stop, but it stopped getting reported. There was a real feel-good factor. That coincided not long after with the Premier League being formed and the emergence of football clubs potentially becoming businesses, so there was a lot going on in the industry. As far as Manchester United were concerned, two things happened. Sales went up through better distribution and there was success on the field. You shouldn't forget that Manchester United has a huge latent support and you know what football supporters are like. You don't change your team just because they're not doing well. They lie dormant and come out when things look up.'

According to Kenyon: 'Edward Freedman did a job for Manchester United that needed doing at the time. At Manchester United all the commercial activities, whether match-day hospitality, kits, went through the commercial department. I think they understood there were more dynamics to this and they needed to bring some professionals in to supplement the others. Bringing Edward in to start a merchandising division was the beginning of that.'

Martin Edwards is keenest to caution against an excessive glorification of Freedman in making him the architect of the corporate giant Manchester United had become: 'Edward built up the turnover and the profit on the merchandising. What you have to be a little bit careful of, and people get a little bit carried away, the merchandising side of our business is a big part of our turnover, but it only operates on normal retail or wholesale margins. There's a big cost of sale involved in that. So the actual contribution to our overall profits sometimes gets exaggerated. Because whereas things like sponsorship and TV income and things like that, they almost fall right through to the bottom line. There's not a huge cost of sale attached to it, whereas with catering and merchandising there's a big cost of sale. We employ 130 full-time staff on merchandising, so we have to pay wages, we have large numbers of stock and all the rest of it.'

In 1997 United declared £27.6 million of profits on ordinary activities before taxation and after net transfer fees of £293,000. The turnover was £87.939 million and merchandising was £28.681 million of that. But how much did merchandising contribute to the £27.6 million profit?

Edwards says: 'The actual merchandising element of that would not be enormous. It'd be sizable, but not enormous. It is a big turnover, low margin, whereas the rest of the business, I mean a lot of it, even gate receipts, is big turnover and pretty high margins. True, even here you have the cost of sale – you've got police and gatemen – but a lot of income from the ticket-holders is retailing profit after you've paid your expenses. People talk about Manchester United's merchandising; don't forget it's bigger than anyone else's. It's big and it makes a contribution but it's not the be-all and end-all. The footballing side, the results on the field, getting into European competitions, getting TV deals, getting sponsorship deals – these are more important profit-wise.'

Merchandising has accounted for around 30% of United's revenue ever since the Freedman marketing revolution. But with a 12% margin on products, it produces 11% of profits.

Edwards and Kenyon fell out with Freedman when, as we shall see, he left United as a result, and their views of him are probably coloured by the desire for post-event justification, to make sure he is not seen as the great marketing Messiah who made United. It could also be argued that this is Martin Edwards seeking to dim some of the glory for the view that the Manchester United corporate revolution was designed by Edward Freedman. But there is some backing for what Martin Edwards says from City analysts.

In November 1996 Julian Easthope, then at UBS Global Research, wrote: 'Gate receipts (which include programme sales) have a gross margin of 90% and are the largest contributor to group profits. It is a high-quality revenue stream, with around 70% received in advance from the sale of season tickets.'

The growth in gate receipts during the 1990s was exceptional, with the compound annual rate amounting to 21%.

A ten-year comparison of gate receipts makes interesting reading:

Year	Gate Receipts (£000)
1988	4,755
1989	5,222
1990	6,227
1991	9,237
1992	11,142
1993	10,676
1994	17,920
1995	19,648
1996	19,588
1997	30,111
1998	29,778
1999	41,908

The gate receipts show how sensitive attendances were to performances on the field. They also reflect Edwards' desire to keep ticket prices low in comparison with other Premiership clubs and often more in line with other clubs in the region. Thus, United's lowest ticket price of £10 in 1994 had gone up to £13 by 1998, an increase of 10% or less a year over the period. The same period had seen its lowest season ticket price of £190 in 1994 increase to £247 by 1998. In real terms, United's season ticket prices had increased between 14.35% for the highest-price ticket between 1993–94 and 1997–98 and 18.35% for the median-priced tickets.

However, even after such increases, United's season ticket prices have been considerably lower than the average highest prices charged by clubs in the Premier League.

In 1994 United's highest-price season ticket was £280, while the average for the Premier League, excluding United, was £307. By 1998 this had risen at United to £361 when the average for the rest of the Premier League, excluding United, was £442. In the 1997–98 season, ten clubs had higher prices than Manchester United at the top end of the season-ticket market and seven clubs had higher prices at the median or bottom end of the market.

But if Edwards kept ticket prices on a strong leash, he was quite happy to charge high prices when it came to merchandising products. A comparison of United's price for merchandising for replica short-sleeve shirts for kids, replica short-sleeve shirts for adults, crew-neck sweatshirts and curtains shows that United's prices for replica shirts were about 5% higher than those of Arsenal; its price for sweatshirts was about 14% higher than Arsenal; but the price of Manchester United curtains 17% less than that of Aston Villa; and the price of duvets was in line with those of Arsenal or Aston Villa (Villa being just over a £1 cheaper than United).

On the United board Edwards had always been the one most reluctant to raise prices and immediately after flotation when prices were put up, it was Roland Smith who insisted that they be raised.

It is interesting to note that when it comes to ticket pricing, Manchester United has often tried to make sure it is not out of line not only with Premiership clubs but even clubs such as Bolton, a neighbour, but one which yo-yos between the Premiership and the Football League. The policy here seems to be that, as ticket prices affect the core fans, United need to make sure it is not much out of line with its rivals in the north. But when it comes to merchandising, which reaches a much wider audience, it can charge higher prices.

So if Edwards believes Freedman wasn't the magician who waved the wand at United, then what did?

Edwards' answer is while Freedman contributed it is wrong to see the financial revolution at United as the work of just one man: 'The turning point was when we started to show results because, don't forget we were floating in the aftermath of Tottenham. The Tottenham experience in the City hadn't been successful at all. In fact it had been a bit of a disaster. So clearly there was a huge nervousness on the part of the institutions to invest on day one. Slowly but surely we started to go and present and the results started to come through. They could see the growth of the company and the promises we'd made at the float suddenly came to fruition. We started to pay a dividend while Tottenham were erratic with the dividend, or didn't pay it at all. One of the things we're proud of is that every dividend since the flotation, every interim, every final, has been increased. They could see that steady increase in the profits and the dividend and suddenly they realised: "Oh, hang on, this isn't just a football club. This is a serious business".'

Edwards can still recall the pain of trying to sell United to the City: 'I think the difficulty we had was selling United in the first place. In other words, getting the float away, because we were going around presenting then and the only experience they had was Tottenham. We had a proper presentation pack, so we took them through the pack: how we saw things going, what our core income was and things like that. But I don't think any of them believed at that stage. Some did because they took it up, but a lot of the institutions who have now invested, at that stage didn't want to know. They didn't believe that a football club could generate profits on a regular basis. They didn't believe that football club directors would be disciplined enough to pay dividends on a regular basis and generally act as proper plc custodians of the business. That doubt was always there. So we've only done it by our results.'

At flotation, as we have seen, Edwards had come down from just over 50%, to 32%, and then down to 14%, and with other directors coming down this meant there were shares to be bought by the institutions.

The City slowly took to United and it was only in 1996 that a majority of United stock, 60%, was in the hands of the City institutions, the percentage creeping up slowly over the years. Edwards says: 'I can't think what the figure was just after the float, but I would suspect it was 20-odd%, maybe 30%. Slowly but surely it's crept up, mainly because the institutions have taken any of the shares sold by the directors. Most of the supporters who had shares, they don't tend to change hands, really, do they? They tend to keep them.'

Cooper supports this assessment by Edwards, that turning United round was not just Freedman working his marketing magic: 'It is not a case that United went nowhere until 1992 and then all of a sudden Freedman came and it came together. That is not quite fair. No, I don't think it is. Earnings started to go up on a trend. We made forecasts in the prospectus and these forecasts were met and exceeded in all cases, which is a very good point for a flotation. As you know, a number of flotations have happened where that wasn't the case. Then, of course, the TV contract came up for renewal. Sky came in 1992 and we began to see for the first time the manifestation of what we are going to talk about now, which is the fact that the recognition that football is an enormously important driver to the viewing public and similarly, obviously, to a satellite public. I mean, everything's changed because when we floated I think we anticipated revenues of £14 million – that was only seven years ago – and now the player wages alone are £22 million. The order of magnitude changed. They've expanded – if you look at the elements of that: TV revenues, commercial revenues. They've radically expanded the size of the ground, so they are getting much more in by way of ticket income, which is still an important aspect of this. Everybody forgets this. They renegotiated all their sponsorship agreements. The deals with Umbro and Sharp. All of those elements together have changed it from what it was in 1991 to what it is in 1999.'

But while Edwards and Cooper are right to emphasise that Freedman on his own did not make the modern United, there can be no denying that it was his marketing success that was driving United's efforts to persuade the City to buy its stock.

The most interesting evidence of this came when United presented its preliminary results for 1995. As with all such result presentations, there were a number of charts showing how the plc had performed and the most prominent figure highlighted was that turnover had increased by 38% This was on the back of Freedman's merchandising, which had increased by 65%, from £14.232 million to £23.488 million. Gate receipts may have contributed more to the bottom-line profits of £16.281 million before transfers and £20.014 million after transfers of £3.733 million, but what caught the City was that merchandising sales had grown by £9.25 million. The presentation laid great emphasis on this.

It was six months after these results were issued in April 1996 that the City first began to take to Manchester United and the first media references to 'Gold Trafford' and Edwards 'the fat cat Gold Trafford chief' began to emerge. On 1 April 1996, Edwards sold 785,000 shares for £2,119,500; his wife Susan sold 350,726 shares for £950,467.46; and the Edwards Family Trust sold 500,000 shares for £1.35 million, making a total take for the Edwards family of £4,419,967.46.

On 2 April 1996, the *Mirror* led its back page with a mock cheque drawn on the Bank of Manchester United reading:

Pay Martin Edwards
Chief executive, Manchester United
£4,419,967.46
FOR ONE DAY

It was also the day that Chelsea floated, but on the AIMs secondary market. Ken Bates' 30 million shares, which had been valued at £16.5 million, went up to £18 million. The *Mirror* did a mock cheque drawn on the Bank of Chelsea reading:

Pay Ken Bates
Chairman, Chelsea
£1,500,000.
FOR ONE DAY

Just a year previously Edwards had got £1.5 million from selling part of his stake and it showed there was now an appetite from institutions for shares. This was a new phenomenon for the back pages. When Tottenham had floated in 1983 nothing like this had happened. Now Edwards could sell part of his holding yet retain control; for the back pages the myth of Edwards the fat cat was born.

However, at this stage, United's shares were still well below £1.50 and, as we have seen, VCI, sensing they were underpriced, made an offer which was not quite a bid.

Glenn Cooper, who was still advising Edwards, albeit informally, when VCI came in, did not think much of the approach and advised against it: 'There was nothing particular to be said about VCI. They seemed like a nice bunch of people. They were small and they made videos. It was a small company offering shares. The subsequent vehicle would have been very, very heavily borrowed. Martin was not tempted by the VCI bid. We chatted about it. My advice was against it, but I don't think he was inclined to take it up anyway.'

Even if Edwards had been tempted, within weeks came the second Sky television deal. As against the previous five-year deal which would expire in 1997–98, and bring in £40 million a year to all the 20 Premiership clubs (United in 1996 could at best hope to get £3.3 million from television) the new deal, which was to start in the 1998–99 season, was for four years and would bring in £135 million a year. With money from the BBC as well, by 1998 United could see its television income treble to £11.4 million.

The first Sky deal, as we have seen, had often been wrongly presented as a £304 million deal as a result of the hype put on by Sky when it did the deal in 1992. It was atually £190 million for five years. As football television deals went, the 1992 deal was big; but it was the second deal that was really different and very huge. The City recognised that and, on the back of it, not only Manchester United but football shares in general took off. The period between March 1996 and October 1997 would see the majority of football clubs that are now on the stock market float, 15 clubs coming to the market in the period. It was the start of the stock market's love affair with football, a love affair that has now ended, and for a time analysts spoke of a separate football sector on the market.

As the City often does, it looked ahead to what else might drive revenues. Encouraged by Chris Akers, then of Caspian, which eventually took over Leeds, pay-per-view became the buzz word for the City. Pay-per-view had been part of the first Sky contract. Indeed, at the meeting in the Royal Lancaster where, in May 1992, the Premier League voted for Sky and rejected Greg Dyke's ITV, Alan Sugar, who was keen on Sky, had lectured the other chairmen on the wonders of pay-per-view. But during the first contract nothing had been done about pay-per-view. However, by 1996, the continent had begun to experiment with pay-per-view and it was the revenue expectations of pay-per-view that began to drive the Manchester United share price and for a time the share prices of other clubs.

Julian Easthope, then of UBS Global Research, writing in November 1996 about Manchester United in a broker bulletin entitled 'Better the Red Devil You Know', while praising its all-round strength also focused on pay-per-view: 'Pay-per-view television provides the biggest medium-term opportunity with our estimates showing a potential profit uplift of between 33% and 100% by 1999.'

Easthope calculated two possible scenarios. One where 750,000 homes would take a Manchester United game which, if the cost per match was £5, would bring in £30 million a year from pay-per-view to United. The other scenario was a season ticket for televised pay-per-view matches which, if 3 million of Sky's 3.8 million subscribers took it up, would generate £153 million of revenue for the Premiership clubs of which United could receive at least £10 million a year. This, Easthope said, would add 33% to the 1999 profit forecast of £30.5 million before tax.

By this time the United share price had begun to climb. Having drifted along the bottom, less than 50p at one stage (the share split of three for one in September 1997 means this price is restated after taking the split into account), it had by 1996 moved up to just over £1 and then, following the announcement of the new Sky contract, moved to nearly £2. (In old-share terms, before the split it was around 427.559p for much of 1996 and had risen to 504p by 13 November 1996. Easthope was confident that it would rise to 680p within a year.)

The City's optimism had already started seeping out into the outside world. Exactly a month before Easthope issued its report, the *People* led its back page with a story of how super-rich Arabs from Abu Dhabi had emerged as the major players in the battle for the ultimate control of Manchester United.

There had been speculation that an Arab group was trying to buy Manchester City and the *People* had then looked at Manchester United's share register and discovered that a range of City institutions now held shares in United including Abu Dhabi Investment Authority. This was the cue for a story to suggest Arabs were into 'Gold Trafford' and for a photograph of Martin Edwards in Arab headgear. The *People* also printed a list of the institutional holders, which ranged from the BBC, the inheritors of Burrows' share holdings, and Post Office pension funds to Mercury, Schroders and the North Yorkshire County Council, which held 0.37%. The *People* wrote: 'The City Suits reckon MUFC stands for Money Unlimited Football Club – because they're a licence to print cash.'

All that had happened was that, five years after United had floated, when within days seen its share price had nearly sunk by a broadside volley by Kevin Maxwell, the City had finally started taking to United shares, and by October 1996, 60% of shares were owned by City institutions.

However, even as this was happening, there was change in the air at United, change just as dramatic as in 1992 when Freedman and Cantona had arrived in quick succession. Now Edwards was planning to bring in someone whose arrival would see Freedman decide he had no future at United. If Freedman's arrival at United was unexpected, then his departure in the summer of 1997 was equally unexpected.

Like so many things at Old Trafford it started with a lunch, a bit like the one with Knighton, on a non-match day overlooking the pitch, but one which ended quite unexpectedly.

11

THE NEW UNITED

In December 1996 Peter Kenyon decided to leave Umbro: 'I'd been with them for ten years. As well as being chief executive, I was responsible for all the commercial plans. I'd taken the company through one sale. When I started, it was £16 million and now it was £600 million. The plan was to take the business to the market in order to sustain its growth potential, but that didn't come to fruition, so in December 1996 I decided to leave. I'd done the original negotiations with Manchester United, I regularly used to contact Martin and when I came back through Europe – I was based in Greenboro in South Carolina – I would have lunch with Martin and discuss the business. Because of the importance of Manchester United and because of the historic business and personal friendship that had built up, I flew over to meet Martin, to let him know I was leaving. That the contract with Umbro was fine and everything would be fulfilled. At this stage I had no plans for my future.'

In February 1997, Kenyon, on his way through to Germany, came to Old Trafford to have lunch with Edwards in the Warwick suite. Says Kenyon: 'It was a typical winter's day in February, a non-match day, and we had lunch overlooking the pitch. We talked about the business and I told him I was leaving. He asked me what I was doing and I said that I was still evaluating what I was going to do. Then he said, "Why don't you come to Manchester United? We've been looking at the structure of the Board. Roland's coming up to 70. I'm looking to get out of the day-to-day running of the business, but I want to retain a definite interest. So I'm looking for somebody to put in that position. Why don't you join us? We've been looking to come and contact you anyway, so you've presented us with an opportunity for you to come in to spend some time as a deputy and the move up to chief executive." I was surprised, flattered, even flabbergasted.

Yes I was, really. I'd never have dreamed of working for a football club.'

However, Kenyon had been born in Manchester, grew up there and supported Manchester United. 'I think, to be fair, Manchester United was the only football club I would work for. Not from a fan's perspective, but from a business and commercial opportunity, an immense heritage in the football club and a huge international opportunity. It was a plc.'

Edwards did not think bringing in Kenyon would cause any problems. However, he was not absolutely certain and, not long after this, just after a Manchester United Board meeting, Edwards approached Freedman. 'It was about six to nine months after the Umbro deal. Martin spoke to me very nervously and asked, "Can we have a chat?" "Yes," I said. He said, "I need your advice." I thought this was strange because he had never asked for advice before. "I'm thinking of bringing in Peter Kenyon. What do you think about it?" I said I wasn't very happy. He said, "Why?" "I don't think we need him or want him," I said. He said, "Would you give it three months and see if you can work together?" I actually said yes.'

Freedman was finding it difficult to reconcile himself to the idea that the man with whom he had negotiated the last Umbro contract, was suddenly no longer a client from whom he could squeeze more money for Manchester United, but a colleague.

However, he was prepared to give it a try. But then came a press release in the programme of the home match against Sheffield Wednesday played on 15 March, a match United won 2–0, which so incensed Freedman that he decided his position at Manchester United was untenable.

Kenyon recalls: 'Martin and I drafted the press release in conjunction with the finance and PR people. It was a press release saying I'd been appointed and part of it said I was being brought in to develop the merchandising and the brand with my past experience and it was a fairly innocuous statement. It was fairly obvious. But the reference to brand and merchandising is what I think upset Edward. He felt that undermined his position in the business and that's the job he was there to do. Manchester United is not about merchandising. Manchester United the brand is all-encompassing.'

The press release did not directly mention Kenyon was coming in as Martin Edwards' deputy but it alluded to it.

Freedman was not at the Sheffield Wednesday match. He picked up the programme which had the press release later and, already unhappy about Kenyon's arrival, decided it was just too much for him. 'It was a very badly worded press release saying that he was going to look after the merchandising and I wasn't very happy about that one iota. I saw him coming in over me, definitely. And I could see no reason for it because Martin had no reason to be unhappy about my work. I told the Board and told Sir Roland Smith and said I wanted to leave.'

Martin Edwards, having decided to bring in Kenyon not to challenge Freedman but to groom Kenyon as his successor as chief executive, was clearly bewildered by this turn of events and could not understand Freedman's distress. Freedman recalls: 'He looked at me and said, "You're older than me, so how can you be the next chief executive?" I said, "That doesn't make sense. I've got different priorities to you."'

Freedman felt very sore about how he was treated: 'I felt I was not treated well. I definitely didn't see the press release, which was a disgrace. In fact I still say it is a disgrace. They probably didn't think I would go. I was earning a lot of money and Martin believes that money is a very important issue. It was important but not that important. Martin was earning a lot more money than me, but I was second largest earner at Manchester United. Of course I had qualms. I saw it as my baby and felt sad and there were a number of people I'd brought in that I'd looked after, built up and treated and whatever. David Gill was shocked when Kenyon came in, that's my opinion. I worked very well with David Gill and liked him. I had no quarrel with him whatever. Maurice Watkins – what can I say? He's a very rich man! I liked the professor. Every time I had dealings with him I found him very straightforward and honest. In fact, he said when I left that if he had been there full time this would never have happened.'

Freedman believes when Edwards brought Kenyon in, he had plans of withdrawing from the scene: 'Yes, his big goal was to win Europe and say goodbye or I definitely think when he's 60, he'll say goodbye. He's 55 now. It is not quite what Irving used to say, you know, to win the European Cup and retire that night. Irving said that but he would have carried on, wouldn't he? Martin sees Kenyon as his successor, which is why he is deputy chief executive.'

So did Freedman leave because he thought Kenyon's arrival meant he could not now succeed Martin Edwards as chief executive? Kenyon does not think so: 'I don't think he ever thought that he would succeed Martin, but Edward lost the plot, in that he thought I was a threat to him. But I would never have come as head of merchandising at Manchester United. It was turning over £25 million and at Umbro I was running an international business turning over £600 million.

Anyway, I was seen as a successor to Martin not Edward Freedman. So there was never a conflict in that respect.'

However, in keeping with the style that Martin Edwards has built up at Manchester United, despite Freedman's anger over the way he was treated, there were no scenes, no public rows. Freedman knew he could not row with Edwards: 'No, you don't have a scene with Martin. He doesn't like confrontation. I went to see him in the morning and said, "I've made my decision. I don't want to stay on." He had obviously thought about it himself because he knew I wasn't very happy. I told him I wanted to leave at the end of August, which is the end of the financial year for Manchester. This would leave everything clean and tidy. I said I would do anything he wanted. I must say they actually gave me a year's pay-off, so I wouldn't go with any other Premier League club during that year, which I honoured and they honoured.'

Officially it was presented as a smooth transition. Kenyon took over as deputy chief executive in May 1997. Freedman went on working with him for a couple of months until August 1997 and was then replaced by Steve Richards from Allsports, who had also had experience of Marks & Spencer.

But even now, two years on, Freedman cannot hide his anger at the way he was treated: 'I worked with Kenyon for two or three months. He never interfered with me but I just didn't see a future for myself. He's read a lot of marketing books and has been very corporate from what I understand. Kenyon trained at Courtaulds and then Umbro. He's very easy-going but I find him very boring and very corporate. He plays very much by the rules.'

This may be more than a harsh view of Kenyon and reflects the hurt Freedman felt in the way he was treated. However, there are people in United, including one Manchester United director, who, despite what Freedman achieved, are keen to debunk the idea that Freedman built the new United. This particular director is scathing about his business practices, alleging he would ask for ideas from suppliers, then use those ideas to market his own United products. However, this is not quite as bad as the director makes it sound, since this is what designers, who attend the fashion shows, do all the time. Freedman had been brought up in the retail trade, where such practices were both commonly accepted and considered very normal. There is, as they say, no copyright in ideas, as any author knows to his cost.

Kenyon skirts such criticism of Freedman saying: 'Edward played a part but he was not an uncontroversial figure. Edward is an entrepreneur. Within a certain business development cycle you need entrepreneurs. Then you reach a point where you've got to be a bit more formal. You've got to delegate. You've got to put structures in place. That's where we are today. I think Edward felt that he contributed to the success but that he wasn't treated as a success at Manchester United. That is because Manchester United is the success at Manchester United. Everybody plays a part. You are talking about something that has international reach, that has heritage. I think Manchester United's success was built on the 50s and the 60s, the heritage, the style of play, the imagery. We go to China, we go to South Africa. We say we've come from England. They know Manchester and they know Bobby Charlton. Bobby Charlton is the biggest name in football next to Pele. If you think of two players, you think of Pele and Charlton. Bobby Charlton is revered. If you've ever travelled anywhere with Bobby or Pele, internationally they are superstars. It transcends generations. I've been in Pele's company when we've been in Tobago and he stood there and signed autographs for three hours. He's humble. Kids who've never seen him play just revere him and it's the same with Bobby. Those are the things that make Manchester United. Players come, players go. Boards come, Boards go, but United goes on.'

Kenyon sees Freedman as having done a particular job for United at a particular time. Exactly a year before he left, another man departed the United management who had also done a particular job at a particular time. The departure of the two men can be seen as the end of the first phase of United's emergence as the top football club in the world.

That man was Robin Launders and although his departure was more low-key than that of Freedman and, almost amicable, during his five years he was a much more controversial figure in the Manchester United management team and created more waves at Old Trafford than Freedman did. So much so that during his five years as finance director, he created a strong impression that there was tremendous tension in the Manchester United boardroom.

Freedman had operated almost like a one-man business within United. Once he had got Edwards to make sure Launders was off his back nobody interfered with Freedman and he was allowed to set his own agenda.

Robin Launders' reign as financial controller was very different. As we have seen, Launders was brought in by Glenn Cooper at the time of the float to reassure the City that a safe pair of hands was running Manchester United's finances. But he actually made his mark at Old Trafford not as an accountant but as an engineer, the man of accounts metamorphosing himself once he got to Old Trafford into a civil engineer.

When Launders arrived at Old Trafford there was little thought that he would fulfil such a dual role. But United soon discovered that they had got two for the price of one.

The prospectus listing Launders' qualifications had stressed his accounting background, but there was nothing in it about his engineering expertise, and not many at Old Trafford, including members of the football club Board, were aware that he had such an engineering background. Edelson was certainly unaware when Launders came that he was also an expert in construction: 'I don't think he was brought in to oversee the construction of the stand. If he was I didn't know. What he did do was oversee the construction of the stand. Whether he was brought in to do that I don't know. But he was a civil engineer as well as an accountant. He had two degrees. Before him we had just had glorified book-keepers, but no accountant. Robin was the first proper accountant we had and I think he did a good job.'

For Martin Edwards, this dual role by Launders was immensely satisfying. The history of English football was of clubs rebuilding their grounds and going into ruinous debt. But here the accountant actually supervised the construction and it seemed ideal. However, Launders combined this with a style and a personality that always grated, and in the process he produced an immense cultural shock for many at Old Trafford. While he was a capable man of figures and could oversee the rise of new stands and engineering structures, he proved a disaster as a man-manager, he was much less successful to put it at its most charitable.

As we have seen, Freedman could not get on with him and while his view is undoubteldy coloured it is instructive, more so as he was not the only one who felt that way about Launders at Old Trafford: 'He was also not very good with people. He wasn't a very good man-manager. He's one of those people who is difficult. Martin calls him a genius, but I don't know. Launders was a pure accountant, a chartered accountant who had also trained as an engineer. His first big project was the rebuilding of the Stretford End and then in 1995 the North Stand went up. Project engineers were responsible for it, but Robin would supervise and look at the building of the stand.'

After the initial problems, Freedman and Launders kept out of each other's way. Ironically, given Launders' accounting qualifications, he did not give Freedman the impression that he was much of a commercial man: 'I did not have much to do with Launders. We had a Board meeting for the separate merchandising division once a month – Martin, Robin and myself. Robin wasn't very commercial and I don't think he understood how the commercial world worked. But after my chat with Martin I never had any problems as such with Robin and to be fair to Robin if you had a problem he was very supportive, but he wasn't commercial.'

Freedman's view of Launders as a difficult man is shared by many at Old Trafford with the exception of Edelson, who did not like Freedman but was very impressed with Launders: 'Robin was a different character. He was an intellectual. Maurice might disagree with me, but he had a great intellect. You just know when you talk to someone that he's on a higher plane than you are. He could certainly quote various things, the Scriptures, the Classics, and when he spoke to you it wasn't down to you but always on your level. He knew nothing about football, nothing at all, and he'd admit that he knew nothing about football. But he had a thirst for knowledge.' However, even Edelson concedes that 'some felt he was pushy and argumentative'.

In essence, what happened with the arrival of Launders was that, for the first time, a man with a public company background came into a business which had been a private company and where individuals had worked and lived together for years. So although much had been made of Les Olive's opposition to the rights issue in 1978, he was still at Old Trafford in 1991 when United floated and the business was run like most private companies where time and events do not dramatically change things and certainly not individuals. In such a situation, Launders was like a man from space bringing the ethos and culture of a very different world, the public company.

Glen Cooper provides an interesting picture of Launders: 'Launders presents himself extremely well and – given the rather reticent and shy Martin Edwards, and a very effusive, very rhetorically able Launders – it isn't very difficult for some of the outside world to form the conclusion that Launders was very much at the heart of Manchester United's success.'

Although Cooper wasn't part of the day-to-day workings of Old

Trafford he heard stories that indicated that 'Launders was not much liked and he was not popular at the time he was at United. But he had come into a private family-style business where, in many ways, people had been working together for many years. A lot of them had been there for a very long time. You inject into that a highly-gifted plc-style person, who has very fixed ideas about how things should be done, and you have a formula for difficulty. I think that in part describes what was happening. There used to be rows with him, so I heard.'

As far as the wider world was concerned, Launders' responsibility was to make sure that the City appreciated that United was not like Tottenham. This was a responsible football club that was run very professionally, the money made would not be frittered away irresponsibly and that dividends would be protected.

As we have seen, Launders had come up with the idea of a Transfer Fee Reserve to reassure the City that there was a definite pot of money for buying players and that there would be no mad splurges. Launders' accounts presentations to the City always made much of this reserve account. A typical presentation was that of the 1995 accounts. He devoted a page of the presentation to Transfer Fee Reserve. It had slowly been built up in the early years of flotation, reaching £4 million by 1994. Then in 1995 a further £4 million had been added to it following United's entry to the Champions League. In 1996 the balance stood at £8 million, the equivalent of £12 million before tax.

As Launders' successor David Gill, who has never looked at that account and never referred to it, says, this was a neat piece of accounting fiction needed at a time when the shadow of Tottenham's stock-market experience still hung over United and United needed to prove to the City that dividends were being protected: 'The Transfer Fee Reserve account was something Robin, Martin and Glen Cooper had devised. If the club made additional profits from participation in cup competitions they would be assigned to Transfer Fee Reserve. If we weren't as successful and we needed to buy players then the accounting reserve – clearly the cash is irrelevant – which had been built up would be used. At the same time dividends were to be protected. In the City this was seen as a dividend protection policy. But now we just ignore the account. I don't believe in it. Since I have been here, there have been no movements. The chairman Roland Smith does not like it; it was created to make the City happy, a cosmetic exercise, and has no cash impact. It has become outdated. And has not been used.'

The fiction of the Reserve is illustrated by the fact that since that £4 million was added in 1995, there have been no further entries in that account despite the many millions United have spent on players. However, if the City no longer requires the fiction, it does still serve a purpose – for the back pages. Every year since then, United's account keeps showing a Transfer Fee Reserve of £8 million, £12 million before tax, which provokes another story in the popular papers of Fergie's war chest of £12 million – but it means nothing. United's spending on players is not determined by what is in this fictional, notional Transfer Fee Reserve account.

Launders needed it for a particular purpose in the years of flotation and he used it well. His style was best exemplified in the 1994–95 season, when in January 1995, in what was seen as a sensational coup, Manchester United bought Andy Cole from Newcastle.

'The Cole deal,' as Martin Edwards recalls, 'started with a conversation with Alex and Kevin Keegan. We'd tried to get Collymore from Forest. Alex had spoken to Frank Clark [then manager of Nottingham Forest] about him. They were prevaricating. They couldn't quite make up their minds about it. [Ferguson tried to contact Clark but was told he had flu.] So then out of the blue Keegan rang Alex about Gillespie. Alex said, "I don't think I could sell Gillespie. I might do. But what about Cole?" That's how it started.'

It was agreed that United would pay £6 million for Cole plus Gillespie, who was a homegrown player but was valued at around a million. So the deal, which filled the back pages of the newspapers, was seen as a £7 million deal. Here it is important to stress how this figure entered the public domain. Unlike America, where players' contracts and transfer fees are disclosed, in keeping with the practice in this country and football clubs' love of secrecy, such details are never disclosed. However, during the publicity surrounding a transfer, journalists are given an unattributable off-the-record briefing about an approximate figure and this is what enters the public domain. And that is how the back pages got the impression that Cole was a £7 million player. At that time it was a British record fee and for weeks the sports pages made much of Cole being the first £7 million player in this country.

However, Manchester United, like all public companies, have to disclose their major contracts to the stock exchange and in the accounts. When these emerged it became clear that Cole was not a £7 million player. In the United accounting books Launders had valued Gillespie not at a million but at £250,000. So the transfer had effectively cost United £6.25 million and this was the figure shown in the 1995 accounts. However, this fact did not hit home until United's accounts were made public, and then there was a great commotion.

Terry McDermott, Kevin Keegan's assistant at Newcastle, poured scorn on the idea that Gillespie was worth only £250,000. How can that be? He was valued by Keegan and Ferguson at a million when he was sold by Manchester United and, if anything, his value since then had gone up to perhaps £2.5 million.

I was asked by my paper to speak to Launders to investigate what seemed like a mystery and it was clear Launders was irritated by what he saw as uninformed questions by sports journalists who did not understand figures or how Manchester United reported them. After he had harangued me for some time about the ignorance of sports journalists, I pointed out that, like him, I was a fellow of the English Institute of Chartered Accountants and had been a partner in a firm before turning to journalism. On hearing this, Launders grew very quiet and our conversation ended soon after.

The story illustrates Launders' style and how he, as the chief accounting officer of a football club that was a public company, had to cope with pressures he would not have had when he was at the car dealers Reg Vardy.

Freedman may be overstating it when he says Edwards considered Launders a genius, but he and Launders were the only two executive directors of the plc in the early years after flotation and Edwards clearly appreciated his work, particularly in relation to the rebuilding of Old Trafford. 'Robin Launders,' says Edwards, 'had a degree in civil engineering. He was quite knowledgeable in that. I don't think David Gill would claim that.'

Edwards can be dismissive about who has made Manchester United. When I put to Edwards that Freedman and Cantona made Manchester United, Edwards said, 'Robin Launders thinks he made Manchester United.'

During the crucial years of 1994–96, Edwards made sure Launders was well rewarded although Edwards remained the top earner. In that time Edwards earned roughly 2.5 times what Launders did. In 1994 Edwards' total remuneration, including bonus, benefits and pension contributions, was £229,000, Launders £104,000. In 1995 Edwards' package had risen to £290,000, Launders to £123,000. In 1996 Edwards had gone up to £321,000, while Launders was at £152,000.

However, by this stage, Edwards had granted Launders lucrative share options in what was to prove a defining moment for Manchester

United. It also had dramatic consequences for Edwards' relationship with Alex Ferguson.

The moment had come sometime in 1992, just after Ferguson had failed to win the League. A meeting was held in the boardroom with Edwards, Launders, Freedman, Ferguson, Danny McGregor, Alex Austin and Ken Merrett present.

The subject was share options and Edwards announced that, while everyone including Ferguson was to get 25,000 of share options, Launders would get four times as much – 100,000 of share options.

Freedman recalls: 'Alex Ferguson was very annoyed that he was getting 25,000 while Launders was getting 100,000. After all he was the manager. He refused to take the 25,000 offered and so did Ken Merrett, who said all the employees should get the share options.'

In 1994 a bonus issue of four shares for every one share held was announced. On 26 March 1996 Launders exercised his share options, now multiplied to 500,000 shares, at 67.8p, when the market price was 282p, making more than £1 million of profit in the process.

Launders would have earned a lot more had he waited a bit longer for, as we have seen, the United share price was to rise sharply within three months. But by the time Launders exercised his options, he appears to have decided that he did not have much of a future at United.

By the spring of 1996, having been finance director for six years and supervised the rebuilding of Old Trafford including the North Stand, the only way for Launders to go was up to become chief executive – but Edwards was clearly not going to make way for him. However, there was another northern club keen to make him chief executive.

Leeds were about to be floated on the market. The club was listed in August 1996 with Caspian, a public company, doing a reverse takeover of Leeds. Chris Akers of Caspian knew Launders and was keen he should become chief executive. Although not everyone at Leeds was keen on Launders (they had heard stories of his Old Trafford style and feared his arrival – he did not last long at Elland Road), he was offered the job by Bill Fotherby. In a sense it was the reverse of the transfer that brought Cantona to United and one where United it seems could not wait to see the back of Launders.

The story goes that Launders went to Edwards and told him that Leeds had made an offer. Edwards, instead of coming up with a counter-offer to persuade him to stay, is supposed to have said, "When are you going?"

This is, probably, one of those apocryphal stories that ought to be true.

Cooper doubts if that is how it happened: 'One of the things about Edwards is that he doesn't respond immediately. He's not at all an instinctive person. So I'd be extremely surprised if, whatever he felt, he said that. He may well have felt it. Again, I don't know. But one result is that whatever tensions there were on the Board were ended with the departure of Robin. I don't think there have been many on this Board, as a matter of fact.'

Freedman believes that when Launders went to Leeds, if the Manchester United boardroom did not exactly dance with joy then, 'I don't think the boardroom were *unhappy*. The reason he left to go to Leeds was I think Robin had put himself down to become the next chief executive of Manchester United. That's my opinion, and when he saw there was no way that was going to happen, he decided to go to Leeds. And he became chief executive there. Martin never held out that hope to him that he would become chief executive. I don't think so ever, but it was in Robin's own mind. It was a natural progression for a financial director to become a chief executive.'

Launders resigned on 14 August 1996. He had also been company secretary and two days later Maurice Watkins was appointed company secretary, although that was temporary as David Beswitherick eventually took over.

The search for a finance director to replace Launders took a little longer, the headhunters finally finding David Gill. The contrast with Launders could not be greater, both physically and in terms of personality. Gill is an enormously tall man who, like all tall men, can belie their physical attributes and be surprisingly gentle and amiable. And, unlike Launders, football is not for him an acquired taste. Gill has been steeped in Manchester United and, what is more, he can claim to be the modern Manchester United supporter, the one born outside Manchester but drawn to United.

Says Gill: 'I grew up in Reading. My father was a Plymouth Argyle fan. My brother chose Tottenham, his son is a big Chelsea fan and I chose United. I started in the 60s, my brother is older than me and was drawn to the double team of Tottenham. George Best and Bobby Charlton were my heroes. I never came up to Old Trafford. I used to go to London to watch them. I can't remember when I first saw them, it must have been either at Chelsea or Tottenham when United went down south to play them.'

For Gill, 'joining United was easy. I had always been interested in sport and always followed United. In the business sense United is in the growth sector, lots of excitement, lots of opportunities to grow the business'.

However, attracted as he was, when the headhunters came calling, Gill did not immediately say yes and had some hard choices to make. He had been in his job only a year and had just moved his family to Sunningdale in Berkshire. There was the question of relocating the family to the north, but in the end he decided the lure of Old Trafford was too great.

Gill was very aware that he was succeeding a man who had left a certain mark at United: 'Robin was clearly an able chap; he had done a lot of good. But I was aware that my predecessor had left a certain perception behind. Through the meetings and interviews, I was aware that his personal chemistry was very different.'

On 7 February 1997, Gill joined Manchester United. Within days, as we have seen, Kenyon came for lunch with Martin Edwards, and this started the chain that was to see the departure of Edward Freedman.

A month after Freedman left in August 1997, on 26 September 1997 Greg Dyke joined the Board as non-executive. Although all these changes at Board and management level meant little to the supporters, who hardly took any notice of them, cumulatively they marked the end of the first phase of Manchester United's existence as a plc and the start of the second phase.

There is a picture which captures this new second phase of United. It is in the annual report of 1997, issued on 16 October 1997. For the first time Manchester United had decided to have pictures in its annual report. The cover had a picture of Ferguson and Kidd holding the Premier League trophy. Roland Smith's chairman statement was illustrated with pictures, converting what in the past had been a rather dull presentation of columns of words into something quite attractive, and it was here that there was the most significant picture.

Most of the pictures were the ones to be expected: Teddy Sheringham, the new £3.5 million signing from Tottenham, an aerial shot of Old Trafford showing the new North Stand. But the most prominent and eye-catching picture was of the Board of directors taken on the Old Trafford pitch. Not players in track suits, but men in suits: Roland Smith looking a little stooped, Greg Dyke bringing up the rear with his hands behind his back and Watkins and Gill looking quite jaunty with one hand in their pockets. This was the new plc face of United and the half-smile on Edwards' face said it all.

The opening page of the accounts had gloried in the fact that on 11 May 1997 United had won the Premier League again, the fourth time in five seasons it had won it. Superimposed on a photograph of Beckham and the boys running on to a packed Old Trafford were the charts showing how well the plc had done, the increases in turnover, profits before tax, earnings per share and the dividend per share. The page was entitled 'The Theatre of Dreams' and Edwards had every reason to feel that United was now fulfilling every fantasy he ever had.

Whereas in the early years of flotation, with Freedman and Launders dominant, Manchester United focused on merchandising and getting Old Trafford right, since then it had diversified the club, becoming more of a group and a rounded organisation.

In the summer of 1996, just after the VCI approach and the new deal with Sky, United had come up with the idea of its own television channel and approached Oliver Olbaum, the television adviser to the Premier League. United was looking for television partners and, says Edwards, Olbaum 'came up with the names. We started talking with Granada, Sky and Flextech. Out of all this came the three-way deal between Sky, Granada and ourselves. TV business is very incestuous. In the end they made a joint approach. We thought the best way to do it was jointly.'

Edwards saw this, the first football channel, not as a channel for screening live Manchester United matches – it would hardly make sense to show it on MUTV where United would have to give two-thirds of its profit away to Granada and Sky – but 'it was purely to nourish the supporter base'.

Paul Ridley, sports editor of the *Sun*, was recruited as its first head. Ridley was about to be poached by former *Sun* editor Kelvin Mackenzie to join a reinvented *Sporting Life*, which the *Mirror* saw as Britain's first sports daily. Stuart Higgins, then editor of the *Sun*, aware of the approach, came up with MUTV to make sure he did not defect. For Ridley, it was both a challenge and a steep learning curve moving from print journalism to television.

Without any live or even recorded matches, except for quite old Premiership ones, programming required dexterity. But Ridley used his journalistic skills to schedule one and formed an effective partnership with Granada, which recruited most of the staff and also got offices in Deansgate near Granada. Ridley says, 'In six and a half months I put together a schedule, first to organise staff, create a television studio built inside Old Trafford and stick rigidly to a £10 million business plan. The challenge was to balance the interests of all three parties, Sky, Granada and United and devise programmes that allowed viewers to get their teeth into. There were endless conversations about MUTV getting either time-delayed rights to matches but with the digital market expanding, no-one was prepared to give an inch to a fledgling channel.'

MUTV was launched in September 1998, which, as it happened, coincided with the Sky bid. But interestingly neither Sky nor United tried to control what MUTV said about the bid. Soon after, Ridley decided to return to London and the *Sun*. Says Edwards: 'Paul Ridley wanted to try his hand in television. He realised he was a journalist, not a TV man, and it was part of his learning curve.'

United, like Sky and Granada, have two directors and Edwards, characteristically, is coy about how much United has invested. 'We have put in money, it's less than our partners, not tens of millions.'

In the 1999 accounts, United disclosed that its investment is capped at £1 million. The accounts also revealed that in the first year its one third share of loss came to £1.7 million. However the share of the net liabilities shown in the balance sheet was £1.2 million, the remaining £0.5 million shown as reserve because Sky and Granada had injected the majority of risk capital by way of share premium.

By the time Ridley was ready with MUTV, Manchester United was also into hotels, having paid £481,000 for a 25% stake in the hotel company Extramini, a company set up to invest in a hotel. The 111-room Quality Inn Hotel, which is just down the road from the ground, has prices ranging from £65 to £70 a night, and provides a grand view of the ground although not the playing surface.

Whereas MUTV was a United initiative and it went looking for partners, the hotel investment resulted from a phone call to Gill early in 1998. Says Gill: 'Robert Race rang me and we had been chatting about how we could take the business forward. You listen to new opportunities all the time and he made an attractive proposal for this hotel investment, then sent me some details and set up a meeting with Peter Roberts, who runs Countrywide Leisure Management, in Rippon in North Yorkshire, and is involved with Langdale Venture in the Lake District. I looked at it, discussed it with Martin and Roland, and we put it to the Board. We were not interested in anything less than 25%, and when that was agreed, we decided to get involved and put our weight behind it. Seventy-five per cent is owned by a number of individual investors.'

United were the second club to have a hotel next to their ground, Chelsea being the first, which is within the Chelsea Village complex. Edwards is adamant that United was not influenced by Chelsea: 'I think we would have done it anyway. It just made sense. It is a bit of a one-off investment for us and if ever the hotel was sold we would have the first option of buying it.'

Gill, in comparing the two hotels, says, 'Compared to Chelsea, ours is a four-star hotel with three-star prices complete with Gary Rhodes' first brasserie outside London. It is not as grandiose as Chelsea's hotel, which, when I visited on match day, struck me as good location, facilities were good, but how busy it is on non-match days is difficult to say.'

The hotel is meant to cater for the fans of United that travel from different parts of the British Isles, or even overseas, to watch them. Edwards says: 'Lots of Irish and Scandinavians come for match days. It would be in hundreds rather than thousands. They are fairly well off. They come to stay the Friday night, take in maybe a show, dinner somewhere, the next day go to Red café for lunch, see the game, probably stay the next night and go home on a Sunday. A proper weekend package. Now they can stay in the Manchester United hotel.'

Gill feels that where United might score over Chelsea is that, while Chelsea is operating in a very competitive London market, the United hotel may also tap into the Manchester hotel trade on non-match days. The area round Old Trafford is now developing and has been transformed from the industrial desert it was even a few years ago into something like the Docklands of London. 'With the Lowry Centre in Salford Quays and Imperial War Museum, it will really be quite a draw for business and leisure perspective,' says Gill.

Gill, who is on the MUTV Board, accepts that compared with the hotel it is the television station that will be the harder work: 'MUTV needs attention and needs work done on it. It will be a harder slog. Critical element is it needs more up-to-date Premier games on it, goals from Saturday's games, which at the moment cannot be shown on it. It can show the games from the first Premier League contract matches, as these have reverted back to the Premier League and the clubs.' The first live action MUTV showed was United's pre-season tour of Australia and the Far East and much was made of it.

Just as the hotel investment was being made, and MUTV was

launched, in June 1998 a property manager, George Johnson, was also acquired. For Edwards this has always been an important strategy: 'We are huge owners of land in Trafford Park. In Trafford Park, apart from Trafford Park estates, we are the biggest owners of land in the area. We always need land and we are always looking to add to facilities on match days. There is match-day car parking needs. When you have 6,000 executive customers, that might mean 4,000 cars plus all the rest of the 55,000, the large majority of whom come by car and want easy access to the ground. We are big acquirers of land for car-parking requirements. We have bought the land round the ground; we are always buying land.'

And in addition to the very big property portfolio, United are 'also always looking out for houses. Foreign players who come over here – the last thing they would want to do is buy a house. When their careers end they may want to go back home. So we need a property portfolio of houses. We have an option at the end of their contract of selling the house or putting in another player in that house. We buy and sell houses. It is mainly in Wilmslow, Brampella areas really. The home-based players own their own homes. But players like Ronny Johnson, Blomquist, Stam, Solskjaer – we buy houses for them. We have to provide rented accommodation for them when they first come. For long-term contracts, it is better to buy them a house. A decision we have to make is whether to buy or rent. Very often we buy, and hope to make capital appreciation and the player gets what he wants.'

By the summer of 1998 United the plc had taken shape. There was the Manchester United UK Merchandising Ltd, run by Steve Richards; Manchester United Catering Ltd, run by Mike Whetton, the man whom Edwards had confused with Michael Knighton when he announced the deal back in 1989; and then in August 1998 came Manchester United International, a new subsidiary set up for the overseas merchandising business, with Mike Farnan as managing director (although Kenyon, with his international business back-ground, takes a special interest in it).

The decision to set up the international merchandising was made at the same time as the Sky bid. For Edwards it was part of the continuous development of United: 'We had been looking at it for a while to take United into China and other places abroad.'

It is an area where Edwards feels United has barely scratched the huge interest and potential: 'The thing abroad hasn't really started yet. That's all in the future. We have big expansion plans abroad. In the Far East, the Middle East and Scandinavia. These are big areas for United.'

Some of these expansion plans started bearing fruit in the month after United won the treble, during the club's pre-season tour of Australia, China and Hong Kong in the summer of 1999. As United played the Australian national team and teams in Shanghai and Hong Kong, business followed United's performance on the field and the opening of new shops was announced. The strategy is for Manchester United to develop its brand across a global stage, building the concept of a theatre of dreams with the retail format varying from shop to shop. So in Dublin, Singapore, Dubai, Shanghai, Hong Kong, United have developed partnerships with regional and local businesses where the locals provide the site – the one in Dublin is of 15,000 square feet in the centre of town – and the staff, while United supply the goods, United make no capital investment and are assured of a profit on the sales of goods they provide.

This marks the final development of the global brand name of Manchester United, seven years after Freedman had first made Old Trafford realise that there was a brand called United to be marketed.

Yet in all these changes of personnel and development of new strategy over the years, and the many things that had had to be done to create the theatre of dreams, one United theatre manager had remained constant, Martin Edwards himself.

12

THE RINGO STARR OF FOOTBALL?

No man in English football has probably had more abuse heaped on him than Martin Edwards. And any assessment of him is, as Carlyle said, when writing of Oliver Cromwell, a bit like trying to excavate the real person from underneath the mound of abuse and myths that have been heaped on him over the years.

For many of the fans he is the ultimate Old Trafford hate figure. Some of this is part of his inheritance – Martin the son suffering for the supposed sins of his father Louis in buying United in the first place and depriving their hero Matt Busby of his rightful place.

This took on a new, and more deadly, form in 1990 when, following the Knighton deal, Michael Crick and David Smith published their *Betrayal of a Legend*. This was one of the first books of its kind – there have been many in this genre since – which, written by committed fans, was meant to be a series of polemical tracts where using their undoubted love and passion for the club, backing it with what they argued were facts, they try and demonstrate what's wrong with their club and English football.

In this case the authors sought to demonstrate that Martin Edwards, developing the ruthless business instincts of his father, had, in his desire to make money, destroyed the legend of the club, hence the title.

There can be no denying the research of Crick and Smith, yet for all their diligence their predictions of where Edwards was leading the club have turned out to be hopelessly wrong. Some of their assumptions are very questionable, to say the least, and underlying the whole book is a depressing suggestion of English snobbery.

One of the chapters of the book is entitled 'The Butcher's Boy'. Butchers, bakers, candlestick-makers are the legendary owners of English football clubs – small-town businessmen who flaunt their wealth by owning their local clubs. The sneer in this chapter and in many parts of the book for Edwards' family background is unmistakable.

But lest anyone miss it Crick and Smith rub it in by highlighting Martin Edwards' alleged educational deficiencies. Young Martin at 13 did so poorly at the Common Entrance that he could not go to Stowe, his parents' first choice and a major public school, and was packed off to Cockethorpe, 'a far from distinguished private school of about 200 boys which had just opened in 46 acres of parkland near Witney in Oxfordshire.'

But even here, say Crick and Smith, he did not do well: he finished with six 'O' levels, in British History, English Literature, Bible Knowledge, Economics and Public Affairs, Economics and English Language, but only after several sittings and even then was not good enough to take 'A' levels. The only option was the family meat business and dealing with the meat industry and butchers' needs at various stores.

It is difficult to resist the conclusion that Crick, who went to New College, Oxford, and was editor of *Cherwell* and President of the Union, not only thinks Martin Edwards is part of the undeserving rich but not very bright to boot. Of course it is not strictly true that you have to be bright to go to a major public school, otherwise the sons of Dukes and Maharajahs would never get to Eton. But if this point made by Crick and Smith is worth stressing it is because, a decade later, it had now developed into the settled myth that Martin Edwards is not bright and he is where he is not because he had earned it, but because of chance and luck. It is something that is voiced, albeit in private, even by some of Edwards' colleagues in the Premier League.

Crick and Smith's other major attack on Edwards has also resonated down the decade. This is that Martin Edwards is not devoted enough to Manchester United. At school he had played rugby. As a grown man back in Manchester he played rugby on Saturday afternoons for Wilmslow and continued to do so even after he got on the Board in 1970. Crick and Smith wrote: 'Many United fans would give the world to sit regularly in the Old Trafford directors' box. Yet even after Louis Edwards had got his son elected to the United Board in March 1970, at the age of 24, Saturdays for Martin Edwards were still devoted to Wilmslow and his "first love" rugby.'

In the eyes of many supporters this is an even greater sin on the part of Martin Edwards than his love of money. It is now an accepted part of the creed of English football that only a fan, preferably an anorak fan, can truly own a club – anyone else must be suspect. The classic of this genre was probably Irving Scholar, who, as Jeff Randall, editor of

Sunday Business, used to joke, would ask a new girlfriend on their first date to name the Tottenham double team. If she failed the date would end with the first drink.

Edwards can get touchy about suggestions that, because he played rugby at school – 'I was at a rugby school. I played rugby, I never played football. I have not touched a rugby ball since 1971' – he does not know enough about football or the history of Manchester United: 'You have a quiz on Manchester United and nobody knows more about it than I do. I did 1,000 questions once and I got 70% right. I know as much about Manchester United as Irving Scholar knows about Tottenham. I've been supporting Manchester United since 1958 on a regular basis. I came here in 1952, first of all as a seven year old. I had six years playing rugby from 1965 to 1971. I have missed very few games since 1971 – that is the last 28 years. I have been a director for 29 years, I have been chairman and chief executive for the last 17 years. If I didn't like football, do you think I could really put up with 29 years on the Board and the last 19 running it every day? Does that really tell you that here is somebody who doesn't like football, because I don't believe it's possible to watch 40 or 50 games every season and not like it. You'd be an idiot.'

The very fact that Edwards has to make such a defence shows that in many ways this is both the most depressing aspect of the attack on him and the most revealing of what is called 'fans psychology'. It suggests that a person's loyalty to a football club must be in doubt if he has any other sporting interest. Crick and Smith make much of the office Edwards has at Old Trafford, their implication being a modern properly furnished office is against the ethos of the club, but do not mention that in the bookcase is a book called *Cricket Crossfire*, a biography of Keith Miller, the great Australian cricketer and a hero of Edwards'.

Edwards is part of the generation who grew up as sports lovers before they became fans of individual clubs. While this did not stop them from developing loyalty to particular clubs, this did not mean they could not enjoy other sports. So Edwards played rugby and cricket and still follows cricket avidly. Indeed, two weeks after United won the Champions League in Barcelona, Edwards was at the other Old Trafford to watch perhaps one of the greatest ever one-day cricket matches, the semi-final of the cricket World Cup between Australia and South Africa. It ended in a tie and Australia just managed to qualify for the final and went on to win the World Cup. Edwards later described the final heart-stopping moments of the match, as dramatic as the United–Barcelona match, with great fervour. While United's victory meant more to him he also enjoyed the cricket semi-final.

However, for the modern football fan, such wide-angled sports following is heresy. A fan must be married to one club and any other interest is akin to betrayal. If having a family which made its money from the meat business was bad enough, and a father who bought his way into United worse, then the fact that Edwards played rugby and likes cricket is the ultimate heresy.

In 1990 such one-eyed love for a club was not quite as prevalent as it is today. But with Crick and Smith, writing just after the Knighton fiasco, and after nearly two decades of underachievement since Busby retired, it was easy to see Martin Edwards as the alien presence in the United boardroom responsible for all its faults: 'As Alex Ferguson's side grappled with the threat of relegation in the 1989–90 season, media speculation inevitably grew that he would become the sixth manager to be dismissed since Sir Matt Busby. Despite the occasional chants of "Fergie Out!", few people associated with United believed that another manager would solve the club's troubles. If change was required, it was at the very top.

'Even the world's most brilliant manager could not transform Manchester United, so long as the club is run from the chairman's office in the way it has been. United have been dragged into mediocrity by both administrative mismanagement and obsession with money which has infected the whole club.'

Even in 1990 such a conclusion was an extreme one, but from a fan's perspective, unable to understand why United were not winning, perhaps understandable. If anyone objected they pointed to what United had then achieved, or rather failed to achieve, under Edwards. Ferguson was Martin Edwards' third manager, after Dave Sexton and Ron Atkinson, and in the 1988–89 season Ferguson, entering his third year at Old Trafford, had won nothing and United that season finished 11th, having lost in the third round of the Littlewoods Cup and the sixth round of the FA Cup.

However, what exposed the weakness of the anti-Edwards brigade was the alternatives they held up as models for United to follow. Crick and Smith held out Liverpool and Everton as the ideal role models. They were, they said, run by chairmen John Smith and Philip Carter, who did not get large dividends and salary bonuses, and everything that was generated went back into the club.

Crick and Smith could not have anticipated how the decade would turn out, but even in 1990 they should have noted that in comparing

Edwards with Carter and Smith they were really comparing apples with pears. There just could not be any direct comparison between John Smith, Philip Carter and Martin Edwards. Edwards was a majority owner, Smith and Carter did not own their respective clubs. As we have seen, one family, the Moores of Littlewoods, owned both Merseyside clubs. Carter was an employee of Littlewoods and while Smith had shares, he was not the majority owner. Some of the shares Smith held were as a nominee of John Moores, head of the Moores family, in order to get round the fact that one person could not own two clubs (John Moores already being a majority shareholder in Everton).

Through the 1990s this joint ownership of the two Merseyside clubs unravelled and, in the case of Everton, it did so with such drama that, as the decade ended, Everton was unable to find anyone to buy out its current majority holder Peter Johnson, despite the fact that League rules, which prohibit one man owning two clubs, require him to sell – and only did so after a long struggle. What is more, Everton's current valuation of £30 million is only £10 million more than what Knighton was prepared to pay for Manchester United in 1989 and 20 times less than Manchester United's current valuation.

And if Liverpool have confined their turmoil to the field, and their boardroom has remained secure, it is precisely because they have chosen to ignore Crick and Smith's advice and continue to be owned by one man, David Moore, the son of Cecil Moore. Imagine the plight of Liverpool today if English football had followed the advice of Crick and Smith: 'The English football authorities would do all fans a service by insisting that no single individual can own a majority of shares in one club.' As it happens this is exactly the situation in Manchester United now where 60% is owned by institutions; no one institution, let alone individual, has a majority but that is not quite what Crick and Smith had in mind.

Nobody can blame Crick and Smith for not predicting the turnround in the fortunes of United, let alone the vast changes that would sweep English football in the 90s. It is, however, remarkable that a book published five years after Bradford and Heysel, and a year after Hillsborough, did not appear to have understood the implications of these awful tragedies or tried to look ahead to the sort of changes they might force on the game and the money demands they would make on the clubs as a result.

Yet there was one possible change Crick and Smith did examine and confidently predicted that it would drive fans away and bring disaster.

This was the idea of what was called the Super League led by the then Big Five of Tottenham, Arsenal, Manchester United, Liverpool and Everton. Fans were opposed to it, said Crick and Smith, and they warned the chairmen planning such a move that if a Super League ever came about it could 'easily kill, or at least seriously maim, the goose that still lays many of their clubs' golden eggs – the supporters who trudge faithfully through the turnstiles'.

Two years after the book was published the Premier League, which was in effect the Super League, did come about and the television money it attracted through Sky helped pave the way for the football revolution of which Manchester United has been such a big beneficiary. The goose, far from being killed, keeps on producing golden eggs, at least for Manchester United.

In such circumstancees it is clubs with stability in the boardroom, like Manchester United and Arsenal, who have had the resources both to make necessary changes to their grounds and successfully compete in the League. Others with less security in the boardroom have floundered or fallen so far behind that it may take them years to catch up, if ever.

Edwards can argue with great conviction that the turnround in Manchester United's fortunes in the 90s owes a great deal to the fact that he owned the majority holding and provided the necessary stability, a turnround which has seen Manchester United reach heights it had not reached even under Busby.

I have dealt at some length with the decade-old book of Crick and Smith because the picture they painted of Martin Edwards, embellished and retouched many times since by the many authors who have followed in their wake, has essentially remained unaltered.

This is that Martin Edwards is not a very bright man who does not love football, let alone Manchester United, merely loves money and if Manchester United has been successful it is not due to him but in some ways in spite of him.

Or as Jim White of the *Guardian* says: 'He is the Ringo Starr of football [the Beatles drummer who inherited the role Pete Best had made and got all the glory when he supposedly really did not deserve it]. Martin Edwards is the luckiest man. This thing has happened despite him not because of him. He is only interested in making money.'

Not surprisingly, Edwards' friends cannot recognise this portrait which they see as a grotesque, cruel caricature. Glenn Cooper, who confesses unashamedly that 'I'm a fan,' says, 'I think he's done a phenomenally good job.'

Nowadays Cooper rarely misses a match at Old Trafford and sits next to Martin Edwards. Cooper exudes an almost paternal feel about Edwards as he says, 'I am in a position of being able to judge and my judgement is that he's done a phenomenal job. I feel very pleased because as a sponsor we took a great risk as underwriter and we underwrote that stock, so what didn't get placed we took on to our own books.'

His view is that while many factors played a part in making United the greatest club in the world, central to it is Martin Edwards: 'A lot is said about how different Manchester United is and that it is successful because of some magic touch that gave it this phenomenal support and took it out of the realms of an ordinary football club and into the realms in which it now finds itself. And while there's a little element of that – certainly Munich gave it recognition and sympathy round the world – and within the Manchester community football is an enormously important aspect. Certainly passion surrounds it, but that doesn't distinguish it entirely. I think what is often overlooked is that this club and this business have been very well run indeed for a number of years. That's not a particularly popular view. In fact, the supporters have always taken a rather harsher view and, I think, wrongly so. The fact of the matter is that, since he's been involved, Martin Edwards has been nurturing that business. A substantial amount of profits that were made out of the business didn't go into his pockets. They went back into the ground and produced Old Trafford, even in 1991, arguably the best club football ground by quite a long way. He's a practised businessman, which is what everybody forgets. He learned his trade in the retail meat business with a pretty harsh father as a taskmaster – and old Louis Edwards, I think, was a pretty hard taskmaster on his son – and Manchester United has had a lot of very good experience. I think what he's done there is perfectly straightforward and has been extraordinarily successful. He recognised the need to develop the commercial business and brought somebody in he thought could do it, in the shape of Freedman. Freedman, on his own admission, barely scratched the surface of what could be done, but what he did do was excellent.'

Cooper would even go further and argue that some of the success Ferguson had enjoyed is due to Edwards and the way he has operated the management team at United: 'I'm not saying it's all his management, but it's certainly part of it. He kept his nerve when the fans wanted Alex Ferguson sacked and one must give him credit for that. In my opinion, he's been very much more instrumental in the way the player end of the business has gone than anybody outside understands. I think he has a considerable influence over who is bought and sold. I mean, Alex Ferguson has a huge influence, but I think Martin is a considerable moderating and thoughtful influence on all of that. In some of the better decisions the hand of Edwards is, I think, to be discerned and Cantona may well be one of them. It wasn't an easy decision because Cantona at the time had a reputation for being extremely destructive.'

But nevertheless is not Martin Edwards the luckiest man in football? After all he did find himself in that position, he did inherit shares from his father, if not a majority holding a substantial chunk?

Cooper will have none of it: 'He's the best manager in football anywhere in the world by a great deal. There's no-one in the world who has had this experience. As for luck, I don't quite see where the luck came in. I think Martin recognised what was going on in the business and the sort of things he had to do. The youth policy wasn't something that just suddenly happened, it was something that had been going on for a period of time. A lot of the other elements that he put in place are bearing fruit today, including one of converting and the development of the ground. He's been very good at beefing up these facilities and balancing player performance with commercial demands of the club.'

It is one of the many paradoxes of the way fans judge Martin Edwards that, even those who are his biggest critics and would love to see his back, resent the fact that he has at times tried to sell and get out. So Jim White echoes many supporters, who may have chanted 'Edwards Out!', but deplore the fact that he has tried to sell: 'On three occasions he has tried to sell United to Maxwell, to Knighton and to Murdoch. He may have been better off sticking to it.'

Here White stresses one of the many contradictions of a fan's attitude to an owner of a club he supports: 'It is a curious thing about football fans, they are happier with an egotist as owner or chairman rather than someone who just takes the money. Their reasoning is an egotist would like the team to be successful. Take Berlusconi who owns AC Milan. He has used football as a platform for his ego. Edwards is no Berlusconi or Doug Ellis. He is perfectly happy to take the money. Edwards sees United as the goose that lays the golden eggs and fans feel he will always put money before success.'

English football has traditionally been happier with football chairmen who were bombastic egotists. The classic of this genre was Bob Lord, also a butcher who was known as the Kruschev of Burnley not only for his physical resemblance, but because of his habit of pounding furniture with his fists and barring reporters from the ground.

Also supporters' views of directors can change very quickly. In the 1960s, when Ken Bates first went to Oldham and started spending money, he received letters praising him as a saviour. But when he put prices up, they denounced him as a 'moneybags' who knew nothing about football.

One reason why Edwards may not have got the recognition that Cooper and his friends think he deserves is his style, which, as Freedman says, is not quite like that of other chairmen: 'I think Martin is very laid back, doesn't panic outwardly or make rash decisions. He's very good at appointing people to do the jobs they do and he doesn't interfere with them, which I think is an asset. I don't think he's really what I'd call a hands-on person. He comes in about 10.30 or so. He looks after himself. He likes his tennis. He leaves at teatime, sometimes later, sometimes earlier. He's a very organised person, mentally, and everything is in place. He likes rugby a lot. He cares very much for Manchester United. People say he's not a football person but I don't know what that's supposed to mean. Are you supposed to have played it? Are you supposed to have played for England? What does it mean? He understands football and likes it. He knows a good player when he sees a good player, and he knows a bad player when he sees a bad player. He was very supportive of Ferguson when another chairman might have sacked him. Absolutely.'

Even White, however reluctantly, is prepared to give credit to Edwards' delegation: 'He has got the best person for the jobs. Ferguson is a good example.'

And it is Edwards' decision to first hire Ferguson, then keep him when fans were baying for his blood, that is at the heart of the modern Manchester United.

Alex Ferguson, who was appointed in November 1986, was Edwards' third manager. Edwards had sacked Dave Sexton, who he had inherited, in 1981 and then hired Ron Atkinson. Under Atkinson, United had won the odd Cup but the League seemed unattainable and this feeling of despair was heightened during the 1985–86 season, when United started with ten wins in a row, looked as if it might overhaul Tottenham's record of 11 in a row at the start of the 1960–61 season, but then stumbled so badly that long before the end United's title chances were gone and it finished the season fourth.

Then in November 1986 came a humiliating defeat in the League Cup at Southampton. On the plane back the talk turned to replacing Atkinson. Edelson was on the flight: 'For away matches, four or five friends would come and we flew to away matches. This one was at Southampton but there were only two of us on the flight, Martin and me. There was a discussion with Martin about what we should do about Atkinson. The next day Martin rang and said the other two directors – Maurice and Bobby – were at Old Trafford and were talking about what we'd been talking about last night. Could I come down? My office is only about ten minutes away, so I went. We discussed it again and narrowed it down to two options: Terry Venables and Alex Ferguson. Terry Venables wasn't really available because he was at Barcelona. They were still in the European Cup and they wouldn't release him, we thought. We decided it wouldn't be worth considering Terry. Alex was obviously the first option, considering the relative merits of the two. The only thing against Alex was no Scottish manager had ever successfully come from Scotland to England. Busby was Scottish but he had never managed in Scotland.'

Earlier that year during the World Cup in Mexico Bobby Charlton had talked to Ferguson on the touch-line, while he was managing Scotland, and said if he wanted to move to England he should think about getting in touch.

Two years earlier in 1984 Ferguson had very nearly moved south, shaking hands on a deal with Irving Scholar to come to Tottenham. They met twice in Paris and everything seemed agreed but then Scholar was told his wife Cathy did not fancy London. Curiously, Ferguson does not give his side of the story in his autobiography and in June 1999, a week after Manchester United won the Champions League, Scholar, waiting by the carousel at Nice airport, saw Ferguson. As they chatted he introduced Scholar to Cathy and Scholar said, 'Ah, you are the woman who stopped him coming to Tottenham.' Cathy Ferguson just looked at Scholar and did not say anything.

Now, in November 1986, in the Old Trafford boardroom, the four United directors discussed how they could approach Ferguson. Maurice Watkins had got to know him when Gordon Strachan had come from Aberdeen. But it was Edelson who volunteered to make the call: 'We were all in the room having the conversation and somebody said, "How can we get in touch with him?" and I said, "I'll phone the club." I did not know him. I just rang him. I spoke to the girl on the switchboard at Aberdeen and asked for Alex Ferguson and she put me through. [According to Ferguson, Edelson told the switchboard girl he was Alan Gordon, Strachan's accountant, and put on a mock Scottish accent.] When Alex came on the phone I told him I was a director of Manchester United and asked him if he'd like to speak to Martin Edwards. Martin said, "Would it be possible to have a chat?" and Alex said he'd clear it with his chairman. He had an option in his contract that if a really big club – Rangers, Tottenham, Manchester United – was interested, he was allowed to speak to them. It was all done within hours. We rang him on Wednesday, Maurice and Martin went up on the Thursday and spoke to him, and Ferguson came down on the Friday. By this time Martin had spoken to Atkinson. Archie Knox stayed in Aberdeen. Alex did the right thing. He left Archie in Aberdeen until they found a replacement.'

It was not so much the money but the lure of managing Manchester United that brought Ferguson to Old Trafford. But three years later in 1989 nobody would have blamed Edwards if he had sacked Ferguson. The results were so bad that the crowds had turned on Edwards.

One of the most dramatic nights was that of 25 October 1989, when Tottenham played Manchester United at Old Trafford in the third round of the League Cup. Tottenham won 3–0 and fans tried to get into the directors' box to assault Martin Edwards. Edwards recalls: 'I was taking a bit of abuse in the box from some supporters. Someone in front of the box did actually try to get into the box and I think a steward or somebody stopped them. I've had abuse before and I'm used to it, really. I mean, there's not many people who actually like abuse. I think there are one or two people in the world who actually quite like abuse. I can't say that most people do and I certainly don't like it. But to my mind it goes with the territory, doesn't it?'

The abuse had got to such a state that often Edwards would vacate the directors' box and watch much of the match from near a box high up in the main stand. Edelson says: 'There was a little box which the announcers used just at the back of the stand – just near the door of the directors' box. The last row of the stand was a bit of glass, about the size of a standard desk, it looked out on the pitch and Martin used to go there.'

The Tottenham defeat had come after what was for Ferguson the lowest point, the 5–1 defeat by Manchester City. At this stage, had Edwards decided to sack Ferguson he could easily have turned the abuse round and become something of a hero with fans, saying the chairman had listened to them. But Edwards would not hear of sacking

Ferguson: 'It was a tough time for us and there was a lot of pressure for us to do something. A lot of supporters and fans don't always realise what's going on in the background in a football club and we knew how hard Alex was working behind the scenes. Don't forget, that year we spent an absolute fortune on players round about that time. We brought in a lot of players – Phelan, Ince, Pallister, Danny Wallace and Webb – and all those players at considerable cost in support of Alex. The last thing we were going to do was suddenly pull the rug from underneath him because we knew how hard he was working. We knew it was going to take time for him to learn the English game, because when he came down from Scotland he didn't know perhaps as much as he thought he did about English players and it does take time. Because we knew how hard he was working, we never lost faith in him. What we were trying to do was to resist all the pressure.' Edwards had not only given Ferguson a new contract at £100,000 a year, but in agreeing to Ferguson's purchases, had taken United into the red, something that Ferguson, at the time fearing Howard Kendall might replace him, was grateful for. As Ferguson said to Hugh McIlvanney at that time, 'I certainly don't regret for a moment asking Martin Edwards to go into the red to buy big in the summer.' Edwards, a cautious man, could not contemplate sacking a manager he was so committed to.

Edwards denies there was ever any pressure from the rest of the Board. However, one story that quickly made the rounds at Old Trafford was that, as Edwards opened one Board meeting, he said, 'If anyone wants to talk about Alex Ferguson leaving they should first leave the Board meeting. Now!'

Edelson is emphatic that the Board did not discuss sacking Ferguson: 'You have to remember that although the years were very tough, Alex was doing all the things, almost replicating what Matt Busby had done. He knew everybody in the ground – the laundry girls, the waiters, the groundsmen – he knew everyone. We were also evolving the more continental style of management where the manager was less and less in charge of everything, because Martin was getting involved more and more. On the commercial side, at that time the manager would not have gone to do a transfer. It was getting to the stage where at least they went together. It was moving on to the new pattern.'

Ferguson had restarted the youth policy first launched by James Gibson and Walter Crickmer back in 1938 and then developed so brilliantly by Busby. Also he had started tackling the drinking school centred round players like Paul McGrath and Norman Whiteside, as he sought to make the club more professional and the players fitter and more capable of coping with a hard league season.

Yet it is indicative of the deep distrust that has developed between some fans and Edwards that even now, ten years later, when Edwards' faith in Ferguson has been completely justified, fans still find it difficult to accept that Edwards did not think of sacking Ferguson. So instead of giving Edwards credit for the decision not to sack him as a shrewd, deeply thought-out one, it is seen as one of those chance events that happened, almost despite Edwards. Like everything else in Edwards' life, it is viewed as something that just turned out lucky for him.

'Yes,' says White, 'Edwards did stick by Ferguson, but I believe there has been post-event rationalisation. I know Bobby Charlton says they did not think of sacking him, but I am sure the axe was poised, and had Ferguson failed to beat Nottingham Forest in the third round of the FA Cup he would have been sacked.'

As we know United was not beaten and Ferguson was not sacked. Ferguson went on to win the Cup, the Cup Winners Cup the next year and in 1993 the League title, and these turned out to be mere appetisers for the sumptuous meal of honours that have followed. Yet, over the years, as trophies accumulated, the relationship between Edwards and Ferguson, far from deepening, appears to have soured.

It could be argued that back in 1989 both Edwards and Ferguson were drawn together by their common predicament, both were rather beleaguered. Edwards was in debt, did not know how he could raise the money to build the Stretford End and the abuse of the fans was getting to him. In the summer of 1989, before Knighton came for his lunch at Old Trafford, Edwards had told Ferguson that he had had enough and was planning to sell. A decade later Edwards has no money problems, Ferguson will rank as one of the great managers of all time and success has driven the two men apart. As Lord Bell was to discover, when he suggested Ferguson be told about the Sky bid in advance, Edwards did not entirely trust his manager.

The level this distrust has now reached, a decade after Edwards held his nerve, is very evident in Ferguson's autobiography, *Managing My Life*, which lays bare the true relationship behind the public façade of the chairman and the manager working together for the good of Manchester United. What emerges is a more complex story of strain and unhappiness.

Ferguson's argument is simply put: 'Conversations with Martin Edwards are usually straightforward and pleasant until you ask him for more money. Then you have a problem.' It is unusual for a serving manager to be quite so blunt of his employer; it probably reflects Ferguson's status as the untouchable of Old Trafford that he can make such statements.

Edwards, true to his style, has refused to respond to Ferguson's attacks. The feeling in the United boardroom is that it is a pity he should have chosen to make the charges. Ferguson's comments show that, if in 1989 Edwards was brave to defend Ferguson, Ferguson, far from feeling any gratitude, is embittered, and since then there have been moments when the two men have come close to parting. In the summer of 1996 Edwards even toyed with the idea of replacing Ferguson and for a time thought of the man they had considered in 1986: Terry Venables.

By then Ferguson's demands for more money and Edwards' refusal to accept them had become something of a boardroom serial, each episode more acrimonious than the previous one. As we have seen, the seeds of this controversy had been sown back in 1992, when there had been the ructions with the share options, with Ferguson feeling less than happy that Edwards had given Launders, the accountant, four times as much as he had given his manager.

In 1993, after Ferguson won his first title and was talking from a position of strength, he had gone to Edwards and asked for a pay rise. Ferguson had been very upset to discover that he earned a lot less than his fellow Scot George Graham. In 1993, George Graham, with two Championships for Arsenal, two Littlewoods Cup and one FA Cup, completing a unique Cup double, was the highest-paid manager in English football. Graham told Ferguson how much he earned and Ferguson mentioned that figure to Edwards, hoping to achieve parity. Edwards checked with Dein and came back to say the figure was not right. Ferguson was crestfallen. He did get a new contract, although it did not quite satisfy him.

The next round of what was now developing into a periodic pay battle came at the end of the 1994–95 season, a season when United looked like repeating their double but won nothing. The season had also seen Paul Ince, Andrei Kanchelskis and Mark Hughes leave the club. Ferguson had instigated Ince's departure but it was not popular at Old Trafford. Moreover, he was not best pleased to be interrupted on holiday by Edwards and told his assistant Brian Kidd was suggesting it was perhaps not such a good move. Also on holiday Ferguson had learnt that Hughes had signed for Chelsea because there were problems over his pension.

Ferguson returned from holiday to find the *Manchester Evening*

News had held a poll asking whether he should be sacked. It was at this point that he went back to Edwards and asked for a pay rise: 'My timing may have been ill-conceived but I still felt seriously aggrieved over having been lumbered with a pay deal that left me trailing so far behind George Graham.'

Edwards could not accept what Ferguson wanted and it was decided that Ferguson would go and see Roland Smith in his Isle of Man home where Maurice Watkins would also be present. Ferguson, having learnt from his 1993 experience, had gone back to George and was now armed with Graham's contract. He was 54 years old, he wanted a new six-year deal which would take him to 60 and he wanted a role in the club after he retired.

As Ferguson showed Roland Smith and Watkins Graham's contract, Sir Roland counterattacked by saying that he might be taking his eye off the ball: 'Well some people at Old Trafford think you are not as focused as you have been.' Soon it was clear he could not get a six-year contract, no United manager ever had such a contract, and there could be no role for him like Busby after retirement. In any case, said Roland Smith and Watkins, the whole thing would have to be held over until June 1996 when the remuneration committee would meet.

Ferguson says he came back from the Isle of Man flattened, confused and worried, but this probably drove him to achieve the second double in 1995–96, with United moving to a higher gear after October 1995 when Cantona returned from suspension.

However, Ferguson's demands for more money and United's refusal to meet them was very much part of the second double season and the night before the Cup Final, when United beat Liverpool in a scrappy match through a Cantona goal, Ferguson had a tremendous row with Watkins about his contract. Wrote Ferguson: 'I was absolutely disgusted. It was annoying that they had insisted on leaving the business until the end of the season in the first place and now their words, "We'll look after you" seemed utterly hollow.' Ferguson was so upset that he was thinking of resigning.

It was at this time that Manchester United came closest to parting with Ferguson. In February 1996, with the FA looking for a successor to Terry Venables, Jimmy Armfield – the man who had headhunted Venables – was charged with finding out who might be interested in succeeding him, told the FA Ferguson might be. Initially he was interested in the Technical Director's job but soon, according to Graham Kelly, then chief executive of the FA, it became clear that Ferguson just liked the idea of taking over from Venables. On 13

March 1996 Kelly went to see Edwards, who doubted whether the board would release him and told him 'No' on the 19th. However, as the season reached its climax, and wage negotiations with Ferguson dragged on, Edwards toyed with the idea of replacing Ferguson with Venables. Edwards was thinking that if Ferguson did resign it would be useful to have someone in mind to replace him. Terry Venables was to become free at the end of June after Euro 96 and, after a Board meeting, Edwards approached Freedman and said they were thinking of Terry Venables. Freedman could barely contain himself: 'What, Terry Venables? You must be mad.'

Nothing came of it and a week after the Cup Final Ferguson's accountant, after six hours of negotiations with the United remuneration committee of Roland Smith and Watkins, hammered out a deal. 'The arguing over the figures I had requested went on all day. To be honest it was pathetic.' Ferguson, having thought of resigning, accepted but remained unhappy: 'I was not given what I believed I was worth but nonetheless I had made huge strides in relation to my existing agreement.'

United had seen off the spectre of Terry Venables at Old Trafford.

Ferguson's book does not dwell much on the final cycle in these pay negotiations which took place just as United did the treble in 1999. Ferguson had a contract going on to 2000. Just before the season began Ferguson came close to resigning. He was on holiday in France, and doing some work during the 1998 World Cup, when he learnt that Kidd had an approach from Everton and United were giving him a new contract to keep him. It seemed to him Kidd always got money whenever an approach came. Then he learnt Kidd was suggesting that, instead of Dwight Yorke, United should buy John Hartson. Enraged, Ferguson flew back from holiday to confront Edwards and Roland Smith at his offices in HSBC and threatened to call it a day. He was pacified but it was clear he would have to be given a new contract.

Then came the bid. Sky was consulted and it was anxious to keep Ferguson. 'We wanted,' says Edwards, 'to give him a new contract but we did not do anything during the bid.'

After the bid was stalled, as Ferguson made his money demands clear, Edwards, having discussed possible terms with the Board, negotiated. The talks went on long and hard but Edwards could not come to an agreement with Ferguson. He returned to the Board only to find that the Board, having previously set down strict guidelines, now amended them and was more prepared to accede to Ferguson than it had been in the past. The whole thing left Edwards unhappy and only helped reinforce Ferguson's image of Martin Edwards as the man who will not loosen the purse strings at Old Trafford.

For detractors of Edwards, this only provides more evidence of his Scrooge-like nature to employees. As the 1999–2000 season began and Roy Keane did not agree to a new contract, which would give him nearly £40,000 a week, one tabloid newspaper totted up all of Edwards' income, dividends, salary, proceeds of share sales since United floated in 1991, divided it by the number of days since flotation, and found it came to £50,000 a day.

So it asked if Roy Keane is not worth more than £40,000 a week, why is this man, Martin Edwards, worth £50,000 a day? Has he really done more for Manchester United?

While Ferguson acknowledges that Edwards has treated him well, never interfered in the slightest about the buying and selling of players and has supported Ferguson's youth policy, he laments the rise of the plc and suggests it is responsible for the cooling of his relationship with Edwards: 'The chairman and I have got on well much of the time but in recent years there have been serious strains in the relationship and always the disharmony has developed over money. There have been difficulties about what I thought should be spent to secure great players for United and about my own wages. I feel I should have received a better salary for my period at United than was forthcoming from Martin, who is extremely guarded with money . . . I appreciate that life at United has changed drastically since the advent of the plc and that Martin Edwards had a difficult job. The new set-up had sadly reduced communication between us. Gone are the days when we maintained a constant, healthy dialogue.'

Ferguson does not mention the transfers Edwards thwarted, but the first one that made the fans feel that Edwards was being the Scrooge concerned Alan Shearer when he moved to Blackburn from Southampton instead of Old Trafford. Freedman says: 'I think the money became excessive in Martin's valuation. Shearer was going to break totally the wage structure of Manchester United, which I don't think Martin wanted to do at the time, or could afford to, come to that. The other thing was I don't think Shearer really made his commitment to United, which I think Alex wanted. Alex didn't want a mercenary saying, "I can get x amount more from you guys." Alex wanted someone to say, "I am committed to United and I'll come for United." I don't think Shearer ever did that.'

The pity about the souring over money is that it obscures how well Edwards and Ferguson could work together. An illuminating illustration of this concerns the decision Manchester United took in the mid-90s not to field its best team in the League Cup, a hugely controversial move when it was first announced. Ferguson argued that, as United searched for the European Cup, this was the only way he could reduce the workload of the first team.

'The Board,' recalls Edwards. 'has never criticised Alex for his policy in the League Cup. I think Alex would mention it and say, "Look, I'm going to struggle in this Cup or that Cup. We'll struggle to win all four. Something's got to let give a little bit. It's a chance for us to play some of our squad players." At the end of the day, team selection is the manager's decision. He has to decide with his resources the competitions he feels he has the best chance of winning. Don't forget when we first did that it was when we played Butt, Scholes and the Neville brothers and all the rest of it. It also gave them great experience at an early stage. We got beaten by York. Yes, and we've been beaten since by other teams, but I remember going to Port Vale with that team and winning down there.'

Edwards is well aware that in this battle between him and Ferguson only Ferguson can win. Many years ago he told Scholar that, 'One thing you should never do is get into an argument with the manager on the back pages. If you do you will lose.' Scholar forgot the advice in 1991, took on Terry Venables, and ended up losing Tottenham. Edwards has never made that mistake.

But he is so reluctant to enter the public arena that, even after Ferguson had revealed details of his pay talks, Edwards refuses to give his side of the story. Asked to comment on how Ferguson had to negotiate with Roland Smith and Watkins to get more money, Edwards says, 'I don't think that was necessarily so. But I don't think it's right for me to discuss.'

A reluctance to engage in any sort of public debate is deeply ingrained in his nature: 'I don't sell myself. I am not interested in PR and having PR people around me saying what a great bloke Martin Edwards is. I am not interested in all that. All I am interested in is doing a job. I do not want any publicity. All I want to do is run a successful business. I feel a sense of hurt about the way my father was treated. I am not impressed by publicity. I am not impressed by people who seek it or want to project themselves. I am not interested if I never appear in a paper. I would be quite happy. I have a slight distrust of journalists because I have been turned over before. Some people won't let anything get in the way of a good story.'

Edwards' reticence can take some extreme forms. For instance, while he is keen to debunk the idea that the high sales Freedman attained meant high profits, he will not reveal the profit margin on merchandising, despite the fact that it is hardly a secret for City analysts who write about it regularly in their circulars. All Edwards will say is 'that it was the normal retail or wholesale business margin, you'd be able to get a handle on it. But it's not as great as people think.'

Edwards' reluctance to talk publicly even goes so far as to keep secret stories which could improve his image and convince the fans that he is one of them. The most illuminating one concerns the 1999 FA Cup semi-final replay match between United and Arsenal, which United won through Ryan Giggs' wonder goal.

Just before he scored, with Arsenal just having missed a penalty and United down to ten men, Edwards could not bear to watch and left the Villa Park directors' box to go downstairs and have a drink and a cigarette. 'I was in a dreadful state. My nerves had gone.' Then, as he was having his drink, Giggs scored and Edwards missed the goal. 'I did not watch the Ryan Giggs goal.' The state Edwards got into is a condition a lot of fans would understand as they must have gone through similar emotions, but Edwards is reluctant to talk about it.

Perhaps the most revealing aspect of his personality came after United drew 2–2 at Anfield, having led 2–0, with Liverpool coming back through a penalty that United hotly disputed. At that stage it seemed the result would benefit Arsenal. That Sunday Joe Melling ran an exclusive story in the *Mail on Sunday* on Martin Edwards' less than complimentary remarks about the referee and it led to the FA writing to find out if he had a case to answer under the catch-all of 'bringing the game into disrepute'. Edwards describes how Melling came to break the story: 'Joe was very very upset. He approached me at the time. I did the interview with you for Sky [just after the MMC report turning down the bid was issued]. Then I did the piece with Steve Curry and with the *Manchester Evening News*. Joe rang me up and said, could he do a piece. I had already done a page in the programme, a page in the *Evening News*, a page in the *Telegraph*, and one with you. He said why can't I be included? I said, if I widen it up I have got to do all. But I felt bad about turning him down. So I felt I owed him a favour. I said I shall repay him. After the Liverpool match I rang him and said Joe, I am sorry about the rest of it. You can have this one. I felt very strongly. The penalty decision. I could not see in a million years how the penalty was given. The sending off [of Denis Irwin for kicking the ball away after a free kick had been given against United] was harsh. It is a judgement thing. The referee could have used a bit of common sense on that. As for the FA letter, I shall reply I can't retract what I said. It was said from the heart. I shall reply in confidence.

'I am,' says Edwards, 'as passionate about Manchester United as anyone, but I don't run around taking my shirt off or breaking the law or run round thumping people or running on the pitch or anything else, but nobody who knows me well enough can question my loyalty towards the team. If you are saying I don't stand on the East End stand and take my shirt off and wave it and swear obscenities at other people – is that what you are trying to say? If that means I am not a tribal supporter of Manchester United, then I am happy not to be.'

But if Edwards is reluctant to court publicity, Ferguson is the master of the back page and his handling of another reporter from Melling's *Mail on Sunday* illustrates this. Bob Cass, who knows Ferguson well, had run a story saying Bryan Robson, who was often injured, was making a come-back in a televised Sunday match. It was the back-page lead, but as the television cameras rolled, there was no Robson, not even on the bench. Roger Kelly, then sports editor of the *Mail on Sunday*, was not best pleased and told Cass so. Kelly then went off to play golf and as he returned home the phone rang. The voice said he was Alex Ferguson: Kelly thought it was a joke; but it was the real man and he told Kelly that Cass had the right story but Ferguson had made a late change and Cass was not to blame. It showed how Ferguson can control the back-page agenda, something Edwards could never hope to match but what is more does not even attempt to try. I have, myself, experienced Ferguson's mastery of the media, and how he can bend journalists to his will. In 1993, the *Manchester Evening News* started a colour magazine and was very keen to do a piece on Ryan Giggs, then seen as another George Best.

Ferguson refused to give permission saying, 'I know you are aware of my reluctance for Ryan to speak with the media, and whilst I realise that everybody wants to interview him, I still feel he's not ready to undertake these activities.' I wrote a piece criticising the way Ferguson was seeking to control Giggs and suggesting the parallels with Best were being overdone.

A few days later Ferguson, having just won the Premiership, was the guest of honour at the launch of a new edition of *Rothmans* and ridiculed me mercilessly, beginning with my name, saying, 'This lad called Booze, I thought that was some Scottish broth, wrote some rubbish about me controlling Ryan Giggs.' The assembled journalists hooted with laughter and nobody raised the question of whether it was right to deny access to Giggs. What was supremely ironical was that the hall was ringed with speakers marked 'Bose' – no relation.

With Edwards not telling his story and Ferguson always on the back pages, evaluation of the Edwards–Ferguson relationship was often based upon the perception of the press – particularly the sports pages, which tend not to reflect reality. There Ferguson is always referred to as the boss of Manchester United when he is in fact an employee – the most important employee but by no means the only figure. Indeed, while Ferguson is supreme in his domain on the field of play, it is quite distinct from the rest of the business.

'We have very defined roles,' says Edwards. So is Ferguson the boss? 'He is not the old-fashioned type of manager. His role is quite sharply defined. Alex would report directly to me as chief executive. Ken Merrett, the secretary of the football club, does a typical job arranging reserve games, deals with team travel and deals with the rule book. Funnily enough, the rule book is mainly done by Maurice Watkins, being a director and solicitor. He can deal with a lot of the rules and regulations.'

United have gone to considerable lengths to separate Ferguson's role as the man who handles the team from the rest of the business. Unlike many other Premiership managers, Arsene Wenger for instance, Ferguson has no office at Old Trafford. His office is at the Cliff, Manchester United's training ground, which is his domain and where he prepares his players for their tasks on the field.

When I mentioned to Edwards that Ferguson gets into his office at the Cliff at 7.30 in the morning, he said, 'It could well be. I don't know. He comes occasionally to the office [at Old Trafford)] His main office is at the training ground. I go very rarely to the training ground. Alex's role would be no different to the coaches in Inter Milan, AC Milan, Barcelona or Real Madrid. I think more and more clubs in this country run it the same way we do. We could not have had a George Graham situation in our club [where as a result of taking a bung over a transfer he was sacked by Arsenal and banned from football for a year] because I do all the buying and I do all the selling. I do all the contracts. So I don't think a George Graham situation could have arisen at Old Trafford. I have had a similar policy to dealing with transfers since Dave Sexton and Ron Atkinson. Alex is, probably, a lot different from Dave Sexton and Atkinson but my policies have not changed.'

As for Ferguson's role in getting the success for United, Edwards is keen to stress that Ferguson has been helped by its structure: 'Structure comes into it a little bit as well. I don't want to take anything away from the manager, he has done a great job team-wise. But he has also benefited from a well-run company at the back of him that takes advantage of the team success, that creates revenue to allow him to buy the best players. Look at 1998 when we won nothing. I don't believe any other club would have gone out and bought Stam, Blomquist and Yorke and spent £28 million. So suddenly when things are getting a bit tough or starting to slow our ascendancy a little bit, we have got the means and the resources to replace them. Had we not done that we would not be winning the treble, no matter how good the manager is.'

Edwards' great pride is he has built a business which will carry on and can even look to a time when Ferguson has gone: 'The fact is business carries on. Somebody else goes, the business carries on. Even when Ferguson goes, the business will carry on. United is constructed in a certain way; it will carry on.'

The fans and the back pages, however, find it difficult to see Ferguson as merely fitting in a well-laid-out United plan. As one colleague put it, Ferguson is more like a pop star who performs with his band of players. Old Trafford may be the theatre of dreams and players great artists, but this comparison does not quite hold. A pop star or a pop group is by definition an anarchic phenomenon, whereas Ferguson is part of a defined system. It is easy to see how the imagery of Ferguson the popstar emerges. In certain areas, the ones that are most visible, his profile is supreme. But in Ferguson's case this status does not make him the master of Old Trafford. Freedman says: 'Ferguson's word is not law at all. That is a myth created by the back pages. There are two different sides to United. On one hand there's the boardroom, plc or whatever, and on the other there's the football side. As regards the football side, the Board listens totally to Alex. He goes to them and tells them what he wants to do. I've never known Martin refuse Alex anything. If he wants to spend £10 million, or £12 million, Martin is totally supportive. Yet on the plc side Ferguson has no role to play.'

It is interesting to observe that Tottenham, despite becoming a plc, still holds on to an old football club tradition at its annual general meetings. At the end of it, after the formal business is over, the shareholders become fans and ask the manager of the day questions about players and tactics. Now this is a tradition of all football clubs. But United treat their annual general meeting like any other plc would. Ferguson does not attend the AGM and there is no forum for shareholders to revert to fans at the end of it and ask him questions.

Some of this reflects Edwards' desire to get things right, his belief that the form should be proper and correct. Some of Edwards' attitude also comes from his natural reticence reinforced from the lessons he drew from his father's relationship with managers. Louis Edwards had got very close to Tommy Docherty. When he had to be sacked, because of his affair with Mary Brown, the wife of the United physio, Laurie Brown, it was very difficult for Louis.

Martin watched this at first hand and was determined that he would never repeat his father's mistake and get too close to the manager or, for that matter, anybody else at Manchester United: 'My father got too friendly with Tommy Docherty. He used to go to races and things like that with him. Then when he got the sack Docherty was quite bitter about it. I think I have a very good working relationship with Alex Ferguson. But if you say do we go out socially together, no we don't. I am as close to Alex as I am to anybody else in the company. I don't socialise with players at all. I have seen other clubs where it has happened, and it always falls out.'

So while Edwards goes to the dressing room, he is never matey with players. He feels, having been involved for 29 years, he knows how people behave: 'I just believe there are certain things you do and certain things you don't do. You have to divorce yourself a little bit. You can never get carried away in football. Liverpool dominated football in the 70s and 80s. Now they have struggled a bit. You cannot take your eyes off the ball in football. Sooner or later something has got to be said or done and if you are friends they don't like it.'

It is this that has shaped his philosophy: 'I don't particularly make great friendship of anyone, my finance director, my deputy managing director. I don't believe in being bosom pals with them; they do not necessarily work. I have seen it go wrong so many times. I am a businessman. I run a business.'

There is only one exception to this iron rule by Edwards and, inevitably, the exception is for Maurice Watkins: 'The exception is Maurice. Maurice is a non-executive director. I don't work with Maurice day in, day out. But even here we don't socialise with our wives hardly at all. I don't mix business with pleasure.'

This aloofness is combined with a nature that is essentially cautious. So, although United were part of the Big Five who played a leading role in eventually forming the Premier League, Edwards followed the lead given by Irving Scholar and David Dein. Edelson says: 'Martin was in the very strong position of knowing that it couldn't take place without Manchester United. It was not a big thing at first and there was a lot of doubt about whether it was going to work or not. It would be fair to say Irving Scholar and David Dein played a more prominent role than

Martin Edwards in the creation of the Premier League and the television deals before that. That is because of the type of people they are. Martin is more careful and there's a lot to be said for not being innovative, for joining immediately after the innovators have done their bit. Martin was there but not initiating the actual steps.'

All this is combined with one other Edwards trait, that he does not really fall out with people. Ron Atkinson, despite being sacked, remains a friend and Glenn Cooper, upset as he was that United changed merchant bankers and moved to HSBC, after the VCI approach, will never even entertain a bad thought about Edwards. Says Cooper: 'I must say, I was upset. But did I have a row with Martin? No. Apart from anything else they were switching from Ansbacher, which is my old haunt, because it had begun increasingly to get out of the corporate finance business, whether willingly or unwillingly, and they knew they were going to have to move financial advisers. They had already moved their PR firm from Brunswick, who I'd brought in for the float, to Financial Dynamics. John Bick, who had been handling the account, moved from one to the other.

'I think they recognised they needed to – as they were getting larger they needed some full-scale financial services. They were looking at the East and they felt they needed some coverage out there. They were looking to start marketing merchandising. So having an Eastern investment banker would help. That's what they said at the time. They didn't come to us because this is a relatively small organisation and they wanted a large one.'

For a man who has done all this, to merely dismiss him as a butcher's boy who was not very bright but happened to have the right genes and then saw everything fall in place, is ridiculous.

Edwards is not charismatic, he is not an innovator, but he is more than the Ringo Starr of football. He has made mistakes and the Knighton saga was unedifying. But he has learnt and can claim great credit for the way Manchester United has now developed.

PART THREE

UNITED AND THE WORLD

13

THE REVENGE OF THE RAGGY-ARSED FANS

In July and August 1998, as Sky had negotiated with Edwards to buy United, the one subject much discussed at Sky's headquarters at Isleworth was: How can we get Alex Ferguson on board? As we have seen, Sky was keen to inform Ferguson before the bid was made official. Edwards, however, had vetoed the plan, feeling that, as Ferguson was not on the plc, he could not be told about it and fearing that if he knew he would leak it.

As Sky executives wrestled with the Ferguson problem, one Sky insider suggested that, 'the way to sell this bid to the fans is to say we have given Alex Ferguson a transfer pot of £20 million or £30 million and he is now free to buy Ronaldo.' However, Sky had been unable to make such an announcement before the bid leaked, and if Mark Booth's failure to identify Denis Irwin on the day the bid was made public was a public relations disaster for Sky, then the failure to declare that Ferguson would have money to buy top players from all over the world would have long-term consequences and provide further grist to the mills of the supporters who were now organising themselves to try to stop the bid going through.

The idea that Sky would buy United and that the very next day Ronaldo would jet in from Milan to Manchester was simplistic in the extreme. But in the eyes of many fans this was how the bid from Sky was seen. Once the bid was announced the one persistent question that was asked repeatedly on phone-ins and other media outlets was: So will United now buy Ronaldo? If the United fans asked the question in hope then fans from other teams, who also asked the question, were fearful that the answer would be 'yes' and would confirm their dread that a United owned by Sky would now rule the world.

The United Board did not see it that way and finance director David

Gill points out that the Sky takeover was never going to affect player purchase dramatically: 'There is a finite number of top class players you can have in the squad. Size of the squad cannot mushroom, you cannot invest in talent for a rainy-day type of thing. Sky coming in would require a return on investment and you have to try to justify the investment. It was up to us to say we need to invest in the players, reason it and get approval. Takeover wouldn't have changed that, but it would have made it less public. Probably less emotive than it is now.'

United, in any case, had never been great buyers of players, the £6.25 million for Andy Cole in January 1995 followed by the £5 million for Henning Berg in August 1997 being the only two purchases over £5 million in the twelve years Alex Ferguson had been there at Old Trafford. But now in July and August 1998 United spent money on players as they had never ever done before. Then, as we have seen, following the heartbreak of May 1998, Edwards had agreed to the purchase of Dwight Yorke for £12.6 million, Japp Stam for £10.6 million and Jesper Blomqvist for £4.4 million, a total of £28 million partly offset by the sale of Gary Pallister and Brian McClair.

Edwards had always looked with horror at the way other clubs had spent most of their income on players' wages. Not for him the ways of Blackburn, spending 98% of their turnover on wages. United in contrast never spent more than a third – in 1998 it was 31%, which was two percentage points lower than what Barnsley spent on wages and salaries in their only ever season in the Premier League. Such tight spending had irked Ferguson, who saw it as the plc holding back the spending on players. This was all the more galling given the Italian rivals he was competing with, where the likes of Inter, AC Milan and others on an average spent more than 50% of their income on wages. So despite all City talk of United's riches, when it came to buying players, United allowed the Italians to outspend it and dominate the international transfer market.

The arrival of Stam, Blomqvist and Yorke, combined with new contracts for six players, meant a very distinct loosening of United's tightly controlled wages structure. In the six months to 1 January 1999 wages and salaries had gone up by 23% to £16.8 million compared with £13.7 million in the six months to 31 January 1998. All this should have convinced United fans that while United did not behave like some English clubs, let alone Italian ones, Edwards and the Board would spend when they thought it was appropriate. But while in any other club the chairman and the Board might have been applauded for such buys, much to Edwards' chagrin, although not to his total surprise, the purchases of Stam, Yorke and Blomqvist did not quite appease the supporters. Stam's early performances for United were uncertain, raising fears that he might be like one of those early Ferguson purchases and prove a dud (and an expensive one at that); Blomqvist was an unknown Swede; and even Yorke's arrival was overshadowed by the fact that United had failed to get Patrick Kluivert.

In reading about how big and powerful United were, the supporters could not understand why in that case Kluivert did not come. He was, says Ferguson, so unimpressed that he would not even come and talk to United preferring to go to Barcelona instead. There were many reasons for this, not least the fact that Barcelona was managed by his fellow Dutchman Louis Van Gaal. But for many supporters, Kluivert not coming to United was not because of Kluivert, it was because the plc drove United and not the needs of football. If United was indeed as rich and powerful, indeed richer than Barcelona, as the City men said, why couldn't it outbid Barcelona? What was the point of having the greatest merchandising machine in the football world, and now being sought by the biggest media mogul in the world, if United could not get Kluivert to talk to it and did not even make an inquiry about Ronaldo? Did this not prove that all this talk of United's riches were not for the glory of Manchester United but to fatten up the plc for the City to bolster the share price and further add to the coffers of the 'greedy butcher's boy Martin Edwards'?

However absurd such accusations may have been, many people made it and the talk of greed, which had been revived with tremendous fury as Sky announced the bid, intensified still further when in February 1999 it was announced that United was not only the biggest club in the land but in the world. This was in a survey done by Deloitte & Touche and published in the magazine *Four Four Two*, which compared the income of football clubs round the globe.

The survey was a bit of hype, the accounting firm deciding to use football's financial figures to generate the right headline. It was not exactly a global comparison: there was only one South American club that figures could be found for and none from Africa or Asia. Deloitte's world was really Europe where it had taken United's turnover and compared it with clubs in Europe. However, even on this limited basis, United's figures were impressive. Their turnover at £87.9 million was very nearly equal to the combined turnover of Juventus (£53.2 million) and Inter Milan (£39.1 million), and comfortably more than Barcelona (£58.9 million), Real Madrid (£55.7 million), Bayern Munich (£51.6 million) and A C Milan (£47.5 million).

Gerry Boone, who had masterminded the survey, had pointed out its limitations, confessing that he was surprised that the only South American team in the survey, Flamengo, had come in 11th with a turnover of £37.4 million. He had also heard that there was another Brazilian club, Vasco da Gama, which had a reported turnover of between £40 and £120 million and was Brazil's best-supported club. In any event, comparison with South America was difficult, partly because of lack of information and also because of the weakness of the South American currencies compared with sterling.

But the press and the public ignored the fine print and made much of the headline of United being the richest club, although Edwards and the Board knew that beneath the headline lurked a less encouraging story of United's marketing drive. There were the first indications that the marketing machine Edward Freedman had fashioned was stuttering. Having reached £28.681 million in 1997, the last year when Freedman was at Old Trafford, in 1998 merchandising was down by 16% to £24.1 million. Much of the reason for it, said Roland Smith, was the decline in sales of home kit, which was in the second year of its two-year life cycle. At the time of the 1998 half-time figures, which had shown a decline in merchandising of 11.4%, Smith had written: 'Clearly the home kit is the most important in our replica kit range and a new kit will be on sale for next season.'

However, by the time he came to make his chairman's statement for the full-year results of 31 July 1998, which he made on 28 September 1998, three weeks after Sky had made its bid for United, he had to admit, 'The new home kit was launched in May 1998 and although sales were satisfactory at the launch they have subsequently been slow as a result of the World Cup and the absence of games at Old Trafford.'

When on 31 March 1999, with Manchester United awaiting the results of the Monopolies and Mergers Commission inquiry into the Sky bid, Smith made his statement for the half-year to 31 January 1999, he had to acknowledge that merchandising had declined still further. While gates were again up, by 18% compared with the previous half year, merchandising turnover was down by 20% for that period and had declined from £15.6 million in the six months to 31 January 1998, to £12.4 million for the six months to 31 January 1999. (By the time the full year figures for 1999 emerged, merchandising had declined by 10% to £21.6 million.) Smith tried to find various explanations for it, including the fact that there had been a change in the replica kit supply arrangements with a major wholesale customer to a royalty basis, but in the end he had to acknowledge that there were reduced home kit sales because people were not buying and consoled the shareholders with the thought: 'The programme to improve the attractiveness of the product range is progressing satisfactorily and the division's profit margins have improved in the half-year.'

All this gave Edwards and the Board pause for thought and, as we have seen, was one of the reasons that persuaded them all the more that the Sky takeover was right. But as far as the fans and the public at large were concerned, Smith's explanations were in the fine print of the chairman's statement that nobody read. United was the richest club in the world, being bought by the media king of the world, but when it came to buying players it still behaved like a small-town provincial English club run, as they alleged, by the butcher's boy more concerned with his own bank balance.

The charge may have been unfair but there was a dichotomy in the way United was perceived in the City and how it came over to its fans and the general football public. In the autumn and winter of 1998 those opposed to the Sky bid now exploited this dichotomy as a mighty populist weapon to make sure that the bid did not go through.

When we left Michael Crick he was on the train back to London on the morning after the Barcelona match, mourning not only United's failure to beat Barcelona after leading 2–0, but not at all confident of his own chances of beating Edwards. The night before the match he had joined forces with Andy Walsh and Jim White to help organise the meeting in Bridgewater Hall, but with nobody at the match much bothering about the bid, Crick's spirits were low and his best hope was that, while United would become part of Sky, 10% or more of the shareholders would reject the Sky offer. As we have seen, Crick had been prompted by the bid to form SUAM (Shareholders Against Murdoch) and despite his feeling of not being able to stop it, he was determined to have a go.

On 5 October 1998 Sky published its offer document to buy United with a joint letter from Booth and Edwards. Crick got to work immediately. It was a classic piece of Crick mischief-making which got him enormous publicity, although in the end it made no difference. The offer document issued to United shareholders had listed the various options open to them. They could accept all shares, all cash or a mixture of cash and shares.

But what if you do not want to accept it at all? This was not mentioned and is never mentioned in any such document. In this country, bid documents are no different from mailshots by supermarkets or mail order firms. When they make an offer, they do not say that you are free to reject the offer, this is always assumed. However, Crick, with a keen eye for the populist angle, saw an opportunity here to embarrass Sky and United, and set about trying to exploit it in some style.

A hotline had been set up to help shareholders. Taking the identity (with consent) of a real life Peter Munday, from 12 Keyside, Macclesfield in Cheshire (Crick divides his time between a home in south London and one in Oxfordshire), Crick rang the hotline and said: 'Well, I'm, um very confused, er, about the document you've sent out.' The woman at the other end answered with a laugh: 'Yes, quite a few people are.' Crick, as Munday, then went through the choices and the woman admitted that the fourth option of not taking up the offer had been missed out and that the document was 'sort of mumbo-jumbo'.

She also admitted that a lot of United shareholders were confused and had been ringing up and asking the same question. Crick immediately made the transcript available and took the matter up with the takeover panel. This resulted in a two-hour meeting with the panel, during which Crick and his SUAM colleagues made it clear that they felt that, by not specifying that the offer could be rejected, the document was misleading and Sky and United should be forced to withdraw it. As it happens the man Crick met there, Mark Curtis, is a Tottenham supporter, although that was not the reason he rejected Crick's complaint. Curtis pointed out that all offer documents were similarly worded, which only strengthened Crick's belief that the takeover panel and the City were out of touch with ordinary punters. 'The takeover panel is a lot of wankers, a racket run for City people and we proved that. Even Lord Wolfenden, chairman of GUS, agreed with us about our views on the takeover panel.'

United and Sky dismissed Crick's comments as just the sort of thing he would make, but he had actually got the PR victory he sought. At this stage, as we have seen, Crick did not think he could stop the bid. All he hoped for was to make sure at least 10% or more of the shareholders rejected the bid and in such a strategy such PR victories were crucial. Also the campaign was reaching unexpected places. Sources close to the Prince of Wales made it known that he was opposed to the bid and the Irish PM, Bertie Aherne came out against it.

While Crick was chalking up PR victories, Walsh and his IMUSA colleagues had begun intensive consultations with Waljee and the lawyers at Lovells. Waljee and her colleagues also saw Crick: 'We could not formally advise him because he could afford it. Occasionally there were certain aspects of company law we explained to him.' But their main work was with Walsh: 'About a week after my initial call to him I met up with Andy Walsh. He came down with his team. They had no idea of the legal complexities. They wanted us to talk through it stage by stage. It was the first of many meetings and they would go on for hours. They were hilarious. There were so many complex factors involved, whole different aspects of looking at the arguments. Andy and his colleagues were dynamic. Andy was trying to understand what was going on. They had an enormous amount of knowledge but it was not refined. The great thing was to see the confidence of the team grow.'

Lovells, who like many law firms are keen to build a profile in sports and have a sports law group, had a team of five people, mainly competition lawyers working with IMUSA. While Waljee was a lawyer she was not a competition lawyer, and in came Lesley Ainsworth, corporate partner Andrew Pearson and assistant Matthew Readings. Readings supported Tottenham, Ainsworth Liverpool and Pearson Millwall, but those differences were forgotten and, says Waljee, 'they worked flat out for two weeks. It was a substantial cost. We had the same level of resources as we would do for anything else. It was a very specific case. Murdoch was going to get hold of Premiership content, he had such dominance in all the other forms of broadcasting, so there was a specific argument relating to him'.

Their first objective at this stage was to make sure that the OFT, which was looking at the bid, would be made aware of the feelings of those who were opposed to the bid. The OFT was due to report to Peter Mandelson, then the Trade and Industry Secretary, and then he would decide whether the bid should be referred to the Monopolies and Mergers Commission.

As we have also seen, Crick, Walsh and White had agreed at the Bridgewater Hall meeting, on the evening before United opened their Champions League campaign with a game against Barcelona, that Crick would look after the City and the shareholders who were supporters, while Walsh would look after the bulk of the other supporters, what he called 'the raggy-arsed lot'. White helped on the media side.

The deadline IMUSA was working to was imposed by the fact that the Office of Fair Trading, under the Fair Trading Act of 1973, had to report to Mandelson by 19 October, although it could ask for another two weeks to deliver its report. Walsh and IMUSA were not only keen to meet the deadline but to make sure that all those opposed to the bid made their views known to the OFT. Walsh sought out people far and wide who could help his cause, including clubs in Mexico, France and other countries where media owners had bought football clubs. He found a man in Berkshire who worked for the large telecommunications company AT&T, who did not agree with Walsh but knew Murdoch and did not like what he did. He provided information on how Murdoch operated in the area of media ownership. Walsh says he sought to discuss issues with United but was turned down. But he and his colleague Chris Robinson had a meeting with Chris Haynes, head of Sky Sports press office and Vic Wakeling in a Manchester bar where Wakeling tried to find out why they were so against the bid.

Waljee can barely contain her admiration for Walsh and IMUSA: 'They became much more aware. In three weeks they produced the most amazing lobbying process going. At one stage Andy rang me up and said he was going to see Karel van Miert [then European Commissioner on Competition] and I told him don't go, they don't have jurisdiction. But he said it was important to go. I said fine and he went and saw Miert and got a statement which said, "I don't have jurisdiction but I am unhappy with the deal."'

If lobbying Miert was a long-shot, there was more intensive lobbying nearer home. Walsh lobbied all the football organisations, including the task force set up by Tony Banks, then sports minister, and headed by former Conservative politician David Mellor. In any case there was already an ally there, Adam Brown, who was also on the executive of the Football Supporters' Association.

The FA had had misgivings almost from the start and its chairman Keith Wiseman made it clear that it did not support the bid a view echoed by the Football League and many other football bodies.

The crucial question was, what would the Labour government say? It was here that both Crick and Walsh concentrated their efforts. Crick says: 'Tony Lloyd [then minister of state in the Foreign Office] was the most serious United fan in the government and he said it was difficult to do anything. However, he advised us to work with Terry Lewis, MP for Eccles. He is a United supporter and a member of IMUSA. Early-Day motions were organised and 150 MPs signed it opposing the bid. We knew Alistair Campbell [a fervent Burnley supporter] was on our side. Stephen Byers was also fairly sympathetic. Labour councillors lobbied him at the Labour Party conference in October and he said "I can't get involved", as he was in the government. But as he walked away, he gave them the thumbs-up sign.'

Both Walsh and Crick were well aware that Tony Blair's government was the most pro-football government that there probably ever has been in this country, which saw football as a useful populist weapon to curry favour with the public (one reason why the government was so involved with the English bid to get the 2006 World Cup). Before his election Blair had been pictured heading the ball with Kevin Keegan, then manager of Newcastle United and Blair's own team, and this was promoted by Campbell as the young prime minister of the new young country he sought to lead. In such a government, many MPs and ministers made sure their own football affiliations were well known and opposing the United bid, more so as it meant a strike against Murdoch, was very popular.

On 12 October, just before they made their submission to the OFT, Walsh and IMUSA came down to London and met Tony Banks at the Department of Culture, Media and Sport and gave them the two papers they were presenting to the OFT: one on public interest, the other on competition. Banks had, on the Sunday the story broke, expressed concern about the bid and now Walsh and his colleagues found he was sympathetic to their views. Banks was supporting football in its battle with the OFT and planned to introduce legislation should the verdict go against football. When his department came to make its submission to the MMC, it voiced several concerns about the bid.

However, one minister who had no interest in sports, let alone football, was Peter Mandelson, and he was the one who would decide whether the bid would be referred to the MMC. All eyes focused on Mandelson with some suggestions that he stay away from the process because of his friendship with Elisabeth Murdoch. However, he could not decide on his own. As in all such situations other government departments like the Department of Culture, Media and Sport and the Treasury had to be consulted.

The Treasury is the most important department in the British state and at the Treasury, then at the right hand of Gordon Brown, the Chancellor, sat Charlie Whelan, Brown's spin doctor but also a fervent Tottenham supporter and a man who had little liking for Murdoch. Wheelan was determined to make sure the bid was referred and that the Treasury made the strongest possible recommendation in that respect.

The Treasury had to fight hard. Mandelson's department, the Department of Trade and Industry, was not at all keen it should be referred and actually prepared a note which said just that. Its lawyers had said there were no competition grounds and there seemed no case for the MMC to look into. But with the Treasury arguing strongly that public interest demanded it be referred, Mandelson was hamstrung.

By now thanks to the efforts of Walsh and IMUSA, the OFT had such a deluge of responses, far in excess of anything it would get in a normal takeover, that it asked for a 15-day extension of the deadline to

2 November. On 27 October IMUSA lobbied Parliament, and while this meant nothing, it ensured that the public pressure was kept on. In an age of soundbites and media images, Walsh was well aware of the need to touch all the keys.

Two days later, on Thursday 29 October, Mandelson announced that he had accepted the advice of Sir John Bridgeman, director-general of the OFT, and referred the bid to the MMC. Bridgeman had advised that the takeover 'raises competition issues in respect of the broadcasting of premium English football, and may have implications more generally for competition in the broadcasting market'. There were also public-interest concerns and the MMC was given until 12 March 1999 to report.

That night Mandelson saw Elisabeth Murdoch and is said to have told her that he felt he had done something to upset her father.

Elisabeth, it seems, reassured Mandelson, saying Murdoch would understand and not to worry about it.

If this suggested a certain sanguine attitude on the part of Sky, and if it was shared by United, then that was because it had long been assured by its lawyers and other professional advisers that while the bid was likely to be referred to the MMC, there was no way the MMC could stop it.

Two weeks before Mandelson had taken his decision, I had met Tim Bell in the course of research for my book. Bell had told me: 'I assume there'll be a reference because I don't see how Mandelson can play it any other way. There's no justification for a reference, except something called public interest, which you can define to your heart's content. There's no competitive reason whatsoever and it would be much healthier if the government would allow only competition as grounds for reference. But you know, it's not, because it's "the people's government" and they're sitting there weighing up whether they lose or win more votes whichever they do. Refer it, don't refer it. Refer it, clear it. Refer it and kill it. It's ridiculous, but there's a massive amount of political interference in the whole thing. It will be denied. Everybody will say that's not what happens, but it is precisely what happens. I suspect it will be referred because the government's view will be, the longer this takes the better.'

However, Bell was sure that referral did not mean the deal was killed; it would delay it and then they would ask for guarantees and it would be allowed: 'Various undertakings might be sought. When Rupert bought the Thompson Newspaper Group he had to put in a new Board at the *Times*, a Times Newspapers Board, as separate from and independent of the News Corp Board. He may be asked to do the same thing. Who knows? It depends what it is they seek, but it will be difficult for them to seek undertakings because undertakings about what? As there is no competition issue here, if there was that would be a legal matter. Here it is public interest, which is a matter of opinion. It's not a legal issue.'

This was the line the lawyers for Sky and United had argued. They saw the referral to the MMC like a skirmish in a war. United and Sky would lose the skirmish, but when it came to the MMC they would win the war. United and Sky just could not lose. Lawyers for both United and Sky had been telling them that there were no competition grounds for the MMC stopping it. Compared with the *pro bono* work of Lovells, United and Sky had some of the best lawyers around. Sky had Herbert Smith, where partners Dorothy Livingston and Jonathan Scott led the team, and United had Freshfields, where its competition experts were Deirdre Trapp and Rod Carlton. These lawyers could not be more confident. Since there were no grounds on which the bid could be stopped, it was not worthwhile getting too worked up about relatively minor matters such as Mandelson referring the bid to the MMC.

Booth says: 'We always anticipated it would be referred to the MMC. But the lawyers also said it would go through. We had unimpeachable advice from everybody without exception.'

David Gill, who had been asked by Roland Smith to take charge of the day-to-day process of controlling United's efforts at the OFT and if necessary MMC, shared Booth's certainty that ultimate victory would be theirs: 'All the advice we received indicated that it would be referred to the MMC. We got advice from Freshfields and Sky got similar advice. We all expected a referral and then to get clearance. We always thought the easy option on such an emotive issue was to refer it. The brave thing was to not refer it. The advice we received from our highly paid lawyers was that it should get through. Get through the MMC reference, not that it would not be referred to the MMC.'

Sky had had a preliminary meeting with the OFT back in August, even as they were negotiating with Edwards and the United Board. It is possible to get pre-bid clearance from the OFT on a confidential basis, but this would have taken weeks and Sky, after an initial meeting, had not pursued the matter.

Interestingly, United's response to the OFT had mirrored that of IMUSA. There, just as IMUSA had taken the lead and Crick's SUAM had associated itself with IMUSA's response, United had tagged along with Sky's presentations to the OFT. It was Sky's bid and at this stage

Sky needed to explain to the OFT what it was doing. Gill says: 'The OFT submission was made by Sky. We didn't do anything directly to the OFT. At the OFT stage we tended to have joint presentations with Sky. Sky was responsible for submitting the merger notices to the OFT, outlining the case and also supplying various documents. We looked at and gave input into the documents. We had a joint meeting with Sky at the OFT and we then had further meetings which Martin and Mark Booth went to. The joint meeting with the OFT in October and Martin and Mark's meeting with the OFT was a week before they made the reference.'

Sky, by now, had acquired some 11% of United by buying in the open market and the companies were keeping in close touch, discussing such issues as expansion plans for Old Trafford and a new contract for Ferguson.

Gill, speaking before the MMC came to its decision, had told me: 'Technically the takeover had lapsed. Freshfields kept saying we as directors have to take a decision in the best interests of Manchester United and we don't believe we are restricted in any way in what we want to do. Obviously, if we believe it is right for the club and it is of sufficient magnitude, Martin might discuss it with Sky, but there is no obligation. I think a lot has been made of such consultation. The reality is somewhat different. Commonsense tells you, if you are going to spend £20 million on a player, anyone with an ounce of sense would know we would chat about it with Sky. For instance, the stadium expansion, which is a £30 million investment. Sky could have thwarted that. They could have said, hold on we may take you over and we may want to revisit it. They voted their shares in support of the resolution to go ahead with the stand.'

Three weeks after Mandelson referred the bid, on 19 November, United held its annual general meeting in the Manchester suite of the North Stand.

Leading up to the AGM, United had announced that it had submitted a planning application to extend the stadium so that it could now seat 67,400. It would cost £30 million and United was seeking shareholders' permission for it. At any other time such an expansion, making Old Trafford the largest football ground in the land apart from Wembley, and almost twice the size of its nearest rival Arsenal, and fit to match the ones in Italy and Spain, would have taken all the headlines and delighted the fans. But now there was only one issue they were interested in: Sky's bid for United.

Roger Brierley, an actor from Manchester who lives in London's

Maida Vale, had bought shares when United had floated in 1991. He had bought 100 shares for £364, then seen them lose their value by a third, but did not much care as he had bought the shares to have them on his wall. He had never liked the Edwards, particularly Louis. He felt no single individual should own the club and preferred ownership in the form of a trust where Granada and the Co-op have shares. When the Sky bid was announced, Brierley had written to the *Guardian*, then reading Crick in the *Evening Standard* and seeing him on *Newsnight*, he had rung him and teamed up with him in SUAM: 'I was the Jack Lemmon to his Walter Matthau; I was trying to implement Michael's thoughts.'

In seven years as a shareholder Brierley had never been to an AGM. Now he helped marshal small shareholders so well that some 1,100 turned up, which meant many had to stand. This prompted Roland Smith to joke about how United did not like people standing and it was the first of many such wise cracks which Smith made at the meeting. He had opened the meeting by looking round at the packed hall and asking, 'I wonder why so many people are here?', which produced one of the few laughs in that fraught, bitter atmosphere. After that, as the *Mail* reported, he acted virtually like a stand-up comedian, which helped him cope with the hecklers and prevent the meeting from descending into anarchy.

Even before the meeting Edwards was aware he would be in for a rough time. The activity on the share register suggested several people had bought shares just to be there and it inevitably turned into a fierce denunciation of Edwards, with one shareholder referring to the fact that he had thrice tried to sell United: to Knighton, Maxwell and now Murdoch. 'Martin Edwards, I hope you get to heaven when your time is up. Surely, though, it's three strikes and you're out. Go Martin Edwards, go!'

The *Mail* wrote: 'Edwards must have felt like King Canute striving to keep his head above water as he was subjected to a merciless pounding by angry shareholders who until yesterday's Old Trafford meeting had been kept at arm's length. This time, flanked by security men in the Manchester suite of the North Stand, he was verbally attacked from all quarters.'

Edwards and the Board had the votes and they carried the day and all the resolutions they wanted were passed. Edwards, in one of his rare interviews, spoke on Radio Five Live and gave a spirited defence of the Sky takeover. He was pretty confident that, despite the fact that Crick and Walsh had made all the noise, the silent majority, as he puts it, were still with him.

Crick, who had led the charge against Edwards and even Roland Smith at the meeting, with disarming frankness admits: 'Eighty-five per cent of the United fans could not give a toss about the takeover. I never heard it mentioned at a game once, not even at the Charlton game which was on the evening the takeover was announced. On the following Saturday when we played Coventry I noticed the directors' box was half empty, so there may have been a protest from the Coventry Board. But apart from that there was never any indication at the games that the United fans cared.'

However, what Crick and Walsh and their allies had done was seize the high-profile moment of the AGM and score another public relations victory. There may only have been a few of them opposing the bid but they were succeeding in giving the impression they spoke for the many.

By this time almost everybody was joining in on whether the bid was a good or bad thing. The very day that Crick, Walsh and company were having a go, Louis van Gaal joined in the act. United were about to travel to Barcelona to play in a Champions League match and the Barcelona coach expressed the opinion that he did not like the Sky bid as he felt commercial interests were taking over in football.

However, there was deafening silence from one group of people and one very important individual.

The silent group was the celebrities who cluster round United. The journalist Jim White says: 'Angus Deayton and the celebs were very quiet. The celebs were very disappointing. Chris Eccleston, he was for us. But Mick Hucknall, Michael Crick's wife's cousin, did not say anything; Martin Edwards is his friend and Angus is a friend of Edwards. They did not wish to be involved. A lot of the celebs are personal friends of Edwards; they did not want to fall out with him. This campaign was not a celeb-driven thing.'

Crick is convinced that the 'celebs were frightened of Murdoch and of getting on the wrong side of Edwards. No celeb joined our cause.'

The other, even more deafening, silence came from Alex Ferguson. After the bid had become public knowledge, Edwards had spoken to him and tried to get him to support it. Edwards says: 'I could not involve him earlier because he is not a member of the plc Board. So you couldn't run the risk of widening it to anybody outside the Board. Even the football club directors did not know about it until it broke. Not even Bobby Charlton. Alex chose not to come out for the bid for whatever reason. I spoke to him more than once. I suspect Alex would have liked the bid to go ahead because he thinks it would have given him more resources. You will have to ask him and he probably would not answer it anyway. He has political leanings and he may have felt this is not the thing to get involved in politically. I don't believe it would have made any difference to the outcome if the manager had said he was in support. I don't think that would have swayed the MMC.'

Kenyon comments: 'Martin spoke to him [Ferguson] on more than one occasion. He took the line "I want to be neutral. I want to talk about football". He took the line, "it is not my position to dissuade people or persuade them. I want to be neutral. I think that is fair."'

Mark Booth, too, spoke to Ferguson but could not get him to commit himself in favour of the bid.

Ferguson, as he had made clear in his autobiography, was not happy with Edwards' reluctance to pay him more and in his public utterances stuck to events on the field.

In February, with the MMC finalising its report, White went up to the Cliff and spent two hours with Ferguson interviewing him for an article he was writing for the *Guardian*. United was about to play Arsenal and it was at this corresponding match in the previous season which Arsenal had won and which had marked the turning of the tide. From that moment on it kept flowing away from United towards Arsenal until the London side finally won the title. The race now was just as tight. Two weeks earlier Manchester United had gone to the top of the table, Arsenal were third and there was much White wanted to talk to Ferguson about. But when it came to the takeover he could not draw him out: 'Ferguson did not commit himself before the Arsenal game. I spoke to him for two hours, but when I asked him about the bid and the boardroom, he said he did not want to talk about it. I think Ferguson spoke to Andy off the record.'

Walsh, understandably, does not wish to comment on that. But the impression that Ferguson indicated to Walsh that he did not approve of the bid is strengthened by the brief but pointed comments he makes in his book: 'Many, but by no means all, bitterly disapproved of the plans for a takeover of Manchester United by BSkyB. But government intervention has killed the proposals, so the dispute is academic now. My own feeling is that the club is too important as a sporting institution, too much of a rarity, to be put up for sale.'

In their campaign Crick and Walsh made clever use of Ferguson. In one of the brochures produced by SUAM, the opening page quoted Ferguson in bold red as saying, 'We are United to the core', and SUAM commented, 'So when Alex Ferguson says, "We are United to the core" – remember so are we and so are you. Show your support for the club as we know it and help to stop this takeover before it makes us into the club we don't know.' The implication was clear: the bid by Sky was an alien thing and it would transform the club in a way Alex Ferguson would not approve.

Meanwhile, soon after the AGM, Edwards was involved in another tussle where the spin on the story on the back pages made it seem that once again the plc Board and Edwards were failing to help Ferguson. This concerned United's coach, Brian Kidd.

For the third time in very nearly a year yet another club had come in for Kidd. On 21 November, two days after the United AGM, following a 2–0 defeat at home to Southampton, Blackburn had slumped to the bottom of the League. It sacked its manager Roy Hodgson and wanted to replace him with Kidd.

As we have seen, at the beginning of the season Kidd had asked for permission to speak to Everton. If this did not please Ferguson, he was further alarmed to hear that Kidd was also suggesting United should sign John Hartson not Dwight Yorke, and over the telephone line from the Riviera, where Ferguson was on holiday, there were terse phone calls to Edwards during which Ferguson had made it clear that he did not think Kidd really wanted to go to Everton or even wanted to be manager. Ferguson felt Kidd was too insecure, too full of doubts about his own ability as a coach to become manager. Ferguson had flown back from holiday to confront Kidd and Edwards, and the issue had been resolved with Kidd getting a new contract which had answered Kidd's moan that Everton had offered more than three times what he was being paid by United.

This made him the best-paid coach in the country, and it was the second contract he had received, having had a new four-year deal in March 1998 when Manchester City had been sniffing around.

However, now Blackburn, desperate to avoid relegation, offered him vast riches, believed to be around £1 million. While United was prepared to offer more and deal with certain other issues, the main problem was, as Kenyon says, 'Brian was offered such an amount of money he could not afford to turn it down. He had a burning desire to be manager, be number one, and there was no guarantee of that at Old Trafford. He did not ask for it because he knew he would not get it, but he implied that. He definitely wanted to prove that he could be number one.'

On the afternoon of 2 December (that evening saw Tottenham meet Manchester United in the Worthington Cup quarter-final) Kenyon, Edwards and Roland Smith had a meeting with Kidd and his adviser at HSBC. Edwards in his previous public statements had said that Kidd would leave Old Trafford over his dead body. But at that meeting it was clear even such a dramatic gesture by Edwards would not stop Kidd from going to Blackburn. He made it clear he wanted to manage. Edwards says: 'Yes, I did not want him to go. When Everton came in we gave him a new contract. When Blackburn came in Brian made it clear at that time he did not want us to match what Blackburn Rovers were offering. Did he want a guarantee of succeeding Ferguson? No.'

It was one of those classic football conversations, in the coded language football loves. At no stage in the conversation did Kidd say he had spoken to Blackburn. But as Kenyon says: 'Well, there are certain things that are accepted but never confirmed. He did not say he had and you don't ask. It was a conversation in football's coded language. It became obvious it was pure money and we couldn't match it. Brian Kidd was the highest-paid coach by miles. Sometimes you have just got to accept things have to be different.'

Keith Harris had booked a car to take them to the game and Kidd, Edwards, Kenyon and Harris piled in. On the way to White Hart Lane, Harris could observe the nuances of football, of how Kidd repeatedly called Edwards chairman but referred to Roland Smith as the 'Prof' and Kenyon by his Christian name. The traffic was heavy that night and as the time for the match approached Kidd was getting anxious about getting to White Hart Lane in time. The driver was asked how far it was; he said it was a mile and Kidd jumped out and decided to run to the ground. But it turned out that it was three miles and it was more than a little breathless and less than composed Kidd who arrived that night at White Hart Lane. The moment they got to Tottenham, Edwards went to see Ferguson and told him Kidd was going, or in the curious jargon used by football, that United had given permission to Blackburn to talk to him. United made sure Blackburn compensated it for this permission. Edwards started by asking for £2 million and settled for £750,000.

However, for all the doubts Ferguson may have had about Kidd's inner resolve, he was less than pleased to see him go. Ferguson may not think Kidd can make a manager, and his subsequent failure at Blackburn suggests that, but he did not want to have to find a new assistant. He was now 57 and the fires of youth and energy were declining. There was no longer the same urge to try to work with a new assistant. Ferguson, as he makes clear in his autobiography, was also not best pleased that whenever a club came in for Kidd he got a new contract, while his own contract negotiations were on hold. As he writes: 'Brian found much less difficulty than I did in gaining improved terms of employment.'

That night Ferguson's mood was really black. Tottenham had beaten United 3–1 and while that did not matter (League Cup defeats in 1998 were a lot different than the ones he had suffered in 1989; now United were secretly relieved to be out of the competition), Kidd's departure put a different gloss on it.

Ferguson came to the post-match press conference, having spoken to Edwards and Kidd, although at this stage the press was not aware Kidd was definitely going. John Dillon of the *Daily Mirror* asked Ferguson whether it was difficult for Kidd to decide between Manchester United and Blackburn, a question that was neither aggressive nor meant to provoke. But Ferguson responded as if it was, saying, 'That's a fucking stupid question.'

Ferguson is well known for his rages at the press but what made this one interesting is how it was treated both by Dillon and the others in the following day's papers. Dillon made no mention of it, indeed wrote a piece very complimentary about Ferguson's style of management. None of the other papers referred to this outburst – by the standards of Ferguson's press conferences this was pretty mild – and all the criticism was reserved for Edwards and the United plc for not doing more to keep Kidd and preserve the Kidd–Ferguson partnership. It showed the unique power Ferguson had over the back pages. At that stage nobody was aware of Ferguson's true feelings for Kidd and it was only nine months later, when Ferguson's autobiography emerged, that the truth of the relationship between Ferguson and Kidd was revealed. Meanwhile as far as the press was concerned, and many of the fans, Edwards and the Board were the villains in this Kidd affair in not doing enough to help Ferguson keep him. The sports pages devoted huge space to discussing this and Talk Radio even had a full afternoon of phone-in on Kidd and the effect of his departure. It was treated as a major blow for Ferguson and United and presented as a story where Edwards and the Board had not helped their manager.

* * *

By this time the MMC was well into its investigations into the Sky bid. Crick and Walsh, having tasted victory at the OFT, now moved to try their luck at the MMC. Walsh had lost his friendly *pro bono* lawyers, who having seen IMUSA to MMC, now returned to their more lucrative, if not quite as exciting, legal work. And at the MMC the paths of IMUSA and SUAM to an extent, if only in presentation terms, diverged. SUAM had gone along with IMUSA's OFT submission, but to the MMC it made its own submission.

Until now everyone had assumed that the only reason the MMC could possibly block the bid was the public interest one. But Crick had found lawyers who were willing to argue that there may be a competition angle why the bid should not be allowed. 'After the OFT, IMUSA carried on with their submission to the MMC, which was essentially what they had given to the OFT, and we went our separate way putting our own submission to the MMC. I discussed with an academic lawyer who is a big United fan. He wants to remain anonymous, because he is involved with the MMC. I was also brought in touch with another lawyer, who was an expert in competition law in the City, who also wishes to remain anonymous. They helped us with a new submission to the MMC. They explained to me why there was a competition ground against the bid which, not being an economist or a lawyer, I understood for about five minutes.'

Then just before Christmas a third lawyer was brought on board – Peter Crowther of Rosenblatt. Not only was he not a United supporter – he was a Leeds supporter – but he was not even a qualified solicitor. He was a consultant to a medium-sized firm called Rosenblatt but with an academic background, having a PhD in Law. Crowther was an old friend of Richard Hytner, co-founder of SUAM with Crick, who had also secured some £15,000 from an anonymous donor to finance SUAM. 'I asked Richard,' says Crick, 'will it embarrass us if it comes out who is funding us. And he said no and I was happy to accept the money.'

Crowther's arrival brought fresh thoughts. 'Peter felt,' says Crick, 'we needed to do more work. We did a supplementary submission to the MMC to the one we had already done, which was way beyond the deadline set by the MMC for submissions, but they accepted it.'

As Crick and the SUAM prepared to try to persuade the MMC, the panel was completing its site visits to both Sky and United. For the Sky bid the five-member panel was chaired by Dr Derek Morris, the chairman of the Commission, and included Nicholas Finney, David Jenkins, Roger Munson and Dr Gill Owen. Morris was an economist,

Finney a businessman, Jenkins a trade unionist, Munson a chartered accountant and Owen an environmental consultant. On 17 November they visited BSkyB and were given a presentation about the broadcaster. Twelve days later the MMC made its trip to Old Trafford.

The reference secretary of the Commission had rung Gill and asked him to arrange a trip to Old Trafford. The idea was to see the size of the operation and what goes on during match days. On Sunday 29 November, as United played Leeds, a 12-strong team from the MMC turned up. Meticulous as ever, they paid for their tickets, £22 each, and did not sit in the directors' box but in the stands.

Gill says: 'We gave them a tour of the ground and the facility. I did a presentation. Then we had a buffet lunch to continue the discussion. They were most interested in the television negotiations. It was critical.'

After the lunch Gill showed them to their seats, where they saw United go behind but win 3–2, and shortly afterwards United received a cheque for £264 for the tickets. United thought it had done a good job of showing the panel how it handled match days and what it was about. But there was no way of knowing. 'The chairman Dr Morris,' says Gill, 'was very even-handed and straight-faced but gave no indication which way he was thinking.'

For the MMC hearings, United had retained Freshfields as its legal representatives; HSBC attended some meetings and United had beefed up the team with Gerry Boon, advising it on certain aspects of the situation, like the evolution of the Premier League. United had an economist, Professor George Yarrow, the director of Economics and Business Policy Research based in Oxford, who was involved in a lot of the drafting sessions. United also engaged GJW as lobbyist to advise it on lobbying ministers and politicians. (IMUSA also had the help of a lobbying firm, but its identity, in line with its policy of secrecy, has never been disclosed.) United and Sky had agreed that Sky would do no formal lobbying of ministers and politicians, that it would be left to United to do that. It was a high-powered, expensive team which would cost United £2.2 million.

United and Sky were the principal players at the MMC hearings. But apart from IMUSA and SUAM there were many others who either appeared before the MMC to give their views or wrote to them. They ranged from broadcasters and those directly involved in football to local authorities and Members of Parliament. There were also some 300 individuals who wrote to the MMC about the bid. But it is the MMC's interaction with United, Sky and the two main organisations opposed to the bid, IMUSA and SUAM, that makes a very interesting timetable.

17 November	Site visit to Isleworth to see Sky
29 November	Site visit to Old Trafford
11 December	IMUSA hearing in Manchester
15 December	1st BSkyB hearing at MMC's Carey Street office
17 December	1st hearing with United at Carey Street
14 January	2nd hearing with BSkyB at Carey Street
14 January	2nd hearing with United at Carey Street
26 January	Hearing with SUAM at Carey Street
11 February 1999	3rd hearing with BSkyB at Carey Street

At the 11 December hearing in Manchester's Picadilly Hotel, the MMC heard not only from IMUSA but also the Professional Footballers' Association and Football Supporters' Association. Walsh had taken a delegation of 12 and was nervous in what was for them an unusual experience. They had been allocated 90 minutes and Walsh joked at the start that he hoped it would not have to go to extra time or penalty shoot-outs. In the event they were there for three hours and Walsh emerged with great satisfaction that the MMC had given them a very good and patient hearing. By the end, some of the IMUSA members were laughing and joking with the MMC members.

Four days later, on the morning of 15 December, at its Carey Street headquarters, the MMC had its first hearing with Sky and the atmosphere was very different from the one in Picadilly Hotel. Sky had taken a full team, including Booth, Martin Stewart, Mike Darcey, economist, Michael Rhodes, lawyer Ian West and Elisabeth Murdoch, in addition to lawyers from Herbert Smith. There was no laughter, no jokes and, according to one Sky source, within the first ten minutes they knew this was going to be a very tough meeting. 'They were,' says the source, 'just so hostile. The meeting was totally out of control. Questions were coming from all directions, from all the panel members. The chairman did not have control. And every time we answered a question we could see they were not believing us.'

However, Booth was not too concerned. This was a first meeting, the MMC was making definitions – the power of Sky, the markets in which it operated – and he had been assured by his professional advisers not to be alarmed. Booth says: 'The first time at the MMC I thought it was very tough. My advisers said that is how such meetings went. The role of the MMC was to take no position and play it down the middle with everybody.'

Two days after meeting Sky, on the afternoon of 17 December, the MMC had its first session with the United Board.

United had made its submission on the day the team travelled to Barcelona, the submission being sent by courier via the lawyers. For the hearing United took what was their strongest team of Edwards, Watkins, Gill, Kenyon and Roland Smith. The questions were tough and Smith, who was the only one among them with City experience of such things, tried to keep everyone's spirits up. At the coffee break he said, 'We have had a good first half, but I hope we don't follow our usual practice this year of having a poor second half.'

Although United and Sky were now making their separate submissions, there was still a lot of contact. Gill recalls: 'We gave them our submission and they gave us their submission. We were sensible. It was an agreed bid, a recommended bid. We felt it was sensible to keep them abreast of what we were doing, how we were approaching it and make sure we were not saying anything different. The issues they were having to address were similar to ours. We needed to make sure we were not coming from opposite ends of the spectrum.'

At the end of this first meeting Gill and Stewart compared notes and they both agreed they were getting a very tough time from the MMC. But again the advisers and the lawyers in particular were reassuring them that this was a first hearing and this was how the MMC operated. There was nothing to worry about – there was no way the bid could be stopped.

Just a week after the MMC had its first hearing with United, on 23 December, Peter Mandelson was forced to resign from the Cabinet. The *Guardian* revealed that he had borrowed money from Geoffrey Robinson, the Paymaster General and a fellow minister, to finance the purchase of a house in Notting Hill, a loan he had not disclosed to his Cabinet colleagues. Mandelson had done nothing illegal, but it was considered bad form, and after resisting the media pressure for a few days he went. He was replaced by Stephen Byers, the man who during the Labour Party conference in October had given what looked like an encouraging thumbs-up sign when Labour councillors had lobbied him against the Sky bid.

Jim White, who never thought the campaign to stop the bid would be successful, is convinced that 'we would have been defeated if Mandelson had not gone'. We cannot be sure. Mandelson will not talk or the MMC reveal its inner workings. But as the MMC resumed its hearing after Christmas it became clear that its position had, if anything, hardened.

On 14 January the MMC had its second session with Sky and United, Sky in the morning and United in the evening.

This second meeting with United was meant to be a follow-up session to discuss issues raised in its submission and by others such as IMUSA and SUAM. This was meant to go into the nitty-gritty of the bid and again, like the first, it proved highly emotive. 'It was,' says Kenyon, 'the first time the majority of us had been to an MMC hearing. The questioning was not hostile but it was certainly probing. I think the first meeting we did feel, yes, it was harder, tougher questioning than we had anticipated. The second meeting we thought had gone extremely well. So over the two meetings we felt we had been given the opportunity of putting our case forward, which we had.'

But if United tried to put on a brave face on the meetings, Sky knew after its 14 January meeting that its cause was a doomed one.

The meeting was better controlled; Morris as chairman asked all the questions; they were not being fired at from all sides. But the questions were, as far as Sky was concerned, just amazing – something that might have been scripted by Michael Crick or Andy Walsh.

One of the first points was: 'It has been put to us that if you take over Manchester United the first thing you will do is buy Ronaldo and this will distort the football market.'

No sooner had Sky explained that this was ridiculous, that it was buying United because it was a good business and Sky intended United's existing management to carry on and for Ferguson to make such decisions, came the second amazing point: 'It has been put to us that if your digital roll-out is in need of more cash you will sell David Beckham to raise cash.'

Sky protested it was absurd to think that way. However valued Beckham was, selling him and getting, say, £25 million would hardly make a dent in a digital business costing millions. A Sky source says: 'We said that is ridiculous. Again, why would we buy something and pay £623 million and destroy it? By that stage we knew there was no rationality to that process. There were also questions about changing the name of the team and moving it. It was very obvious that the two panel members who were so hostile to us simply didn't believe us. Their whole facial expression and body language said that. We were answering their questions truthfully, and were simply not being believed. We did not think we got a fair ride.'

Booth emerged from the second session convinced the bid had enormous problems: 'The second time we went back I felt we had problems. Reading the room, the body language. There was some argument which was pretty straightforward which we thought was not controversial and we felt we were having problems with. If that is the case you have got problems. The most obvious was how the rights are voted on for television rights. We said there is no veto. BSkyB as owners of Manchester United will have one vote out of 20. One vote out of 20. It is ludicrous to assume you can drive the television proposition. You have 19 self-interested clubs out there. We were prepared to have them not vote on the television rights. When that kind of discussion did not seem to be going very well I was pretty sure we had problems. I did not feel they were giving us the benefit of the doubt. On things like that, that are straightforward and clear cut and we were not getting through, my view was we were struggling. I told Deanna Bates that it had gone very badly. She agreed.'

The session was particularly telling for Booth, whose idea the bid was. He could sense that every time the MMC looked at him, it did not see a cuddly American but the figure of the demonised Murdoch, the red devil who was going to gobble up this unique British institution. Walsh and Crick's strategy of always insisting it was a Murdoch bid, one they said had been planned and designed by Murdoch himself, had paid off. Crick, in one of his SUAM leaflets, had listed every possible Murdoch misdemeanour he could find, including the fact that there were arrest warrants for him in India for something one of his television channels had shown. Now at the MMC hearing Booth and his Sky colleagues sat there, thinking they were representing a major public company, but the MMC saw only Murdoch in front of them.

Until now Sky had tended to shrug off the many outside voices that were telling the MMC it must reject the bid. These ranged from Labour and Conservative MPs to the Manchester City Council to the Portsmouth Trades Council. Also not one of the 300-odd individuals who wrote to the MMC supported it. However, the response of the

Premier League was critical and Sky wanted to make sure it did not join the growing anti-lobby.

The MMC had asked the Premier League for its views. As we have seen, initially many clubs had been opposed and talked of expelling United. This had come to nothing and Leaver decided that since there was no collective view he would make a personal response. The League had not taken a view on the bid or even discussed it. Six clubs – Arsenal, Aston Villa, Leeds, Newcastle, Southampton and Tottenham – had made their own submissions supporting the bid, but these were voices in the wilderness given the weight of opposition to the bid that was growing. Leaver did not quite go along with them. He was also not aware that the clubs had supported the bid and only learnt about it when he read the MMC report.

His view was that if the Premier League won its case against the OFT and collective selling was still allowed, then the merger would have some adverse effects and would require some safeguards. If the OFT case went against the Premier League then 'the adverse effects would be marked'.

Leaver's submission had infuriated Manchester United and marked another low point in the relationship. The relationship had never been very good. Soon after he had arrived, towards the end of the 1996 season, he and Sir John Quinton, chairman of the Premier League, had turned down United's request to extend the season. United had taken the case to arbitration and lost. United won the League that season, and indeed did the double, but when Leaver went up for the final match against West Ham, a match that was in effect a celebration, he, his wife and Sir John and Lady Quinton felt humiliated by the treatment they had received at the hands of the United Board which they felt was very discourteous. They were also upset that United had ignored Bass, the sponsors, and West Ham. They had been left alone in the United boardroom without anyone chatting to them. United in turn was amazed to learn that Leaver was upset.

Then there had been problems with the perimeter advertising boards. These were meant to be centrally sold by the League. United disputed that and claimed it had sold its own boards and that it could do a better job for the whole League than the League's own marketing set-up. The result was Leaver and United had got involved in a tussle which surfaced during several tense meetings of the Premier League and at times a stand-off between Leaver and Maurice Watkins. Leaver felt United was not being very straightforward, particularly Edwards. He even had to deal with it once while on holiday on the *QE2*. It ended in a messy compromise but further strained relations between Leaver and United.

Then as we have seen there had been the problems with United's involvement with Media Partners. When we left the story, Leaver had warned United and Arsenal not to talk to Media Partners on their own and United, despite being unhappy about it, had complied. By then, the time the MMC hearings began, it was clear Media Partners had lost. UEFA had got its act together.

On 10–11 December the UEFA executive meet in Beau Rivage Hotel in Lausanne and approved a plan which meant the 1999–2000 season would see a major shake-up of European competitions. The Cup Winners Cup would be merged with the UEFA Cup into a new UEFA Cup competition expanded to 96 teams. And the Champions League would be a 32-strong league where England could have three representatives, Italy and others could have four, with the winner getting as much as £40 million, almost five times what the winner of 1998–99 would get. Media Partners was reduced to writing letters to clubs asking for money claiming that its efforts at a breakaway had led to the UEFA changes. While the Italian clubs favoured paying Media Partners, United did not.

United may have started the process by talking to Media Partners, but after September, it had played little role in the UEFA negotiations, which were handled mainly by Leaver and Rick Parry. In November United had been invited by AC Milan, as were Liverpool, to form part of G-14, a group of 14 clubs which had won the European Cup in the past and saw themselves as representing club power to keep UEFA on its toes. But the main action was at the UEFA stage where United had much less input.

As it happens, just as UEFA were meeting in the Beau Rivage to finally kill off Media Partners, in London there was the row over the consultancy contract Leaver had given to Sam Chisholm and David Chance, the former Sky executives, which would see Leaver himself getting the sack in March 1999.

Nobody doubted Leaver's skill as QC or his devotion to football – he watched his first match at his favourite club Tottenham when he was a boy and still referees football matches on Sundays – but what was proving his undoing was what was seen by some as a certain hectoring style which went down very badly with the chairmen. One of them described it as like being back at school lectured to by a stern master who could never accept he had made a mistake.

In many ways it was perception of Leaver's style that would

contribute to his problems and had made the whole issue of the contract he had given former Sky executives Sam Chisholm and David Chance such an explosive one.

Leaver sought out the two men as the League's television advisers after the death of its previous television adviser Richard Dunn. Leaver saw the pair as good negotiators and crucial to the Premier League's chances of having its own dedicated football channel. Leaver felt that by creating the possibility of a credible Premier League channel, he could make sure there was a genuine bid for the next television contract. If the television companies felt there were no rivals, they would not offer much of an improvement on the present contract and the League would lose out.

Chisholm and Chance extracted a high price for their services – £650,000 for each of them every year for three years, plus either 5% of any increase in a new television contract or a 5% stake in a Premier League channel. All this could earn them £50 million.

To make matters worse, Leaver initially refused to tell the chairmen of the 20 clubs that make up the Premier League the terms of the contract. In November, at a northern regional meeting of the clubs, Martin Edwards had asked for details but Leaver refused. He is reported to have said, 'I cannot tell you the terms because if I do it will end up in Mihir Bose's column in the *Daily Telegraph*.'

On 3 December the Premier League had met for one of its regular sessions. The issue was raised and Leaver eventually relented and agreed to the clubs seeing the contract provided they signed a confidentiality clause. Six clubs including Manchester United stayed behind to see the contract and were horrified by the terms, which they felt were outrageous. Such was the intensity of feeling that Leaver considered resigning – he had been talking of going since August, now he felt utterly fed up. Dein persuaded him not to, and it was agreed that an emergency meeting should be called on 11 December, where clubs voted by 19–1 to reject the contract, only West Ham voting in favour. They also formed a sub-committee to try to renegotiate the contract.

It was against this fractious background that Booth sought out Leaver, aware of how incensed United was with his views on the takeover, and suggested they meet for lunch. The lunch took place at Harry's Bar just before Leaver went to the MMC.

Booth says: 'Peter, I and Vic Wakeling were there. Peter told me he was very supportive and did not see a problem with it. He told us he had no problems with the Sky bid. This was before he had made his submission to the MMC. He told us categorically he did not have problems with Sky and its proposed takeover of Manchester United. But clearly at the MMC hearing he was saying something different which was not very helpful. All I can tell you is most of the Premier League clubs I talked to thought it was a very good thing. Couple of clubs called us and said wish you had picked us. Peter's judgement of that was not very good. It was unhelpful to any club if you rule out media companies as potential owners. You are cutting out a lot of potential value that can be reared. That is something no chief executive would like to constrict.'

Leaver says he did not tell the MMC anything different from what he told Booth and Wakeling at the Harry's Bar lunch. The MMC were very interested in finding out how the television negotiations worked, and since they had been done by Rick Parry, he had taken him along to the hearing. It was Parry who explained how they worked. As for his views about the bid, he was making his own personal points as a man of football and a QC that there could be problems. In company law, the takeover presented no problem. But in terms of football, there could be problems.

The lunch was overshadowed by the fact that by this time Leaver was very unhappy about the fact that some Sky officials were briefing against him. Says Booth: 'Peter Leaver felt a lot of things were going wrong. He felt there were leaks from Sky about him which was not helpful. I said I would look into that.'

Whether a ringing endorsement by Leaver of the bid would have made any difference is impossible to say. The dice appears to have been already heavily loaded, not helped by the fact that Peter Rogers, chief executive of the Independent Television Commission, came out against the bid. It was to be further tilted on 26 January when SUAM and Crick made their presentation to the MMC.

Crick was extremely nervous about the hearing. Adam Brown had come from his hearing and said he had a rough time. Crick got hold of the transcript and studied it. It was decided to have a dress rehearsal of the MMC hearings and this was held in Crowther's offices. Crowther brought along a serving MMC member who was not on the panel, an economist Crowther had worked with. Present were the two other lawyers Crick had used to make his first submission to the MMC. Also there was the academic professor Jonathan Michie.

Although a Scot and originally a Glasgow Rangers supporter, Michie had taken to United after marrying into a Manchester United family and was a member of both IMUSA and SUAM. From the moment the bid was announced he had set about organising his academics against the bid, writing to various people, including Tony Blair, and even holding a conference on the subject. He and his fellow academics had made their own submission against the bid but he was also part of SUAM.

There was one other individual present for the MMC dress rehearsal at Crowther's office. This was Stefan Szymanski, a lecturer in economics at Imperial College, who had written many academic papers on football. He was advising the OFT on its case and had co-authored a book on football, *Winners and Losers*, which had considerably upset United. It had extensively used the material in Crick and Smith's book on United and in the process recycled some of the myths about Edwards – for instance, that he stopped Ferguson buying Gascoigne when, as Scholar pointed out back in 1992 and Ferguson has since confirmed it, it was Gascoigne and his agent who had opted for Tottenham, with Gascoigne even going so far as to deceive Ferguson.

The rehearsal in Rosenblatt's boardroom, which went on for three hours from 6.00 to 9.00pm, far from encouraging Crick had made him even more depressed. Crowther, too, felt it had gone badly: 'It was nerve-racking.' Crick felt 'so awful, I was so terrified about how it would go'.

They all went off to have dinner at a restaurant in Aldwych. Crick, suffering from nerves and worry about the hearing, hardly ate anything, but he and Michie paid the bill, which came to about £200.

However, the next morning at the MMC, the hearing which lasted about an hour and a half, was very different. Crick had gone with his team and, says Crowther, 'the hearings went better than expected. I knew the MMC was very reluctant to block a merger outright. But what struck me was a throwaway line when we said you can't trust Murdoch, there can be no safeguards, just look at his record. That was picked up immediately. I was pleasantly surprised and they asked us to draft a submission on precise undertakings.'

The moment Crick said Murdoch had not kept a single promise he had made on a takeover, the MMC asked him for examples, and Crick said, 'I can send you more details if you give me time.' The MMC's response to Murdoch was the first inkling Crick had it might go their way: 'I was surprised they were interested in that. I thought, we have a chance here.'

Crick soon provided the details. Then, when it was announced that Canal Plus were in negotiations with Sky, Crick got back to the MMC and suggested this might mean that with Canal Plus owning Paris St Germain there could be conflicts of one owner having two clubs.

Moreover, since both clubs were in Europe, United may not be able to play in the Champions League. 'I got on to the MMC telling them of the Canal Plus negotiations. They asked me to provide something in writing. I drafted a thing and sent it by eight o'clock in the evening. By two the next afternoon I had received a draft back of what they were going to put in our submission. It proved to me that they were looking around for all the arguments they could find to stop the bid.' Soon after, Crick's optimism increased when he had a leak from within the government which said it was going their way.

However, at this stage in February, this mood of optimism had not spread to United's entire anti-Sky camp. White, who had never quite shared Crick's optimism (he could not see a competition argument against the bid), also found Walsh very pessimistic: 'Andy was very frustrated. In February Andy was banging his head against the brick wall about the lack of publicity and I got an article in the *Guardian* about him and what he was doing.'

However at Sky the gloom was now universal. On 11 February, Sky had a third meeting with the MMC. The point the MMC repeatedly made was what would happen in any television negotiations if Sky took over. Booth wrote offering guarantees: 'We wrote after the third meeting. At this point I was very pessimistic. I thought it was a very small probability of a favourable outcome.'

The MMC by now had collected a voluminous amount of information, although it was not going to publish all of it. It sent back to everyone who had given evidence a draft, factual summary of what they had said. United along with its lawyers looked at it and, says Gill, 'we got them to rework quite a lot to make sure our case was put correctly. We had them remove the financial information we felt sensitive, about how HSBC had come up with a valuation of the business, and a bit on players' wages would have been taken out.'

On 12 March, a Friday, the MMC presented its report to Stephen Byers. The next day Walsh left a message on Byers' home phone reminding him of how important the decision was and asking him to jump the right way. That day on the *Mirror*'s back pages, Harry Harris had an 'exclusive' story saying the bid had been allowed through. A similar story, but not quite so certain, was on the front page of the *Guardian* under the joint byline of Martin Thorpe, their soccer writer and a news reporter. Harris and Thorpe had collaborated on the story. Harris had just won the Sports Reporter of the Year award and recalls: 'Martin had rung me a couple of weeks earlier saying he had heard the deal would go through. Then in that week I heard similar stories and I felt duty-bound to tell him since he had told me first and we decided to go with it. We got it wrong, but if you have to get something wrong, that was probably the story.'

Over at the *Daily Telegraph*'s City offices, Alistair Osbourne, who had excellent MMC contacts, had for weeks been working on it. He finally pieced together that the deal had stopped. However, since a previous MMC story on Ladbrokes had caused problems, it was decided to have it bylined by Ben Potter, another City reporter.

The moment Booth read the *Telegraph*, he was convinced his worst fears had come true: 'When I read the *Telegraph* story I was convinced that was it. I told Jeremy and Rupert and a couple of other Board members. I said it was very unlikely it would go through.'

Sky wrote a letter asking the MMC whether the *Daily Telegraph* story was true or not, and what was the source, only to get a dusty reply from the MMC, who said it was not responsible for newspaper stories.

Sky then decided to disclose to the *Financial Times* that it had written to the MMC, that it would be happy to have Manchester United withdraw from the television negotiations. But Sky learnt later that Bridgeman took the view that it was unenforceable.

Sky's decision to leak its letter to the MMC, saying it was willing to give guarantees, showed it had conceded; it knew it was going to be beaten but it was too late to make any difference.

On 9 April Stephen Byers announced he had blocked the Sky bid. In the light of the MMC's recommendations there was nothing he could have done. He did not have to read far into the report to discover what the MMC had decided. The two and a bit pages at the start of the 254-page report said it all: the bid had to be blocked; there were no guarantees that could possibly make it acceptable; and there were not only public interest grounds but competition grounds for stopping the takeover.

The night before, United and Sky had been informed that the report was coming the next day, but not what the contents were. That would be known only at 3.00pm on 9 April, at the same time as the stock exchange was informed. However, on the morning of the 9th, at around 8.30, Tim Allan found out and he swiftly informed Booth.

The question was: How would Sky react to it? Tim Bell spoke to Booth about two or three times that morning to discuss media responses from Sky. Says Bell: 'It was mainly when we were going to meet and who we should put up for television. We were originally going to go to Isleworth. Mark didn't come because there was nothing for him to do. He had done his quotes. The argument was, Vic Wakeling would do it better. He was the face of sport. What we had to say was, this is a blow for football, this is not a blow for Sky. We've still got plenty of sport. We met at about two o'clock at my Westminster offices. I was sitting with Vic Wakeling, who had been put up to speak and Tim Allan came in.'

The moment Allan came in, he said, 'Let's do the negative scenario.'

Bell was convinced it had been blocked: 'We were all convinced by then it would be turned down and we only rehearsed the negatives.'

Booth could see little logic in the MMC decision: 'I think it was an example of emotion outweighing facts and that is what a body like the MMC is supposed to see through. When you see the numbers of submission and they talk so much against the bid, then logic becomes less important. This was not to do with right or what the facts were but just human nature carrying itself to an illogical end-point.'

Not long after, Booth himself had gone, moving on to work on the Internet for Murdoch, having turned down an offer to join Bill Gates. He stoutly maintains: 'I did not move on because it was a reprimand by Rupert. No, there was no row. If this had been a strategic or vital component of our business, that would be different. The fact is Sky digital was a very big success. Sky stock outperformed the market. The day the MMC turned down the bid the stock went up. Everybody thought this would have gone through based on the facts. I did not go with Bill Gates because I saw an opportunity to be an entrepreneur. I got a chance of having a tremendous amount of freedom and it is a nice problem to have.'

Booth still maintains that his strategy of not just buying Martin Edwards' stake was right: 'I had thought of buying Martin's stake. I thought it would be cleaner to have a bid.'

Yet within months this was exactly what Granada, a rival Booth had feared might make a bid for United, and Sky itself, was doing. Granada bought a 9.09% stake in Liverpool, valuing the club at £200 million, getting a seat on the Board and the right to do all its marketing. Sky, having been allowed to retain its 11% stake in United (it has since had to sell under Premier League rules), then paid £13.8 million for a 9.9% stake in Leeds. Sky's bid for United had been revolutionary and, like so often in England, revolution had failed but change was coming, if in a different way.

Unlike Sky, United, despite the hard time it had at the MMC, was not expecting to be rejected and was much more surprised by the decision. As the news was announced Gill was with Sir Roland Smith in the offices of their PR consultant John Bick in London, while Edwards and Kenyon were at Old Trafford.

The reaction of Kenyon (like Booth, he just could not understand why the MMC came to their decision) showed how difficult it was for United to believe the MMC could have found a competition ground against the bid: 'We didn't believe there was ever any competition ground, right from the start. That was the legal advice. Never believed during the process that it became a competition question, so it was a public interest one on which this turned. Public interest is difficult to define.'

But did that not mean it was fan power that converted the MMC? 'I don't believe the thing was turned down because of fan power. If you talk to supporter groups, people on the terraces, huge amounts of fans individually, they were in favour. As demonstrated, be it IMUSA or Michael Crick, they mobilised a small but extremely vocal group of people.'

White, like Crick, readily concedes that the majority of United fans 'did not give a toss', but as Crick and his friends celebrated with a party at Roger Brierley's house, the MMC decision was seen as a great victory for fan power and they could proclaim, in the words of White, 'it was the most sophisticated football campaign that there has ever been'.

Edwards would like to believe that there was a silent majority to be mobilised, which clearly the United Board failed to do. When Kenyon is asked, Where was the silent majority? Why was it not mobilised? he says, 'It is a good question.'

In many ways the most interesting response was from Gill. He had been at the heart of United's efforts at the OFT and MMC for four and a half months. Just before the decision was announced, I asked him how he would react if it went against United: 'Personally I won't be heartbroken. I get heartbroken for personal things that happen to me. Having been close to it day in, day out I can see major benefits in Sky taking over or United staying as it is. I am excited by it. Either way I am relaxed. Having been in charge of the project for four and a half months I will be disappointed. I firmly believe that our shareholders should decide whether we should be taken over by Sky. It would be a wrong decision if we are not allowed to make the bid. This has wider implications for English football. My personal view, having lived and breathed it for four and a half months, I feel it should be allowed to go ahead with conditions. If it does not go through, part of the attraction for media companies to get leverage out of content will go. Other entities perhaps can come in and try and buy us, but whether they can justify £2-plus per share we shall see. We were always in play as a separately quoted company. You have to accept it. If the partner is right and the acquisition is the right price, if they can add something to the business, we would look at it. If it does not go ahead, we have got an exciting future and lots of opportunity ahead of us. We have got to go ahead and manage. If it means we stay independent, it is great to stay on as finance director of an independent company.'

White spoke for the fans who had organised against Murdoch when he said: 'Martin Edwards was bad enough; Murdoch would have been worse. At least Edwards was the devil we knew. At least Edwards turns up for matches. Edwards is interested in football. He asked Ferguson when he went up to Scotland to meet a Scottish great, I think it was Jim Baxter, and Ferguson arranged tea for him. I know people will say wake up, smell the coffee, this is the real world. But Murdoch saw United as you might see a car on the starting grid of Formula One, positioning itself for the start of the race. If Murdoch had got hold of it, prices would have gone up, pay-per-view would have come, season tickets would have gone up, no purchases made whatsoever. Murdoch had the big guns on his side and they thought they could win the argument. There was a knee-jerk reaction against Murdoch. If it had been Lord Hollick or Michael Green there would not have been the instinctive knee-jerk reaction. We were driven by the knee-jerk reaction, but we were right.'

It is not a view echoed on the Board. However, there is one thing on which both the fans and the Board are in agreement and that is, as White says, 'Manchester United's PR is terrible. For a company with £110 million income they do not have a proper PR structure.'

As Tim Bell points out, the amazing thing about the MMC report was that in the general public nobody supported the bid, not even the Manchester City Council. United, once the best-loved club in the country, could no longer get its way. For the United Board, this revealed a problem that needed to be addressed. But even as it turned to it, another, quite unexpected issue rose – one that was the result of United's success both on and off the field and revealed the power of United and the perils of having such power.

14

THE BURDEN OF BEING THE BEST

It is a measure of the unique nature of Manchester United that despite the enormously distracting year it had off the field, it did not seem to affect its performances on it. Kidd, the man seen as vital to the Ferguson machine, had gone mid-season, and until 9 April, the Board was fighting fans over who should own United.

But now the season was coming to a climax. United and the team Ferguson had fashioned seemed to shrug it off and just powered on. Two days before the MMC report, on 7 April, United could only draw with Juventus in the first leg of the Champions League semi-final and only then with a goal in injury time by Ryan Giggs.

The goal was seen as a consolation. Juventus had outplayed United for an hour at Old Trafford, and worryingly, United had never beaten an Italian team in Italy. The comment of the Juventus general manager, that United's marketing was better than Juventus' (Juventus are now looking to own their own stadium to rectify matters) seemed to sum up for many fans the new United: great at selling itself, not so good at winning on the field against Europe's best. Juventus may learn marketing from United but expected to wrap up the tie back in Turin and once again dash United's hopes of winning the elusive Champions Trophy.

At that stage it looked like United might end up as in 1998 with nothing to show for the season. It faced Arsenal in the Cup semi-final and Arsenal was also the team to beat for the League. The first match in the semi-final was drawn; then in the second match United turned its season on its head. Roland Smith had said after the MMC hearings United did not play well in the second half. That may have been true at the start of the season, it was certainly the case when they opened their Champions League campaign against Barcelona, but now they showed how to finish. A goal behind to a Bergkamp special, United were down to ten men, then Bergkamp missed a penalty and Giggs scored a wonder goal. As we have seen, Edwards showed his true fan's instincts by being unable to watch and taking shelter in the Villa Park directors' bar. Giggs' goal meant United was on course for the double.

It became the treble a week later when, in a pulsating match at Turin, United, 2–0 down to Juventus in eleven minutes, came back to win 3–2. United were now in their first Champions League Final since 1968 and faced Bayern Munich.

However, the night they won, a decision was taken in Tel Aviv, where the UEFA executive committee was meeting, which was to have dramatic consequences for United and English football.

After the Turin result there were a few stutters, away draws to Leeds, Liverpool and Blackburn, but otherwise United seemed to have a momentum that was awesome. On Sunday, 16 May, Tottenham came to Old Trafford, with United needing to win to make sure Arsenal did not retain its title. After 25 minutes United went behind to an unlikely goal by Ferdinand but, if before the MMC United began well and then folded, now they roared back and won 2–1, their fifth Premier League title in seven years. A week later they overran a poor Newcastle side in the FA Cup Final to complete their third double in five years.

Only the treble remained and on Wednesday 26 May, at Barcelona's Nou Camp, once again displaying their newly found skill of coming from behind, United scored in injury time to win.

It was an important result for both United and England. United had done so only for only the second time, still well behind Liverpool's record of four wins, and it only put them equal with Nottingham Forest, by then relegated back to the First Division. More crucially, for the first time since 1984, an English team had won the premier club trophy in Europe and, for the first time since 1985 and Heysel, had even got to the final.

The match also demonstrated that the old English quality so admired and envied round the world, of never giving up was still intact. Bayern was the better team, and while this may have been heightened by the fact that United was without Keane and Scholes, there were questions to be raised about using Beckham in central midfield. However, the most impressive memory was how United, despite being outplayed and at times outclassed, never gave up and in the end English grit overcame a classier German side. United in 1968 had been the first English club to win the then European Cup, now they were the first to complete a unique treble.

But within a week of this epic triumph, United was faced with a challenge that was quite unprecedented.

The challenge was that the champion of England and Europe now had to campaign for England and make sure England got the right to stage the 2006 World Cup. United had to use its prowess on the field of play to influence decisions taken in smoke-filled committee rooms of FIFA, world football's governing body.

The weekend after United's triumphs in Barcelona had seen limp-wristed England performances against Sweden and Bulgaria, giving rise to jokes that United would do better against them. The fact is that on a different level this is exactly what the England bid committee for the 2006 World Cup was thinking. For them United was crucial in making sure England, who were contesting with Germany, South Africa, Brazil and Morocco for 2006, got the votes.

For this United had to participate in a pet project of Sepp Blatter, the president of FIFA. This pet project was a World Club championship between the leading club sides of the world. On 12 March, at a meeting of the FIFA executive in Zürich, Blatter had got the proposal through for an eight-team tournament to be played sometime in the year 2000. On 16 March he had written to UEFA and the other confederations asking them to nominate their teams.

UEFA, still smarting over the way the clever Swiss had beaten their candidate Lennart Johansson for the presidency of FIFA in June 1998 – just before the start of the World Cup in France – was not at all keen on yet another tournament. It had just managed to shelve a Blatter idea for two-year World Cups, but in order to avoid a confrontation UEFA agreed on a one-off basis to participate. This was the decision taken at Tel Aviv as United were winning in Juventus. And the decision was that the winner of the Champions League final would go. UEFA expected that team to come from a country which had a winter break, and since Germany had a winter break and England did not, it was expected that whatever happened in Barcelona, Bayern Munich would go to humour Blatter.

However, in England nobody focused on this decision by UEFA. They were more concerned about how many tickets United fans would get for the final and there was the now familiar cry, raised minutes after United had won at Turin, from fan pressure groups that United fans were not going to get enough tickets.

The FA got busy with this fan concern and appeared to have done well, for it seemed United fans ended up with some two-thirds of the seats at the Nou Camp on the night.

Whether this distracted the FA or not is unclear, but the FA missed a trick here. While FIFA had decided it wanted to hold the tournament and had decided it should be staged in January 2000, it had not decided where to hold it. In March, when it wrote to UEFA about this, FIFA also contacted the FA, along with other countries, asking if the FA would be prepared to host the event. By this stage United was in the semi-final of the Champions League. However, the FA decided that the dates in January 2000 were not suitable and, in any case, with UEFA not sure it wanted a European team to take part, the FA did not see much relevance for this tournament.

It is quite clear FIFA was struggling to get a decent country to bid for Blatter's pet project, which, despite Europe's reservation, he was determined to host if not every year, perhaps every two years.

Initially nine countries expressed interest: Tahiti, Paraguay, Uruguay, China, USA, Turkey, Mexico, Saudi Arabia and Brazil. But five of them, Tahiti, China, Paraguay, USA and Turkey, dropped out.

Brazil, England's rival for 2006, emerged as the favourite. But the formal decision was not made until the emergency committee meeting of FIFA in Cairo on 7 June, ten days after United had won in Barcelona. It seems that had England expressed an interest then even at that stage the FA probably would have got the nod ahead of Brazil. The chairman of the organising committee, the Saudi Arabian executive member of FIFA, Abdullah Al-Dabal, has a flat in London and had been wooed by the FA in an attempt to get his vote for the 2006 bid. But England did not.

United was unaware of this FA refusal until Monday 2 August, long after the row about its participation in the tournament had become public. That evening United was about to fly to Australia to begin its pre-season tour when I, as a result of my investigation on this story, rang Maurice Watkins, who was at Manchester airport waiting to board the flight to Frankfurt and then Melbourne. He was astonished, informed Edwards and Kenyon, who were standing next to him in the departure lounge, and when they got to Frankfurt, Watkins spoke to FA officials and expressed concern that United was not told about it before it made its decision to go to Brazil, a decision which was to have such dramatic consequences. Had the tournament been held in this country, not only would it have been easier for United to play, but another English team could have played and the FA, as the Brazilians undoubtedly will, could show off the English stadiums and skills at hosting international events to FIFA executive members.

The FA first realised the importance of Blatter's tournament when

England played against Sweden at Wembley. Three members of FIFA made it clear to Tony Banks that if United did not go they would change their votes and desert England. This set alarm bells ringing.

It dawned on the FA that if United did not go, Bayern Munich would represent Europe in the tournament. Those leading the English campaign felt if United's place was taken by Bayern Munich, it would mean more brownie points for Germany in the eyes of Blatter and FIFA. Germany was already representing Europe, replacing world champions France, in the Confederation Cup, another of Blatter's pet projects, which was played in Mexico between 24 July and 4 August 1999.

Blatter, who was in Barcelona to watch United triumph, had made it clear he was very keen that United, as the champions of Europe, should be in Brazil. The FA and the 2006 bid committee were convinced that in order to keep Blatter and his executive sweet, United should take part in the competition, even though it could mean quite a disruption to both the FA Cup and the Premier League programme.

The tournament would see two groups of four, with the winner of each group playing in a grand final in Rio. There would be a team from Brazil invited as host and one from each confederation. Real Madrid as winner of last season's Toyota Cup (the match between the champion club of Europe and that of South America) was also invited. With travelling time back and forth, the whole thing would take up to two weeks.

For Bayern it would come in its winter break. But for United two weeks off in January meant something would have to be sacrificed in the English domestic calendar.

United, worried about fixture congestion and the fact that, in defending its Champions League trophy, it would have to play 17 matches to get to the final, had made it clear that it did not much care for this new Blatter project. Something had to give.

Davies spoke to Edwards, who was just going on holiday. It was decided to call a meeting for 10 June in the Bobby Moore room of the FA's headquarters at Lancaster Gate. Kenyon and Roland Smith represented United; Davies and the FA and Premier League officials were present, as was Tony Banks. Banks had decided to put his ministerial authority behind trying to persuade Manchester United to play in the World Club Championship in Brazil.

It was at this meeting that United was told it must reconsider its decision not to go to Brazil for England's sake. The meeting considered that if United went to Brazil in January it would have to rearrange two

Premiership fixtures and, if United got that far, the fourth round of the FA Cup and the semi-final of the Worthington Trophy.

Banks now decided to put further pressure on United.

Immediately after the meeting, Banks wrote to Sir Roland Smith. After noting that United had declined the invitation to go to Brazil, he told Sir Roland, 'A refusal could have serious ramifications for England's 2006 World Cup bid. I have been personally informed by three FIFA executive members, all of whom had previously committed themselves to England's cause, that they will not vote for us in the event of Manchester United's non-appearance. I can appreciate how unfair it is to put such a burden upon you but it is clearly in the national interest for your club to compete in the FIFA championships.'

Banks went on to say that while the government had no powers to instruct the FA, he would make it clear to the FA 'that in the event of Manchester United agreeing to compete, we would expect the most sympathetic consideration being given to easing the inevitable fixture problems'. The letter was copied to Number 10 and to Chris Smith, the Secretary of State for Culture, Media and Sport, and Banks' boss.

Exactly a week later, on the morning of Thursday 17 June, as Banks flew back from an overseas mission to try to garner votes for England's 2006 bid, he met Edwards, back from holiday, Kenyon, David Davies and officials of the FA and Premier League at the Hilton Hotel near Heathrow.

Banks at this stage had criss-crossed the globe many times to try to secure the 2006 World Cup for England by lobbying the 24 members of the executive committee of FIFA who decide on the bid. He was now even more convinced he knew how these members felt. He had no doubts that United's presence in Brazil next January was essential if England was to maintain the momentum of its campaign.

For two hours various ways were discussed of easing the fixture problem. The semi-final of the Worthington Trophy was the least of United's headaches, for United had long since seen this competiton as one to be used to field essentially reserve sides.

However, the FA Cup and the Premiership were different. Could United field weakened teams, could the season be extended, could there be a bye into the fourth or even fifth round of the FA Cup? Although in recent seasons the Premiership programme has always ended on the same day, there is no rule which says it must, and the FA, which has a golden share in the Premier League, can, if it feels necessary, extend the League.

But none of the options seemed feasible and all of them would increase the number of matches United would have to play. Towards the end of the meeting Edwards proposed that United be given the right to withdraw from the FA Cup.

This was a sensational request. Davies thought it was unlikely the FA would allow United to withdraw but he promised to look into it.

Over the next few days Banks, Davies and bid officials of the 2006 campaign discussed plans. A United withdrawal fom the FA Cup would have implications for the sponsors and Banks and Davies summoned AXA to a meeting at the House of Commons, where the issues were further discussed.

As far as Banks and the 2006 campaign were concerned, time was pressing. On 5 July, FIFA was holding an extraordinary congress in Los Angeles, where the great and good of football, including the FIFA executive members, would gather, and Banks wanted a decision before that. Also, on the afternoon of Monday 28 June Banks was due to answer questions on sport in the House of Commons.

On the evening of 26 June, a Saturday, with the FA gathered in Chester for its annual summer meeting, where it had just elected Geoff Thompson as chairman and Ian Stott as vice chairman, Banks rang Davies to say he needed a decision. That evening Davies and his officials went round gathering members of the FA executive, as many as he and his officials could find, and an emergency meeting of the FA executive was held on Sunday morning at 8 o'clock. Davies asked the meeting to approve giving United an exemption from the FA Cup for the 1999–2000 season, and after a two-hour discussion, it decided to allow Manchester United to withdraw from the FA Cup.

Publicly the FA presented this as a decision that United had to take and insisted that there was no pressure on United from the FA.

Tony Banks, answering questions on sport in the House of Commons on the Monday, when asked by Michael Foster, the Labour member for Worcester, to justify the FA's decision, said, 'It is my considered opinion that in such an event [United not going to Brazil] significant damage would be inflicted on England's chances of hosting the World Cup in 2006.'

However, Banks did not say there was any government pressure on United and presented it as a decision United must take.

On Wednesday 30 June, United announced it had accepted the FA's invitation and would withdraw fom the FA Cup to play in Brazil.

A public storm broke out with the *Mirror* leading a campaign to get United back into the Cup. But for weeks the FA and government clung to their line, much to the anger of Manchester United, that they had put no pressure on United to make the decision to go to Brazil. The fact that Banks copied the letter he wrote to Sir Roland Smith had convinced Manchester United that Number 10 supported the pressure Banks was putting on and they saw Banks' request as having the authority of the highest in the land.

When I revealed the letter in the *Daily Telegraph*, it exploded the myth that Banks and the government did not put any pressure on the club to go to Brazil. When I asked Banks about it, he admitted that he had told Manchester United about the threat from FIFA members, but said, 'I was told to my face by three members of FIFA. No, I will not name them but I am not making it up. What was I supposed to do with this information? Keep this to myself? What would you have said then if it had come out?'

Asked if this did not mean the government put pressure on Manchester United, Banks still insisted there had been none: 'There was no pressure. When you are doing something like this you are all under pressure. There was government pressure on Manchester United, but there was pressure on all of us, there was the pressure of events. The idea that we can pressurise Manchester United is grotesque. I don't know why you are trawling through all this now, it is an old story.'

Banks' successor, Kate Hoey, was clearly unaware of all this and in particular Banks' letter. The day she took over from Banks (on 28 July), she told me that United should play in the Cup. Her comments on radio that United had treated its fans shabbily by withdrawing from the Cup incensed Martin Edwards, who rejected this.

A week later, with United playing in the Charity Shield Final, Hoey attending as sports minister sat next to Edwards. Hoey's team, Arsenal, beat United 2–1 and the *Mirror* got the moment when Hoey cheered the Arsenal winning goal. Next to her Edwards looked glum. Desperate to keep its campaign going, the *Mirror* imagined words of rebuke Edwards had spoken to Hoey at that moment. In fact their meeting at Wembley had been pleasant and Hoey recognised United had been put in an impossible position.

For Edwards it was yet another case of United not being understood. It had been asked to do it for England, to carry on the legacy left behind by Matt Busby. Just as Busby was the first to take English football to Europe, defying the then League leadership, the modern United of Ferguson was to carry England's flag to the new frontier.

Yet critics of Edwards claimed the real reason United was going to Brazil was for the money and the fact that it would enhance the global brand name. The fact was United did not know how much the tournament would bring and television rights had not even been sold when it gave in to FA and Banks' pressure.

The United of Busby had boldly gone into Europe in a simpler, less complex age and enhanced the glory of United and made a case for England. There was no commercialism then, or at least that was how it was perceived. Now, bowing to pressure from the FA and Banks, United was doing something considered even more vital for England but was condemned for its greed.

The whole situation once again raised the gap between what United felt it was doing and how it was perceived. Kenyon argues that while in public perception United's role in society may appear to have diminished since the days of Busby, 'the reality is it has not diminished. We have been reluctant to tell the story.'

I had spoken to Kenyon on 14 May, two days before United's triumph over Tottenham, which secured them the first leg of the treble, and it was clear Kenyon and the United Board were wrestling with the problems the MMC rejection of the bid had thrown up. Everybody had come out against the bid, even the Manchester City Council. I asked him was that not a surprise? 'What we give back to the Manchester community is a huge amount. We don't have a relationship problem with the council. We are major promoters of Manchester, major tourist attractions, major attractions for people coming to the city. When you look at our various activities across Greater Manchester and its boroughs, then we have contributed huge amounts of time, money and exposure. Manchester City does not have a better relationship. The difference is they tell people what they do. Every time they do something they tell people. We tend not to tell people. Because we are almost embarrassed to tell people. We are slowly coming out of our shell. We have to because, ultimately, it is damaging the next generation.'

It is possible to detect a sense of the siege mentality here. In the weeks and months following the rejection of the bid, the United Board has discussed this image problem. Kenyon says: 'We are very conscious about it. And we intend to do something about it. I think what Manchester United hasn't done enough is to talk to people about what its real plans are or what its real objectives are, what we are doing in the community, what we are doing for football in general. We have become the epitome of corporate football. If you talk to Martin Edwards, given the chance of talking about football, he will be the most passionate, articulate, supporter of sport in general and football in particular. But people don't go to him for that type of discussion. So it has become: if it's business it is Martin, if it's football it is Alex. It is the way it has been portrayed.'

But had not United and its Board contributed to it? As Roger Brierley, while luxuriating in the victory over Edwards, had said, 'the Manchester PR was absolutely dreadful'. Kenyon would agree: 'You create your own image, don't you, by design or default? That is how we have come to be perceived. If you look at Manchester United under Martin Edwards it had had tremendous success in a lot of fields. That is the reality of it. That is what makes Manchester United different, almost unique in football, success both on and off. Lots of football clubs are very successful on but are doing nothing off and there are not that many that are successful on the field but are successful off. But what Manchester United have been able to do is achieve both. One feeds the other, and it is a vicious circle, and that is how we have become successful. Unfortunately we are portrayed or are being portrayed as two separate ends of the same business which are in constant conflict. That is great headlines but it is not true. If we don't disabuse people and start telling the real story, that is how it will go on.'

How United can solve their communications problem is not clear. As Kenyon says: 'The only communication that has come from the chairman or the Board is through the City. Consequence of being a plc and all the rest of it. And in all the soccer aspects of Manchester United being a football club the Board is sidelined. There has to be a change in presentation. There isn't a successful business or club who does not look for its fans or supporters. We are looking at that now. What does it mean? Who do we talk to, how do we talk? What tone do we take? Manchester United is an enormous organisation with supporters in the four corners of the world. We cannot afford to neglect the local community; neither can we ignore the people in Hong Kong.'

This still, however, would not mean Edwards would sound off about football: 'Martin and I won't be taking a more upfront view on football. It is more rounded communication. That is what is important. The balanced message coming across.'

Kenyon is very aware that United has to give something back to the game: 'Manchester United has to get involved in the fabric of the sport. We have kept it at a distance. It is probably a bit of both, a conscious thing and a reflection of the personality of Martin. Manchester United is a business and it is a football club. We have done the business side very well and we have done the football on the field very well. But we have a lot to offer and we have got to give back, and giving back is sitting on some committee which is time-consuming but important. This is for the next generation. A strategy is being discussed. Manchester United will be moving in different business activities and we have to be very clear how we address those. The idea is to continue the tremendous success we have had in a very different environment over the next five years.'

It was two weeks after this conversation that the first pressures from the FA and Banks came to go to Brazil. United saw it as part of its duty of giving to the wider English football community, only to find it was perceived as yet another marketing exercise by the Board.

In the long term, the most important challenge facing United is working out its succession both at the boardroom level and on the field of play, as Kenyon admits: 'We have to get the succession on the field and in the boardroom. Absolutely.'

Unlike in 1968, when United won the European Cup for the first time, there is no immediate crisis. Ferguson has a new contract taking him to 60, which means the next three years are not a problem. But there will be a problem after that and it will have to get the transition right. United did not get it right after Busby, Liverpool after Dalglish and Tottenham after Nicholson. Kenyon has great faith in 'Ferguson's ability is to see things through', which could mean some involvement by Ferguson in the process of his succession.

There are in some ways more pressing problems at change at the boardroom and they may be just as fascinating. When, soon after the MMC decision, it also emerged that Greg Dyke was becoming Director General of the BBC, it was clear that he would have to leave the Board, which he duly did on 1 October 1999, just as the United Board signed off the 1999 results.

Edwards had made it clear that United might have to look for not one but two non-executive directors, as with Watkins having been there for more than 10 years and being involved in a great deal of work, he may no longer be seen as per new City rules as a non-executive. And with Roland Smith due to retire in March, Edwards also suggested he might like to become chairman of the plc.

But he could hardly be chairman of the plc and still be the largest shareholder, and so within days of the MMC turning down the Sky bid there was speculation that Edwards was selling. In June, following United's triumph in Barcelona he was approached by racing interests led by the Irish racing man J. P. McMannus, acting on behalf of a syndicate believed to include horse race owners John Magneier and

Michael Tabor. But Edwards, who talked to McMannus, turned down their offer, aware that there were voices in Old Trafford who were not happy at the prospect of a racing syndicate owning a large slice of shares.

But on 5 October, just a day after United announced their 1999 results, Edwards announced he had sold 7.5% of his stake for just under £41 million. This meant that including the money he had got at the float, shares sales since then had brought him just under £79 million.

The sale was prompted by several City institutions looking for Manchester United shares following the results announcement which showed that on the back of their treble success last season, United's turnover had exceeded £110 million, double that of Juventus and Barcelona, and its operating profit increased by 20% to £32.3 million.

However there were not many shares on the market and the brokers contacted Edwards who clearly felt this was too good an opportunity to miss. Most of the shares sold were owned by Edwards but some were sold through the trust fund he has for his children and some by his wife Susan.

The City has long felt that it would not be right for a chairman of a plc to have a large stake in the company and even the present stake may be reduced by next March, particularly if United's share price continues to rise.

The sale meant that for the first time since Louis Edwards had taken control, an Edwards was not the largest shareholder. That honour went, ironically to BSkyB who had acquired 11% of United during the bid process – since reduced to comply with Premiere League rules.

The share sales revived cries of 'greedy Edwards'. Edwards had in twenty years converted what was an investment of around £600,000 into just under £79 million and the 6.5% he held was worth another £30 million. Given the fact that Louis had paid between £31,000 and £41,000 for his 54% controlling interest in the club, the fans who had opposed the bid made much of this supposed Edwards greed. However, as we have seen, back in 1964 the BBC had paid £5,000 a year for its television contract for recorded highlights, United's share was £50 and nobody could have anticipated the riches television would bring that would help make United the richest club in the world.

The question that remains to be decided is whether Edwards, on becoming chairman of the plc, will continue to be chairman of the football club or whether he will distance himself further from the day to day involvement in the football club he has run for twenty years.

Kenyon, who is likely to take over as chief executive in March, says 'The make-up of the board in total, given certain aspirations, ambitions and retirement, will have to change, but change in a way that takes us forward.' The question is how can this change be made so United do go forward?

When Busby retired in 1968 the Edwards family was already established in the boardroom and, for all the heartache it caused when Busby opposed the rights issue, they provided the boardroom stability that has been so crucial to United's success. By the time Ferguson goes in three years' time, Edwards may also have gone and how United will cope with this double change will determine whether the club goes forward, and how this club, which has blossomed so brilliantly in the closing years of the twentieth century, does in the beginning of the twenty-first century.

The task for United and for Peter Kenyon when he becomes chief executive is clear. At the beginning of this century when Manchester United was changing its name from Newton Heath L and YR Cricket and Football Club and moving to Old Trafford it was unknown outside Manchester and even little known within the city. Manchester was already a great city, the shock city of the age, the Venice of the north Ruskin had called it and the city that could boast of being the nursery of the industrial revolution, the home of nineteenth century economic liberalism, host to the First Trade Union Congress and home of Britain's oldest symphony orchestra. Some writers likened it to the city states of antiquity and its roll call of honour includes: Bright, Cobden, Hallé and Richter. And its sports was led by the Lancashire cricketing greats of McLaren, Spooner, Tyldesley, and the immortal Hornby and Barlow.

Neville Cardus, the father of modern sports journalism, was a product of this Manchester, by Old Trafford he meant cricket, and had he been alive today he would have been amazed at how Manchester United has now joined the historic greats of his old home town and become a symbol of the city. Old Trafford football has long pushed Cardus's beloved Old Trafford cricket into obscurity and Manchester United has been so successful in projecting itself and its city that in a country where everything is so London-centred, Manchester is a name to conjure with in far corners of the world.

However as we have seen, the price of such success has been a sense of alienation with some fans, and an increasing distrust, if not hatred, from neutrals. Of course football clubs can flourish in such a situation. Barcelona is a prime example of a club loved by its followers but hated by everyone else in Spain. But Barcelona is a symbol of Catalan nationalism – Manchester United does not carry the flag for some Red Rose Lancashire political revival. It seeks to be a global brand, instantly accepted by people all over the globe. If that be so then Edwards, and in particular his successor Kenyon's task, will be to make sure that as Manchester United go marching on and seek success on and off the field it also lessens the distrust some of its fans instinctively feel for the Board and the hostility many of the neutrals harbour.

It will not be an easy task but the way it tackles this will show how the post-Edwards/Ferguson phase of Manchester United is developing.

POSTSCRIPT

O n 19 December 1999, as the storm over the first edition of my book broke, Jim White wrote in the *Guardian*: 'The intriguing question is why Bose's book was leaked now, just as Gardner [Roy Gardner, Ian Much and Philip Yea had just become new non-executive members of the United's Board in a reorganisation following the departure of Greg Dyke] takes up his position in the Old Trafford directors' box. The author would have been anxious not to release anything ahead of publication, not least to satisfy the papers he actually works for, but he was pre-empted. And the fact that the juicy details came out in the *Sun*, which is part of the same empire as Sky, suggests another agenda.

'It is known that there are those within Sky who were not impressed by Edwards' handling of the putative takeover. As Bell suggested at the time, a basic grasp of PR would have told anyone that the bid needed public support of the two figures who were noticeably missing: Ferguson and Bobby Charlton, still the presentable international face of the club.

'It allowed opponents all the space they needed to spin stories of rifts which it seems were there all along. Just at the time when the chief executive needs to impress his new directors, the *Sun* is keen to lay the blame for the PR disaster with Edwards. Worse he is portrayed, fairly or otherwise, as acting not in a dispassionate manner of the potential chairman of a significant plc but out of personal grudge. As untimely revelations go, news of an affair with the club physiotherapist's wife would have been less damaging.'

As I have already explained, a plot by the *Sun* to damage Edwards using my book could not have been further from the truth, since my book was not leaked to the *Sun* or any other paper but was officially released in a press conference to which White's *Guardian* was invited but did not turn up. However, such a simple fact could hardly have served this purpose which was to construct a myth that my book, much to my displeasure, had been leaked to the *Sun*, a construction, however fantastic, that helped the *Guardian* launch another myth about Edwards and Manchester United grandly entitled 'The Battle for United's Soul'.

If this was yet another illustration of the fact that those who write in condemnation of other people's spin are themselves quick to see intrigue and agendas where none exists, as far as the Manchester United story is concerned, this comes as no surprise. As we have seen there is no shortage of myths that surround the club and in the nine months since the first edition was published we have had further myths.

The most persistent myth was that the club would lose the services of Roy Keane because the Board was too tightfisted. The publication of my book came as the papers endlessly debated Keane's future, to which they soon added other problem stories from Old Trafford, in particular of rows with David Beckham and the United management, with some newspapers freely predicting that he was almost certain to leave United in the summer. His wife Victoria 'Posh Spice' Adams was quoted as saying, 'At the moment David is happy up there. I'm happy up there. But I think that playing abroad is something he would like to do.'

As it happened Keane, having got an offer of over £50,000 a week, decided not to exercise his rights under the Bosman freedom of contract and move and though Beckham has had some public problems with Ferguson, including being sent home from training once, his departure from Manchester United, like the death of Mark Twain, has proved a bit premature.

That United should generate such stories is not surprising. It's success has made it the ultimate sporting soap opera particularly in the tabloid press which, at times, is even more compelling than *Coronation Street*, with daily speculation both on what is happening on the training ground and the Boardroom.

Yet amidst all this media drama the club in the last year has serenely sailed along, deftly converting certain defeats into improbable victories.

The Brazilian trip, at the beginning of 2000, was a classic one. Having got an exceptional exemption from the FA Cup to try and shore up England's bid for the 2006 World Cup, United went to Rio with high hopes of proving it was the best club side in the world. But despite the fact that the Rio adventure was a disaster, United in their characteristic style made the best of turning disaster abroad into triumph at home.

The upside of the Rio journey was that it provided, in effect, a month's rest from the Premiership, Manchester United's very own mid-winter break in the sun, a luxury not afforded to its rivals in the Premiership. When United returned to England they proved irresistible and literally walked away with the Premiership title, their sixth in eight seasons of the Premiership. True by then they had lost their European crown to Real Madrid, but their form in this country showed that at their best, they were still an awesome side, one which had few equals in this country or even in Europe.

Similarly, off the field United's march has gone on. Even as the dust was settling over my book, United were finalising a new sponsorship deal, replacing their long standing sponsor Sharp with Vodaphone, a deal carefully planned and executed by Peter Kenyon and which could fetch United upwards of £30 million in four years, nearly three times as much as their nearest rivals Arsenal had negotiated after the Highbury club had done the double two years earlier.

Further impetus for the Manchester United money machine came with the renegotiation of television rights for the Premier League. Even before it began United had stolen a march on its Premiership rivals. Since the inception of the Premiership, every Saturday has seen one match from the Premiership televised live round the world, selling English soccer to a vast global audience and making it the biggest and most watched League in the world. In the past this match has nearly always been the match the BBC selected for its extensive coverage on *Match of the Day* and did not always feature Manchester United.

However, from the beginning of the 1999 season, with United having done the treble of Premiership, FA Cup and Champions League, foreign television stations could not get enough of Old Trafford and made it clear they wanted to see Manchester United every week. Since then all United's Saturday games have been beamed live overseas, adding to United's appeal and making it that much easier for Kenyon and his men to market United to customers in the Far East and Australia.

The new Premiership television deal opens other doors. Clubs are now allowed to make their own Internet arrangements. The main television deal, which now includes pay-per-view, is still a collective agreement and while Manchester United's success will bring more money, it cannot get the sort of mega-money that Barcelona, which under Spanish League rules can make its own television deal, can command. But on the Internet United can name its price and, with the Premiership allowing them to show their domestic matches live, after a 24- or 48-hour delay on the Internet, United with its vast worldwide following can use it to generate income that would take it yet another step closer to the Italian and Spanish giants and the millions they make from television.

However, in one sense Jim White was right to say that there were other agendas, maybe even plots at United, although his identification of the plot with Murdoch and the *Sun* was woefully off the mark. If there has been a plot in the last year at Old Trafford then it has centred round the intriguing question of the future of Martin Edwards. When I completed my research for the first edition of this book in September 1999, the confident assumption was that by March 2000 Edwards would move up from chief executive to chairman of the public company in place of Sir Roland Smith.

Smith's term was due to expire then and Edwards, as we have seen, had made no secret of the fact that he wanted Peter Kenyon to take over as chief executive and that he, himself, wanted to become chairman, a non-executive position which would allow him, in his own way, to slowly disengage himself from what had been his life for more than two decades.

But as the millennium came to an end, so wheels began to turn in the United boardroom, helped by events outside, that began to raise doubts on this well laid out plan.

The start of the millennium was a horrendous time for Edwards. If United's Brazilian foray was bad enough, worse still was the torrid time Edwards was having personally. His public image, never the best, touched a new nadir. He was being relentlessly hunted by the *Mirror* which included scrutinising his personal life in lurid detail with allegations made about certain Brazilian beauties he is alleged to have consorted with while in Rio, allegations Edwards denied but was powerless to prevent being bandied about.

At the same time there were noises coming from the boardroom that maybe Edwards would not become chairman.

The first indication of this had come even as Manchester United were looking to appoint non-executive directors to the plc. In the summer of 1999 the Board had appointed Heidrick Struggles, a firm of head-hunters, to sound out various candidates and, according to one candidate who was approached, 'one of the questions I was asked was how do you feel about becoming chairman? I said I wouldn't want it; I thought that job was going to Martin Edwards'.

The candidate was sufficiently perturbed to tell Edwards that seeking out a new chairman seemed to be part of the agenda. This person has deep suspicions as to who on the Board might have put the headhunters up to asking this question.

Another candidate who was also interviewed was Keith Harris. He, too, was asked whether he would like the idea of becoming chairman and said, 'I am surprised you have to ask me that question.'

But far from being made chairman Harris did not even get on the

Board and there is a mystery as to why this was. Was he considered perhaps a bit too much of a supporter and in the end the preference was for non-executives who were perhaps a little removed from the club? Or was it felt that he was a bit too close to Martin Edwards and to be a true non-executive he should not be that friendly with Edwards? At least one Board member is said to have felt that Harris was too close to Edwards to be a truly independent non-executive director of the plc.

Harris says he does not know. But in the process his close association with Roland Smith, the man he had brought to HSBC, seemed to become more distant. Harris was asked to help out with appeals from Manchester Grammar and UMIST, Smith's university. He helped Manchester Grammar and Smith appears to have been miffed.

By this time there were also indications that Smith was changing his mind about going in March 2000. Several ideas had been floated to persuade Smith to leave Old Trafford. The Premier League was looking for a chairman and, after Smith made an excellent presentation to it with regard to the work of the government appointed Task Force, there were many who saw him as a good chairman, but, of course, he would then have to sever his links with Old Trafford.

Then there was talk that the government might set up a regulatory body to oversee football and provide fans with a forum to raise issues. Smith had served on the Task Force, which had led to the idea of such a regulatory body, and in the early discussions as to who might serve on such a regulatory body the football authorities had, themselves, proposed Smith's name. But this suggestion was not pursued.

Come March it was clear Smith was going nowhere but staying on at Old Trafford. So the question arose: What would Martin do? As we have seen he had brought in Kenyon back in 1997 on the basis that with Smith soon to become 70 and Edwards, himself, seeking to slowly disengage, Kenyon would take over as chief executive while Edwards moved upstairs. But even if Edwards' route upstairs was now blocked by the very man he had brought to Old Trafford, should he in turn block Kenyon's move to the position of chief executive?

By June Edwards decided that irrespective of what Smith did he could not keep Kenyon hanging around. He told friends he was finding it difficult to come to terms with the increasing use of new technology, and at the summer meeting of the Premier League, told some of his fellow chairmen that he had decided to end his day-to-day running of Manchester United. The Board of the plc met on 30 June and this matter was discussed and soon it was decided that an announcement would be made to the Stock Exchange in a couple of weeks' time.

United were also about to get a full-time group PR, a need that had long been recognised by both Edwards and Kenyon and it seemed a good time to change. As we have seen the United Board, and in particular Kenyon, had long been aware that for all their success they needed to improve their public image, particularly on the corporate side. Given the size of the business, worth over £1 billion, Kenyon was determined to set this right.

On the morning of 17 July Manchester United informed the Stock Exchange that from 1 August Edwards would relinquish his job as chief executive and, while he would remain chairman of the football club, this would now be a non-executive role, effectively ending his day-to-day involvement with Old Trafford. David Gill would become Kenyon's deputy while remaining financial director.

Edwards has not completely left Old Trafford but plans to go in a couple of days a week. He, also, of course still retains his 6% holding of the Manchester United stock, which means he remains one of the major shareholders, the stake being worth more than £60 million, not far short of the money he had already made over the years in diluting down his once majority stake of over 50% at the time of the float in 1991.

One suggestion from Old Trafford has been that Edwards is now likely to take a more active role in European football, particularly in relation to the activities of G-14, the association of top European clubs. It was expected that the chairmanship of G-14 would rotate with whichever club holds the Champions League and as such Edwards should have taken over from Lorenzo Sanz, then President of Real Madrid last year following United's success in Barcelona in May 1999. But he did not. However, high UEFA officials have made it clear that if they have to deal with G-14 they would prefer to deal with Edwards rather than Sanz. Now that G-14 is getting a more permanent office in Brussels, Edwards, who is already involved with UEFA activities, may be more heavily involved.

But what about Edwards becoming chairman of the plc and Smith retiring? This matter is still unresolved. Glenn Cooper, who organised the Manchester United float and advised that Edwards he needed a prominent City figure as chairman of the plc, which led Edwards to recommend Smith, makes no bones about his intense irritation with the fact that the plan for Edwards to move up as chairman has not yet been completed.

'I brought Roland in as chairman at the time of the float. I said given the Tottenham experience, which had made the City very nervous of football clubs, we needed an independent City figure. Martin said would

Roland do and I said yes. I feel very cross that Roland Smith has now not gone. I do not know what his intentions are. He was expected to go in March. Then he suddenly decided to stay on and I am not sure what his real reasons were. One of the reasons he gave was that the television negotiations for the Premier League was about to take place and he wanted to be there while it was completed. This was a transparent excuse. He has no expertise in television, and in any case, the Premier League carried out the negotiations. And what I find upsetting is that he has steadfastly refused to do what he should have done: name Martin as his successor. He feels Martin has had enough, taken a lot of flak, and that he should not take any more flak. I know Martin's family, and in particular his wife, want him to get out of Old Trafford. Martin has done well for himself and she would like to see more of him. My view is that as long as Martin is at Old Trafford, in any capacity, he will get flak. I have always felt that he should be allowed to work himself out of the job and the best way to do so would be by becoming non-executive chairman. I am a great fan of Martin; he is the unsung hero of the success at Old Trafford and the Board should do nothing to lose his knowledge and unique expertise. United do not want to be deprived of his hand on the tiller. I have spoken to institutional shareholders of United and they recognise this and would want Martin Edwards as the next chairman. I do not know now what Roland Smith is playing at. He knows he will have to go, he is over 70, and although Martin has not yet become chairman, I would not rule him out. He will remain a very powerful figure at Old Trafford as indeed he should.'

As far as Smith is concerned he, as we have seen, is one of the few who refused to talk to me, but some indications of his thoughts were provided in an interview he gave to *Cheshire Life* which, interestingly, was published in March 2000, the very month he was expected to step down. It was entitled: 'Mr Manchester United'.

The introduction to the piece said, 'It's not Sir Alex, or even Martin Edwards. Wilf Altman catches up with the real power broker behind Manchester United. He is Professor Sir Roland Smith.'

Then, underneath a photograph showing Eddie George, the governor of the Bank of England, presenting an honorary degree to Smith, the author wrote: 'He rarely talks publicly about his role as chairman of Manchester United but he is clearly a powerful influence on the business.' Then the author quotes Smith as saying: 'As chairman you must have a vision of what you wish to achieve with the company. I wanted to see Manchester United as the most successful and profitable soccer business in Britain and then in Europe. We have achieved that vision. Since I have never held any shares in Manchester United plc, my vision was solely for the benefit of the club and for the business. Being a public company has proved an outstanding success both on and off the field and for me as chairman it has been an exciting and successful experience.'

The author then went on to say that at some stage in the first year of the millennium Smith would retire as chairman.

Those brief remarks are quite telling. Smith's emphasis that he does not own shares contrasts sharply with Edwards' still considerable share ownership.

However, the chances are that Smith will retire come March 2001 and that Edwards will take over. There has been press speculation that Roy Gardner of Centrica may be a candidate, but if it came to a vote, Edwards might still command a majority on the plc Board and achieve his one last ambition.

The departure of Edwards reignited the speculation about Ferguson. It is well known that Smith has had good relations with Ferguson on whom he conferred an honorary degree as chancellor of Manchester Metropolitan University. Kenyon's arrival as chief executive is also seen as further improving Board relations with Ferguson. This is in contrast with the strain in the Edwards–Ferguson relationship, a strain that nearly led to full scale legal action when Ferguson, upset by revelations in the first edition of my book, made his annoyance very clear and there were meetings between Ferguson, Smith, Edwards and Watkins.

In the final chapter, printed in the paperback edition of this book, Ferguson wrote: 'Somewhere in the middle of the protracted commotion over our absence from the FA Cup, the newspapers found another justification for working Manchester United into a few provocative headlines. They were based on criticisms of me attributed to Martin Edwards but this particular story was so lacking in credibility that it was petering out almost as soon as it was launched. It had originated in a book written by Mihir Bose, which contained claims that Martin described me as being useless with money. Bose is usually defined as an investigative journalist but I would have to question the quality of his investigation. Martin wrote to me categorically denying that he had ever spoken to the man about me. The remarks quoted amounted to such blatant nonsense that I had never for one moment believed the chairman could find himself capable of uttering them. For a start, Martin has no knowledge whatsoever of my personal finances so in that area there could be no foundation for comments of any kind. Suggestions that my record with United had shown me to be useless with money would be rather difficult to sustain, considering that

Martin's fortune has swollen by upwards of £120 million over the past ten years as a result of his shareholdings in the club. There was no substance to the story and I can only assume that Bose had been listening to a lot of tittle-tattle which, as I observed earlier, is always plentiful around a big organisation like ours.'

It was just the sort of robust defence one would expect from Ferguson, including questioning my abilty to research. But what was interesting was Edwards had denied saying the remarks about Ferguson to me when, as I had made clear, he had said it not to me, but at a meeting at HSBC in the days leading up to the leak of Sky's bid for United and so he was denying something I had never claimed.

There has been some press talk of Ferguson going on the Board when he retires. However, not only is there the memory of Busby and how his move to the Board backfired, but there is also the question of what Ferguson would do when he got there. As it is as manager he is on the football Board. It is unlikely that he would be proposed for the plc Board, so the question Manchester United have to consider is whether he should stay on the football Board and how this might affect a new manager. The day after the Edwards announcement was made, Ferguson, in the words of the *Sun* headline writer, 'opened his heart to the Sun' and said that he had wanted to stay on but as he had not heard from Edwards he had decided to make other arrangements. Ferguson is known for playing mind games with other football managers, and it is possible that this was another of his mind games but being played with his own directors.

For United, of course, how they manage the change to the post-Ferguson era remains the biggest challenge. They must make sure they avoid the problems that were caused when they failed to get the succession to Busby right.

But such has been the success story at Old Trafford that while the tabloids, or for that matter the broadsheets, may go on spinning new material for the United soap opera and present the club in a state of perpetual turmoil, it seems unlikely that anything can affect its continued rise. If the transition to the post-Ferguson era is mishandled then success may turn sour. So far, however, the men who run United have shown such a sure management touch it seems very likely they can handle this transition well. Edwards may be taking a back seat but the management duo of Kenyon and Gill he has left behind at Old Trafford suggest that there will be no lack of a clear strategy, or the ability and the willingness to pursue the policies that have made Manchester United such a unique sporting institution.

APPENDIX I

MANCHESTER UNITED'S CONSOLIDATED PROFIT AND LOSS ACCOUNTS, 1995 TO 1999

	1999 £'000	1998 £'000	1997 £'000	1996 £'000	1995 £'000
Turnover	110,674	87,875	87,939	53,316	60,622
Operating profit before amortisation of players and exceptional item	32,310	26,996	26,201	14,167	15,649
Amortisation of players*	(10,192)	(4,723)	–	–	–
Exceptional item	(1,807)	–	–	2,173	–
Operating profit	20,311	22,273	26,201	16,340	15,649
Share of results of joint venture and associated undertaking	(1,777)	–	–	–	–
Total operating profit (Group and share of joint venture and associate)	18,534	22,273	26,201	16,340	15,649
Profit on disposal of players*	2,193	2,947	–	–	–
Net transfer fees*	–	–	293	(1,300)	3,733
Net interest receivable	1,684	2,619	1,083	359	632
Profit on ordinary activities before taxation	22,411	27,839	27,577	15,399	20,014
Taxation	(7,023)	(8,211)	(8,549)	(4,126)	(5,792)
Profit for the year	15,388	19,628	19,028	11,273	14,222
Dividends	(4,676)	(4,416)	(4,026)	(3,221)	(2,737)
Appropriation to transfer fee reserve	–	–	–	–	(4,000)
Retained profit for the year	10,712	15,212	15,002	8,052	7,485
Shareholders' funds	107,936	97,132	72,418	40,762	32,072
Earnings per share (pence)	5.9	7.6	7.4	4.6	5.9
Dividends per share (pence)	1.800	1.700	1.550	1.300	1.125
Dividend cover (times)	3.3	4.4	4.7	3.5	5.2

* The results for 1998 have been restated following the adoption of FRS 10, 'Goodwill and Intangible Assets' in 1999. Therefore, the results for 1997 to 1995 are not directly comparable with those for 1998 and 1999 below the level of operating profit before amortisation of players and exceptional item.

Source: Manchester United published accounts

APPENDIX II

ACTIVITIES AND CORPORATE STRUCTURE OF MANCHESTER UNITED

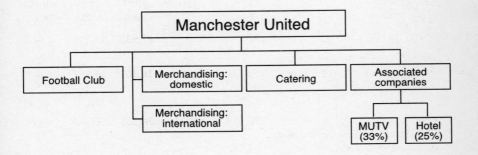

APPENDIX III

BREAKDOWN OF MANCHESTER UNITED'S TURNOVER AND OPERATING PROFIT

MANCHESTER UNITED CONTRIBUTION BY REVENUE CATEGORY TO TOTAL TURNOVER, 1995 TO 1999

per cent

	Years ended 31 July				
	1995	*1996*	*1997*	*1998*	*1999*
Gate receipts	32	35	34	34	38
TV	11	11	14	18	20
Sponsorship and royalties	12	12	13	13	16
Conference and catering	6	7	6	7	6
Merchandising and other	39	35	33	28	20
	100	100	100	100	100
Total turnover (£m)	61	53	88	88	111

Source: Manchester United published accounts and MMC calculations.

BREAKDOWN OF MANCHESTER UNITED'S OPERATING PROFIT FOR 1998 AND 1999

£ million

	Domestic	*European*	*1998 Total*	*1999 Total*
Gate receipts	27	3	30	42
TV	10	6	16	23
Sponsorship and royalties	12	–	12	17
Conference and catering	6	–	6	7
Merchandise and other	24	–	24	22
Turnover	79	9	88	111
Cost of sales	(21)	(1)	(22)	
Operating expenses	(38)	(1)	(39)	
Operating profit	20	7	27	
Operating profit as a percentage of total operating profit (%)	74	26	100	

Source: Manchester United, MMC calculations.

Note: in 1999, Manchester United played 31 home games against 25 in 1998, averaging 54,000 a game against 54,900 in 1998. But the aggregate attendance for 1999 was 1.674 million as against 1.371 million in 1998 because of more games in the treble-winning season.

APPENDIX IV

MANCHESTER UNITED PLC AVERAGE SHARE PRICE

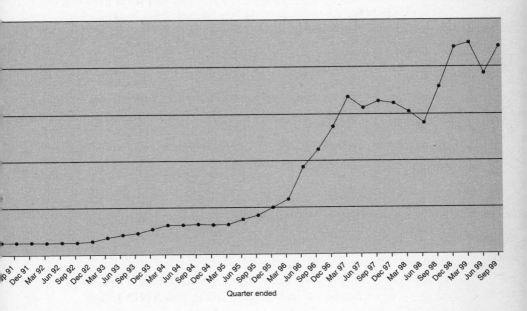

Quarter ended

APPENDIX V

EXTRACTS FROM THE SUMMARY OF THE
MONOPOLIES AND MERGERS COMMISSION REPORT
ON THE PROPOSED MERGER OF MANCHESTER
UNITED PLC AND BSKYB, APRIL 1999

1.2. BSkyB is a vertically integrated broadcaster which buys TV rights, including those for sporting events, makes some of its own programmes, packages programmes from a range of sources into various channels, and distributes and retails these channels to its subscribers using its direct-to-home satellite platform as well as selling them wholesale to other retailers using different distribution platforms.

1.3. On all relevant measures, Manchester United is the strongest English football club. Its football-related activities include the supply of TV rights for its matches. At present the rights to Manchester United's Premier League matches, together with those of other Premier League clubs, are sold collectively by the Premier League itself.

1.6. In considering the public interest consequences of the merger, we looked primarily at its effects on competition among broadcasters for live Premier League rights. Because of uncertainties about the outcome of the RPC case on the collective selling of Premier League rights, we considered four scenarios, one or other of which may be expected to occur.

1.7. Our first scenario involved the continuation of existing collective selling arrangements and no other mergers between broadcasters and Premier League clubs. We have concluded that under this scenario, BSkyB would, as a result of the merger, gain influence over and information about the Premier League's selling of rights that would not be available to its competitors. It would also benefit from its ownership stake in Premier League rights, providing a further advantage in the bidding process.

1.8. Taken together, these factors would significantly improve BSkyB's chances of securing the Premier League's rights. We would expect this to influence the behaviour of BSkyB's competitors causing them to bid more cautiously than would otherwise be the case and, in some cases, even not to bid at all. This would enhance BSkyB's already strong position arising from its market power as a sports premium channel provider and from being the incumbent broadcaster of Premier League football. The effect would be to reduce competition for Premier League rights leading to less choice for the Premier League and less scope for innovation in the broadcasting of Premier League football.

1.9. Under our other scenarios we have concluded that:

(a) If the live rights of Premier League clubs were to be sold on an individual basis and there were no other mergers between broadcasters and clubs, BSkyB would, as a result of the merger, have substantial advantages over other broadcasters competing for the rights. This would have adverse effects for competition similar to those we identified under our first scenario.

(b) If existing selling arrangements continued and the BSkyB/Manchester United merger were to precipitate a further merger between a broadcaster and a Premier League club, the effects on competition of the merger between BSkyB and Manchester United would be broadly similar to those of our first scenario. If there were several mergers between broadcasters and Premier League clubs precipitated by the BSkyB/Manchester United merger, then we believe that collective selling would continue only if broadcasters agreed among themselves to share the rights, which would have at least as adverse an effect on competition as our first scenario.

1.10. If rights were sold on an individual basis and there were several mergers between broadcasters and Premier League clubs precipitated by the BSkyB/Manchester United merger, all of the feasible outcomes would be less competitive than the situation in which rights were individually sold and no broadcaster/Premier League club mergers had occurred.

1.11. In most of the situations described in paragraphs 1.7 to 1.9, the merger would enhance BSkyB's ability to secure Premier League rights in future. We would expect this further to restrict entry into the sports premium channel market by new channel providers, causing the prices of BSkyB's sports channels to be higher and choice and innovation less than they otherwise would be. Reduced entry by sports premium channel providers would feed through into reduced competition in the wider pay TV market.

1.12. We conclude that, under all of the scenarios described in paragraphs 1.7 to 1.9, the merger may be expected to reduce competition

Manchester Unlimited

for Premier League rights with the consequential adverse effects we have identified.

1.13. We have based our public interest conclusions mainly on the effects of the merger on competition among broadcasters. However, we also think that the merger would adversely affect football in two ways. First, it would reinforce the existing trend towards greater inequality of wealth between clubs, thus weakening the smaller ones. Second, it would give BSkyB additional influence over Premier League decisions relating to the organization of football, leading to some decisions which did not reflect the long-term interests of football. On both counts the merger may be expected to have the adverse effect of damaging the quality of British football. This adverse effect would be more pronounced if the merger precipitated other mergers between broadcasters and Premier League clubs.

1.14. We were unable to identify any public interest benefits from the proposed merger. We therefore conclude that the proposed merger between BSkyB and Manchester United may be expected to operate against the public interest.

1.15. We considered whether the adverse effects we have identified could be remedied by undertakings by BSkyB. We did not find any that we regarded as effective. We think that the adverse effects are sufficiently serious that prohibiting the merger is both an appropriate and a proportionate remedy. Accordingly, we recommend that the acquisition of Manchester United by BSkyB should be prohibited.

Source: HMSO